Criminal Justice

Contemporary Literature in Theory and Practice

Series Editors

Marilyn McShane

Frank P. Williams III

California State University–San Bernardino

GARLAND PUBLISHING, INC.

New York & London

1997

Contents of the Series

1. Law Enforcement Operations and Management
2. Drug Use and Drug Policy
3. Criminological Theory
4. The Philosophy and Practice of Corrections
5. The American Court System
6. Victims of Crime and the Victimization Process

The Philosophy and Practice of Corrections

Edited with introductions by
Marilyn McShane
Frank P. Williams III
California State University – San Bernardino

GARLAND PUBLISHING, INC.
New York & London
1997

Library of Congress Cataloging-in-Publication Data

The philosophy and practice of corrections / edited with introductions
by Marilyn McShane, Frank P. Williams III.
p. cm. — (Criminal justice ; v. 4)
Includes bibliographical references.
ISBN 0-8153-2510-X (alk. paper)
1. Corrections—United States. 2. Prisons—United States.
I. McShane, Marilyn D., 1956– . II. Williams, Franklin P.
III. Series: Criminal justice (New York, N.Y.) ; 4.
HV9471.P47 1997
365'.973—dc21 96-45337
CIP

Printed on acid-free, 250-year-life paper
Manufactured in the United States of America

Contents

vii Series Introduction

xiii Volume Introduction

1 Factors Influencing Probation Outcome: A Review of the Literature
Kathryn D. Morgan

9 Does Correctional Treatment Work? A Clinically Relevant and Psychologically Informed Meta-Analysis
D.A. Andrews, Ivan Zinger, Robert D. Hoge, James Bonta, Paul Gendreau, and Francis T. Cullen

45 Essential Components of Successful Rehabilitation Programs for Offenders
Daniel H. Antonowicz and Robert R. Ross

53 Correctional "Good Time" as a Means of Early Release
Ellen F. Chayet

71 Patriarchy, Prisons, and Jails: A Critical Look at Trends in Women's Incarceration
Meda Chesney-Lind

89 No Soul in the New Machine: Technofallacies in the Electronic Monitoring Movement
Ronald Corbett and Gary T. Marx

99 Is Incarceration Really Worse? Analysis of Offenders' Preferences for Prison Over Probation
Ben M. Crouch

121 Communication Policy Changes from 1971 to 1991 in State Correctional Facilities for Adult Males in the United States
George E. Dickinson and Thomas W. Seaman

133 The Privatization of Prisons in Historical Perspective
Malcolm M. Feeley

144 Reaffirming Rehabilitation in Juvenile Justice
Dan Macallair

167 Probation and Parole: Public Risk and the Future of Incarceration Alternatives
Michael R. Geerken and Hennessey D. Hayes

183 The Response of the Criminal Justice System to Prison Overcrowding: Recidivism Patterns Among Four Successive Parolee Cohorts
William R. Kelly and Sheldon Ekland-Olson

203 The Meaning of Correctional Crowding: Steps Toward an Index of Severity
John M. Klofas, Stan Stojkovic, and David A. Kalinich

222 The Impact of Shock Incarceration Programs on Prison Crowding
Doris Layton MacKenzie and Alex Piquero

251 Adapting Conservative Correctional Policies to the Economic Realities of the 1990s
Alida V. Merlo and Peter J. Benekos

267 A Comparison of Programming for Women and Men in U.S. Prisons in the 1980s
Merry Morash, Robin N. Haarr, and Lila Rucker

292 Growth-Centered Intervention: An Overview of Changes in Recent Decades
Ted Palmer

299 Using Situational Factors to Predict Types of Prison Violence
Pamela Steinke

314 Imprisonment in the American States
William A. Taggart and Russell G. Winn

328 Democratizing Prisons
Hans Toch

339 Measuring Prison Disciplinary Problems: A Multiple Indicators Approach to Understanding Prison Adjustment
Patricia Van Voorhis

371 Acknowledgments

Series Introduction

At the turn of the century the criminal justice system will be confronting many of the same demons, although the drugs of choice, the technology of crime fighting, and the tools and techniques of management have evolved. Despite the enhancements of twenty-first century technologies, funding, crowding, and public concerns about effectiveness continue to be discussed in "crisis" terminology, and criminal justice scholars remain somewhat cynical about the ability to reform the criminal justice system. This pessimistic attitude may be fueled, at least in part, by the drama of real-life crime that plays itself out in courtrooms, newspapers, and talk shows across America every day. The combination of emotional political maneuvering and campaigning on punitive rhetoric assures us of a steady stream of legislation designed to reflect a zero tolerance for crime.

Testing the constitutional limits of our times, we have devised even more ways of imposing severe punishments, seizing assets, reinstituting corporal punishment, and penalizing the parents of delinquents. We have also created new offenses, such as recruiting someone into a gang, transmitting "indecent" images on the Internet, and knowingly passing along a disease. Despite these politically popular solutions to crime, problems of enforcement, equity, and affordability remain. The public's preoccupation with "what works?" and quick fixes to crime problems have never been reconciled with the more realistic ideas of "what can we live with?" and long-range preventive solutions.

Ironically, despite public perceptions that crime has been getting worse, statistics seem to indicate that the rates for virtually all offenses are either no worse than they were in 1980 or are now lower. Drug-related arrests and the rates for most forms of adult crime (in particular, most violent crimes) have actually decreased. Against this general backdrop, the rate of violent juvenile crime appears to be the sole increasing trend, leading to a situation in which risks of victimization by violent crime have also increased for juveniles. The contrary public perception of a massive and growing crime problem has created a situation in which the number of cases of juveniles transferred to adult court has increased, as has the proportion of inmates facing life sentences, life in prison without parole, and death sentences. On the other hand the risk of incarceration also appears to have increased for minorities, directing attention to questions of racial and economic disparity in the quality of protection and justice available in this country today.

While all this has been happening over the past two decades, academia has rather quietly developed an entire discipline dedicated to the study of crime and the criminal justice system. Though crime policy is still dominated largely by political interests swayed by public opinion, crime scholars have begun to have an impact on how crime is viewed and what can be done about it. While this impact is not yet a major one, it continues to gain weight and shows promise of some day achieving the influence that economists have come to wield in the realm of public policy-making.

Simultaneously with this growing scholarship comes an irony: academic journals, the major repository of scholarly wisdom, are being discontinued by libraries. Access, although ostensibly available in an electronic form, is decreasing. In many academic libraries, only a few select, "major" journals are being retained. Clearly, there is so much being done that the few "top" journals cannot adequately represent current developments (even if these journals were not focused in particular directions). Thus, the knowledge of the field is being centralized and, at the same time, more difficult to obtain. The multitude of criminal justice and criminology degree programs now face an interesting dilemma: how do students and faculty access current information? Or put differently, how does the field distribute its hard-gained knowledge to both assure quality of education and pursue efforts to offset the often ill-informed myths of public opinion?

Electronic access would appear to be one possible answer to the problem, especially with libraries facing yet another squeeze, that of space. On-line and media-based (CD-ROM) services promise quick availability of periodical literature, but remain futuristic. The costs associated with downloading articles can approximate the cost of the journal subscriptions themselves and many libraries cannot afford to participate in on-line periodical services. In addition, there is the inconvenience of translating the electronic images into the user's still-preferred paper-based format. Moreover, the paper-based serendipitous value of "browsing" decreases as only specific articles appear on-line, without surrounding materials.

An alternative solution is to review the range of journals and collect the "best" of their articles for reprinting. This is the approach this criminal justice periodical series has taken. By combining both depth and scope in a series of reprints, the series can offer an attractive, cost-effective answer to the problem of creating access to scholarship. Moreover, such a compact format yields the added advantage that individuals searching for a specific topic are more likely to experience the serendipity of running across related articles. Each of the six volumes presents a comprehensive picture of the state of the art in criminal justice today and each contains articles focused on one of the major areas of criminal justice and criminology: Police, Drugs, Criminological Theory, Corrections, Courts, and Victimology. Each volume contains approximately twenty articles.

The Article Selection Process

The articles appearing in the series represent the choices of the editors and a board of experts in each area. These choices were based on four criteria: (1) that the articles were from the time period of 1991–1995, (2) that they represent excellent scholarship, (3) that collectively they constitute a fair representation of the knowledge of the period, and (4) that where there were multiple choices for representing a knowledge area, the articles appeared in journals that are less likely to be in today's academic library holdings. We believe the selection criteria and the board of experts were successful in compiling truly representative content in each topical area. In addition, the authors of the selected articles constitute a list of recognizable experts whose work is commonly cited.

Finally, there is one other advantage offered by the volumes in this series: the articles are reprinted as they originally appeared. Scholars using anthologized materials are commonly faced with having to cite secondary source pages because they do not have access to the original pagination and format. This is a difficulty because mistakes in reprinting have been known to alter the original context, thus making the use of secondary sources risky (and synonymous with sloppy scholarship). In order to overcome this problem, the series editors and the publisher made the joint decision to photoreproduce each article's original image, complete with pagination and format. Thus, each article retains its own unique typesetting and character. Citations may be made to pages in confidence that the reproduced version is identical in all respects with the original. In short, the journal article is being made available exactly as if the issue had been on a library shelf.

We believe this series will be of great utility to students, scholars, and others with interests in the literature of criminal justice and criminology. Moreover, the series saves the user time that would have otherwise been spent in locating quality articles during a typical literature search. Whether in an academic or personal library, the only alternative to this collection is having the journals themselves.

Volume Introduction

This volume attempts to clarify some of the issues in corrections that may have become, for the reader, a blur of campaign rhetoric and dueling statistics. For the most part, our image of convicted offenders has been distorted by the media's emphasis on bizarre serial killers and a parade of celebrity prisoners. The less sensational but more realistic features of modern corrections are highlighted in the articles presented here. They cover everything from the contracting of private facilities to the continued debate over rehabilitation and the promises of community corrections. Contemporary research, as illustrated in this work, has provided more sophisticated models for examining complex phenomenon, such as crowding and recidivism. The current status of inmate rights is discussed as well as the progress toward equitable programming for female offenders. As the expanding "corrections industry" continues to demand greater proportions of state and federal budgets, it is important for us to monitor and evaluate operations and to suggest alternatives to incarceration. This volume provides the basis for the readers' understanding of just how great a task that will be.

The Crisis in Corrections

Correctional crowding has been described as a crisis for so long, the term is cliche, as are the other references to the current state of corrections as a "runaway train" (Hassine, 1996) and the "prison-building frenzy" (Martin, 1996). As Alida Merlo and Peter Benekos explain, a constant stream of conservative legislation propelled by emotion with no concern for fiscal or practical implementation has bred a correctional system we cannot afford. The short-term political gains of "get tough" grandstanding has mortgaged our society into an incarceration industry.

Prison overcrowding is among the more prevalent problems created by a continued increase in the use of incarceration. John Klofas, Stan Stojkovic, and David Kalinich attempt to develop the crowding concept into a more sophisticated model with measures that can be applied directly into management. It recognizes that crowding is not based on numbers alone, but on the direct effects that each additional body has on a variety of institutional support services. The impact of crowding will also vary from facility to facility based on its unique physical and organizational features.

Privatization has been touted as a cost-effective and expedient way to address the current crowding dilemma. However, using an historical perspective, Malcolm Feeley is able to demonstrate how the growth of privatization only increases the capacity of the state to punish and creates new forms of control. He points out that the distinction between corrections and law enforcement is blurred by new private entrepreneurs.

Another approach to decreasing prison crowding is the use of shock incarceration programs to diminish an inmate's length of stay in prison. Doris MacKenzie and Alex Piquero examine boot camp records from five states to determine their potential for reducing prison populations. They note that the degree to which program participants would otherwise have been incarcerated is critical. If the programs are unsuccessful, they actually may increase the number of offenders in prison. If recidivism, dropout, and washout rates are lowered, then prison crowding may be positively affected. However, another effect of the boot camp programs may be that of net-widening, with a long-term, higher probability of incarceration for a greater number of people.

With the possibility of prison overcrowding solutions backfiring, William Kelly and Sheldon Ekland-Olson examine collective solutions to prison overcrowding in Texas at a time of maximum pressure on prison capacity. Their analysis suggests that attempts to reduce prison crowding inadvertently resulted in higher reincarceration among parolees. Among the precipitating factors were public pressure, legislation increasing incentives for "technical" parole violations, and a potential reduction in deterrence.

In a final article related to the topic of overcrowding, William Taggart and Russell Winn attempt to explain why incarceration rates vary from state to state. Using data from 1984, they produce eight possible explanations ranging from crime to economics to criminal justice reforms to ideology and culture. Their findings show that the two most important factors are crime and ideology and crime and culture. Other factors may affect the prison rates, but only indirectly and not as strongly.

Prison Conditions

Several of the cases of judicial intervention in state prison systems and jail facilities have been justified under the general rubric of imprisonment under unconstitutional conditions. However, recent conservative court decisions have expressed a reluctance to involve the judiciary in correctional management. Research and commentary on the issues, ranging from violence to disciplinary systems to food, have been abundant. The authors in this section contribute to the most critical of those issues.

After summarizing the state of the art in prison discipline research, Patricia Van Voorhis analyzes the utility of various measures of prison adjustment. Using a sample of federal inmates, she constructs four different indicators of prison adjustment and compares them to four different outcome measures. She concludes that, while all four approaches give reasonable results, each has different sources of bias and error and predicts some outcome behaviors better than others.

Pamela Steinke, in a research study attempting to predict prison violence, separates aggression into four areas: toward staff, toward other inmates, toward self, and toward property. She finds personality characteristics are not particularly useful in predicting incidents and suggests situational factors must be considered. Aggressiveness toward staff tended to occur in activity areas, but where inmates were largely alone. Aggressiveness toward other inmates tended to occur in congregation areas, and incidents involving self and property largely occurred in the inmate's own cell or dorm area.

Throughout the 1980s, prisons struggled to equalize conditions between men and women who were incarcerated. Although some claim that women's facilities are, by nature and design, more hospitable and relaxed, others argue that standards and spending for women's programming still lags far behind that of male prisoners. Merry Morash, Robin Haarr, and Lila Rucker compare programming for men and women in 1980s prisons. They conclude that prison programs still reflect gender stereotypes, resulting in fewer programs and substantial lack of opportunities for incarcerated women. In addition, the programs that do exist tend to foster workplace marginalization and provide training and treatment that is not relevant to the women's problems.

In another essay on females in prison, Meda Chesney-Lind probes the data on female crime and incarceration and brings a feminist analysis to the issue of incarcerated women. Reflecting on the Hawaiian female prison experience, she notes that many liberal approaches to improving the condition of women in prison have backfired. Thus, she cautions that the political and correctional proponents of women's prisons have proven tenacious and able to sway liberal arguments to their own ends. As one alternative, Chesney-Lind argues for a non-incarcerative response to women's crimes.

In a final essay on prison conditions, Hans Toch argues for a management approach to improving inmate life. Consonant with participative and TQM management schemes, democratic prison reform would include both staff and inmate involvement in decision-making. This is particularly true for inmates in making classification and programming decisions as well as policies that affect the quality of prison life. In addition to improving management and prison life, Toch believes that democratization would also serve to prepare offenders for life outside prison.

The Continued Controversy Over Rehabilitation

More sophisticated research methodology and a sensitivity toward the complexity of the concept of rehabilitation has allowed us to examine correctional programming in more detail than ever before. Guided by more specific questions than the previous generation of "what works?" endeavors, several researchers scrutinized contemporary intervention strategies and their evaluation. D. A. Andrews, Ivan Zinger, Robert Hoge, James Bonta, Paul Gendreau, and Francis Cullen perform a meta-analysis of studies on juvenile and adult correctional treatment. Their conclusions are that effective treatment programs, no matter what their specific focus may be, have a component that allows for psychological evaluation and delivery of appropriate correctional services.

Another review of treatment studies is performed by Daniel Antonowicz and Robert Ross. They focus on rigorous experimental studies published between 1970 and 1991, some of which were found to be quite effective. The most effective programs followed a cognitive-behavioral conceptual model, worked with variables directly related to reoffending, and were multifaceted in their programming.

Ted Palmer's essay continues his long-standing probing of rehabilitative programs to determine what works for whom. Beginning with the 1970s, he reviews the history of rehabilitation—demonstrating a movement from pessimist to guarded optimism. Palmer suggests that new rehabilitative programs need to be sensitive to the needs and characteristics of their clients. The best of the emerging modalities appears to be growth-centered intervention.

While many program reviews have focused on adult corrections, Dan Macallair expressly treats the juvenile system. He documents the decline in rehabilitation programs since the 1970s, mostly in favor of a justice model. Presenting evidence that the justice model has unexpectedly resulted in worsening conditions, Macallair notes the irony of more favorable evidence for rehabilitative treatment modalities. Pointing out the promising results amassed in four states, he argues for a return to a progressive agenda for juvenile justice.

Individual programs, while not as easy to review and evaluate as multifaceted programs, are still being assessed in the literature. Ellen Chayet looks at "good time" credit and, as might be expected, the results are mixed. Positive features are that good time is a useful management tool and helps control prison population size. Moreover, there is little effect on public safety. On the negative side, the use of good time credits may serve to aggravate sentencing differentials. Another individual program, encouraging outside communications, is examined by George Dickinson and Thomas Seaman. Examining communications policies over a twenty-year span, they note that most correctional institutions attempted to liberalize their policies. Positive effects have been an increase in inmate morale, fewer assaults, and more time made available for counselors.

The Promise of Community Corrections

Some have theorized that prison crowding has pressured communities into retaining many serious offenders with more intensive supervision strategies. Others argue that probation has simply been subject to the same "get tough" adjustments as prisons. Either way, recent studies have examined the phenomenon of punitive trends and offenders' perceptions of prison, probation, and parole. While there is no support for the idea that any one disposition is more preferable, as the public may claim, demographic factors play an important role in preferences for certain types of sanctions (Petersilia and Deschenes, 1994).

Ben Crouch conducted interviews with male felons in Texas on the question of sanction preference. His findings suggest that offenders perceive probation to be more harsh than the public does. Giving the respondents' choices between probation sentence lengths compared to one year in prison, he reports that somewhere between one-third to two-thirds would choose incarceration.

The traditional emphasis on recidivism as a measure of success and the disproportionate media emphasis on a small number of unusual, sensational case failures have no doubt limited the acceptance of probation and parole by the general public. Given current resources and the inevitability of alternatives to incarceration, one must redefine goals or reinterpret results in a way that will be politically acceptable. Michael

Geerken and Hennessey Hayes argue that we should perhaps look at proportions of the total number of offenses committed by those on community supervision when trying to evaluate the incapacitative effects of these alternatives to incarceration.

Finally, one of the major tools of community corrections is electronic monitoring, a standard "get-tough" measure for those on probation or parole. Ronald Corbett and Gary Marx find no evidence that electronic monitoring has thus far been successful. Given this, they discuss fallacies and problems related to electronic monitoring and warn that expectations may be unrealistic.

* * * * * *

We would like to thank the board members of this volume who assisted us in the selection of articles. Because only a limited number of pieces could be selected for this volume, an expanded bibliography is included to provide additional materials. Articles marked with an asterisk (*) are included in this anthology.

Alexander, Rudolf, Jr. (1993). Slamming the federal courthouse door on inmates. *Journal of Criminal Justice* 21(2): 103–16.

*Andrews, D.A., Ivan Zinger, Robert Hoge, James Bonta, Paul Gendreau, and Francis Cullen (1991). Does correctional treatment work? A clinically relevant and psychologically informed meta-analysis. *Criminology* 28: 369–404.

*Antonowicz, Daniel and Robert Ross (1994). Essential components of successful rehabilitation programs for offenders. *International Journal of Offender Therapy and Comparative Criminology* 38(2): 97–104.

Ashford, Jose and Craig LeCroy (1993). Juvenile parole policy in the United States: Determinate versus indeterminate models. *Justice Quarterly* 10(2): 179–95.

Backstrand, John, Don Gibbons, and Joseph Jones (1992). Who is in jail? An examination of the rabble hypothesis. *Crime and Delinquency* 38(2): 219–29.

Belenko, Steven, Martha Schiff, and Mary Phillips (1994). Modeling the prison displacement effects of alternative sanctions programs: A case study. *Prison Journal* 74(2): 167–97.

*Chayet, Ellen (1994). Correctional "good time" as a means of early release. *Criminal Justice Abstracts* 26(3): 521–38.

*Chesney-Lind, Meda (1991). Patriarchy, prisons and jails: A critical look at trends in women's incarceration. *The Prison Journal* 71(1): 51–67.

*Chilton, Bradley and David Nice (1993). Triggering federal court intervention in state prison reform. *The Prison Journal* 73(1): 30–45.

*Corbett, Ronald and Gary Marx (1994). No soul in the new machine: Technofallacies in the electronic monitoring movement. *Journal of Offender Monitoring* 7(3): 1–9.

*Crouch, Ben (1993). Is incarceration really worse? Analysis of offenders' preferences for prison over probation. *Justice Quarterly* 10(1): 67–88.

Cullen, Francis, Edward Latessa, Velmer Burton Jr., and Lucien Lombardo (1993). The correctional orientation of prison wardens: Is the rehabilitative ideal supported? *Criminology* 31(1): 69–92.

Cullen, Francis, Edward Latessa, Renee Kopache, Lucien Lombardo, and Velmer Burton Jr. (1993). Prison wardens' job satisfaction. *The Prison Journal* 73(2): 141–61.

*Dickinson, George and Thomas Seaman (1994). Communication policy changes from 1971–1991 in state correctional facilities for adult males in the U.S. *Prison Journal* 74(3): 371–82.

Durham III, Alexis (1991). Then and now: The fruits of late 20th century penal reform. *Federal Probation* 55(3): 28–36.

Ekland-Olson, Sheldon, William Kelly, and Michael Eisenberg (1992). Crime and incarceration: Some comparative findings from the 1980s. *Crime and Delinquency* 38(3): 392–416.

Feeley, Malcolm and Jonathan Simon (1992). The new penology: Notes on the emerging strategy of corrections and its implications. *Criminology* 30: 449–74.

*Feeley, Malcolm (1991). The privatization of prisons in historical perspective. *Criminal Justice Research Bulletin* 6(2): 1–10.

Fields, Charles, ed. (1994). *Innovative trends and specialized strategies in community-based corrections.* New York: Garland.

Flanagan, Timothy and Kathleen Maguire (1993). A full employment policy for prisons in the United States: Some arguments, estimates and implications. *Journal of Criminal Justice* 21(2): 117–30.

Flynn, Edith (1992). The graying of American's prison population. *The Prison Journal* 72(1-2): 77–98.

Gabel, Katherine and Denise Johnston (1995). *Children of Incarcerated Parents.* New York: Lexington Books.

*Geerken, Michael and Hennessey Hayes (1993). Probation and parole: Public risk and the future of incarceration alternatives. *Criminology* 31(4): 549–64.

Harris, Patricia (1994). Client management classification and prediction of probation outcome. *Crime and Delinquency* 40(2): 154–74.

Hassine, Victor (1996). *Life without parole: Living in prison today.* Los Angeles: Roxbury.

Heard, Chinita (1993). Forecasting models for managing a changing inmate population: Implications for public policy. *Criminal Justice Review* 18(1): 1–11.

Innes, Christopher (1993). Recent public opinion in the United States toward punishment and corrections. *Prison Journal* 73(2): 220–36.

Jacobs, Susan (1995). AIDS in correctional facilities: Current status of legal issues critical to policy development. *Journal of Criminal Justice* 23(3): 209–21.

Johnson, Wesley, Greg Dunaway, Velmer Burton Jr., James Marquart, and Steven Cuvelier (1994). Goals of community-based corrections: An analysis of state legal codes. *American Journal of Criminal Justice* 18(1): 79–93.

Johnston, Norman (1994). *Eastern State Penitentiary: Crucible of Good Intentions.* Philadelphia: University of Pennsylvania Press.

*Kelly, William and Sheldon Ekland-Olson (1991). The response of the criminal justice system to prison overcrowding: Recidivism patterns among four successive parolee cohorts. *Law and Society Review* 25(3): 601–20.

Kinkade, Patrick and Matthew Leone (1992). Issues and answers: Prison administrators' responses to controversies surrounding privatization. *The Prison Journal* 72(1-2): 57–76.

*Klofas, John, Stan Stojkovic, and David Kalinich (1992). The meaning of correctional crowding: Steps toward an index of severity. *Crime and Delinquency* 38(2): 171–88.

Lawrence, Richard (1991). Re-examining community corrections models. *Crime and Delinquency* 37(4): 449–64.

Lemert, Edwin (1993). Visions of social control: Probation reconsidered. *Crime and Delinquency* 39(4): 447–61.

Liberton, Michael, Mitchell Silverman, and William Blount (1992). Predicting probation success for the first time offender. *International Journal of Offender Therapy and Comparative Criminology* 36(4): 335–47.

Logan, Charles (1992). Well-kept: Comparing quality of confinement in private and public prisons. *Journal of Criminal Law and Criminology* 83: 577–613.

*Macallair, Dan (1993). Reaffirming rehabilitation in juvenile justice. *Youth and Society* 25(1): 104–25.

*MacKenzie, Doris and Alex Piquero (1994). The impact of shock incarceration programs on prison crowding. *Crime and Delinquency* 40(2): 222–49.

MacKenzie, Doris (1991). The parole performance of offenders released from shock incarceration (boot camp prisons): A survival time analysis. *Journal of Quantitative Criminology* 7: 213–36.

McShane, Marilyn and Frank Williams III (1993). *The management of correctional institutions*. New York: Garland.

*Merlo, Alida and Peter Benekos (1992). Adapting conservative correctional policies to the economic realities of the 1990s. *Criminal Justice Policy Review* 6(1): 1–16.

*Morash, Merry, Robin Haarr, and Lila Rucker (1994). A comparison of programming for women and men in U.S. prisons in the 1980s. *Crime and Delinquency* 40(2): 197–221.

Morgan, Kathryn (1993). Factors influencing probation outcome: A review of the literature. *Federal Probation* 57(2): 23–29.

Owen, Barbara and Barbara Bloom (1995). Profiling women prisoners: Findings from national surveys and a California sample. *The Prison Journal* 75(2): 165–85.

*Palmer, Ted (1992). Growth centered intervention: An overview of changes in recent decades. *Federal Probation* 56(1): 62–67.

Palmer, Ted (1991). The effectiveness of intervention: Recent trends and current issues. *Crime and Delinquency* 37: 330–46.

Petersilia, Joan and Elizabeth Deschenes (1994). What punishes? Inmates rank the severity of prison vs. intermediate sanctions. *Federal Probation* 58(1): 3–8.

Renzema, Marc and David Skelton (1991). The scope of electronic monitoring today. *Journal of Offender Monitoring* 4(4): 6–11.

Senese, Jeffrey (1992). Intensive supervised probation and public opinion: Perceptions of community correctional policy and practices. *American Journal of Criminal Justice* 16(2): 33–56.

Shichor, David (1993). The corporate context of private prisons. *Crime, Law and Social Change* 20(2): 113–38.

Smykla, John and William Selke, eds. (1995). *Intermediate Sanctions: Sentencing in the 1990s.* Cincinnati: Anderson.

Steadman, Henry, Edward Holohean, and Joel Dvoskin (1991). Estimating mental health needs and service utilization among prison inmates. *Bulletin of the American Academy of Psychiatry and the Law* 19(3): 297–307.

*Steinke, Pamela (1991). Using situational factors to predict types of prison violence. *Journal of Offender Rehabilitation* 17(1-2): 119–32.

Stohr, Mary, Nicholas Lovrich, and Gregory Wilson (1994). Staff stress in contemporary jails: Assessing problem severity and the payoff of progressive personnel practices. *Journal of Criminal Justice* 22(4): 313–27.

*Taggart, William and Russell Winn (1993). Imprisonment in the American states. *Social Science Quarterly* 74(4): 736–49.

*Toch, Hans (1994). Democratizing prisons. *Prison Journal* 74(1): 62–72.

*Van Voorhis, Patricia (1994). Measuring prison disciplinary problems: A multiple indicators approach to understanding the prison experience. *Justice Quarterly* 11: 679–709.

Wooldredge, John (1991). Identifying possible sources of inmate crowding in U.S. jails. *Journal of Quantitative Criminology* 7(4): 373–86.

Wooten, Harold and Mary Shilton (1993). Reconstructing probation: What prosecutors, defense attorneys and judges can do. *Criminal Justice* 7(4): 12–15, 48–50.

Zimring, Franklin and Gordon Hawkins (1995). *Incapacitation.* New York: Oxford University Press.

Zupan, Linda (1992). Men guarding women: An analysis of the employment of male correction officers in prisons for women. *Journal of Criminal Justice* 20(4): 297–309.

Factors Influencing Probation Outcome: A Review of the Literature

By Kathryn D. Morgan, Ph.D.
Assistant Professor, Department of Criminal Justice, University of Alabama at Birmingham

Introduction

FOR MUCH of correctional history, the criminal justice community has relied upon various programs designed to serve as alternatives to ıcarceration. Probation has been and continues to e one of these correctional alternatives. Recent staistics published by the Department of Justice (Bueau of Justice Statistics, 1992) indicate that in)ecember 1990, there were approximately 3 million ffenders under Federal and state probation supervi-ion with 83 percent of the total being under active upervision. Petersilia (1985) estimates that beween 60 percent and 80 percent of all convicted riminals are sentenced to probation. Despite the roliferation of intermediate punishments such as ntensive probation, home confinement, and elecronic surveillance, probation has survived as a senencing alternative.

Although used extensively, probation has been the enter of much controversy and criticism for its failure o rehabilitate and deter offenders placed under the upervision of probation departments. Much of this riticism can be attributed to the decline of the rehailitative ideal and the rise of the Justice Model in the 970's and the "get tough on crime" philosophy of the 980's. The controversy and criticism that have surounded probation since the 1930's focus on several ssues which include: having caseloads too large for upervising officers to be effective; inadequate funding vhich often results in understaffed and underpaid robation departments; and failure of probation to ehabilitate offenders or deter their future criminal ıctions.

Because such a large number of correctional clients ıre under probation supervision, it is important that ve understand the effectiveness and outcome issues elated to probation and assess factors which influence robation outcome and probation effectiveness. Past esearch has provided some important insight into vhat factors influence probation outcome and which ffenders are more likely to succeed or fail under robation supervision.

Review of the Literature

Although used extensively, probation has been criticized for its failure to rehabilitate and deter offenders. Many studies have shown that the failure rate for robationers under supervision is high. Tippman 1976), who studied 790 male felons, found the failure rate to be 40 percent. Rogers (1981), with a sample of 1,014 probationers, concluded that 60 percent of those placed under probation supervision fail. Many studies have cited such factors as age, gender, employment, educational attainment, and marital stability as related to probation success or failure. Roundtree, Edwards, and Parker (1984) and Tippman (1976) found prior criminal record to be the most significant predictor of probation outcome. Other studies have identified probation supervision variables including the length of sentence and types of conditions assessed as being predictors of probation outcome. The studies which focus on probation outcome can be classified into three categories: (1) studies that report probation failure rates only (Irish, 1977; Rogers, 1981; General Accounting Office, 1976); (2) studies that report failure rates but also indicate significant factors correlated with that failure (Caldwell, 1951; England, 1955; Frease, 1964; Davis, 1964; Landis, Mercer, & Wolff, 1969; Tippman, 1976; Kusuda, 1976; Missouri Division of Probation and Parole, 1976; Roundtree et al., 1984); and (3) studies that discuss factors influencing probation outcome only (Ditman, 1967; Lohman, 1966; Wisconsin Corrections Division, 1972; Bartell & Thomas, 1977; Renner, 1978; New Jersey Administrative Office of the Courts, 1980; Holland, Holt, & Beckett, 1982; Scott & Carey, 1983; Cuniff, 1986; McCarthy & Langworthy, 1987; Petersilia, 1987; Kane County Diagnostic Center, no date; California Bureau of Statistics, 1977).

Studies Reporting Probation Failure Rates

The first group of studies report failure rates for probation samples (see table 1).

The General Accounting Office (1976) studied probation outcome in four counties in the United States: Maricopa County, Arizona; Multnomah County, Oregon; Philadelphia County, Pennsylvania; and King's County, Washington. In these counties, approximately 77 percent of all offenders were placed under probation supervision. The sample consisted of 1,100 closed probation cases which were tracked for 22 months after discharge from probation and 50 current cases. Recidivism was defined as having probation revoked while still on probation or during the followup period. The results showed that only 4 or 5 out of every 10 complete their probation without arrest, conviction, or revocation.

Irish (1977) attempted to assess probation effectiveness by examining probation outcome. His conclusions indicated that three-fourths of those under study made a successful adjustment while on probation, and two-thirds conformed to law-abiding behavior after probation. Thus, he concluded that probation was successful in accomplishing its outcome.

Rogers (1981) analyzed data on 1,104 male and female probationers to identify factors related to recidivism. She used three measures of recidivism: reconvictions during probation; reconvictions between date that the probation order was issued and 24 months following termination; and sentences assessed between the date the probation order was issued and 24 months following termination. She found that one of every five probationers was convicted while under probation supervision. Within the 24-month period following termination, the number had increased to one in three probationers being convicted with 60 percent of those convicted being given sentences of incarceration. Among probationers receiving intensive probation supervision, reconviction rates were much higher (60 percent) than for probationers given minimum or no supervision.

Vito (1985) concluded that felony probation is effective in controlling recidivism when his examination of 317 felony probationers in Kent, Ohio, indicated a failure rate of 22 percent.

TABLE 1. SUMMARY OF STUDIES REPORTING FAILURE RATES ONLY

Year	Researcher	Failure Rate
1976	General Accounting Office	55%
1977	Irish	30%
1981	Rogers	60%
1985	Vito	22%

Studies Reporting Failure Rates and Related Factors

The second category of studies reports probation failure rates but also describes factors significantly correlated with probation failure and success (see table 2).

Caldwell (1951) studied Federal probationers whose cases had been terminated during the period of July 1, 1937, through December 31, 1942. In the analysis of 337 probationers who violated conditions while under supervision, youthfulness and low socioeconomic status were characteristics of violators. Educational attainment was similar for both recidivists and nonrecidivists. In the second part of the study, 403 postprobationers were selected to examine postprobation outcome. Results indicated that there were 66 probation failures or probationers who were convicted of crimes following probation release. Fifty-eight of the 66 failures were due to arrests for minor offenses. Factors related to postprobation success included high occupational skill, full employment, adequate income, and marriage with children.

England (1955) studied 500 Federal offenders whose probation was terminated between January 1, 1939, and December 31, 1944. He followed these offenders for a period of 6 to 12 years. He defined failure as convictions for misdemeanor and felony offenses. With a 17 percent failure rate, factors associated with failure included previous criminal record, youthfulness, personal instability, and lower socioeconomic background. Most postprobation convictions were for minor offenses such as gambling, theft, and disorderly conduct. England (1955) used findings from his study of 490 adult felony and misdemeanor probationers who had completed terms between 1939-44 to suggest that selection for probation and daily probation operations might provide more insight into understanding probation outcome. These probationers were not subjected to any intensive, individualized social casework procedures. They were simply exposed to routine surveillance. The data showed that by 1951, only 17.7 percent of the offenders had recidivated. He argued that other variables besides "social work" are important in the probation experience including the fact of being under surveillance; being publicly branded an offender; and the threat of a jail term.

Frease (1964) studied 605 probationers under supervision from July 1, 1961, through June 30, 1962, to identify factors related to probation outcome. He defined failures as those who had been served a bench warrant or whose probationary status had been revoked. The data indicated the following factors to be associated with probation success: being female; no prior felony commitments; 5 years or more residence in Washington; a fourth grade education or more; nondrinking; married; and positive family support.

Defining failure as two or more violations and revocation, Davis (1964) used a cohort approach to study probation effectiveness. The sample consisted of a cohort made up of all defendants granted probation in 56 California counties in the years 1956 (3,199); 1957 (3,970); and 1958 (4,469). The highest revocation rate was for probationers convicted of minor offenses including forgery and check offenses. The lowest revocation rate was for homicide and sex offenses. Age and sex were more significantly correlated with probation outcome; females and older people are more successful on probation.

Landis et al. (1969) analyzed variables related to success or failure on probation for 791 adult offenders in California. Three categories of variables for the 415 probation successes and 376 failures were identified: social background, antisocial behavior, and conditions of probation. Social background variables included educational achievement, occupational achievement, work history, marital status, and use of intoxicants. Antisocial behavior variables included type of military discharge, prior juvenile record, prior adult record, type of offense, and type of property offense. Conditions of probation were length of probation, jail as a probation condition, and restitution as a condition of probation. Of the three categories of variables, antisocial behavior variables were more highly correlated to probation failure. Probationers with a past history of disciplinary problems, a juvenile record, or an adult record are more likely to fail on probation. Probation failures commit more property crime. As it relates to social background, failures are more likely to have lower educational achievement and lower socioeconomic status, marital instability, and a tendency to move from job to job.

Of the 2,726 offenders convicted of criminal offenses in Alberta Canada, in the years 1967-71, Cockerill (1975) took a subsample of those offenders who had been placed on probation. The data showed that the group had a failure rate of 39 percent with employment, marital status, and time of most recent conviction being significantly related to failure. He also found that racial origin was a significant variable.

Tippman (1976) studied 790 male felons 1 year after they were placed on probation. Within a year after placement on probation, 17 percent had committed new felonies, and 23 percent had committed misdemeanors or violated probation conditions. He found the best predictor of recidivism to be adult criminal record with race, age, and juvenile record having only a slight impact on recidivism. He concluded that recidivism rates can be predicted and explained by prior criminal record. He also found that large numbers of poor probation risks are being placed under probation supervision.

Kusuda (1976) examined factors related to recidivist behavior for 7,147 male and female probationers who had been terminated from the Wisconsin Division of Corrections. The study defined failure as revocation of probation for a new offense, rules violation, or absconding. The results indicated a 19 percent failure rate with failures being due to absconding and minor offenses. Success was linked to such factors as stable marriage; full-time employment; per month income of more that $400; nonuse of drugs and alcohol; and probation terminated at age 55 or older.

The Missouri Division of Probation and Parole (1976) examined probation and postprobation outcomes using data for 5,083 probationers placed under supervision from July 1, 1968, to June 30, 1970. Data indicated that approximately 20 percent of the probationers under supervision failed with failure being related to age, educational attainment, marital status, employment, adequate income, prior incarceration, and alcohol and drug abuse. The results also indicated that the type of conviction offense is related to failure. Those convicted of armed robbery, forcible rape, motor vehicle theft, and forgery are likely to fail. A simple random sample of 216 cases was selected from the population of probationers who had successfully completed probation. During the followup period which lasted from 6 months to 7 years, 30 percent of the 216 cases failed. Of the failures, only one probationer was arrested for a crime similar to the original conviction offense.

Roundtree et al. (1984) isolated offender characteristics related to recidivism. A random sample of 100 probationers was selected from a total population of 2,419 adult probation cases that had been closed between January 1, 1975, and December 31, 1978. Of the cases making up the sample, 14 percent were revoked and 86 percent completed probation successfully. Significant relationships were found between recidivism and school grade completed, prior criminal record, age at first arrest, number of prior arrests, offender classification, and length of probation sentence. Factors not significantly related to recidivism included race, sex, age left school, marital status, employment status at the time of the offense, age at the time of present offense, and time of the offense.

Petersilia (1987) conducted research to determine how felons perform under probation supervision. Taking a sub-sample of 1,672 from a sample of 16,000 felons convicted in the California Superior Court, she reported a 51 percent failure rate for probationers. Data showed that those originally charged with property crimes were more likely to recidivate; they tended to be arrested more than those convicted of violent or drug offenses. Factors correlated to probation failure included prior juvenile and adult convictions, income at arrest, and household composition. The greater the number of prior convictions, the higher the probability of probation failure; regardless of the source or amount, the presence of income at the time of arrest reduces possibility of failure; and living with spouse and/or child reduces the probability of failure.

In a study of 266 felony probationers in Tennessee, Morgan (1991) found probation failure significantly related to employment, hourly wage, marital status, prior felony commitments, and conviction offense. Probationers who are unemployed, making less than minimum wage, unmarried, with two or more prior felony commitments and a conviction for a property offense are more likely to experience probation failure. In this study, failure was measured by revocation, absconding, or being sentenced for a new offense.

TABLE 2. SUMMARY OF STUDIES REPORTING FAILURE RATES AND RELATED FACTORS

Year	Researcher	Failure Rate	Related Factors
1951	Caldwell	19% (termination)	Failure correlated with youth and low socioeconomic status.
		16% (postprobation)	Postprobation success related to full employment, adequate income, marriage with children.
1955	England	17%	Failure related to instability, prior criminal record, low socioeconomic status, and youth.
1964	Frease	20%	Success related to being female, no felony commitments, educational attainment, marriage, positive family support.
1964	Davis	30%	Age and sex highly related to outcome.
1969	Landis et al.	52%	Failure related to frequent job changes, prior criminal record,marital instability, and low educational attainment.
1975	Cockerill	39%	Failure related to employment, marital status, time of most recent previous conviction.
1976	Tippman	40%	Failure correlated with adult criminal record.
1976	Kusuda	18%	Success correlated with full employment, realistic goals, stable marriage, nonuse of alcohol and drugs, being 55+, and income of $400 or more per month.
1976	Missouri Dept. of Corrections	20%	Failure related to age, educational attainment, marital status, employment, adequate income, prior incarceration, alcohol and drug use, and conviction offense.
1984	Roundtree et al.	14%	Failure related to prior arrests, length of supervision, age at first arrest, school grade completed.
1987	Petersilia	51%	Failure related to conviction offense, prior juvenile and adult convictions, income at arrest, living arrangements.

Studies Reporting Factors Related to Probation Outcome

The third category of studies report findings of research that focus primarily on factors that are highly correlated to probation success or failure (see table 3). Whereas the second category of studies focuses on failure rates and factors highly correlated to those failure rates, this third category attempts to identify factors related to probation outcome.

Ditman (1967) examined the relationship between alcohol rehabilitation treatment and probation success rates. He defined success as not having any rearrests. The study tracked 2,713 offenders for a 6-month treatment period. For the 6-month treatment period, 472 offenders had successful probation outcomes. Of the 146 probationers who had violated probation conditions during this 6-month period, 62 percent were successful and had no further violations after serving a 30-day sentence and receiving additional alcohol treatment.

Lohman (1966) found little difference in the type of supervision and success or failure. He compared intensive, ideal, and minimal supervision and their relationships to probation outcome. Using a sample size of 307, he studied males and females between the ages of 20-60 who had been under ideal, intensive, or minimal supervision status. The study found that violation rates for intensive supervision were much higher than for ideal and minimal supervision.

Data from the Wisconsin Corrections Division (1972) provide insight into probation outcomes for adult and juvenile probationers. They defined outcome as success or failure under supervision. Data regarding successful outcomes indicate that females are more successful under supervision than males. Drug and alcohol use, being unemployed, and long periods of supervision were highly correlated with failure.

Bartell and Thomas (1977) studied recidivist practices for 100 probationers and incarcerated felons. They found that the best predictor of failure for both groups was age which was inversely related to recidivism. Those who were the lowest risks for recidivism were offenders age 28 and above. Offenders arrested for burglary are more likely to be rearrested with the new charge most often being another burglary.

Renner (1978) profiled 1,905 probationers in Ontario and concluded that the factors most often related to failure were employment, alcohol and drugs, and longer and more intense periods of probation supervision.

A 1980 study by the New Jersey Administrative Office of the Courts analyzed recidivism rates for 651 probationers who had been terminated in 1975. The study found that one-third of all probationers recidivated either prior to termination or after discharge. Employment status and a prior criminal record were strongly related to recidivism rates.

Holland et al. (1982) studied probation outcome for 198 male offenders over a period of 32 months. The researchers concluded that nonviolent failure is more common; the nonviolent criminal is more likely to recidivate. Persistent nonviolent criminality reflects a propensity for criminality. Because violence is a transitory psychological state, it is not a good predictor of future criminality.

Using 498 felons placed on probation and in a residential treatment facility, Scott and Carey (1983) found failure to be highly correlated with unemployment, prior incarcerations, and whether or not there was serious physical injury in the previous offense. Age, race, and prior convictions had no significant effect on outcome for probationers or inmates.

Cuniff (1986), taking a subsample of 226 from a larger sample, found that probation failures are more likely to be males, in the mid-twenties, living at home with family and convicted of property crimes. When probationers are rearrested, it is most often for burglary.

McCarthy and Langworthy (1987) compared probationers aged 50 and older (N=95) with younger probationers (N=82). They argued that being older, married, and employed with no drug use contributed to a higher success rate for older offenders. They also stated that older offenders are usually violent offenders rather than property offenders, a fact which possibly contributes to higher success rates for older offenders.

Kane County Diagnostic Center in Illinois found variables most related to probation outcome included highest grade completed, income, number of dependents, prior incarceration, and marital status. McGinnis and Klocksiem (1976) concluded that employment is the most important factor in probation success.

When comparing probationers given straight probation time with offenders given probation and jail time and offenders given straight jail time, a California (1977) study found that probationers with straight probation time did better than the other two groups. With straight probation, females were more successful than males; sex offenders were more successful than property offenders; and younger offenders (<30) were the most likely to fail within the first year. The study indicated age, race, prior criminality, and being convicted of a property offense were significantly correlated to probation outcome.

Summary of the Literature Review

Much of the prior research on probation outcome measures outcome as success or failure while under supervision or during the postprobation period. Failure in a majority of these cases was measured by reconviction, revocation, or absconding. Success was measured by the completion of the probation term without reconviction, revocation, or absconding. Much of the reviewed research indicated that probation is effective as a correctional alternative. Failure rates ranged from 14 percent (Roundtree et al., 1984) to 60 percent (Rogers, 1981). Factors most often associated with failure included employment status, prior criminal record, low income, age, sex, and marital status. Young males who are unemployed or underemployed with a low income and prior criminal record are more likely to fail. Instability, as measured by employment status, marital status, and length of stay at residence, was also related to probation failure or success. Probationers who were married with children, adequately employed, and had lived in an area for more than 2 years, were often successful under supervision. When discussing probation failures, most of the studies indicated that reconviction offenses tended to be minor misdemeanors rather than felonies.

According to Latessa, Eskridge, Allen, and Vito (1985), it is important to exercise care when reporting the results of probation research. He points out that methodological problems occur when trying to assess probation effectiveness from past research. Defini-

TABLE 3. SUMMARY OF STUDIES IDENTIFYING FACTORS RELATED TO PROBATION INCOME

Year	Researcher	Related Factors
1967	Ditman	Failure correlated with alcohol abuse.
1966	Lohman	Failure correlated with level of supervision.
1972	Wisconsin Corrections Division	Failure correlated with age, drug and alcohol abuse, employment, and length of probation sentence.
1976	McGinnis & Klockseim	Most important factor related to success is employment and length of supervision.
1977	Bartell & Thomas	Best predictors of probation failure are age, prior arrests, and burglary as a conviction offense.
1977	California Bureau of Statistics	Probation outcome related to age, race, prior criminality, and being convicted of a property offense.
1978	Renner	Failure related to employment, alcohol, drugs, and longer periods of supervision.
1980	New Jersey Administrative Office of the Courts	Failure related to unemployment and prior criminal record.
1982	Holland et al.	Failure highly related to being a property offender.
1983	Scott & Carey	Failure related to serious physical injury in the conviction offense, unemployment, and prior incarcerations. Age, race, and prior convictions have no significant effect.
1986	Cuniff	Failure related to being convicted of property offense (burglary), age, employment, and sex.
1987	McCarthy & Langworthy	Failure highly related to age—males 50 and over are more successful.
no date	Kane County Diagnostic Center	Probation outcome most significantly related to highest grade completed, income, number of dependents, prior incarcerations, marital status.

tions of failure, followup periods, and types of offenders used in the sample often differ from study to study. These problems prevent adequate assessment of probation and determination of effectiveness.

In the literature review for the present study, there were questions and issues in the different studies which are crucial to probation research designed to assess the effectiveness of probation as a correctional alternative. In the studies reviewed, there was little uniformity in the definition of failure. Many of the studies used failure to indicate termination from probation due to reconviction, revocation, or absconding. Other studies used failure to refer to arrests for both misdemeanors and felonies, reconvictions, and revocation. In these studies, absconding or disappearance without notification was not considered to be failure.

None of the studies indicated the use of a control group for comparison. Although the experimental design with random assignment represents the best way for determining effectiveness, it is seldom possible in corrections research. However, the use of a comparison group based on matching would be beneficial to probation research.

Studies of postprobation outcome used different followup periods. Some used 6 to 12 years; 4 to 11 years; 22 months; 5½ to 11 years; 3 to 4 years; and 6 months to 7 years.

Study populations were different. Some studies used only felons, while others used both felons and misdemeanants. Federal probationers comprised the population in two studies, while the remaining studies used probationers supervised by state probation agencies.

The purpose of this article was to examine past research regarding probation outcome. A major underlying theme of this past research has been whether probation as a nonincarcerative alternative is fulfilling its objectives. There is a tremendous need for more empirical investigation of probation as a correctional alternative. More research is needed into issues including whether probation "widens the net" of social control, what probation can and cannot do, and for whom probation works best.

References

Bartell, T., & Thomas, W. (1977). Recidivist impacts of differential sentencing practices for felony offenders. *Criminology, 15*, 387-396.

Bureau of Justice Statistics. (1992). Probation in 1990. *Correctional populations in the United States, 1990*. Washington, DC: Department of Justice.

Caldwell, M. (1951). Preview of a new type of probation study made in Alabama. *Federal Probation, 15*(2), 3-11.

California Bureau of Statistics. (1977). Superior court probation and/or jail sample.

Cockerill, R. (1975). Probation effectiveness in Alberta. *Canadian Journal of Criminology and Corrections, 17*(4).

Comptroller General of the United States. (1976). *State and county probation: Systems in crisis.* Washington, DC: U.S. Government Printing Office.

Cuniff, M. (1986). *A sentencing postscript: Felony probationers under supervision in the community.* Washington, DC: National Criminal Justice Planning Association.

Davis, G. (1964). A study of adult probation violation rates by means of the cohort approach. *Journal of Criminal Law, Criminology and Police Science, 55,* 70-85.

Ditman, K.S. (1967). A controlled experiment on the use of court probation for drunk arrests. *American Journal of Psychiatry, 124*(2), 160-163.

England, R. (1955). A study of postprobation recidivism among five hundred federal offenders. *Federal Probation, 19,* 10-16.

Frease, D. (1964). Factors related to probation outcome. Olympia, WA: Department of Institutions, Board of Prison Terms and Parole.

General Accounting Office. (1976). *State and county probation systems in crisis.* Washington, DC: U.S. Government Printing Office.

Holland, T., Holt, N., & Beckett, G. (1982). Prediction of violent versus nonviolent recidivism from prior violent and nonviolent criminality. *Journal of Abnormal Psychology, 91,* 178-182.

Irish, J. (1977). Probation and its effect on recidivism: An evaluative study of probation in Nassau County, New York. Mineola NY: Nassau County Probation Department.

Kane County Diagnostic Center. (no date). *Probation prediction models and recidivism.* Geneva, IL.

Kusuda, P. (1976). *1974 probation and parole terminations.* Madison, WI: Wisconsin Corrections Division.

Latessa, E., Eskridge, C., Allen, H., & Vito, G. (1985). *Probation and parole in America.* New York: The Free Press.

Landis, J., Mercer, J., & Wolff, C. (1969). Success and failure of adult probationers in California. *Journal of Research in Crime and Delinquency, 6,* 34-40.

Lohman, J. (1966). *Ideal supervision caseload: A preliminary evaluation.* (The San Francisco Project Research Report #9). Berkeley, CA: University of California School of Criminology.

McCarthy, B., & Langworthy, R. (1987). *Older offenders: Perspectives in criminology and criminal justice.* New York: Praeger.

McGinnis, R., & Klockseim, K. (1976). *Probation and employment: A report to the Bergen County, New Jersey Probation Department.*

Missouri Division of Probation and Parole. (1976). *Probation in Missouri, July 1, 1968-June 30, 1970: Characteristics, performance and criminal reinvolvement.* Jefferson County, MO: Division of Probation and Parole.

Morgan, K. (1991). *An analysis of factors influencing probation outcome.* Unpublished dissertation, Florida State University.

New Jersey Administrative Office of the Courts. (1980). *Adult probation in New Jersey: A study of recidivism and a determination of the predictive utilities of a risk assessment model.* Trenton, NJ.

Norland, S., & Munn, P. (1984). Being troublesome: Women on probation. *Criminal Justice and Behavior, 11,* 115-135.

Petersilia, J. (1985). *Granting felons probation: Public risks and alternatives.* Santa Monica, CA: The Rand Corporation.

Petersilia, J. (1987). Probation and felony offenders. *Federal Probation, 51*(2), 56-61.

Renner, J. (1978). *The adult probationer in Ontario.* Ontario, Canada: Ministry of Correctional Services.

Rogers, S. (1981). *Factors related to recidivism among adult probationers in Ontario.* Ontario, Canada: Ontario Correctional Services Ministry.

Roundtree, G., Edwards, D., & Parker, J. (1984). A study of personal characteristics related to recidivism. *Journal of Offender Counseling Services and Rehabilitation, 8,* 53-61.

Scott, M., & Carey, H. (1983). Community alternatives in Colorado. *Criminal Justice and Behavior, 10*(1), 93-108.

Tippman, D. (1976). *Probation as a treatment alternative for criminal offenders: An analysis of variables related to performance on probation in a sample of men placed on probation.* Ph.D dissertation, Wayne State University.

Vito, G. (1985). Probation as punishment: New directions and suggestions. In L. Travis III (Ed.), *Probation, parole and community corrections.* Prospect Heights, IL: Waveland Press.

DOES CORRECTIONAL TREATMENT WORK? A CLINICALLY RELEVANT AND PSYCHOLOGICALLY INFORMED META-ANALYSIS*

D.A. ANDREWS
IVAN ZINGER
ROBERT D. HOGE
Carleton University

JAMES BONTA
Ottawa–Carleton Detention Centre

PAUL GENDREAU
Centracare Saint John, New Brunswick

FRANCIS T. CULLEN
University of Cincinnati

Careful reading of the literature on the psychology of criminal conduct and of prior reviews of studies of treatment effects suggests that neither criminal sanctioning without provision of rehabilitative service nor servicing without reference to clinical principles of rehabilitation will succeed in reducing recidivism. What works, in our view, is the delivery of appropriate correctional service, and appropriate service reflects three psychological principles: (1) delivery of service to higher risk cases, (2) targeting of criminogenic needs, and (3) use of styles and modes of treatment (e.g., cognitive and behavioral) that are matched with client need and learning styles. These principles were applied to studies of juvenile and adult correctional treatment, which yielded 154 phi coefficients that summarized the magnitude and direction of the impact of treatment on recidivism. The effect of appropriate correctional service (mean phi = .30) was significantly (p <.05) greater than that of unspecified correctional service (.13), and both were more effective than inappropriate service (−.06) and nonservice criminal sanctioning (−.07). Service was effective within juvenile and adult corrections, in studies published before and after 1980, in randomized and nonrandomized designs, and in diversionary, community, and residential programs (albeit, attenuated in residential settings). Clinical sensitivity and a psychologically informed perspective on crime

* This paper is dedicated to Daniel Glaser, Ted Palmer, and Marguerite Q. Warren.

may assist in the renewed service, research, and conceptual efforts that are strongly indicated by our review.

During the 1970s, the ideological hegemony of the individualized treatment ideal suffered a swift and devastating collapse (Rothman, 1980). Previously a code word for "doing good," rehabilitation came to be seen by liberals as a euphemism for coercing offenders and by conservatives as one for letting hardened criminals off easily. Although the public's belief in rehabilitation was never eroded completely (Cullen et al., 1988), defenders of treatment were branded scientifically and politically naive apologists for the socially powerful, self-serving human service professionals, or curious relics of a positivistic past. Thus, a number of jurisdictions in the United States (Cullen and Gilbert, 1982) and Canada (Andrews, 1990; Leschied et al., 1988) embarked on sentencing reforms that undercut the role of rehabilitation in justice and corrections.

The decline of the rehabilitative ideal cannot be attributed to a careful reading of evidence regarding the effectiveness of rehabilitative treatment. As will be shown, reviews of the effectiveness literature routinely found that a substantial proportion of the better-controlled studies of rehabilitative service reported positive effects, and did so for programs that operated within a variety of conditions established by criminal sanctions, such as probation or incarceration. We will also show that criminal sanctions themselves were typically found to be only minimally related to recidivism. Thus, rather than a rational appreciation of evidence, the attack on rehabilitation was a reflection of broader social and intellectual trends. This is evident upon consideration of the particular historical timing and intensity of the attack on rehabilitation.

First, the rapidly changing sociopolitical context of the decade preceding the mid-1970s propelled conservatives to seek "law and order," while liberals attached to class-based perspectives on crime became discouraged about the benevolence of the state and the promise of direct intervention (Allen, 1981; Cullen and Gendreau, 1989). Second, an emerging social science, informed by labelling and critical/Marxist approaches, embraced antipsychological and often anti-empirical themes (Andrews, 1990; Andrews and Wormith, 1989). These emergent perspectives played an important role in legitimating the decision of many academic criminologists and juridical policymakers to declare rehabilitation fully bankrupt. Most noteworthy was Robert Martinson's (1974:25) conclusion that "the rehabilitative efforts that have been reported so far have had no appreciable effect on recidivism." In short order, with the blessing of a major academy of science (Sechrest et al., 1979), the notion that "nothing works" became accepted doctrine (Walker, 1989). "Nothing works" satisfied conservative political reactions to the apparent disorder of the 1960s, liberal sorrow over perceived failures of the Great Society, and the ideological persuasions of those academicians whose truly social visions of deviance asserted that only radical social change could have an impact on crime.

In the 1980s, however, rehabilitation and respect for evidence made at least a modest comeback. As will be noted, a number of revisionist scholars have observed that the marriage of conservative politics and leftist social science—in both its "discouraged liberal" and "critical/Marxist" versions—has neither improved justice nor increased crime control. In any case, it is our thesis that evidence of effective treatment was there from the earliest reviews, now is mounting, and constitutes a persuasive case against the "nothing works" doctrine.

Even so, criticisms of rehabilitation are not in short supply. As Walker (1989:231) comments: "It is wishful thinking to believe that additional research is going to uncover a magic key that has somehow been overlooked for 150 years." Other scholars—as exemplified most notably and recently by Whitehead and Lab (1989; Lab and Whitehead, 1988)—continue to participate in the scientific exchange on intervention and to present evidence ostensibly bolstering the "nothing works" message.

Whitehead and Lab's (1989) report is very much in the tradition of the reviews and conclusions that are challenged in this paper. Before detailing our position, however, we note that the Whitehead and Lab review is important for several reasons. First, having searched the psychological, sociological, and criminological journals, they produced an impressively complete set of controlled evaluations of juvenile treatment for the years 1975 to 1984. They coded the setting of treatment and distinguished among diversion programs (within and outside the juvenile justice system), probation and other community-based programs, and residential programming. Moreover, they coded type of treatment within these settings as either behavioral or nonbehavioral and considered recency (year of publication) and quality of research design. Focused exclusively upon evaluations employing recidivism as an outcome variable, their conclusions actually had to do with crime control. Clearly then, the negative conclusion of Whitehead and Lab is worthy of serious consideration by those in criminal justice.

Most serious, and unlike most earlier reviews—including the Martinson (1974) review—portions of the Whitehead and Lab (1989) paper support a very firm version of "nothing works." That is, the methodological, clinical, and sampling caveats typically listed by earlier reviewers were discounted systematically in Whitehead and Lab (1989). Regarding quality of the research, the more rigorous studies were reported to find correctional treatment to have effects even more negative than did the less rigorous studies. As to standards of effectiveness, Whitehead and Lab advised that their standard (a phi coefficient of .20 or greater) was so generous that evidence favorable to treatment would certainly have emerged had positive evidence, in fact, existed. In regard to type of treatment, they admitted that behavioral forms of intervention may be effective with outcomes other than recidivism, but they found behavioral treatment to be no more effective than nonbehavioral approaches in the control of recidivism.

Our meta-analysis includes, but is not confined to, the Whitehead and Lab (1989) sample of studies. Challenging sweeping conclusions regarding program ineffectiveness, we reaffirm a line of analysis for developing meaningful conclusions on the conditions under which programs will work. Our challenge is informed by considerations of research and theory on the causes of crime and by research and theory on behavioral influence processes. In particular, a growing number of scholars and practitioners now agree with what was always the starting point of the Gluecks (1950), the Grants (1959), Glaser (1974), and Palmer (1975): The effectiveness of correctional treatment is dependent upon what is delivered to whom in particular settings. Certainly that has been our view[1] and the view of many other reviewers and commentators.[2]

CLINICALLY RELEVANT AND PSYCHOLOGICALLY INFORMED PROGRAMMING, EVALUATION, AND META-ANALYSIS

The psychology of criminal conduct recognizes multiple sources of variation in criminal recidivism (Andrews, 1980, 1983; Andrews and Kiessling, 1980; Andrews et al., 1990; Cullen and Gendreau, 1989; Hoge and Andrews, 1986; Palmer, 1983; Warren, 1969). These major sources of variation are found through analyses of the main and interactive effects of (a) preservice characteristics of offenders, (b) characteristics of correctional workers, (c) specifics of the content and process of services planned and delivered, and (d) intermediate changes in the person and circumstances of individual offenders. Logically, these major sources of variation in outcome reside within the conditions established by the specifics of a judicial disposition or criminal sanction. Thus, there is little reason to expect that variation among settings or sanctions will have an impact on recidivism except in interaction with offender characteristics and through the mediators of intervention process and intermediate change. We develop this "criminal sanction" hypothesis first and then compare it with hypotheses regarding the effectiveness of a correctional service approach that attends to preservice case characteristics, to

1. Andrews (1980, 1983, 1990), Andrews and Kiessling (1980), Andrews et al. (1990), Cullen and Gendreau (1989), Gendreau and Ross (1979, 1981, 1987).

2. Basta and Davidson (1988), Currie (1989), Garrett (1985), Geismar and Wood (1985), Greenwood and Zimring (1985), Izzo and Ross (1990), Lipsey (1989), Martinson (1979), Mayer et al. (1986), Palmer (1983), Ross and Fabiano (1985).

the process and content of intervention, and to intermediate change within particular sanctions.

IN THEORY, WHY SHOULD CRIMINAL SANCTIONING WORK?

A focus upon variation in official disposition is a reflection of one or more of the three sets of theoretical perspectives known as *just deserts, labelling*, and *deterrence*. The just deserts or justice set is not overly concerned with recidivism, but on occasion the assumption surfaces that unjust processing may motivate additional criminal activity (Schur, 1973:129). It appears, however, that the devaluation of rehabilitation—in the interest of increasing "just" processing—has been associated with increased punishment and decreased treatment but not with reduced recidivism (Cullen and Gilbert, 1982; Leschied et al., 1988).

The labelling and deterrence perspectives actually yield conflicting predictions regarding the outcomes of different dispositions (Rausch, 1983). Labelling theory suggests that less involvement in the criminal justice system is better than more (because the stigma is less), while deterrence theory suggests the opposite (because fear of punishment is greater). The assumptions of both labelling (Andrews and Wormith, 1989; Wellford, 1975) and deterrence (Gendreau and Ross, 1981) have been subjected to logical and empirical review, and neither perspective is yet able to offer a well-developed psychology of criminal conduct. Basic differentiations among and within levels and types of sanctions have yet to be worked out (Smith and Gartin, 1989), type of offender is likely a crucial moderating variable (Klein, 1986), and the social psychology of "processing" is only now being explored (Link et al., 1989).

IN FACT, DOES CRIMINAL SANCTIONING WORK?

To our knowledge, not a single review of the effects of judicial sanctioning on criminal recidivism has reached positive conclusions except when the extremes of incapacitation are tested or when additional reference is made to moderators (e.g., type of offender) or mediators (e.g., the specifics of intervention). Reading Kirby (1954), Bailey (1966), Logan (1972), and Martinson (1974) reveals the obvious but unstated fact that their negative conclusions regarding "treatment" reflected primarily the negligible impact of variation in sanctions such as probation and incarceration. Thus, we agree with Palmer (1975): The main effects of criminal sanctions on recidivism have been slight and inconsistent.

This hypothesis is extended to judicial "alternatives," because there are no solid reasons for expecting alternative punishments, such as community service or restitution, to have an impact on recidivism. Any anticipated rehabilitative benefit of "alternatives" is based on the hope that offenders will learn that crime has negative consequences, and yet the enhancement of cognitive and interpersonal skills (e.g., future-orientation and perspective-taking) are dependent upon systematic modeling, reinforcement, and graduated practice (Ross and Fabiano, 1985). Given little reason to expect much from the incidental learning opportunities provided by such sanctions as restitution, correctional treatment service is a crucial supplement to a criminal justice approach that is preoccupied with avoiding stigma while delivering "just" and "innovative alternative" punishment.

CORRECTIONAL TREATMENT SERVICES

Reviewers of the literature have routinely found that at least 40% of the better-controlled evaluations of correctional treatment services reported positive effects (Andrews et al., 1990). For example, considering only the better-controlled studies, the proportion of studies reporting positive evidence was 75% (3/4) in Kirby (1954), 59% (13/22) in Bailey (1966), 50% (9/18) in Logan (1972), 78% (14/18) in Logan when Type of Treatment × Type of Client interactions are considered, 48% (39/82) in Palmer's (1975) retabulation of studies reviewed by Martinson (1974), 86% (82/95) in Gendreau and Ross (1979), and 47% (40/85) in Lab and Whitehead (1988). This pattern of results strongly supports exploration of the idea that some service programs are working with at least some offenders under some circumstances, and we think that helpful linkages among case, service, and outcome are suggested by three principles known as risk, need, and responsivity (Andrews et al., 1990).

The risk principle and selection of level of service

The risk principle suggests that higher levels of service are best reserved for higher risk cases and that low-risk cases are best assigned to minimal service. In the literature at least since the Gluecks (1950), the risk principle has been restated on many occasions (e.g., Glaser, 1974). Although the parameters remain to be established, evidence favoring the risk principle continues to grow (Andrews et al., 1990). In brief, when actually explored, the effects of treatment typically are found to be greater among higher risk cases than among lower risk cases. This is expected unless the need and/or responsivity principles are violated.

The need principle and selection of appropriate intermediate targets

Risk factors may be static or dynamic in nature, and psychology is particularly interested in those dynamic risk factors that, when changed, are associated with *subsequent* variation in the chances of criminal conduct. Clinically, dynamic risk factors are called *criminogenic needs*, and guidelines for their assessment are described elsewhere (Andrews, 1983; Andrews et al., 1990).

The most promising intermediate targets include changing antisocial attitudes, feelings, and peer associations; promoting familial affection in combination with enhanced parental monitoring and supervision; promoting identification with anticriminal role models; increasing self-control and self-management skills; replacing the skills of lying, stealing, and aggression with other, more prosocial skills; reducing chemical dependencies; and generally shifting the density of rewards and costs for criminal and noncriminal activities in familial, academic, vocational, and other behavioral settings.[3] Theoretically, modifying contingencies within the home, school, and work by way of an increased density of reward for noncriminal activity may reduce motivation for crime and increase the costs of criminal activity through having more to lose (Hunt and Azrin, 1973).

Less-promising targets include increasing self-esteem without touching antisocial propensity (e.g., Wormith, 1984), increasing the cohesiveness of antisocial peer groups (e.g., Klein, 1971), improving neighborhood-wide living conditions without reaching high-risk families (the East Side, Midcity, and other community projects in Klein, 1971, and Schur, 1973), and attempts to focus on vague personal/emotional problems that have not been linked with recidivism (Andrews and Kiessling, 1980).

THE RESPONSIVITY PRINCIPLE AND SELECTION OF TYPE OF SERVICE

The responsivity principle has to do with the selection of styles and modes of service that are (a) capable of influencing the specific types of intermediate targets that are set with offenders and (b) appropriately matched to the learning styles of offenders. We begin with the general literature on the treatment of offenders and then turn to specific Responsivity × Service interactions.

Responsivity: General principles of effective service. Drawing upon our earlier review (Andrews et al., 1990), appropriate types of service typically, but not exclusively, involve the use of behavioral and social learning principles of interpersonal influence, skill enhancement, and cognitive change. Specifically, they include modeling, graduated practice, rehearsal, role playing, reinforcement, resource provision, and detailed verbal guidance and explanations (making suggestions, giving reasons, cognitive restructuring). Elsewhere (Andrews and Kiessling, 1980), we describe the applications of these practices as (a) use of authority (a "firm but fair" approach and definitely not interpersonal domination or abuse), (b) anticriminal modeling and reinforement (explicit reinforcement and modeling of alternatives to procriminal styles of thinking, feeling, and acting), and (c) concrete problem solving and

3. For example, Andrews et al. (1990), Andrews and Wormith (1989), Glueck and Glueck (1950), Johnson (1979), Loeber and Stouthamer–Loeber (1987), Wilson and Herrnstein (1985).

systematic skill training for purposes of increasing reward levels in anticriminal settings. High levels of advocacy and brokerage are also indicated as long as the receiving agency actually offers appropriate service. Finally, Andrews and Kiessling (1980) recommended that service deliverers relate to offenders in interpersonally warm, flexible, and enthusiastic ways while also being clearly supportive of anticriminal attitudinal and behavioral patterns. Interestingly, social learning approaches receive strong, albeit indirect, support from the prediction literature on the causal modeling of delinquency (Akers and Cochran, 1985; Jessor and Jessor, 1977).

Responsivity: Ineffective service. Some types and styles of services should be avoided under most circumstances (Andrews et al., 1990). Generally, programming for groups is to be approached very cautiously because the opening up of communication within offender groups may well be criminogenic (Andrews, 1980). In group and residential programming, clinicians must gain control over the contingencies of interaction so that anticriminal, rather than procriminal, patterns are exposed and reinforced (Buehler et al., 1966). For example, Agee's (1986) programmatic structures supporting positive change may be contrasted with the failure of unstructured, peer-oriented group counseling and permissive, relationship-oriented milieu approaches. The failure of these unstructured approaches is well documented in open community settings (e.g., Faust, 1965; Klein, 1971), in group homes operating according to the essentially nondirective guidelines of "guided group interaction" (Stephenson and Scarpitti, 1974:Ch. 8), in hospitals (Craft et al., 1966), and in prisons (Kassebaum et al., 1971; Murphy, 1972). There are also no convincing theoretical grounds for believing that young people will be "scared straight" (Finckenauer, 1982). Fear of official punishment is not one of the more important correlates of delinquency (Johnson, 1979), and yelling at people is counter to the relationship principle of effective service (Andrews, 1980).

Finally, traditional psychodynamic and nondirective client-centered therapies are to be avoided within general samples of offenders (Andrews et al., 1990). These therapies are designed to free people from the personally inhibiting controls of "superego" and "society," but neurotic misery and overcontrol are not criminogenic problems for a majority of offenders. Authorities such as Freud (in his introductory lectures on psychoanalysis, 1953) and the Gluecks (in their classic *Unraveling*, 1950) warned us about evocative and relationship-dependent psychodynamic approaches with antisocial cases.

Specific responsivity considerations. The success of highly verbal, evocative, and relationship-dependent services seems to be limited to clients with high levels of interpersonal, self-reflective, and verbal skill. The "I-Level" (Harris, 1988) and "Conceptual Level" (Reitsma–Street and Leschied, 1988) systems provide guidance regarding the types of offenders who may respond in positive ways to services that are less structured than those we have been describing as appropriate for antisocial samples in general.

SUMMARY

Our clinically relevant and psychologically informed principles of treatment predict that criminal sanctioning without attention to the delivery of correctional service will relate to recidivism minimally. Additionally, we suggest that the delivery of services, regardless of criminal sanction or setting, is unproductive if those services are inconsistent with the principles of risk, need, and responsivity. Positively, we predict that appropriate treatment—treatment that is delivered to higher risk cases, that targets criminogenic need, and that is matched with the learning styles of offenders—will reduce recidivism.

METHOD

SAMPLES OF STUDIES

We subjected 45 of the 50 studies included in the Whitehead and Lab (1989) review to content and meta-analysis.[4] The Whitehead and Lab sample included only studies of juvenile treatment that appeared in professional journals between 1975 and 1984 and that presented effects of treatment on binary (less–more) measures of recidivism. Studies that focused on imprisonment or the treatment of substance abuse were not included.

We also explored a second sample of studies in order to check on the generalizability of any findings based on the Whitehead and Lab sample. Sample 2 included 35 studies in our research files as of February 1989 that were not included in the Whitehead and Lab set but had employed binary measures of recidivism. Studies in sample 2 date from the 1950s through 1989, but they are not purported to be a representative sample of any particular time period. Sample 2 provides a convenient means of exploring, albeit tentatively, how well conclusions based on the Whitehead and Lab sample may generalize to adult samples.

ESTIMATES OF TREATMENT EFFECT

The Whitehead and Lab sample yielded a total of 87 2×2 contingency

---

4. Douds and Collingwood (1978) and Collingwood and Genthner (1980) were excluded because their samples appeared to overlap those of either Collingwood et al. (1976) or Williams (1984). Similarly, Fo and O'Donnell (1975) was dropped because of overlap with O'Donnell et al. (1979). The Baer et al. (1975) report on Outward Bound was excluded because the independent variable did not involve variation in service. Beal and Duckro (1977) was dropped because the outcome seemed to be court proceedings on the offense that led to a program referral.

tables reflecting the strength and direction of the association between two levels of treatment and recidivism-nonrecidivism. Whitehead and Lab, on the other hand, tabled a single phi coefficient for each study. With our approach, distinct phi coefficients were computed when distinct samples and distinct treatments were reported in a paper (e.g., Klein et al., 1977), and rather than compare two "appropriate" styles of service, we compared each service with its respective control (e.g., Jesness, 1975; Mitchell, 1983; in the latter study we estimated that the experimental recidivists were averaging twice the number of new offenses found among control recidivists). Tests of Type of Offender × Type of Treatment interactions were represented only incidentally in Whitehead and Lab. In our report, services to higher and lower risk cases yield separate estimates of treatment effects.

Sample 2 yielded 67 treatment-recidivism tables, 44 based on studies of juveniles and 23 based on adults. (Romig's 1976 analysis of parole supervision is entered as part of the Whitehead and Lab sample, and the analysis of months incarcerated is entered as part of sample 2). The studies and treatment comparisons are outlined in detail in the appendix (Table A1) for readers who may wish to reconstruct our analyses. Phi was employed as the measure of treatment effect because it provides a convenient summary of the direction and magnitude of the association between two binary variables, is equivalent to the Pearson product-moment coefficient, is more conservative than gamma, and was used by Whitehead and Lab.

CONTENT ANALYSIS

The potential covariates of phi estimates were coded as follows:

1. Setting: The Whitehead and Lab codes for setting were accepted uncritically: nonsystem diversion, system diversion, probation/parole/community corrections, and institutional/residential. Preliminary analyses confirmed that the effects on phi coefficients of the three different community settings were statistically indistinguishable. Hence, setting was employed as a two-level, community-residential factor in further analyses. Table A1, however, includes the elaborate code.
2. Year of publication: before the 1980s/in the 1980s.
3. Quality of research design: Studies employing random assignment were coded "stronger design." Nonrandom assignment was coded "weaker design," except when information on risk factors (e.g., prior offense or "bad attitude") allowed the computation of separate treatment comparisons for lower and higher risk cases. When risk was so controlled, the design was coded "stronger."
4. Sample of studies: Whitehead and Lab/sample 2.
5. Justice system: Juvenile system/adult system.

6. Behavioral intervention: Programs described as behavioral by the authors of an evaluation study were coded "behavioral," as were those that systematically employed behavioral techniques.[5]
7. Type of treatment: Following the principles discussed above, the four levels of type of treatment were as follows:
   a. Criminal sanctions: This code involved variation in judicial disposition, imposed at the front end of the correctional process and not involving deliberate variation in rehabilitative service (e.g., restitution, police cautioning versus regular processing, less versus more probation, and probation versus custody).
   b. Inappropriate correctional service: Inappropriate service included (1) service delivery to lower risk cases and/or mismatching according to a need/responsivity system, (2) nondirective relationship-dependent and/or unstructured psychodynamic counseling, (3) all milieu and group approaches with an emphasis on within-group communication and without a clear plan for gaining control over procriminal modeling and reinforcement, (4) nondirective or poorly targeted academic and vocational approaches, and (5) "scared straight."
   c. Appropriate correctional service: Appropriate service included (1) service delivery to higher risk cases, (2) all behavioral programs (except those involving delivery of service to lower risk cases), (3) comparisons reflecting specific responsivity-treatment comparisons, and (4) nonbehavioral programs that clearly stated that criminogenic need was targeted and that structured intervention was employed.[6]

---

5. The interventions of Hackler and Hagan (1975) were coded as nonbehavioral. William's (1984) Dallas program was coded behavioral in our study, in line with Whitehead and Lab's coding of the Collingwood et al. (1976) report on the same program as behavioral. Both studies of restitution were coded nonbehavioral in our study (only one of which was coded nonbehavioral by Whitehead and Lab). The Ross and Fabiano behavioral skills program was coded as unspecified because it was a comparison condition for a more appropriate program.

6. Treatments admitted to the "appropriate" category by criterion "4" were appropriate according to the principles of need and responsivity (although some readers might disagree): Kelly et al. (1979) encouraged delinquents to explore alternative values and behavior patterns; the transactional program (Jesness, 1975) established individualized targets based on criminogenic need; the family counseling program of McPherson et al. (1983) targeted discipline and self-management; Bachara and Zaba (1978) focused on specific learning problems; Shore and Massimo (1979) studied very intensive, highly individualized, vocationally oriented counseling. Some difficult calls, which we ultimately coded as unspecified, included the following: Druckman's (1979) family counseling, which hinted at a nondirective client-centered approach but lacked a clear statement of same; the paraprofessional advocacy program of Seidman et al. (1980), Wade et al.'s (1977) family program, and Sowles and Gill's (1970) counseling programs all included references to both

d. Unspecified correctional service: Unspecified service was a residual set for those comparisons involving treatments that we could not confidently label appropriate or inappropriate.

HYPOTHESES

Our first hypothesis is that Type of Treatment is the major source of variation in estimates of effect size (phi coefficients).[7] Specifically, the contributions of Type of Treament to the prediction of effect size will exceed the predictive contributions of year of publication, quality of design, setting, behavioral-nonbehavioral intervention, justice system (juvenile or adult), and sample of studies examined.

Our second hypothesis is that appropriate correctional service will yield an average estimate of impact on recidivism that is positive and exceeds those of criminal sanctions, unspecified service, and inappropriate service.

RESULTS AND DISCUSSION

A preliminary comparison of the two samples of studies was conducted on various control variables. The comparisons reflected an obvious concern that any systematic differences between the Whitehead and Lab sample and sample 2 be documented. Overall, apart from the inclusion of studies of adult treatment in sample 2, the two samples of studies were found to be reasonably comparable across the various potential predictors of treatment effect size explored in this paper (see row 2 of the intercorrelation matrix in Table 1).[8]

---

appropriate and inappropriate elements. Some "treatments" in Rausch (1983) may have involved unspecified service components, but they were assigned to the criminal sanction set in the spirit of the Rausch analysis of labelling and deterrence theory.

7. Reliability and validity in coding the type of treatment are obvious concerns. One of our ongoing research efforts involves building a psychometrically sound instrument that can be used to assess the correctional appropriateness not simply of printed program descriptions but also of ongoing programs. The psychometrics of this instrument will be the focus of future reports. For now, we have indicated in Table A1 what comparisons were assigned to what categories, and they are thereby appropriately and easily the focus of critical review.

8. The Whitehead and Lab sample ($n = 87$) and sample 2 ($n = 67$) were virtually identical in the proportion of tests falling in the three categories of treatment services: inappropriate (20/87 vs. 16/67), unspecified (16/87 vs. 16/67), appropriate (30/87 vs. 24/67). The nonsignificant trend was an underrepresentation of comparisons involving criminal sanctions in sample 2 (21/87 vs. 9/67, $r = .08$). Because the Whitehead and Lab sample was limited to studies of juveniles, there was an expected and substantial correlation between Justice System and Sample of Studies (phi $= .48$, $p < 0.01$). Not as obviously deducible from the descriptions of the samples provided in the methods section, sample 2 included a statistically significant overrepresentation of institution-based treatments (phi $= .21$, $p < .05$).

Table 1. Intercorrelation Matrix, Correlations with Phi Coefficients (N = 154), and Mean Phi Coefficients at Each Level of Each Variable

	A Type of Treatment	B Sample of Studies	C Justice System	D Year of Publication	E Quality of Design	F Setting
A.		.08	.01	−.14	.10	.11
B.			.48**	.11	.14	.21*
C.				.23*	.15	−.01
D.					−.10	−.33**
E.						−.17
Simple Unadjusted Correlation with Phi (Mean Phi = .104, SD = .234)						
	.69**	.18*	.02	.09	−.03	−.07
Unadjusted Mean Phi Coefficient (n) at Each Level of Each Variable						
1.	−.07 (30)	.07 (87)	.10 (131)	.08 (76)	.11 (81)	.11 (119)
2.	−.06 (38)	.15 (67)	.11 (23)	.13 (78)	.10 (73)	.07 (35)
3.	.13 (32)					
4.	.30 (54)					
F Values for Unadjusted Effects						
	45.62**	5.27*	0.49	1.33	0.11	0.74
Partial Correlation with Phi, Controlling for Other Variables						
	.72**	.15*	.02	.18*	−.07	−.16*
Adjusted Mean Phi Coefficient (n) at Each Level of Each Variable						
1.	−.08 (30)	.07 (87)	.10 (131)	.06 (76)	.11 (81)	.12 (119)
2	−.07 (38)	.14 (67)	.11 (23)	.14 (78)	.08 (73)	.03 (35)
3.	.10 (32)					
4.	.32 (54)					
F Values for Adjusted Effects						
	57.15**	6.99*	0.33	9.80**	1.18	7.43**

* $p < .05$ ** $p < .01$

Note: The levels of the variables are as follows: Type of Treatment (criminal sanctions, inappropriate service, unspecified service, appropriate service), Sample of Studies (Whitehead and Lab, sample 2), Justice System (juvenile, adult), Year of Publication (before 1980, 1980s), Quality of Research Design (weaker, stronger), and Setting (community, institutional/residential).

A qualitative and nonparametric summary of findings is appended, but here the hypotheses are tested directly.

HYPOTHESIS 1: RELATIVE PREDICTIVE POTENTIAL OF TYPE OF TREATMENT

Inspection of the first column of Table 1 reveals that the correlation between Type of Treatment and phi coefficients was strong (Eta = .69) and, with simultaneous control introduced for each of the other variables through analysis of covariance techniques in a multiple classification analysis, the correlation increased to .72 (Beta). The only other significant unadjusted predictor of phi coefficients was Sample of Studies (.18, unadjusted; .15, adjusted). With controls for Type of Treatment introduced, the magnitude of correlation with phi coefficients increased to significant levels for Year of Publication (from .09 to .18) and for Setting (from −.07 to −.16).

Comparisons from sample 2, recency of publication and community-based treatment, were each associated with relatively positive effects of treatment. These trends, however, were overwhelmed by Type of Treatment. In a stepwise multiple regression, the only variables contributing significantly ($p < .05$) to variation in phi estimates were Type of Treatment (beta = .69) and Year of Publication (beta = .19), $F(^2/_{151}) = 68.01$, $p < .000$, adjusted R square = .47. In summary, our first hypothesis was strongly supported: Type of Treatment was clearly the strongest of the correlates of effect size sampled in this study.

HYPOTHESIS 2: THE IMPORTANCE OF APPROPRIATE CORRECTIONAL SERVICE

As described above, the main effect of Type of Treatment on phi estimates was strong and positive, with or without adjustment for control variables. Scheffe tests confirmed that the mean phi coefficient for appropriate correctional service (.30, n = 54) was significantly ($p < 0.05$) greater than that for criminal sanctions (−.07, n = 30), inappropriate service (−.06, n = 38), and unspecified service (.13, n = 32). In addition, Scheffe tests revealed that the average effect of unspecified correctional service significantly exceeded the mean phi coefficients for criminal sanctions and inappropriate service.

Mean phi coefficients for each of the four types of treatment are presented in Table 2 at each of the two levels of the various control variables. Inspection reveals a robust correlation between Type of Treatment and effects on recidivism at each level of Sample of Studies, Justice System, Year of Publication, Design, and Setting.

The only variable to interact significantly ($p < 0.05$) with Type of Treatment was Year of Publication. It appears that criminal sanctions yielded more negative phi estimates in the earlier literature than in the more recent literature (−.16 versus −.02, $F[^1/_{28}] = 8.98$. $p < .006$). This reflects a greater representation of residential studies in the earlier years (the negative implications of residential programs will be discussed below). More interestingly, studies of appropriate correctional treatment in the 1980s yielded a much higher mean phi estimate than did earlier studies of appropriate treatment (.40 versus .24, $F[^1/_{52}] = 8.40$, $p < .005$). Most likely, this reflects three trends. First, the earlier studies included what are now recognized to be unsophisticated applications of token economy systems (see Ross and

McKay, 1976). Second, studies of the 1980s paid greater attention to cognitive variables (Ross and Fabiano, 1985). Third, the positive effects of short-term behavioral family counseling have been replicated in the 1980s (Gordon et al., 1988). In summary, Hypothesis 2 was supported to a stronger degree than was initially anticipated: Both appropriate and unspecified correctional services were significantly more effective in reducing recidivism than were criminal sanctions and inappropriate service.

NOTE ON BEHAVIORAL INTERVENTION

The use of behavioral methods was a major element in the coding of appropriateness according to the principle of responsivity. Not surprisingly, in view of our coding rules, 95% ($^{38}/_{41}$) of the behavioral treatments were coded as appropriate treatment and 70% ($^{38}/_{54}$) of the appropriate treatments were behavioral. Thus, the correlation between Behavioral Intervention and Type

Table 2. The Effect of Type of Treatment on Recidivism at Each Level of the Control Variables: Mean Phi Coefficients (N)

	Criminal Sanctions	Correctional Service		
		Inapp.	Unspec.	Appropriate
Sample of Studies				
Whitehead and Lab	−.04 (21)	−.11 (20)	.09 (16)	.24 (30)
Sample 2	−.13 (9)	−.02 (18)	.17 (16)	.37 (24)
Justice System				
Juvenile	−.06 (26)	−.07 (31)	.13 (29)	.29 (45)
Adult	−.12 (4)	−.03 (7)	.13 (3)	.34 (9)
Year of Publication				
Before the 1980s	−.16 (10)	−.09 (22)	.17 (11)	.24 (33)
1980s	−.02 (20)	−.03 (16)	.11 (21)	.40 (21)
Quality of Research Design				
Weaker	−.07 (21)	−.04 (10)	.15 (18)	.32 (26)
Stronger	−.07 (9)	−.08 (22)	.11 (14)	.29 (28)
Setting				
Community	−.05 (24)	−.14 (31)	.12 (27)	.35 (37)
Institution/Res.	−.14 (6)	−.15 (7)	.21 (5)	.20 (17)
Behavioral Intervention				
No	−.07 (30)	−.06 (36)	.13 (31)	.27 (16)
Yes	—	−.09 (2)	.23 (1)	.31 (38)
Overall Mean Phi	−.07 (30)	−.06 (38)	.13 (32)	.30 (54)
S.D.	.14	.15	.16	.19
Mean Phi Adjusted for Other Variables	−.08 (30)	−.07 (38)	.10 (32)	.32 (54)

of Treatment was substantial ($r = .62$). As expected, Behavioral Intervention, on its own, yielded a significantly greater mean phi coefficient than did non-behavioral treatment. The mean phi coefficients were .29 (SD = .23, n = 41) and .04 (SD = .20, n = 113) for behavioral and nonbehavioral interventions, respectively ($F[^1/_{152}] = 46.09, p < .000$, Eta = .48). Once controls were introduced for Type of Treatment, however, the contribution of Behavioral Intervention was reduced to nonsignificant levels, $F(^1/_{151}) < 1.00$, Beta = .07. It appears, then, that use of behavioral methods contributes to the reduction of recidivism, but those contributions are subsumed by the broader implications of risk, need, and responsivity as represented in our Type of Treatment variable.

NOTE ON RESIDENTIAL PROGRAMMING

The minor but statistically significant adjusted main effect of setting is displayed in column six of Table 1. This trend should not be overemphasized, but the relatively weak performance of appropriate correctional service in residential facilities is notable from Table 2 (mean phi estimate of .20 compared with .35 for treatment within community settings, $F[^1/_{52}] = 5.89, p < .02$). In addition, inappropriate service performed particularly poorly in residential settings compared with community settings (−.15 versus −.04, $F[^1/_{36}] = 3.74, p < .06$). Thus, it seems that institutions and residential settings may dampen the positive effects of appropriate service while augmenting the negative impact of inappropriate service. This admittedly tentative finding does not suggest that appropriate correctional services should not be applied in institutional and residential settings. Recall that appropriate service was more effective than inappropriate service in all settings.

CONCLUSIONS

The meta-analysis has revealed considerable order in estimates of the magnitude of the impact of treatment upon recidivism. As predicted, the major source of variation in effects on recidivism was the extent to which service was appropriate according to the principles of risk, need, and responsivity. Appropriate correctional service appears to work better than criminal sanctions not involving rehabilitative service and better than services less consistent with our a priori principles of effective rehabilitation. This review has convinced us that the positive trends that we and others detected in the literature of the 1960s and early 1970s were indeed worthy of serious application and evaluation. There is a reasonably solid clinical and research basis for the political reaffirmation of rehabilitation (Cullen and Gilbert, 1982).

The importance of clinical and theoretical relevance in programming and in meta-analysis has been demonstrated—the sanction and treatment services should be differentiated, and the action in regard to recidivism appears to reside in appropriate treatment. Much, however, remains to be done. We look forward to critiques and revisions of the principles of risk, need, and responsivity as stated and applied herein. What comparisons were assigned to what analytic categories is described in our report and is thereby easily and appropriately the focus of critical review (see note 7). Reserved for future reports are the many issues surrounding therapeutic integrity (Gendreau and Ross, 1979), the measurement of recidivism (Andrews, 1983), and methodological issues such as sample size (Lipsey, 1989). Similarly, we anticipate exploring in detail the value of alternatives to ordinary least squares analyses (for now, nonparametric tests of Type of Treatment are appended). Gender effects and the treatment of sex offenders, substance abusers, and inmates of long-term institutions require detailed analyses. Toward these ends, our meta-analytic data base is being extended. Our focus here, however, remains on type of service and effect size.

Of immediate concern is the meaning of an average phi coefficient of .30 for comparisons involving appropriate correctional service. First, until convinced otherwise, we will assume that an average phi of .30 is more positive, clinically and socially, than the mean effects of the alternatives of sanctioning without regard for service or servicing without regard to the principles of effective correctional service. Casual review of recidivism rates will reveal that, on average, appropriate treatment cut recidivism rates by about 50% (in fact, the mean reduction was 53.06%, SD = 26.49). Thus, we do not think that the positive effects are "minimal". Second, the correlation between effect size estimates and type of treatment approached .70. Correlations of this magnitude are unlikely to reflect "lucky outliers" (Greenwood, 1988), although more systematic sources of error may indeed inflate correlation coefficients. Third, issues surrounding the assessment of the clinical and social significance of diverse measures of effect size are indeed worthy of ongoing research. Future reports on our expanding data bank will compare various estimates of effect size, including some direct estimates of clinical/ social significance. For now, we are interested in discovering ethical routes to strengthened treatment effects, but we are not talking about magical cures.

Critics of rehabilitation are correct when they note that the average correlation between treatment and recidivism is not 1.00. At the same time, critics might be asked to report on the variation that their "preferred" variable shares with recidivism. For example, if their preferred variable is social class, they may be reminded that some reviewers have estimated that the average correlation between class and crime is about −.09 (Tittle et al., 1978). If their preferred approach is incapacitation or community crime prevention, they may be reminded of the minimal effects so far reported for these strategies (Rosenbaum, 1988; Visher, 1987). Critics, be they supporters of social class or incapacitation, likely will respond with examples of particular studies that yielded high correlations with indicators of crime. We remind them that the largest correlations are no better estimates of the average effect than are the least favorable estimates. We also remind them that the positive evidence regarding appropriate rehabilitative service comes not from cross-sectional research—the typical research strategy of critics of rehabilitation—but from deliberate and socially sanctioned approximations of truly experimental ideals. Finally, we remind the critics that one can be interested in the effects of class, punishment, and prevention programs on individual and aggregated crime rates while maintaining multiple interests and without letting one interest justify dismissal of the value of another.

This meta-analysis has done more than uncover evidence that supported our a priori biases regarding the importance of appropriate correctional service. The finding that the effects of inappropriate service appeared to be particularly negative in residential settings while the positive effects of appropriate service were attenuated was something of a surprise. While sensitive to the difficulties of working with antisocial groups, we did not predict this incidental affirmation of a widely shared preference for community over residential programming. Institutions and group homes, however, remain important components of correctional systems and hence active but thoughtful service is indicated. The literature should be carefully scrutinized in order to avoid inappropriate service, and follow-up services in the community may be necessary in order to maximize effectiveness. Finally, the suppressive impact of residential programming suggests that the negative effects of custody are better established than we anticipated.

The effect of the quality of the research design on estimates of effect size was relatively minor. Even if some design problems do inflate effect size estimates (Davidson et al., 1984; Lipsey, 1989), the interesting finding was that comparisons involving more and less rigorous research designs agreed as to what types of treatment were most effective. Program managers and frontline clinicians who find truly randomized groups to be practically or ethically impossible may consider conducting an evaluation that approximates the ideals of a true experiment. In particular, we strongly endorse the use of designs that introduce controls for the preservice risk levels of clients and that actually report on risk × service interactions. In addition, even evaluations that rely upon comparisons of clients who complete or do not complete treatment may be valuable.

Finally, the number of evaluative studies of correctional service should increase dramatically over the next decade. Although millions of young people were processed by juvenile justice systems during the past decade, the total number of papers in the Whitehead and Lab (1989) set that involved systematic study of appropriate service was 21. Were it not for behavioral psychologists, the number of papers involving appropriate service would have been nine. From a positive perspective, there is renewed interest, vigor, and sensitivity in the study of the psychology of criminal conduct (Andrews and

Wormith, 1989; Loeber and Stouthamer–Loeber, 1987; Wilson and Herrnstein, 1985) and of correctional service and prevention (e.g., Andrews et al., 1990; Cullen and Gendreau, 1988; Currie, 1989; Gendreau and Ross, 1987). There are solid reasons to focus in ethical and humane ways on the client and the quality of service delivered within just dispositions.

REFERENCES

Adams, R. and H.J. Vetter

1982 Social structure and psychodrama outcome: A ten-year follow-up. Journal of Offender Counseling, Services, and Rehabilitation 6:111–119.

Agee, V.L.

1986 Institutional treatment programs for the violent juvenile. In S. Apter and A. Goldstein (eds.), Youth Violence: Program and Prospects. Elmsford, N.Y.: Pergamon.

Akers, R.L. and J.K. Cochran

1985 Adolescent marijuana use: A test of three theories of deviant behavior. Deviant Behavior 3:323–346.

Alexander, J.F., B. Cole, R.S. Schiavo, and B.V. Parsons

1976 Systems-behavioral intervention with families of delinquents: Therapist characteristics, family behavior, and outcome. Journal of Consulting and Clinial Psychology 44:556–664.

Allen, F.A.

1981 The Decline of the Rehabilitative Ideal: Penal Policy and Social Purpose. New Haven: Yale University Press.

Andrews, D.A.

1980 Some experimental investigations of the principles of differential association through deliberate manipulations of the structure of service systems. American Sociological Review 45:448–462.

1983 The assessment of outcome in correctional samples. In M.L. Lambert, E.R. Christensen, and S.S. DeJulio (eds.), The Measurement of Psychotherapy Outcome in Research and Evaluation. New York: John Wiley & Sons.

1990 Some criminological sources of antirehabilitation bias in the Report of the Canadian Sentencing Commission. Canadian Journal of Criminology. Forthcoming.

Andrews, D.A. and J.J. Kiessling

1980 Program structure and effective correctional practices: A summary of the CaVIC research. In R.R. Ross and P. Gendreau (eds.), Effective Correctional Treatment. Toronto: Butterworth.

Andrews, D.A. and J.S. Wormith

1989 Personality and crime: Knowledge destruction and construction in criminology. Justice Quarterly 6:289–309.

Andrews, D.A., J.J. Kiessling, D. Robinson, and S. Mickus

1986 The risk principle of case classification: An outcome evaluation with young adult probationers. Canadian Journal of Criminology 28:377–396.

Andrews, D.A., J. Bonta, and R.D. Hoge
1990 Classification for effective rehabilitation: Rediscovering psychology. Criminal Justice and Behavior 17:19–52.

Bachara, G.H. and J.N. Zaba
1978 Learning disabilitites and juvenile delinquency. Journal of Learning Disabilities 11:242–246.

Baer, D.J., P.J. Jacobs, and F.E. Carr
1975 Instructors' ratings of delinquents after Outward Bound survival training and their subsequent recidivism. Psychological Reports 36:547–553.

Bailey, W.C.
1966 Correctional outcome: An evaluation of 100 reports. Journal of Criminal Law, Criminology and Police Science 57:153–160.

Baird, S.C., R.C. Heinz, B.J. Bemus
1979 Project Report #14: A Two Year Follow-up. Bureau of Community Corrections. Wisconsin: Department of Health and Social Services.

Barkwell, L.J.
1976 Differential treatment of juveniles on probation: An evaluative study. Canadian Journal of Criminology and Corrections 18:363–378.

Barton, C., J.F. Alexander, H. Waldron, C.W. Turner, and J. Warburton
1985 Generalizing treatment effects of functional family therapy: Three replications. The American Journal of Family Therapy 13:16–26.

Basta, J.M. and W.S. Davidson
1988 Treatment of juvenile offenders: Study outcomes since 1980. Behavioral Sciences and the Law 6:355–384.

Beal, D. and P. Duckro
1977 Family counseling as an alternative to legal action for the juvenile status offender. Journal of Marriage and Family Counseling 3:77–81.

Berman, J.J.
1978 An experiment in parole supervision. Evaluation Quarterly 2:71–90.

Buckner, J.C. and M. Chesney-Lind
1983 Dramatic cures for juvenile crime: An evaluation of a prisoner-run delinquency prevention program. Criminal Justice and Behavior 10:227–247.

Buehler, R.E., G.R. Patterson, and J.M. Furniss
1966 The reinforcement of behavior in institutional settings. Behavioral Research and Therapy 4:157–167.

Byles, J.A.
1981 Evaluation of an attendance center program for male juvenile probationers. Canadian Journal of Criminology 23:343–355.

Byles, J.A. and A. Maurice
1979 The Juvenile Services Project: An experiment in delinquency control. Canadian Journal of Criminology 21:155–165.

Clarke, R.V.G. and D.B. Cornish
1978 The effectiveness of residential treatment for delinquents. In L.A. Hersov, M. Berger, and D. Shaffer (eds.), Aggression and Anti-social Behavior in Childhood and Adolescence. Oxford: Pergamon.

Collingwood, T.R. and R.W. Genthner
1980 Skills trainings as treatment for juvenile delinquents. Professional Psychology 11:591–598.

Collingwood, T.R., A.F. Douds, and H. Williams
1976 Juvenile diversion: The Dallas Police Department Youth Services Program. Federal Probation 40:23–27.

Craft, M., G. Stephenson, and C. Granger
1966 A controlled trial of authoritarian and self-governing regimes with adolescent psychopaths. American Journal of Orthopsychiatry 34:543–554.

Cullen, F.T. and P. Gendreau
1989 The effectiveness of correctional rehabilitation. In L. Goodstein and D.L. MacKenzie (eds.), The American Prison: Issues in Research Policy. New York: Plenum.

Cullen, F.T. and K.E. Gilbert
1982 Reaffirming Rehabilitation. Cincinnati: Anderson.

Cullen, F.T., J.B. Cullen and J.F. Woznick
1988 Is rehabilitation dead? The myth of the punitive public. Journal of Criminal Justice 16:303–317.

Currie, E.
1989 Confronting crime: Looking toward the twenty-first century. Justice Quarterly 6:5–25.

Davidson, W.S. and T.R. Wolfred
1977 Evaluation of a community-based behavior modification program for prevention of delinquency. Community Mental Health Journal 13:296–306.

Davidson, W.S., L. Gottschalk, L. Gensheimer, and J. Mayer
1984 Interventions with Juvenile Delinquents: A Meta-analysis of Treatment Efficacy. Washington, D.C.: National Institute of Juvenile Justice and Delinquency Prevention.

Davidson, W.S., R. Redner, C. Blakely, C. Mitchell, and J. Emshoff
1987 Diverson of juvenile offenders: An experimental comparison. Journal of Consulting and Clinical Psychology 55:68–75.

Douds, A.F. and T.R. Collingwood
1978 Management by objectives: A successful application. Child Welfare 57:181–185.

Druckman, J.M.
1979 A family-oriented policy and treatment program for female juvenile status offenders. Journal of Marriage and the Family 41:627–636.

Dutton, D.G.
1986 The outcome of court-mandated treatment for wife assault: A quasi-experimental evaluation. Violence and Victims 1:163–175.

Empey, L.T. and M.L. Erickson
1972 The Provo Experiment: Evaluating Community Control of Delinquency. Lexington, Mass.: Lexington Books.

Farrington, D.P. and T. Bennett
1981 Police cautioning of juveniles in London. British Journal of Criminology 21:123–135.

Faust, D.
1965 Group counseling of juveniles by staff without professional training in group work. Crime and Delinquency 11:349–354.

Finckenauer, J.O.
1982 Scared Straight! and the Panacea Phenomenon. Englewood Cliffs, N.J.: Prentice-Hall.

Fo, W.S.O. and C.R. O'Donnell
1975 The buddy system: Effect of community intervention on delinquent offenses. Behavior Therapy 6:522–524.

Freud, S.
1953 A General Introduction to Psychoanalysis. Reprint ed. New York: Permabooks.

Garrett, C.J.
1985 Effects of residential treatment of adjudicated delinquents: A meta-analysis. Journal of Research in Crime and Delinquency 22:287–308.

Geismar, L.L. and K.M. Wood
1985 Family and Delinquency: Resocializing the Young Offender. New York: Human Sciences Press.

Gendreau, P. and R.R. Ross
1979 Effectiveness of correctional treatment: Bibliotherapy for cynics. Crime and Delinquency 25:463–489.
1981 Correctional potency: Treatment and deterrence on trial. In R. Roesch and R.R. Corrado (eds.), Evaluation and Criminal Justice Policy. Beverly Hills, Calif.: Sage.
1987 Revivification of rehabilitation: Evidence from the 1980s. Justice Quarterly 4:349–408.

Gensheimer, L.K., J.P. Mayer, R. Gottschalk, and W.S. Davidson
1986 Diverting youth from the juvenile justice system: A meta-analysis of intervention efficacy. In S.J. Apter and A. Goldstein (eds.), Youth Violence: Programs and Prospects. Elmsford, N.Y.: Pergamon.

Gilbert, G.R.
1977 Alternate routes: A diversion project in the juvenile justice system. Evaluation Quarterly 1:301–318.

Glaser, D.
1974 Remedies for the key deficiency in criminal justice evaluation research. Journal of Research in Crime and Delinquency 11:144–153.

Glueck, S. and E.T. Glueck
1950 Unraveling Juvenile Delinquency. Cambridge, Mass.: Harvard University Press.

Gordon, D.A., J. Arbuthnot, K.E. Gustafson, and P. McGreen
1988 Home-based behavioral systems family therapy with disadvantaged juvenile delinquents. Unpublished paper, Ohio University.

Grant, J.D.
1965 Delinquency treatment in an institutional setting. In H.C. Quay (ed.), Juvenile Delinquency: Research and Theory. Princeton, N.J.: Van Nostrand.

Grant, J.D. and M.Q. Grant
1959 A group dynamics approach to the treatment of nonconformists in the navy. Annals of the American Academy of Political and Social Science 322:126–135.

Greenwood, P.W.
1988 The Role of Planned Interventions in Studying the Desistance of Criminal Behavior in Longitudinal Study. Santa Monica, Calif.: Rand.

Greenwood, P.W. and F.E. Zimring
1985 One More Chance: The Pursuit of Promising Intervention Strategies for Chronic Juvenile Offenders. Santa Monica, Calif.: Rand.

Gruher, M.
1979 Family counseling and the status offender. Juvenile and Family Court Journal 30:23–27.

Hackler, J.C. and J.L. Hagan
1975 Work and teaching machines as delinquency prevention tools: A four-year follow-up. Social Service Review 49:92–106.

Harris, P.W.
1988 The interpersonal maturity level classification system: I-level. Criminal Justice and Behavior 15:58–77.

Hoge, R.D. and D.A. Andrews
1986 A model for conceptualizing interventions in social service. Canadian Psychology 27:332–341.

Horowitz, A. and M. Wasserman
1979 The effect of social control on delinquent behavior: A longitudinal test. Sociological Focus 12:53–70.

Hunt, G.M. and N.H. Azrin
1973 A community-reinforcement approach to alcoholism. Behavior Research and Therapy 11:91–104.

Izzo, R.L. and R.R. Ross
1990 Meta-analysis of rehabilitation programs for juvenile delinquents. Criminal Justice and Behavior 17:134–142.

Jackson, P.C.
1983 Some effects of parole supervision on recidivism. British Journal of Criminology 23:17–34.

Jesness, C.F.
1975 Comparative effectiveness of behavior modification and transactional analysis programs for delinquents. Journal of Consulting and Clinical Psychology 43:758–779.

Jessor, R. and S.L. Jessor
1977 Problem Behavior and Psychosocial Development: A Longitudinal Study of Youth. New York: Academic Press.

Johnson, R.E.
1979 Juvenile Delinquency and Its Origins: An Integrative Theoretical Approach. New York: Cambridge University Press.

Johnson, B.D. and R.T. Goldberg
1983 Vocational and social rehabilitation of delinquents. Journal of Offender Counseling, Services, and Rehabilitation 6:43–60.

Kassebaum, G., D. Ward, and D. Wilner
1971 Prison Treatment and Parole Survival: An Empirical Assessment. New York: John Wiley & Sons.

Kelley, T.M., A.K. Havva, and R.A. Blak
1979 The effectiveness of college student companion therapists with predelinquent youths. Journal of Police Science and Administration 7:186–195.

Kirby, B.C.
1954 Measuring effects of treatment of criminals and delinquents. Sociology and Social Research 38:368–374.

Kirigin, K.A., C.J. Braukman, J.D. Atwater, and M.W. Montrose
1982 An evaluation of Teaching Family (Achievement Place) Group Homes for juvenile offenders. Journal of Applied Behavior Analysis 15:1–16.

Klein, M.W.
1971 Street Gangs and Street Workers. Englewood Cliffs, N.J.: Prentice-Hall.
1986 Labeling theory and delinquency policy: An experimental test. Criminal Justice and Behavior 13:47–79.

Klein, N.C., J.F. Alexander, and B.V. Parsons
1977 Impact of family systems intervention on recidivism and sibling delinquency: A model of primary prevention and program evaluation. Journal of Consulting and Clinical Psychology 3:469–474.

Kratcoski, P.C. and L.D. Kratcoski
1982 The Phoenix Program: An educational alternative for delinquent youths. Juvenile and Family Court Journal 33:17–23.

Kraus, J.
1978 Remand in custody as a deterrent in juvenile jurisdiction. British Journal of Criminology 18:17–23.
1981 Police caution of juvenile offenders: A research note. Australian and New Zealand Journal of Criminology 14:91–94.

Lab, S.P. and J.T. Whitehead
1988 An analysis of juvenile correctional treatment. Crime and Delinquency 34:60–83.

Leschied, A.W., G.W. Austin, and P.G. Jaffe
1988 Impact of the Young Offenders Act on recidivism rates of special needs youth: Clinical and policy implications. Canadian Journal of Behavioural Science 20:322–331.

Lewis, R.V.
1983 Scared straight—California style: Evaluation of the San Quentin Program. Criminal Justice and Behavior 10:209–226.

Link, B.G., F.T. Cullen, E. Struening, P.E. Shrout, and B.P. Dohrenwend
1989 A modified labeling theory approach to mental illness. American Sociological Review 54:400–423.

Lipsey, M.W.
1989 The efficacy of intervention for juvenile delinquency: Results from 400 studies. Paper presented at the 41st annual meeting of the American Society of Criminology, Reno, Nev.

Lipsey, M.W., D.S. Cordray, and D.E. Berger
1981 Evaluation of a juvenile diversion program using multiple lines of evidence. Evaluation Review 5:283–306.

Loeber, R. and M. Stouthamer–Loeber
1987 Prediction. In H.C. Quay (ed.), Handbook of Juvenile Delinquency. New York: John Wiley & Sons.

Logan, C.H.
1972 Evaluation research in crime and delinquency: A reappraisal. Journal of Criminal Law, Criminology and Police Science 63:378–387.

Martinson, R.
1974 What works? Questions and answers about prison reform. The Public Interest 35:22–54.
1979 New findings, new views: A note of caution regarding prison reform. Hofstra Law Review 7:243–258.

Maskin, M.B.
1976 The differential impact of work vs communication-oriented juvenile correction programs upon recidivism rates in delinquent males. Journal of Clinical Psychology 32:432–433.

Mayer, J.P., L.K. Gensheimer, W.S. Davidson, and R. Gottschalk
1986 Social learning treatment within juvenile justice: A meta-analysis of impact in the natural environment. In S.J. Apter and A. Goldstein (eds.), Youth Violence: Programs and Prospects. Elmsford, N.Y.: Pergamon.

McPherson, S.J., L.E. McDonald, and C.W. Ryder
1983 Intensive counseling with families of juvenile offenders. Juvenile and Family Court Journal 34:27–33.

Mitchell, C.M.
1983 The dissemination of a social intervention: Process and effectiveness of two types of paraprofessional change agents. American Journal of Community Psychology 11:723–739.

Mott, J.
1983 Police decisions for dealing with juvenile offenders. British Journal of Criminology 23:249–262.

Murphy, B.C.
1972 A Test of the Effectiveness of an Experimental Treatment Program for Delinquent Opiate Addicts. Ottawa: Information Canada.

O'Donnell, C.R., R. Lydgate, and W.S.O. Fo
1979 The buddy system: Review and follow-up. Child Behavior Therapy 1:161–169.

Ostrum, T.M., C.M. Steele, L.K. Resenblood, and H.L. Mirels
1971 Modification of delinquent behavior. Journal of Applied Social Psychology 1:118–136.

Palmer, T.
1975 Martinson revisited. Journal of Research in Crime and Delinquency 12:133–152.
1983 The effectiveness issue today: An overview. Federal Probation 46:3–10.

Palmer, T. and R.V. Lewis
1980 A differentiated approach to juvenile diversion. Journal of Research in Crime and Delinquency 17:209–227.

Persons, R.
1967 Relationship between psychotherapy with institutionalized boys and subsequent adjustments. Journal of Consulting Psychology 31:137–141.

Petersilia, J., S. Turner, and J. Peterson
1986 Prison versus Probation in California: Implications for Crime and Offender Recidivism. Santa Monica, Calif.: Rand.

Phillips, E.L., E.A. Phillips, D.L. Fixen, and M.W. Wolf
1973 Achievement Place: Behavior shaping works for delinquents. Psychology Today 6:75–79.

Quay, H.C. and C.T. Love
1977 The effect of a juvenile diversion program on rearrests. Criminal Justice and Behavior 4:377–396.

Rausch, S.
1983 Court processing vs. diversion of status offenders: A test of deterrence and labeling theories. Journal of Research in Crime and Delinquency 20:39–54.

Redfering, D.L.
1973 Durability of effects of group counseling with institutionalized females. Journal of Abnormal Psychology 82:85–86.

Regoli, R., E. Wilderman, and M. Pogrebin
1985 Using an alternative evaluation measure for assessing juvenile diversion. Children and Youth Services Review 7:21–38.

Reitsma-Street, M. and A.W. Leschied
1988 The conceptual level matching model in corrections. Criminal Justice and Behavior 15:92–108.

Romig, D.A.
1976 Length of institutionalization, treatment program completion, and recidivism among delinquent adolescent males. Criminal Justice Review 1:115–119.

Rosenbaum, D.P.
1988 Community crime prevention: A review and synthesis of the literature. Justice Quarterly 4:513–544.

Ross, R.R. and E.A. Fabiano
1985 Time to Think: A Cognitive Model of Delinquency Prevention and Offender Rehabilitation. Johnson City, Tenn.: Institute of Social Sciences and Arts.

Ross, R.R. and H.B. McKay
1976 A study of institutional treatment programs. International Journal of Offender Therapy and Comparative Criminology 21:165–173.

Ross, R.R., E.A. Fabiano, and C.D. Ewles
1988 Reasoning and rehabilitation. International Journal of Offender Therapy and Comparative Criminology 32:29–35.

Rothman, D.J.
1980 Conscience and Convenience: The Asylum and Its Alternatives in Progressive America. Boston: Little, Brown.

Sarason, I.G. and V.J. Ganzer
1973 Modeling and group discussions in the rehabilitation of juvenile delinquents. Journal of Counseling Psychology 20:442–449.

Schneider, A.L. and P.R. Schneider
1984 A comparison of programmatic and ad hoc restitution in juvenile court. Justice Quarterly 1:529–547.

Schur, E.M.
1973 Radical Nonintervention: Rethinking the Delinquency Problem. Englewood Cliffs, N.J.: Prentice-Hall.

Sechrest, L., S.O. White, and E.D. Brown
1979 The Rehabilitation of Criminal Offenders: Problem and Prospects. Washington, D.C.: National Academy Press.

Seidman, E., J. Rappaport, and W.S. Davidson
1980 Adolescents in legal jeopardy: Initial success and replication of an alternative to the criminal justice system. In R.R. Ross and P. Gendreau (eds.), Effective Correctional Treatment. Toronto: Butterworth.

Shichor, D. and A. Binder
1982 Community restitution for juveniles: An approach and preliminary investigation. Criminal Justice Review 7:46–50.

Shore, M.F. and J.L. Massimo
1979 Fifteen years after treatment: A follow-up study of comprehensive vocationally-oriented psychotherapy. American Journal of Orthopsychiatry 49:240–245.

Shorts, I.D.
1986 Delinquency by association. British Journal of Criminology 26:156–163.

Smith, D.A. and P.R. Gartin
1989 Specifying specific deterrence. American Sociological Review 54:94–105.

Sorenson, J.L.
1978 Outcome evaluation of a referral system for juvenile offenders. American Journal of Community Psychology 6:381–388.

Sowles, R.C. and J. Gill
1970 Institutional and community adjustment of delinquents following counseling. Journal of Consulting and Clinical Psychology 34:398–402.

Stephenson, R.M. and F.R. Scarpitti
1974 Group Interaction as Therapy: The Use of the Small Group in Corrections. Westport, Conn.: Greenwood Press.

Stringfield, N.
1977 The impact of family counseling in resocializing adolescent offenders within a positive peer treatment milieu. Offender Rehabilitation 1:349–360.

Stuart, R.B., S. Jayaratne, and T. Tripodi
1976 Changing adolescent deviant behaviour through reprogramming the behaviour of parents and teachers: An experimental evaluation. Canadian Journal of Behavioural Science 8:132–143.

Tittle, C.R., W.J. Villimez, and D.A. Smith
1978 The myth of social class and criminality: An empirical assessment of the empirical evidence. American Sociological Review 43:643–656.

Viano, E.C.
1976 Growing up in an affluent society: Delinquency and recidivism in suburban America. Journal of Criminal Justice 3:223–236.

Vinglis, E., E. Adlap, and L. Chung
1982 The Oshawa Impaired Drivers Programme: An evaluation of a rehabilitation programme. Canadian Journal of Criminology 23:93–102.

Visher, C.A.
1987 Incapacitation and crime control: Does a "lock 'em up" strategy reduce crime? Justice Quarterly 4:513–544.

Vito, G.V. and H.E. Allen
1981 Shock probation in Ohio: A comparison of outcomes. International Journal of Offender Therapy and Comparative Criminology 25:70–76.

Wade, T.C., T.L. Morton, J.E. Lind, and N.R. Ferris
1977 A family crisis intervention approach to diversion from the juvenile justice system. Juvenile Justice Journal 28:43–51.

Walker, S.
1989 Sense and Nonsense about Crime: A Policy Guide. Pacific Grove, Calif.: Brooks/Cole.

Walsh, A.
1985 An evaluation of the effects of adult basic education on rearrest rates among probationers. Journal of Offender Counseling, Services and Rehabilitation 9:69–76.

Walter, T.L. and C.M. Mills
1980 A behavioral-employment intervention program for reducing juvenile delinquency. In R.R. Ross and P. Gendreau (eds.), Effective Correctional Treatment. Toronto: Butterworth.

Warren, M.Q.
1969 The case for differential treatment of delinquents. Annals of the American Academy of Political and Social Science 381:47–59.

Wellford, C.
1975 Labelling theory and criminology: An assessment. Social Problems 22:332–345.

Whitaker, J.M. and L.J. Severy
1984 Service accountability and recidivism for diverted youth: A client- and service-comparison analysis. Criminal Justice and Behavior 11:47–74.

Whitehead, J.T. and S.P. Lab
1989 A meta-analysis of juvenile correctional treatment. Journal of Research in Crime and Delinquency 26:276–295.

Williams, L.
1984 A police diversion alternative for juvenile offenders. Police Chief (Feb), 54–56.

Willman, M.T. and J.R. Snortum
1982 A police program for employment and youth gang members. International Journal of Offender Therapy and Comparative Criminology 26:207–214.

Wilson, J.Q. and R.J. Herrnstein
1985 Crime and Human Nature. New York: Simon & Schuster.

Winterdyk, J. and R. Roesch
1982 A Wilderness Experimental Program as an alternative for probationers. Canadian Journal of Criminology 23:39–49.

Wormith, J.S.
1984 Attitude and behavior change of correctional clientele: A three year follow-up. Criminology 22:595–618.

Wright, W.E. and M.C. Dixon
1977 Community prevention and treatment of juvenile delinquency. Journal of Research in Crime and Delinquency 14:35–67.

Zeisel, H.
1982 Disagreement over the evaluation of a controlled experiment. American Journal of Sociology 88:378–389.

D.A. Andrews is a professor of psychology at Carleton University and co-director of the Laboratory for Research on Assessment and Evaluation in the Human Services. His research interests include the assessment of risk, need, and responsivity factors among clients of correctional, youth, family, and mental health agencies, as well as the analysis and evaluation of effective treatment services. Additionally, he is interested in the social psychology of criminological knowledge.

Ivan Zinger, a recent graduate from Carleton University, is currently a student of law at the University of Ottawa. His research interests include the clinical/community psychology of crime and the social psychology of law and justice.

Robert D. Hoge is a professor of psychology at Carleton University and co-director of the Laboratory for Research on Assessment and Evaluation in the Human Services. His major areas of research interest concern problems in psychological assessment, with a particular concern for educational and criminal justice settings.

James Bonta is Chief Psychologist at the Ottawa–Carleton Detention Centre, clinical associate professor at the University of Ottawa, and research adjunct professor at Carleton University. His research interests include the assessment of offenders, the effectiveness of correctional rehabilitation, and the effects of incarceration.

Paul Gendreau is a professor of psychology at the University of New Brunswick (Saint John), consultant and past-director of research at Centracare Saint John, and consultant to Saint John Police Services. His research interests include assessment, treatment, and consultation.

Francis T. Cullen is a professor of criminal justice at the University of Cincinnati. His research interests include theories of crime and deviance, white-collar crime, correctional policy, and the attitudes of the public and professionals toward deviance and official processing.

APPENDIX: NONPARAMETRIC SUMMARY AND OVERVIEW OF THE STUDIES

Descriptions of the 154 explorations of treatment and recidivism are presented in Table A1. The major subheadings in the table identify Type of Treatment. Levels of the remainder of the variables are indicated in the columns labeled Sample, System, Design, Setting, Beh., and Phi. As noted at the bottom of the table, numeric codes reflect the levels for each Sample of Studies, Justice System, Quality of Research Design, Setting, and Behavioral Intervention. The minor subheadings in Table A1 enhance descriptions of type of treatment but did not enter into the analyses. The Comments column is intended as a guide for readers who wish to recreate the 2 × 2 tables that we drew from the original studies. Many of the comments will make little sense without reference to those original studies.

CRIMINAL SANCTIONS

Inspection of Table A1 provides an overview of the 30 "criminal justice" comparisons. Phi coefficients were signed positive when lower recidivism rates were found under "more" processing conditions. The first eight comparisons were culled from four studies of diversion through police cautioning versus regular processing, and only one phi estimate, a negative one, reached the .20 level (the standard of effectiveness in Whitehead and Lab was a positive phi coefficient of at least .20). The next set of 20 comparisons involved less versus more severe judicial dispositions, and six of the phi coefficients, all negative, equaled or exceeded .20. The final two studies in the criminal justice set reveal that completion of restitution contracts was only mildly associated with reduced recidivism rates. One might expect that the confound with selection factors would have had a stronger inflationary effect on the phi estimates. Overall, the findings of the 30 criminal justice comparisons were consistent with expectations: Only seven (20%) phi coefficients reached the criterion of .20 and, more consistent with labelling than deterrence theory, they were each negative in sign.

INAPPROPRIATE CORRECTIONAL SERVICE

Thirty-eight comparisons involved "inappropriate" treatments—treatments that we predicted would be either unrelated to recidivism or have a negative effect. Inspection confirms that only five phi coefficients reached the .20 level, and each was negative in sign. The mean phi coefficient was −.06. The only surprises in this set of comparisons were the positive phi coefficients, albeit statistically insignificant, yielded by Davidson et al.'s (1987) paraprofessional relationship-oriented program. Overall, the hypothesized ineffectiveness of inappropriate service was supported.

UNSPECIFIED CORRECTIONAL SERVICE

Table A1 provides an overview of 32 comparisons involving unspecified correctional service. The number of positive phi coefficients equaling or exceeding .20 was 10 (34%), and the mean phi was clearly positive but low (.13). In regard to our hypothesis, we now begin to uncover evidence of the effectiveness of rehabilitative service. Note, in addition, the many significant but low phi estimates. Obviously, many weak effects emerged significant statistically because of the large samples studied. Not as obvious, except upon a reading of the original papers (e.g., Palmer and Lewis, 1980), several Type of Client × Type of Service interactions were found in this set of studies. Hence, some of the tabled effect size estimates are misleading because they reflect an averaging of what were actually positive and negative effects dependent upon type of case. For example, Palmer and Lewis (1980) reported that nonspecific family counseling for female first offenders was associated with clearly negative effects, apparently replicating the Druckman (1979) study. Unfortunately, these interactions were not reported in a manner that allowed the simple effects of treatment to be coded by type of case. Klein (1986) also reported some intriguing interactions that suggest weak or negative effects with low-risk cases. This pattern would be consistent with those tests of treatment in the inappropriate service set that involved the delivery of services to low-risk cases (studies 58-66 in Table A1).

APPROPRIATE CORRECTIONAL SERVICE

The overall pattern here reveals that 70% ($^{38}/_{54}$) of the comparisons within the appropriate service set yielded a positive phi of at least .20, and the overall mean phi coefficient was .30. In every comparison but two, which involved token economy programs in residential settings, the phi coefficients were positive. Appropriate treatment appears to work at least moderately well. Note that many of the studies in the appropriate set involved small samples (and sample size is inversely correlated with effect size: Lipsey, 1989). Future research will explore the relative contributions of methodological, statistical, and therapeutic integrity factors to this correlation between sample size and effect size. Preliminary explorations, however, have revealed that the effect of Type of Treatment on phi estimates is found in both smaller and larger sample studies. For example, 30 of the 54 tests of appropriate service involved a control group with 30 or fewer cases, compared with only 28 of the 100 other tests of treatment. Among the small sample tests, 77% ($^{23}/_{30}$) of the tests of appropriate treatment yielded a positive phi of at least .20 compared with 21% ($^{6}/_{28}$) of the tests of less appropriate treatments. The corresponding figures among the tests based on larger samples were 63% ($^{15}/_{24}$) for appropriate treatment and 7% ($^{5}/_{72}$) for other treatments.

NONPARAMETRIC SUMMARY

The proportion of coefficients within each of the four levels of Type of Treatment reaching or exceeding the Whitehead and Lab (1989) standard of effectiveness were .00, .00, .34, and .70 for the criminal sanction, inappropriate service, unspecified service, and appropriate service sets, respectively; chi-square = 68.83, $p < .000$, Eta = .67, r = .64, gamma = .92.

Table A1. Summary of 154 Tests of Correctional Treatment

ID Author (Year)	Sample	System	Design	Setting	Beh	Phi	Rec Rate: % (n) Treat		Control		Comments
TYPE OF TREATMENT: 1) CRIMINAL SANCTIONS											
Sanctioning vs Cautioning											
1 Kraus (81)	1	1	1	1NSD	1	−15	41	(78)	27	(78)	
2 Klein (86)	2	1	2	1NSD	1	−25*	73	(81)	49	(82)	Release vs Petition
Studies with Higher Risk Cases											
3 Mott (83)	1	1	2	1NSD	1	−08	58	(167)	46	(26)	
4	1	1	2	1NSD	1	19	53	(30)	80	(5)	(girls)
5 Farrington & P (81)	1	1	2	1NSD	1	04	45	(11)	50	(8)	
Studies with Lower Risk Cases											
6 Mott (83)	1	1	2	1NSD	1	−03	33	(57)	30	(174)	
7	1	1	2	1NSD	1	−05	14	(7)	9	(75)	(girls)
8 Farrington & P (81)	1	1	2	1NSD	1	10	0	(2)	12	(24)	
More vs Less Severe Disposition											
9 Viano (76)	1	1	1	1 SD	1	−08	26	(35)	19	(21)	
10	1	1	1	1 SD	1	−20	26	(35)	10	(38)	Informal adjustment
11	1	1	1	1 SD	1	−12	19	(21)	10	(38)	Dismissal
12 Rausch (83)	1	1	1	1 SD	1	−01	47	(196)	44	(18)	
13	1	1	1	1 SD	1	−02	47	(196)	45	(91)	Probation
14	1	1	1	1 SD	1	−05	47	(196)	47	(45)	Maximum Community
15	1	1	1	1 SD	1	04	40	(45)	44	(18)	Community agent
16	1	1	1	1 SD	1	05	40	(45)	45	(91)	Probation
17	1	1	1	1 SD	1	00	45	(91)	44	(18)	Community agent
18 Kraus (78)	1	1	1	1PPC	1	−28*	64	(90)	37	(90)	
19 Horowitz & W (79)	1	1	2	1PPC	1	−22	91	(196)	75	(67)	
20	1	1	2	1PPC	1	−32*	83	(29)	43	(106)	Lower risk
21 Stephenson & S (74)	2	1	1	2	1	−23*	61	(44)	39	(44)	Prob vs Group Home
22	2	1	1	2	1	−20*	59	(44)	39	(44)	Inst vs Prob
23	2	1	1	2	1	02	59	(44)	61	(44)	Inst vs Group Home
24 Phillips P F & W (73)	2	1	1	1PPC	1	01	53	(15)	54	(13)	Inst vs Prob
25 Vito & A (81)	2	2	1	1PPC	1	−07*	17	(585)	12	(938)	Shock Incar vs Prob
26 Petersilia T & P (86)	2	2	1	2	1	−07	41	(162)	34	(162)	I vs P (viol offs)
27	2	2	1	2	1	−18*	61	(219)	43	(219)	I vs P (prop offs)
28	2	2	1	2	1	−17*	35	(130)	20	(130)	I vs P (drug offs)
Restitution (Successful Completion of)											
29 Schicor & B (82)	1	1	1	1NSD	1	14	7	(59)	15	(55)	
30 Schneider & S (84)	1	1	1	1PPC	1	18*	60	(190)	80	(61)	

Table A1. (continued)

ID Author (Year)	Sample	System	Design	Setting	Beh	Phi	Rec Rate: % (n) Treat		Control		Comments
TYPE OF TREATMENT: 2) INAPPROPRIATE CORRECTIONAL SERVICE											
Intensive Non-Behavioral Group Interaction (including Recreation)											
31 Byles (81)	1	1	1	1PPC	1	−11	71	(31)	60	(35)	Attendance Centers
32	1	1	1	1PPC	1	08	68	(25)	76	(49)	
33 Shorts (86)	2	1	1	1NSD	1	−01	48	(43)	47	(19)	
34	2	1	1	1NSD	1	03	10	(31)	12	(17)	
35 Winterdyk & R (82)	2	1	2	1 SD	1	00	20	(30)	20	(30)	Wilderness Program
Non-Directive Client-Centered/Psychodynamic Counselling											
36 Klein A & P (77)	1	1	2	1 SD	1	−11	60	(30)	49	(56)	
37	1	1	2	1 SD	1	−17	61	(30)	40	(10)	(Sibs)
38 Adams & V (82)	1	1	2	2	1	−44*	100	(14)	69	(13)	Group Psychodrama
39 Davidson R B M & E (87)	2	1	1	1NSD	1	06	33	(12)	43	(112)	Rel vs Beh/Adv/Act
40	2	1	1	1NSD	1	16	33	(12)	58	(89)	Rel vs Controls
41 Berman (78)	2	2	2	1PPC	1	00	25	(16)	25	(16)	Non-Bev Para-prof
Non-Behavioral Milieu Therapy/Guided Group Interaction											
42 Stringfield (77)	1	1	1	1PPC	1	−31*	56	(32)	25	(20)	Milieu vs Fam
43 Clarke & C (78)	1	1	2	2	1	−01	70	(86)	69	(87)	
44 Stephenson & S (74)	2	1	1	1PPC	1	−20*	59	(44)	39	(44)	GGI vs Prob
45	2	1	1	2	1	00	59	(44)	59	(44)	GGI vs Inst
46	2	1	1	2	1	02	59	(44)	61	(44)	GGI vs Group Home
47 Empey & E (72)	2	1	2	1PPC	1	−03	58	(71)	54	(79)	GGI vs Prob
48	2	1	1	1PPC	1	16*	64	(44)	79	(132)	GGI vs Incar
49 Craft S & G (64)	2	1	2	2	1	−13	58	(24)	46	(24)	Milieu vs Auth
Non-Behavioral Weakly-Focused Academic/Vocational Approaches											
50 Willman & S (82)	1	1	1	1 SD	1	−11	71	(68)	60	(68)	
51 Maskin (76)	1	1	1	2	1	−39*	50	(30)	13	(30)	
52 Hackler & H (75)	1	1	2	1NSD	1	−05	33	(85)	29	(70)	
53	1	1	2	1NSD	1	07	25	(67)	32	(131)	
54 Zeisel (82)	2	2	2	1PPC	1	00	49	(???)	49	(???)	(TARP)
Confrontational Groups (Scared Straight)											
55 Buckner & C-L (83)	1	1	1	1 SD	1	−04	41	(100)	37	(100)	
56	1	1	1	1 SD	1	11	22	(50)	32	(50)	(female)
57 Lewis (83)	1	1	2	1 SD	1	−16	67	(55)	81	(53)	
Mismatched According to Risk or Responsivity/Need Systems											
58 Sorenson (78)	1	1	2	1NSD	1	−35*	30	(30)	4	(45)	
59 Byles & M (79)	1	1	2	1 SD	1	−12	57	(94)	43	(114)	
60 Gruher (79)	1	1	2	1 SD	1	06	32	(38)	38	(40)	
61 Quay & L (77)	1	1	2	1NSD	1	07	28	(268)	36	(92)	
62 O'Donnell L & F (79)	1	1	2	1NSD	2	−07	25	(169)	19	(130)	
63	1	1	2	1NSD	2	−10	18	(116)	11	(65)	(female)
64 Baird H & B (79)	2	2	2	1PPC	1	−13	10	(58)	3	(58)	
65 Andrews & K (80)	2	2	2	1PPC	1	−09	17	(58)	11	(62)	Para-prof prog
66 Andrews K M & R (86)	2	2	2	1PPC	1	−09	14	(98)	2	(28)	Para-prof prog
67 Grant & G (59)	2	2	2	2	1	−14*	52	(91)	38	(144)	Low maturity
68 Andrews & K (80)	2	2	2	1PPC	1	11	42	(23)	48	(13)	Low Emp/High Risk

Table A1. (continued)

ID	Author (Year)	Sample	System	Design	Setting	Beh	Phi	Rec Rate: % (n) Treat		Control		Comments
TYPE OF TREATMENT: 3) UNSPECIFIED CORRECTIONAL SERVICE												
Service-Oriented Diversion												
69	Regoli W & P (85)	1	1	1	1NSD	1	19*	2	(52)	11	(52)	Complete prog vs pre-program controls
70		1	1	1	1NSD	1	16*	8	(98)	21	(98)	
71		1	1	1	1NSD	1	31*	6	(61)	32	(61)	
72		1	1	1	1NSD	1	12	10	(72)	18	(72)	
73		1	1	1	1NSD	1	−06	29	(119)	24	(119)	
74		1	1	1	1NSD	1	−05	26	(107)	24	(107)	
75	Lipsey C & B (81)	1	1	1	1 SD	1	18*	26	(776)	44	(476)	Complete vs Incomplete
76		1	1	1	1 SD	1	10*	27	(870)	37	(533)	
77		1	1	1	1 SD	1	10*	35	(543)	45	(333)	
78	Whitaker & S (84)	1	1	1	1NSD	1	10*	33	(???)	46	(???)	More vs Less Diverse
79	Palmer & L (80)	1	1	1	1 SD	1	07*	25	(1345)	31	(1192)	Unspec quasi control
80	Gilbert (77)	1	1	1	1 SD	1	30*	34	(58)	65	(78)	Assign vs Preprog conts
81	Klein (86)	2	1	2	1NSD	1	17*	57	(88)	73	(81)	Ref vs Petition
82		2	1	2	1NSD	1	12	62	(55)	73	(81)	Ref+ vs Petition
83		2	1	2	1NSD	1	−08	57	(88)	49	(82)	Ref vs Release
84		2	1	2	1NSD	1	−13	62	(55)	49	(82)	Ref+ vs Release
Appropriateness Uncertain On Targets/Style												
85	Romig (76)	1	1	1	1PPC	1	15*	14	(301)	27	(127)	Parole Supervision
86	Jackson (83)	1	1	2	1PPC	1	03	82	(198)	84	(98)	Parole Supervision
87	Barkwell (76)	1	1	2	1PPC	1	−16	88	(16)	75	(16)	Prob Serv vs Surveill
88	Druckman (79)	1	1	1	1NSD	1	−17	50	(14)	33	(15)	Family Counseling
89	Seidman R & D (80)	2	1	2	1NSD	1	46*	50	(12)	90	(12)	Parapro Advocacy
90	Wade M L & F (77)	2	1	1	1NSD	1	51*	15	(34)	70	(77)	Family crisis
91	Romig (76)	2	1	1	2	1	10*	12	(177)	20	(251)	Mths served/rel order
92	Johnson & G (83)	2	1	2	1PPC	1	05	3	(87)	5	(87)	State Vocational Serv
93	Sowles & G (70)	2	1	2	2	1	22	37	(30)	60	(15)	Ind/Group (boys)
94		2	1	2	2	1	38	0	(10)	20	(5)	(girls)
95	Ostrum S R & M (71)	2	1	2	1 SD	1	22	26	(19)	48	(19)	Mixed socio-psych prog
96	Redfering (73)	2	1	1	2	1	29	35	(17)	64	(14)	Cl-Ce Group (appro tar)
97	Jesness in grant (65)	2	1	2	2	1	05	73	(11)	77	(13)	Small vs Large Units
98	Ross F & E (88)	2	2	2	1PPC	2	23	47	(17)	70	(23)	Life Skill vs Reg Prob
99	Vinglis A & C (82)	2	2	2	1PPC	1	−05	15	(58)	19	(62)	Impaired Driving
100	Walsh (85)	2	2	1	1PPC	1	21*	24	(50)	44	(50)	Gen Equiva Prog

Table A1. (continued)

ID	Author (Year)	Sample	System	Design	Setting	Beh	Phi	Rec Rate: % (n) Treat		Control		Comments
TYPE OF TREATMENT: 4) APPROPRIATE CORRECTIONAL SERVICE												
Short-Term Behavioral/Systems Family Counseling												
101	Alexander C S P (76)	1	1	1	1 SD	2	64*	0	(12)	56	(9)	
102	Klein A & P (77)	1	1	2	1 SD	2	23*	26	(46)	48	(56)	
103		1	1	2	1 SD	2	18	20	(46)	40	(10)	(sibs)
104		1	1	2	1 SD	2	31*	26	(46)	57	(30)	
105		1	1	2	1 SD	2	41*	20	(46)	60	(30)	(sibs)
106	McPherson M & R (83)	1	1	2	1 SD	1	20*	33	(15)	58	(60)	(target = discipline)
107	Gordon A G & M (88)	2	1	1	1 SD	2	83*	0	(12)	75	(4)	(girls)
108		2	1	1	1 SD	2	44*	20	(15)	65	(23)	(boys)
109	Stuart J & T (76)	2	1	2	1NSD	2	19	0	(30)	7	(30)	
110	Barton A W T & W (85)	2	1	1	2	2	41*	60	(30)	93	(44)	
Structured One-on-One Paraprofessional/Peer Program												
111	Kelly H & B (79)	1	1	1	1NSD	1	26*	0	(65)	12	(63)	(target = thinking)
112	Mitchell (83)	1	1	1	1PPC	2	29*	14	(29)	43	(63)	
113	Ross & M (77)	1	1	1	2	2	33	7	(15)	33	(15)	
114		1	1	1	2	2	46*	7	(15)	60	(45)	
115	Seidman R & D (80)	2	1	2	1NSD	2	51*	48	(25)	100	(12)	Beh/adv vs Controls
116		2	1	2	1NSD	2	60*	25	(12)	92	(12)	Beh vs Controls
117		2	1	2	1NSD	2	17	25	(12)	50	(12)	Beh vs Advocacy
118	Davison R B M & E (87)	2	1	1	1NSD	2	15*	43	(112)	58	(89)	Beh/Adv/Action vs C
119	Andrews (80)	2	2	2	1PPC	2	15*	15	(72)	28	(116)	Hi Emp Hi So Officers
Specialized Academics/Vocational Services												
120	Bachra & Z (78)	1	1	1	1NSD	1	38*	7	(31)	42	(48)	(specific focus)
121	Kratcoski & K (82)	1	1	1	1PPC	2	65*	42	(38)	100	(83)	
122	Walter & M (80)	2	1	1	1PPC	2	62*	9	(53)	70	(23)	
123	Shore & M (79)	2	1	2	1NSD	1	52*	40	(10)	90	(10)	(intense/ individualized)
Intensive Structured Skill Training												
124	Collingwood D & W (76)	1	1	1	1 SD	2	41*	11	(813)	51	(196)	Participants vs Nonpar
125	Williams (84)	1	1	1	1 SD	2	33*	21	(564)	64	(77)	Participants vs Nonpar
126	Sarason & G (73)	2	1	2	2	2	18*	19	(64)	34	(64)	Modeling vs Contr
127		2	1	2	2	2	24*	14	(64)	34	(64)	Discuss vs Control
128	Ross F & E (88)	2	2	2	1PPC	2	52*	18	(22)	70	(23)	Cog-Beh vs Reg Prob
129		2	2	2	1PPC	2	31*	18	(22)	47	(17)	Cog-Beh vs Life Skill
130	Dutton (86)	2	2	1	1PPC	2	43*	4	(50)	40	(50)	Cog-beh (wife batter)
Introduction of Individualized Rehabilitative Regime												
131	Jesness (75)	1	1	1	2	2	10*	32	(398)	42	(499)	Token Eco vs Pre-Prog

Table A1. (continued)

ID	Author (Year)	Sample	System	Design	Setting	Beh	Phi	Rec Rate: % (n) Treat		Control		Comments
132		1	1	1	2	1	14*	33	(453)	47	(660)	(target=ind crimino need)
133	Ross & M (76)	1	1	1	2	2	27	10	(10)	33	(15)	
134		1	1	1	2	2	38*	10	(10)	60	(45)	
Token Economy												
135	Kirigin B A & W (82)	1	1	1	2	2	21	27	(38)	47	(30)	(girls)
136		1	1	1	2	2	12	57	(102)	73	(22)	(boys)
137	Davidson & W (77)	1	1	1	2	2	−26*	??	(??)	??	(??)	
138	Ross & M (77)	1	1	1	2	2	−23	60	(45)	33	(15)	
139	Phillips P F & W (73)	2	1	1	2	2	36*	18	(16)	53	(15)	Ach Place vs Inst
140		2	1	1	2	2	37*	18	(16)	54	(13)	Ach Place vs Prob
Individual/Group Counselling												
141	Persons (67)	2	1	2	2	2	29*	32	(41)	61	(41)	Ind + Group
Appropriately Matched According to Risk or Responsivity/Need Systems												
142	Sorenson (78)	1	1	2	1NSD	1	06	25	(44)	31	(26)	
143	Byles & M (79)	1	1	2	1 SD	1	27*	68	(60)	92	(37)	
144	Gruher (79)	1	1	2	1 SD	1	07	56	(16)	63	(30)	
145	Quay & L (77)	1	1	2	1NSD	1	23*	36	(164)	65	(40)	
146	O'Donnell L & F (79)	1	1	2	1NSD	2	20	62	(37)	81	(21)	(boys)
147		1	1	2	1NSD	2	08	38	(13)	50	(2)	(girls)
148	Barkwell (76)	1	1	2	1PPC	1	35*	56	(16)	88	(16)	
149		1	1	2	1PPC	1	20	56	(16)	75	(16)	
150	Baird H & B (79)	2	2	2	1PPC	1	17*	16	(184)	30	(184)	
151	Andrews K M & R (86)	2	2	2	1PPC	1	31*	33	(54)	75	(12)	Para-prof prog
152	Andrews & K (80)	2	2	2	1PPC	1	82*	0	(11)	80	(10)	(Hi Emp & Risk)
153	Grant & G (59)	2	2	2	2	1	09	29	(135)	38	(141)	(High Maturity)
154	Andrews & K (80)	2	2	2	1PPC	1	27*	31	(34)	58	(23)	Para-prof prog

* $p < .05$ (Chi square)

Note: The value labels for codes "1" and "2" are as follows: Sample of Studies (Whitehead & Lab, Sample 2), Justice System (juvenile, adult), Quality of Research Design (weaker, stronger), Behavioral Intervention (no, yes) and Setting (community, institutional/residential). The letters beside code "1" for Setting refer to different types of community settings (NSD: nonsystem diversion; SD: system diversion; PPC: probation, parole, community).

Essential Components of Successful Rehabilitation Programs for Offenders

Daniel H. Antonowicz
Robert R. Ross

Abstract: *A quantitative analysis of 44 rigorously controlled offender treatment studies, published between 1970 and 1991, was undertaken to determine if the factors suggested by previous reviewers to be essential to program success are in fact related to efficacy. The results indicated that only six factors were significantly associated with the efficacy of programs. These factors included: (a) a sound conceptual model; (b) multifaceted programming; (c) the targeting of "criminogenic needs"; (d) the responsivity principle; (e) roleplaying and modeling; and (f) social cognitive skills training. The study raised several questions about the adequacy of research on offender rehabilitation and about the validity of many assertions that have been made about the essential characteristics of effective programs.*

A growing body of research literature attests to the fact that *some* rehabilitation programs are successful with *some* offenders in *some* settings when applied by *some* staff (e.g., Andrews et al., 1990; Gendreau & Ross, 1979, 1987; Lipsey, 1991). Researchers now appear to be less preoccupied with the decades long debate as to whether or not rehabilitation "works" and more concerned with determining under what conditions rehabilitation works. The present investigation examined a large number of factors that practitioners and researchers have suggested are associated with success to determine whether the presence or absence of each of these factors is in fact related to the efficacy of programs published in the literature.

Our examination of all the published reviews of the correctional treatment literature conducted from 1970 to 1991 identified factors that the reviewers had suggested were crucial to the success of programs. Rigorously controlled evaluations of rehabilitation programs were then analyzed to determine whether the presence of each of these factors was associated with the effectiveness of programs.

Eligible evaluation studies were identified by (a) examining previous reviews of the literature (Andrews et al., 1990; Cullen & Gendreau, 1989; Gendreau & Ross, 1979, 1987; Ross & Fabiano, 1985; Ross & Gendreau, 1980), and (b) searching criminological, sociological, psychological, and substance abuse journals. Only studies that dealt with officially adjudicated offenders, were published between 1970 and 1991, had experimental or quasiexperimental designs, and reported on community-based followup outcome measures such as rearrest, reconviction, and reincarceration, were included. In order to ensure a standardized test of outcome we conducted a

International Journal of Offender Therapy and Comparative Criminology, 38(2), 1994 chi-square test of the difference in recidivism between treatment and control groups. Programs were judged to be effective if there was a significant difference in favour of the treatment group.

RESULTS AND DISCUSSION

One of our major findings was that there is not a large number of published, rigorously controlled studies. Many published studies have either inadequate control/comparison groups, do not report on sample size, use sample sizes that are too small to enable statistical tests, or fail to examine outcome. In the period 1970–1991, only 44 published studies were found that met our requirement of adequate evaluation. We recognize that our criteria were more stringent than some others have employed. We wished to ensure that our investigation was based only on good quality evaluation research. Moreover, it was found that only 20 (45%) of the 44 controlled studies were effective. Twenty effective programs in 21 years indicates that effective programs are truly exceptional.

In spite of the fact that all of the studies that qualified were published in refereed journals or edited books, most had serious limitations in their reporting, which subsequently made determining what they actually did an impossible task. It also made the analysis of the factors problematic. The limitations included inadequate reporting of offender characteristics (e.g., age, sex, criminal history), impressively inadequate program description, and inadequate description of staff. We could find no empirical evidence to suggest that the efficacy of programs was related to the inclusion or exclusion of most of the factors that the literature suggests are key to program success. This is because (a) too few reports provide adequate information on which to judge whether the factor was present or not, or (b) there were simply too few studies that did employ these factors to make valid comparisons possible. In fact, in sharp contrast to the long list of factors that various reviewers have identified, this study found only six characteristics to be associated with program efficacy:

1. Sound Conceptual Model. The conceptualization of delinquency or criminal behavior on which the program is based determines what intermediate targets the intervention should focus on in order to reduce recidivism—the primary target. It also serves as a guide for program planners and practitioners in terms of the techniques that should be applied.

Consistent with previous reviews, the present study found that programs that were based on a cognitive-behavioral theoretical model were the most beneficial. Seventy-five percent of successful programs were cognitive-behavioral in nature, compared to only 38% of unsuccessful programs ($X^2(1) = 6.188$; $p = 0.013$). Other models such as deterrence, psychodynamic, or sociological models received little or no support.

2. Multifaceted Programming. Multifaceted programs incorporate a variety of techniques in their intervention strategy; unlike many correctional programs, they do not rely on a single method. Offenders are complex; therefore, programs designed to help them must also be complex. In accord with most previous reviews of the literature, we found that multifaceted programs are more effective than ones that are not (Agee, 1986; Gendreau & Ross, 1979, 1981, 1984; Lipsey, 1991; Ross & Lightfoot, 1985). Seventy percent of successful programs were multifaceted as compared to only 38% of unsuccessful programs ($X^2(1) = 4.619$; $p = 0.032$).

3. Targeting "criminogenic needs." It has been argued that successful treatment programs must target the "criminogenic needs" of offenders (Andrews et al., 1990), that is, program targets must be factors that are known to be linked with recidivism: social cognition (Ross & Fabiano, 1985), or:

> changing antisocial attitudes, changing antisocial feelings, reducing antisocial peer associations, promoting familial affection/communication, promoting familial monitoring and supervision, promoting identification and association with anticriminal role models, increasing self-control, self-management and problem solving skills, replacing the skills of lying, stealing and aggression with more prosocial alternatives, reducing chemical dependencies, shifting the rewards and costs for criminal and noncriminal activities in familial, academic, vocational, recreational and other behavioural settings, so that noncriminal alternatives are favoured, providing the chronically psychiatrically troubled with low pressure, sheltered living arrangements, changing other attributes of clients and their circumstances that, through individualized assessments of risk and need, have been linked reasonably with criminal conduct, and insuring that the client is able to recognize risky situations, and has a concrete and well-rehearsed plan for dealing with those situations. (Andrews, 1989, p. 15)

The results of the present study indicate that targeting of the "criminogenic needs" of offenders is crucial to program efficacy: 90% of successful programs targeted "criminogenic needs," whereas only 58% of unsuccessful programs did so ($X^2(1) = 5.515$, $p = 0.019$). It appears that it is essential to have appropriate targets if one is to achieve success in offender rehabilitation.

4. Responsivity Principle. It has been asserted that program efficacy depends on matching styles and modes of service to the learning styles and abilities of offenders. Many previous investigators have suggested that offenders seem to respond best to a cognitive-behavioral approach (e.g., Andrews et al., 1990).

In the present study, the responsivity principle was judged to be present if behavioral or social learning techniques such as modeling, graduated practice, rehearsal, roleplaying, reinforcement, or cognitive restructuring were utilized or if specific responsivity considerations such as the Interpersonal Maturity Level System (I-Level) or Conceptual Level Systems, which attempt to match clients to style of intervention/supervision on the basis of their characteristics (social maturity or cognitive style), were utilized. The responsivity principle was supported by the results of this study: 80% of successful programs employed behavioral or social learning techniques compared to 50% of the unsuccessful programs ($X^2(1) = 4.243$; $p = 0.039$).

5. Role-playing/Modeling. Previous reviewers have argued that it is essential to the efficacy of programs that correctional workers/agents model anticriminal attitudes and behavior (Andrews & Kiessling, 1980; Sarason & Ganzer, 1973). Researchers have also asserted that modeling and roleplaying techniques are valuable in that they can be used as a basis for the training of empathy, interpersonal problem-solving, and social skills that can enable offenders to cope prosocially with adverse or criminogenic environmental experiences (Ross & Fabiano, 1985). In the present investigation 50% of successful programs included a roleplaying/modeling component, whereas only 17% of unsuccessful programs did ($X^2(1) = 5.587$; $p = 0.018$).

6. Social Cognitive Skills Training. A common component of many effective correctional programs is some technique that could be expected to have an impact on the offender's thinking (Ross & Fabiano, 1985). Qualitative analyses, component analysis, and meta-analyses have demonstrated the importance of including cognitive techniques in rehabilitation programs (Andrews et al., 1990; Garrett, 1985; Izzo & Ross, 1990; Ross & Fabiano, 1985).

The present study also found that including program techniques that can have an impact on the offender's thinking was of critical importance. More specifically, social cognitive skills training and roleplaying and modeling were found to be related to program efficacy.

Moreover, behavioral programs that included a cognitive component were very likely to be effective: 75% of successful programs were behaviorally oriented and included a cognitive component, whereas all behavioral programs that did *not* include a cognitive component were unsuccessful.

It should be noted that although we found that training in social cognitive skills (including negotiation, interpersonal skills, assertiveness, and communication) were effective, no valid conclusions could be made on the basis of the data of this study pertaining to the efficacy of cognitive *therapy* as opposed to cognitive skills training techniques. Cognitive therapy (e.g. Ellis, 1973) or cognitive behavior modification (e.g. Mahoney, 1974) is designed to modify *what* a client thinks; cognitive skills training is designed to teach a client *how* to think. Perhaps offenders need to be taught *how* to think before we can expect to modify what they think. Perhaps cognitive therapy with offenders needs to incorporate, or be preceded by, cognitive skills training.

Although the value of including a social cognitive skills component in programs has consistently been shown to be critical to successful program outcome, no study has yet examined whether the use of a specific cognitive skills training technique, by itself, is associated with program efficacy. The present study sought to address this question. None of the specific cognitive techniques by themselves were found to be statistically significant although in each case there were more successful than unsuccessful programs that used these techniques: training in social perspective-taking (10% vs. 0%), self-control (15% vs. 8%), interpersonal problem-solving (30% vs. 13%), and values enhancement (30% vs. 8%). Unfortunately, in many cases there was insufficient data to make statistical comparisons and we still cannot determine *which* cognitive techniques are essential; we can only conclude broadly that cognitive skills training techniques are essential. Recent studies of a cognitive skills training program have found: (a) a 60% reduction in recidivism among high-risk penitentiary inmates compared to untreated controls (Porporino, Robinson, & Fabiano, 1992); (b) a 70% reduction in revocation rates for drug-abusing offenders in an intensive probation program with cognitive skills training compared to probation controls (Johnson & Hunter, 1992); (c) only one of 12 high-risk prisoners in a Spanish prison recidivated in a one-year follow-up compared to 12 of 12 untreated controls (Morales, 1992); and (d) a 74% reduction in recidivism among cognitively trained high-risk Canadian probationers compared to untreated controls (Ross, Fabiano, & Ewles, 1988).

The results of the present study also found that some important and widely held assumptions about correctional rehabilitation programs were not supported by the research literature: (1) there was no significant difference between high-risk and low-risk offenders in terms of their response to varying intensity of services—success *can* be found with both high and low-risk offenders; (2) some programs can be effective in prisons at least if they somehow escape from or diminish the usual prison ambience and create an "alternative community" within the institution in which the program is either housed in separate buildings away from the general offender population or is conducted in an educational or therapeutic community that isolates the offenders from the antisocial prison subculture (e.g., Ayers, Duguid, Montague, & Wolowidnyk, 1980; Linden, Perry, Ayers, & Parlett, 1984; Platt, Perry, & Metzger, 1980; Wexler, Falkin, & Lipton, 1990); (3) no support was found for the view that programs can only be effective with motivated offenders who voluntarily engage in programs. Coercing offenders into programs by court order or by a probation or parole requirement, and so on, has been viewed as counterproductive to program efficacy. In fact some widely endorsed correctional models and criminal justice models (e.g. Fogel's "justice model", 1979) are based on the rejection of mandatory treatment. We could find no empirical evidence to support that view. In this study, only 8% of all successful programs actually were conducted with well-motivated clients. Since 92% of successful programs were actually conducted with offenders who were mandated into the program or enticed by promise of reduction in supervision/control, one must seriously rethink the notion of limiting rehabilitation programs to motivated offenders. Clearly, the offenders who are in greatest need of programs are those who are the least motivated!

CONCLUSIONS

The major finding of this study is that there is very little empirical support for the validity of many of the suggestions and assertions that appear in the literature about the essential characteristics of effective programs. In fact, given the distressingly poor quality of research and reporting of research, it is not yet possible to adequately test most of these suggestions. Few study reports describe their clients, their staff, their programs, their results, or the analysis of their results in sufficient detail or with sufficient clarity to enable the reader to determine who did what to whom, why, how much, how often, and with what results.

All we can conclude with confidence at this stage of research on rehabilitation is that adequately evaluated, effective rehabilitation programs are exceptional. They are exceptional not only in their small numbers but in at least *some* of their characteristics. However, the magnitude of the reductions in recidivism may be very large—as high as 90% (range: 27%-90%).

It does appear that our best chances for successful rehabilitation will come from implementing programs based on a cognitive-behavioral model, target offender characteristics known to be associated with reoffending, are multifaceted and include roleplaying, modeling, and social cognitive skills training. Moreover, they may not have to be restricted to community settings or to well-motivated or low-risk clients.

REFERENCES

Agee, V. L. (1986). Institutional treatment programs for the violent juvenile. In S. Apter & A. Goldstein (Eds.), *Youth violence: Program and prospects* (pp. 75-88). New York: Pergamon Press.

Andrews, D. A. (1989). Recidivism is predictable and can be influenced: Using risk assessments to reduce recidivism. *Forum on Corrections Research, 1*(2), 11-18.

Andrews, D. A., & Kiessling, J. J. (1980). Program structure and effective correctional practices: A summary of the CAVIC research. In R. R. Ross & P. Gendreau (Eds.), *Effective correctional treatment* (pp. 441-463). Toronto: Butterworths.

Andrews, D. A., Zinger, I., Hoge, R. D., Bonta, J., Gendreau, P., & Cullen, F. T. (1990).

Does correctional treatment work? A clinically-relevant and psychologically-informed meta-analysis. *Criminology, 28,* 369-404.

Ayres, A., Duguid, S., Montague, C., & Wolowidnyk, S. (1980). *Effects of University of Victoria Program: A post-release study.* Ottawa: Ministry of the Solicitor General of Canada.

Cullen, F. T., & Gendreau, P. (1989). The effectiveness of correctional rehabilitation: Reconsidering the "Nothing Works" doctrine. In L. Goodstein & D. L. Mackenzie (Eds.), *The American prison: Issues in research policy* (pp. 23–44). New York: Plenum.

Ellis, A. (1973). *Humanistic psychology: The rational-emotive approach.* New York: Julian Press.

Fogel, D. (1979). *". . . We are the living proof. . . ": The justice model for corrections.* Cincinnati: W.H. Anderson Company.

Garrett, C. J. (1985). Effects of residential treatment on adjudicated delinquents: A meta-analysis. *Journal of Research in Crime and Delinquency, 22,* 287–308.

Gendreau, P., & Ross, R. R. (1979). Effectiveness of correctional treatment: Bibliotherapy for cynics. *Crime and Delinquency, 25,* 463–489.

Gendreau, P., & Ross, R. R. (1981). Offender rehabilitation: The appeal of success. *Federal Probation, 45*(4), 45–48.

Gendreau, P., & Ross, R. R. (1984). Correctional treatment: Some recommendations for successful intervention. *Juvenile and Family Court Journal, 34*(4), 31-40.

Gendreau, P., & Ross, R. R. (1987). Revivification of rehabilitation: Evidence from the 1980s. *Justice Quarterly, 4,* 349–408.

Izzo, R. L., & Ross, R. R. (1990). Meta-analysis of rehabilitation programs for juvenile delinquents: A brief report. *Criminal Justice and Behavior, 17,* 134-142.

Johnson, G., & Hunter, L. (1992). *Evaluation of the specialized drug offender program.* Report for the Colorado Judicial Department. Boulder: University of Colorado, Center for Action Research.

Linden, R., Perry, L., Ayers, D., & Parlett, T. A. A. (1984). An evaluation of a prison education program. *Canadian Journal of Criminology, 26,* 65-73.

Lipsey, M. (1991). Juvenile delinquency treatment: A meta-analytic inquiry into the variability of effects. *Meta-analysis for explanation: A casebook.* New York: Russell Sage Foundation.

Mahoney, M. J. (1974). *Cognition and behavior modification.* Cambridge, MA: Ballinger.

Morales, S. (1992). *Tenerife prison study.* Manuscript in preparation, University of LaLaguna, Tenerife, Canary Islands.

Platt, J. J., Perry, G. M., & Metzger, D. S. (1980). The evaluation of a heroin addiction treatment program within a correctional environment. In R. R. Ross & P. Gendreau (Eds.), *Effective correctional treatment* (pp. 421-437). Toronto: Butterworths.

Porporino, F., Robinson, D., & Fabiano, E. A. (1992). *Application of the cognitive skills training approach in Canada's prisons.* Prepublication summary, Ottawa: Correctional Service of Canada.

Ross, R. R., & Fabiano, E. A. (1985). *Time to think: A cognitive model of delinquency prevention and offender rehabilitation.* Johnson City, TN: Institute of Social Sciences and Arts.

Ross, R. R., Fabiano, E. A., & Ewles, C. D. (1988). Reasoning and rehabilitation. *International Journal of Offender Therapy and Comparative Criminology, 32,* 29-35.

Ross, R. R., & Gendreau, P. (1980). *Effective correctional treatment.* Toronto: Butterworths.

Ross, R. R., & Lightfoot, L. O. (1985). *Treatment of the alcohol-abusing offender.* Springfield, IL: C.C. Thomas.

Sarason, I. G., & Ganzer, V. J. (1973). Modeling and group discussions in the rehabilitation of juvenile delinquents. *Journal of Counseling Psychology, 20,* 442-449.

Wexler, H. K., Falkin, G. P., & Lipton, D. S. (1990). Outcome evaluation of a prison therapeutic community for substance abuse treatment. *Criminal Justice and Behavior, 17,* 71-92.

Request for reprints: Robert R. Ross, Ph.D.

Daniel H. Antonowicz, M.C.A.
Doctoral Candidate
Department of Psychology
Carleton University
Ottawa, Ontario
Canada K1S 5B6

Robert R. Ross, Ph.D.
Professor
Department of Criminology
University of Ottawa
1 Stewart St.
Ottawa, Ontario
Canada K1N 6N5

Correctional "Good Time" as a Means of Early Release

Ellen F. Chayet
Associate Editor, *Criminal Justice Abstracts*

The practice of credit-based early release from prison or jail—also known as "good time," "gain time," "sentence remission," or "time off for good behavior"—is an area of increasing importance for criminal justice policy. Contemporary corrections administrators and decision makers, coping with ever-larger numbers of offenders committed or returned to prisons, are recognizing that a judicious use of good time—a long-standing "back-door" response to prison crowding—may be the most immediate and promising tool available to accelerate the release of incarcerated offenders and alleviate population pressures.

The routine acquisition and accumulation of good-time credits can affect time served either by shortening the length of sentence to be served, or by advancing the date when inmates become eligible for parole consideration (*see* Davis, 1990). This definition sets good time, remission, and earned-release practices apart from other discretionary correctional release programs such as furloughs, work release, and halfway houses. A good-time sentence reduction may, however, have the effect of speeding up the eligibility of certain inmates for these programs.

Policies allowing for good time are nearly universal in the U.S. Almost every state retains a form of good time permitting inmates to be released before completing their imposed sentences. A 1989 survey of laws and policies showed that 43 of 49 responding correctional jurisdictions in the U.S. provided good time (Davis, 1990). The survey illustrated the variability in good-time practices across the country. Depending on the state, inmates could reduce their sentences by as little as 4.5 days or as many as 75 days for each month incarcerated. In 17 states, inmates could acquire 30 days or more per month served, and only six states offered no good-time credits.

Good time is not used only in the U.S. In Canada, earned remission is analogous to good time, allowing a 10 to 15 day reduction in the sentence served (Davis, 1990). In Great Britain, prior to the Criminal Justice Act of 1991—which replaced previous distinctions between remission and parole with the single concept of early release—remission could reduce an inmate's served sentence and also be taken away through prison disciplinary proceedings (Wasik, 1992). Remission policies have also operated in contemporary penal systems in Australia (Chan, 1992), and in France, where 70% of inmates benefit from the maximum amount of good time allowable. French prisoners can also earn time reductions by passing educational and vocational exams, and by making "...exceptional efforts at rehabilitation" (Lloyd, 1991:234).

Despite its use in prison systems throughout the world, credit-based release is a subject that has received limited research attention. The process of awarding credits is often automatic, but decisions to award good time can also be discretionary, as when prison classification or reclassification committees place inmates in a specific status that increases or decreases the rate at which credits can be accrued. Moreover, the discretion to take away credits is often exercised by corrections officers in the context of prison disciplinary hearings that are typically closed to public scrutiny.

This review summarizes the major empirical, theoretical, legal, and practical works on correctional good time, focusing primarily on North American systems.

A HISTORY OF GOOD TIME

Good time in the U.S. was developed in conjunction with prison reform and the problems associated with the American penitentiary in the first half of the nineteenth century (Parisi and Zillo, 1983). In 1817, New York enacted the first good-time law. Inspectors at a new prison in Auburn, N.Y. were empowered to reduce inmates' sentences by up to 25% for good behavior and work habits. This policy was initiated as a population-reducing alternative to the overuse of pardons at the time. Good-time laws gave prison officials some control over inmate behavior, while relieving prison crowding and enhancing rehabilitation (Bottomley, 1990).

These developments in the U.S. mirrored a concurrent trend in overseas penal systems, such as: Alexander Maconochie's system for earning release from the penal colony at Norfolk Island, Australia (1840 to 1844); the Irish prison system reforms of Sir Walter Crofton (1850s); and progressive earned release and remission systems implemented by Montesinos y Molina in Italy in 1835 (Barry, 1956; Ross and Barker, 1986). These reformers believed that prison was a place to modify the attitudes and behavior of inmates (Ross and Barker, 1986). Maconochie pioneered a system of earned release based on good works and self- discipline, and the accumulation of "marks" in recognition of positive behavior (Barry, 1956). Similarly, Crofton's system advanced concepts of reward, including release, based on industry and behavior. By 1876, some 29 states in the U.S. and the federal system had enacted good-time laws (Parisi and Zillo, 1983).

Canada has had a remission system since 1868, also based on the principles enunciated by Maconochie. The Penitentiary Act in that year rewarded a 5-day-per-month deduction from sentences of inmates displaying "...positive attitudes, cooperative behaviour and industrious work habits" (Ross and Barker, 1986:8). Legislation passed in 1883 and 1906 instituted a system whereby more credits were progressively earned, and introduced the punitive aspect of remission for certain misbehavior. During the twentieth century, refinements such as distinct statutory and earned remissions, and mandatory supervision were added (Ross and Barker, 1986; Cole and Manson, 1990).

GOOD TIME TODAY

The practice of good time in the U.S. today is quite complex, and varies considerably among jurisdictions. At least four forms of credit-based early release can be identified: statutory or administrative; earned; meritorious; and emergency credits. Statutory good time is typically awarded automatically to prison inmates, who are often credited with all potential credits they can receive upon commitment to custody. In 1989, statutory good time was used in 39 correctional jurisdictions, with 27 states having some provision for crediting time "up front" (Davis, 1990). (In some of these jurisdictions, good-time provisions were only applicable to inmates sentenced under earlier laws. For example, in Oregon, statutory good time was granted to inmates sentenced before November, 1989, when sentencing guidelines went into effect.) Good time awarded in this way, upon entering prison, is affected primarily by credits revoked as penalty for misbehavior. Thus, some call it a disincentive or punishment system (Ross and Barker, 1986; 1988).

Earned-credit systems are closer to the original concept of good time as an incentive and reward for positive behaviors. They allow inmates to reduce their sentences by participating in prison programs or activities such as education or vocational training. This method was offered in 37 states in 1989, often in combination with statutory (administrative) good time (Davis, 1990).

Meritorious or special credits, are usually a form of statutory good time provided to inmates who perform exceptional acts such as donating blood or for exemplary behavior during emergencies.

Finally, today's overcrowded prisons and frequent court- ordered population caps have encouraged the use of special emergency credit awards. Eligible inmates may be granted a usually predetermined number of credits to accelerate their discharge dates or advance a parole hearing. These awards are often enabled under existing administrative or meritorious good-time statutes vesting the discretion for responding to population crises in prison administrators.

One example of emergency credit awards is the Illinois Forced Release and Meritorious Good Time Program, begun in 1980, which used administrative time-credit provisions to reduce sentences by 90 days. The subsequent Supplemental Meritorious Good Time Program in 1990 allowed an additional three months deduction for certain inmates. Since 1980, more than a dozen states have implemented similar programs (Austin, 1986; Austin and Bolyard, 1993). In Michigan, the legislatively initiated Emergency Powers Act granted additional good-time credits to accelerate parole hearing dates under indeterminate sentencing. This provision was used nine times between 1980 and 1984 (Austin, 1987). Texas also adds good-time credits under emergency circumstances, which has the effect of moving up an inmate's parole eligibility date (Ekland-Olson and Kelly, 1993).

Relationship to Sentencing and Parole

Credit-based early release exists in all types of sentencing systems. In some indeterminate sentencing jurisdictions, its coexistence with parole may undermine the value of good time as a correctional tool. For example, good time may be deducted only from the maximum sentence, while parole eligibility is calculated from the minimum term. In this system, the parole date almost invariably precedes the date of credit-based discharge (NYS Coalition, 1982). Critics have called for applying good time to minimum sentences, thereby restoring the use of good time as a behavioral incentive as well as enhancing control over prison population size (NYS Coalition, 1982; Zimmerman, 1982; Huling, 1990).

In determinate sentencing states, good time often remains as a predominant release mechanism despite reformers' intention to introduce greater certainty in sentencing. Among eight states that enacted determinate sentencing laws and abolished parole by 1982, all but one retained statutory good time (Jacobs, 1982). In Illinois, determinate sentencing, along with more efficient prosecutions, contributed to burgeoning prison populations as prison exits declined, admissions rose, and length of stay increased. In response, the Illinois Department of Corrections expanded its time credit-granting program using both statutory and meritorious good time. As a result, "(d)espite the passage of determinate sentencing, inmates were beginning to be released in greater numbers after serving shorter prison terms" (Austin, 1987:22). However, according to Goodstein and Hepburn (1986), routine good-time policy did not undermine the principles of determinacy in Illinois, although the excessive use of meritorious good time did increase inmates' uncertainty about their release dates. In two other determinate sentencing systems studied—Minnesota and Connecticut—the use of good time did not seriously compromise sentence certainty (Goodstein and Hepburn, 1985; 1986).

Florida enacted a series of mandatory minimum sentences by 1990 (Bales and Dees, 1992) that may affect gain time and early release awards by either: (1) denying any award until the mandatory part of the sentence is served; or (2) allowing credit awards but not permitting them to reduce the mandatory minimum. Forecasts of the effects of this approach suggested that, while the number of inmates ineligible for early release would rise, the sentences of those eligible for credits would be reduced even further (Bales and Dees, 1992).

In Texas, severe crowding in correctional facilities and the need to comply with court-ordered population ceilings under *Ruiz vs. Estelle* led to legislation that affected good time in a number of ways. Along with generally liberalized good-time statutes, the Prison Management Act (PMA), first enacted in 1983 and revised in 1987, provided that when prison populations reached 95% of capacity, 30-day increments of administrative good time could be granted to eligible inmates. Additional good time (up to 90 days) or advanced parole eligibility could also be awarded to inmates meeting certain conditions if overcrowding persisted. As a result, between 1982 and 1990, the proportion of sentences that was actually served dropped from 35% to 20%, and the average length of time served in prison decreased from 2.3 years to 1.9 years (Ekland-Olson and Kelly, 1993).

Subsequent legislation in Texas permitted the corrections director to restore good time earned during a parole violator's initial period of incarceration. This policy, an additional measure to help in managing the size of the prison population, allowed parole violators to be re-released as quickly as three months after their revocation. However, Winfree and colleagues (1990a; 1990b), found that the overall behavior and effects of the parole board's decisions were not significantly altered by the law.

Finally, good-time discharges may be accompanied by a formal supervision period in the community. In Canada, such a period of mandatory supervision for federal inmates was enacted in 1970 and survived several legal challenges. Inmates are expected to comply with certain conditions of release imposed by the National Parole Board (Cole and Manson, 1990).

EFFECTS OF GOOD TIME

(1) Offender Rehabilitation and Public Safety

Originally, good time was said to contribute to *prisoner reform* by encouraging participation in programs aimed at offender rehabilitation. As an incentive to good behavior, good time was also believed to strengthen pro-social skills necessary for a law-abiding life in the community. It is, however, particularly difficult to attribute aspects of offender reform that may reflect these skills—such as obtaining stable employment and residence—specifically to credit-based release.

Risk posed to the community is one measurable aspect of rehabilitation, although no controlled studies could be found that specifically examined recidivism among inmates discharged early as a result of routine allocations of administrative good time or earned credits. However, one bivariate analysis suggested that inmates in Texas who lost good time had higher rates of return to prison than those with no revocations (Eisenberg, 1985). Moreover, a body of research does exist on the public safety risk posed by special early release programs (Malak, 1984; Austin, 1986; Austin and Bolyard, 1993; Ekland-Olson and Kelly, 1993). These studies indicate that special early release programs do not adversely affect public safety by resulting in additional crimes committed.

Two research projects examined special good-time allocations in Illinois (Austin, 1986; Austin and Bolyard, 1993). The use of Meritorious Good Time (MGT), which accelerated an inmate's discharge date by 90 days, presented only a small risk to public safety.

According to a variety of recidivism measures, inmates released early were no more likely to commit crimes than other inmates, and, when arrested, their crimes were typically nonviolent offenses. Overall, the Illinois early release policy increased the amount of reported crime by less than 1% (Austin, 1986). In part, MGT's success was attributable to careful screening by the Illinois Department of Correction, which selected inmates who had good conduct records and lower security levels.

In 1990, to cope with persistent prison crowding, Illinois offered an additional 90 days of Supplemental MGT for selected inmates. Austin and Bolyard (1993) could find no differences in recidivism for SMGT and MGT inmates, compared with those not released under these programs. Other public safety indicators were also positive. Reported reoffending was lower for discharges with 180 SMGT days compared to inmates released with 90 MGT days. These positive impacts saved $98.7 million in prison construction/operating costs in FY 1991. Austin and Bolyard concluded that "...offenders can be punished with significantly shorter sentences with no adverse risk to public safety and at considerable savings to state government" (1993:63).

Research conducted in Colorado also suggested that public safety is not compromised by special early release. The court ruling in *People vs Chavez* (1983) resulted in the awarding of substantial good time to inmates confined in jails prior to sentencing. Among 126 inmates receiving accelerated release, there was no evidence of increased likelihood in the number or rate of rearrests during the first eight months following discharge (compared to full-term inmates), even though the early-released inmates could be considered higher-risk offenders (Malak, 1984).

Somewhat contrasting findings are reported in Ekland-Olson and Kelly's (1993) evaluation of Texas policy changes that granted both 90 days of additional good time and advanced parole review dates under "emergency" conditions. Early releasees were reincarcerated for a technical parole violation more quickly than inmates not benefiting from accelerated release. While perhaps not representing a major threat to the community, the authors concluded that the PMA actually contributed to crowding by "...speeding up the cycle time of release and return" (Ekland-Olson and Kelly, 1993:103).

Does good time enhance the rehabilitative potential of prison programs? Although empirical research on this issue is sparse, there may be rehabilitative promise in the restoration of credits. Keltner and Gordon (1976) found that carefully restoring lost days of earned remission was successful in modifying drug abuse and violent behavior among inmates. These results should be regarded cautiously, however, since the sample consisted of only 16 cases.

In Canada, prisoners themselves considered the incentive value of remission to be overrated (Ross and Barker, 1986). Most Canadian inmates favored retaining the remission system, however, although the majority would favored abolishing the mandatory supervision of earned remission discharges because it "...considerably devalues the motivating effect of earned remission in prison" (Ross and Barker, 1986:31).

In 1982, the New York State Coalition for Criminal Justice queried inmates and correctional employees about the good-time system then in operation. Concerns were expressed about its questionable reward value, as well as about eligibility factors, credit revocations for disciplinary infractions, and good time's relationship to parole decisions (NYS Coalition, 1982). Employees shared the concern that good time does not have much incentive value. While fully 80% of the inmates, and between 71% and 84% of employees, believed that good time should motivate participation in educational programs, only 55% of the inmates and 35% to 56% of employees felt that it did so (NYS Coalition, 1982:25).

The public, often assumed to oppose good time, may support these policies under limited circumstances. One study, evaluating public preferences for various potential responses to prison crowding, found that 80% of the respondents in Cincinnati and 70.7% of those in Cleveland favored a program of incentive good time earned for "good behavior and participation in educational and work programs in prison" (Skovron, Scott, and Cullen, 1988:157). A Canadian study interviewed over 1,000 adults in 1986, focusing on public knowledge of and attitudes towards two forms of early release from prison: earned remission and parole (Roberts, 1988). Few adults were aware of the distinctions between the two programs, although 63% supported early release. Specifically, 59% of the respondents preferred release through earned remission over parole, typically favoring a reduction of 20 to 29% of the inmate's sentence.

(2) Prison Management

The power to shorten time served may provide corrections officials with a tool for *maintaining institutional control* and discipline. Surveys of prison managers conducted in Canada and the U.S. during the 1980s found support for remission policies (Ross and

Barker, 1986). While managers expressed concern about the limited effectiveness of credit-based release, they agreed that remission was important in helping administrators to control their prisons. These *perceptions* that good time helps to control inmate behavior may be as important as the actual control conferred by these policies (Emshoff and Davidson, 1987; Ross and Barker, 1988).

Does good time help maintain prison discipline? The research evidence is indirect and far from clear. A "natural experiment" on the ability of good time to modify behavior occurred in Michigan, where correctional policy prohibited certain classes of inmates from earning good-time deductions from the minimum sentence. Emshoff and Davidson (1987) concluded that expectations that good time deprivation would increase inmate misbehavior could not be supported by the data.

In Indiana, it was predicted that a change from earned statutory good time to a system of formula-based classes of credit time under sentencing reform would make the prisons more difficult to control. In fact, while predatory behavior offenses did not increase, a rise in more minor offenses was reported (Schaefer, 1982). Although possibly attributable to the change from good time to credit time, these results also likely represent "an increase in formal enforcement of prison regulations by staff" (Schaefer, 1982:157).

A California study, while primarily evaluating the impact of determinate sentencing and the abolition of parole release on prison unrest, suggested that serious prison rules violations increased despite substantially strengthened and specifically articulated good-time provisions (Forst and Brady, 1983). California prison officials felt that good time was an ineffective deterrent to misconduct since the number of days forfeitable was limited, and thus the potential to reduce sentences relatively small. Forst (1981) argued that inmates in that case were unlikely to change their behavior based on anticipated rewards that would occur at release, a time often far in the future.

(3) Prison Population Management

Release via good time as a *"back-end" solution to prison overcrowding* has recently become more critical. Does good time enable administrators to manage the size of their prison populations, and is it an effective safety valve? Research on this question is generally affirmative.

The Illinois program of emergency meritorious good time (MGT) produced a 10% reduction in the size of the projected prison population (Austin, 1986). The later SMGT policy reduced populations by 1,490 inmates; combined with MGT, population decreased by 4,529. By the year 2,000, both policies are projected to reduce the inmate population by 8,951 residents (Austin and Bolyard, 1993).

In Florida, a federal court consent decree prohibited prison crowding. A nearly universal policy of granting unlimited extra good-time credit successfully controlled prison population growth, shortening the average time served from two years in 1980 to less than one year in 1989 (Austin, 1991).

Simulation studies, which project the impact of various good time policies on the size of the prison population, can be particularly instructive. In 1982, New York State estimated the effects of three alternative proposals. The most liberal good- time policy would have resulted in greater numbers of inmates released each year and would have generated the slowest growth in prison populations (Zimmerman, 1982). In Maine, the use of an enhanced good-time policy was predicted to save 233 beds over four years compared to a continuation of previous policy (Ehrenkrantz Group, 1984). A more recent projection of the impact of abolishing both parole and good time on the numbers incarcerated in Texas prisons predicted dramatic and immediate increases over a six-year period, requiring the construction of 184,000 new prison beds (Texas Criminal Justice Policy Council, 1992).

GOOD TIME ADMINISTRATION AND PRACTICE

The administration of good time, involving granting, revoking, and restoring forfeited credits, is often complex. Its very complexity has led to criticisms that its practice undermines its intentions. Frequently, no formal policy or procedural guidance is available to enable informed or consistent decision making, with revocation criteria often particularly ambiguous. Decisions to revoke credits are typically made by corrections officers and staff in disciplinary hearings, during which prison rules infractions may be penalized by a variety of sanctions. In some states, however, provisions for vesting credits prohibit the forfeiture of credits already accrued (Jacobs, 1982).

Little research exists on the routine administration of good-time policies. The administration and effects of routine good-time allowances on felony and misdemeanor sentences in Connecticut were examined by Parker (1978). This descriptive research showed that good time was rarely revoked—only 20% of the felons experienced revocation—and that about one-third of the forfeited time was ultimately restored. In British prisons, however, forfeiture of remission was found to be the most frequent sanction imposed by the Board of Visitors for a breach of discipline (Iles et al., 1984).

Gifis described disciplinary committee decision making in a Massachusetts prison (Gifis, 1978). The purpose of the hearing was to decide upon appropriate sanctions, which most commonly included a loss of good time. Sanction selection was highly variable, and the range of actions possible was quite wide and based on a number of factors. Nationally, inmates are theoretically entitled to minimum due process safeguards when determining their guilt or innocence of charges potentially involving a loss of good time (*see Wolff vs. McDonnell* (1974)). Subsequent court decisions, however, have largely eroded this protection (Jones, 1992).

Lost credits may typically be restored by prison authorities, usually when the inmate nears release. But this last-minute restoration, intended to accelerate release and free up prison beds, may further undermine the value of good time for controlling inmates' behavior. Moreover, the reinstatement of a potentially substantial number of days is usually not governed by standards specifying the circumstances and amount of time to be restored, and is subject to variation among decision makers (Jacobs, 1982). For example, in New York, inmates felt that the restoration process was biased partly because of the composition of the time-allowance committees and also "because of procedural limitations which inhibit their ability to make a credible case for themselves" (NYS Coalition, 1982:20).

Treatment Disparity and Equity

Placing substantial discretionary autonomy over decisions that affect time served in the hands of corrections officers and staff, without effective controls over its use, may exacerbate or shift disparities introduced at sentencing (Clear, Hewitt, and Regoli, 1978). Examining the effect of Indiana's determinate sentencing system, this research suggested that attempts to constrain discretion at one stage of the criminal justice system often inflate discretion at later stages. While one goal of abolishing parole release decisions was to limit the availability of discretion, the enhanced credit-time provisions made extensive discretion available to corrections administrators (Clear, Hewitt and Regoli, 1978:440).

Good-time-revocation decisions may involve differential treatment on the basis of characteristics unrelated to seriousness of the misbehavior. Studies of penalties imposed for disciplinary offenses suggest that sanction imposition and severity are often associated with non-behavioral or extra-legal attributes such as race, age, gender and place of incarceration, as well as infraction severity (Flanagan, 1979, 1982; Poole and Regoli, 1980; Keenan, 1982; Iles et al., 1984). Moreover, inmates in a large Northeastern state who were characterized as "long- term" prisoners were significantly more likely to be sanctioned with loss of good time (11%) than "short-term" prisoners (less than 2%), despite evidence that long-termers misbehaved less often than prisoners serving less time in prison (Flanagan, 1979).

A study of responses to institutional rule breaking in a southern prison revealed race differentials, with blacks being significantly more likely to receive a disciplinary report than whites (Poole and Regoli, 1980). These disparities existed despite self-reports indicating equal participation of black and white inmates in rule breaking. Prior record also influenced disciplinary sanctions that could be expected to produce a loss of good time.

In Georgia, the earned-time system included a disciplinary sanction of "time-out" from accruing credits. Keenan's (1982) analysis revealed variability in the length of time-outs imposed, although the exact nature of race differentials depended upon the type of facility and violations. Despite this variability, Keenan concluded that "relative equity" existed in the time-out system (Keenan, 1982:32).

Earned-credit systems present a special potential for treatment inequities (see Chayet and Weisburd, in press). Unless inmates have access to credit-granting programs, decisions about who may participate can be biased if offenders are excluded on non-defensible grounds. And, as Jacobs (1982) pointed out, waiting lists to join programs often exist. Moreover, questions can be raised about which programs carry the opportunity to earn credits, and the relative amount of credits to be earned in each. These kinds of credit differentials can lead inmates to appraise programs on their credit value rather than on their rehabilitative or other personal merit (Weisburd and Chayet, 1989). Another equity consideration is what happens to offenders who are willing and appropriate, but otherwise ineligible to earn credits by participating in programs. Do sick inmates or those in protective custody have an alternative means to reduce their sentences by accruing good time credits? What happens when inmates are transferred among institutions, curtailing their involvement in programs and credit earnings?

Additional factors have been identified that raise further questions about the fairness of good-time policies and practices. Institutional differences exist within many prison systems in the number of credits revoked for particular offenses. For example, in four New York facilities, good-time loss ranged from 11% to 46% of cases heard (NYS Coalition, 1982). Similarly, restoration of lost credits ranged from about 12% to over 60% of the days revoked. A survey of prisoners and corrections staff in New York found that both groups believed that good-time benefited a small segment of the prison population, and that the same amount of good time was awarded to inmates who actively participated in prison programs as to those who merely avoided misbehavior (NYS Coalition, 1982).

Significant institutional differences in remission forfeitures have also been reported in England (Iles et al., 1984). Variations by geographic region in both the proportion of inmates losing remission as a disciplinary penalty, and in the number of days forfeited, were also found in Canadian federal penitentiaries (Solicitor General of Canada, 1981). This Canadian study further identified revocation disparities related to an inmate's security level. In addition, good-time forfeiture for parole revocations in Wisconsin varied depending upon which officers sat at hearings (Wagner, 1980).

Different classification statuses, length of sentence, time served, and type of program may entitle inmates to accrue credits at different rates, as reflected in differential earnings rates for convicted offenders housed in jails versus prisons. A recent study in Virginia found that, due to good-time policies, inmates incarcerated in local jails served more time than "similarly situated felons" in prison. Jail inmates who were parole eligible received, at least initially, less good time than their prison counterparts (Virginia State Crime Commission, 1993).

In Illinois, Goodstein and Hepburn (1986) observed that most inmates continued to earn all potential credits available to them, and that much of what was revoked was ultimately restored. They concluded, however, that good-time revocations may compromise sentence equity and predictability if inmates with revocations served longer sentences than similar inmates with no time forfeited. Large differences between prisons in handling revocations and restorations, coupled with the prisoner review board's inability to eliminate these differences, "...underscores sentence equity problems on a state-wide basis" (Goodstein and Hepburn, 1986:315). These equity problems were also affected by an excessive use of meritorious good time.

CONCLUSION

The foregoing literature review suggests that little is known about how correctional good time operates on a routine basis and what effects it has on the criminal justice system, inmates or the community (Weisburd and Chayet, 1989). Much of what is known is indirect or focuses on special early release programs, rather than on the everyday instances of prison decision making whereby time served is continually modified.

The evidence available to date suggests that the effects of good time are mixed. Good time makes a positive contribution to controlling the size of prison populations, while apparently having little or no negative effect on public safety. It is not clear whether good time improves the in-prison behavior of inmates, but correctional administrators and staff believe that it assists them in maintaining institutional control. There is, however, no evidence that good-time credits have rehabilitative benefits, although in earned release programs, under certain conditions, credits may provide inmates with an incentive to engage in self-improvement. Finally, there is significant evidence to suggest that good time contributes to disparities in sentences served and correctional treatment inequities.

Perhaps the most cogent and enduring criticism of good time was made by James Jacobs (1982). He argued that good time, as a highly invisible discretionary system for resentencing inmates, has failed to meet its goals for prison discipline, offender reform, and attaining "just deserts." Other goals of good time, such as mitigating sentence severity and managing populations, can be more efficiently or appropriately addressed through more visible alternative approaches that would limit potential abuses of discretion, according to Jacobs. Recognizing the potential for abuse, he concluded that good time should be phased out, or at least strictly curtailed and controlled. Ross and Barker (1986; 1988) added that the numerous, often conflicting goals for good time or remission, have led to a "constant tinkering" with the system that may have hampered the ability of credit-based release to achieve its goals.

Similarly, recent "truth-in-sentencing" legislation (North Carolina Governor's Crime Commission, 1987; Davis, 1990) calls for the curtailment or elimination of statutory good time and minimal use of earned credits. However, without a solid base of empirical research to describe how good time works—especially its advantages and deficiencies—major changes may be unnecessary or, at best, misdirected (Weisburd and Chayet, 1989).

Good time remains an integral part of correctional systems throughout the U.S. and Europe. Indeed, the enduring prisoner population crisis in corrections, combined with reduced judicial and parole discretion, has led to an increased reliance upon good time to alleviate prison crowding. This review demonstrates an even greater need to examine and understand dimensions of these routine, but important correctional decisions.

Acknowledgments. The author would like to thank Professor David Weisburd, Director of the Center for Crime Prevention Studies at Rutgers University, for his collaboration on earlier works on good time, and for making unlimited support of the center available to prepare some of the work represented in this paper. Robyn Mace Fisher, also at the center, was instrumental in locating many of the documents in the review. Special thanks are due Robert Kidd and Richard Allinson for their knowledgeable and skillful editing of the manuscript.

REFERENCES

Austin, James (1986) "Using Early Release to Relieve Prison Crowding: A Dilemma in Public Policy." *Crime & Delinquency* 32(4):404-502.

—— (1987). "The Use of Early Release and Sentencing Guidelines To Ease Prison Crowding: The Shifting Sands of Reform." In: Dale K. Sechrest, Jonathan D. Caspar and Jeffrey A. Roth (eds.), *Prison and Jail Crowding: Workshop Proceedings*. Washington, DC: National Research Council.

—— (1991). "The Consequences of Escalating the Use of Imprisonment: The Case Study of Florida." *Focus*, National Council on Crime and Delinquency (June).

—— and Melissa Bolyard (1993). *The Effectiveness of Reduced Prison Terms on Public Safety and Costs: The Evaluation of the Illinois Supplemental Meritorious Good Time Program*. San Francisco, CA: National Council on Crime and Delinquency.

Bales, William D. and Linda G. Dees (1992). "Mandatory Minimum Sentencing in Florida: Past Trends and Future Implications." *Crime & Delinquency* 38(3):309-329.

Barry, John Vincent (1956). "Pioneers in Criminology: Alexander Maconochie (1787-1860)." *Journal of Criminal Law, Criminology, and Police Science* 47(2):145-161.

Bottomley, A. Keith (1990). "Parole in Transition: A Comparative Study of Origins, Developments, and Prospects for the 1990s." In: Michael Tonry and Norval Morris (eds.), *Crime and Justice: A Review of Research*, volume 12. Chicago, IL: University of Chicago Press.

Chan, Janet B.L. (1992). *Doing Less Time: Penal Reform in Crisis.* Sydney, AUS: Institute of Criminology, Sydney University Law School.

Chayet, Ellen F. and David Weisburd (in press). "Good Time Credit in American Prisons." In: Marilyn D. McShane and Frank P. Williams, III (eds.), *Encyclopedia of American Prisons.* New York, NY: Garland.

Clear, Todd R., John D. Hewitt, Robert M. Regoli (1978). "Discretion and the Indeterminate Sentence: Its Distribution, Control, and Effect on Time Served." *Crime & Delinquency* (October):428-445.

Cole, David P. and Allan Manson (1990). *Release From Imprisonment: The Law of Sentencing, Parole and Judicial Review.* Toronto, CAN: Carswell.

Davis, Su Perk (1990). "Good Time." *Corrections Compendium* XV(4):May.

Ehrenkrantz Group, P.C. (1984). *State of Maine Department of Corrections Legislation Impact Study.* New York, NY: author.

Ekland-Olson, Sheldon and William R. Kelly (1993). *Justice Under Pressure: A Comparison of Recidivism Patterns Among Four Successive Parolee Cohorts.* New York, NY: Springer-Verlag.

Eisenberg, Michael (1985). *Factors Associated with Recidivism.* Austin, TX: State of Texas Board of Pardons and Paroles.

Emshoff, James G. and William S. Davidson (1987). "The Effect of 'Good Time' Credit on Inmate Behavior: A Quasi-Experiment." *Criminal Justice and Behavior* 14(3):335-351.

Flanagan, Timothy (1979). *Long-Term Prisoners: A Study of The Characteristics, Institutional Experience and Perspectives of Long-Term Inmates in State Correctional Facilities.* Ph.D. Dissertation, SUNY-Albany. Ann Arbor, MI: University Microfilms International.

—— (1982). "Discretion in the Prison Justice System: A Study of Sentencing in Institutional Disciplinary Proceedings." *Journal of Research in Crime and Delinquency* 19(2):216-237.

Forst, Martin L. (1981). "Effects of Determinate Sentencing on Prison Disciplinary Procedures and Inmate Misconduct." Unpublished manuscript.

—— and James M. Brady (1983). "The Effects of Determinate Sentencing on Inmate Misconduct in Prison." *Prison Journal* LXIII(1):100-113.

Gifis, Steven (1978). "Decision-making In A Prison Community." In: Burton Atkins and Mark Pogrebin (eds.), *The Invisible Justice System: Discretion and the Law* (second edition). Cincinnati, OH: Anderson.

Goodstein, Lynne and John Hepburn (1985). *Determinate Sentencing and Imprisonment: A Failure of Reform.* Cincinnati, OH: Anderson.

—— (1986). "Determinate Sentencing in Illinois: An Assessment of Its Development and Implementation." *Criminal Justice Policy Review* 1(3):329-343.

Huling, Tracy (1990). *Anti-Crime Strategies at a Time of Fiscal Constraint.* New York, NY: Correctional Association of New York.

Iles, Susan, Adrienne Connors, Chris May and Joy Mott (1984). *Punishment Practice By Prison Boards of Visitors.* London, ENG: Home Office Research and Planning Unit Paper 26.

Jacobs, James B. (1982). "Sentencing by Prison Personnel: Good Time." *UCLA Law Review* 30(2):217-270.

Jones, Charles J. (1992). "Recent Trends in Corrections and Prisoners' Rights Law." In: Clayton A. Hartjen and Edward E. Rhine (eds.), *Correctional Theory and Practice*. Chicago, IL: Nelson-Hall.

Keenan, John P. (1982). *The Earned Time System: Third General Evaluation.* Atlanta, GA: Georgia Department of Offender Rehabilitation.

Keltner, Alfred A. and Arthur Gordon (1976). "Functional Analysis of a Reinforcer in a Prison Population." *Corrective and Social Psychiatry and Journal of Behaviour Technology, Methods and Therapy* 22(2):42-44.

Lloyd, Margaret Gwynne (1991). "Early Release of Prisoners in France: Plus Ca Change, Plus C'est la Meme Chose." *Howard Journal* 30(3):231-237.

Malak, Patricia A. (1984). *Early Release.* Denver, CO: Colorado Division of Criminal Justice (March).

New York State Coalition for Criminal Justice (1982). *Earned Good Time... A Concept Whose Time Has Returned.* Albany, NY: author.

North Carolina Governor's Crime Commission (1987). *Truth in Sentencing: A Report to the Governor.* Raleigh, NC: author.

Parisi, Nicolette and Joseph A. Zillo (1983). "Good Time: The Forgotten Issue." *Crime & Delinquency* 29:228-237.

Parker, Donald M. (1978). *An Analysis of Good Time Allowances in Connecticut Correctional Facilities and the Effects on Misdemeanant and Felon Sentences.* Hartford, CT: Connecticut Department of Correction.

Poole, Eric D. and Robert M. Regoli (1980). "Race, Institutional Rule Breaking, and Disciplinary Response: A Study of Discretionary Decision Making in Prison." *Law & Society Review* 14(4):931-946.

Roberts, Julian (1988). "Early Release From Prison: What Do the Canadian Public Really Think?" *Canadian Journal of Criminology* (July):231-249.

Ross, Robert R. and Tonia G. Barker (1986). *Incentives and Disincentives: A Review of Prison Remission Systems.* Toronto, CAN: Ministry of the Solicitor General of Canada.

—— (1988) "Prison Remission Systems: Incentive or Disincentive: Control or Reform?" *Crimcare Journal* 4(2):111-131.

Schaefer, N.E. (1982). "Good Time and Prisoner Misconduct: A Preliminary Examination." In: Nicolette Parisi (ed.), *Coping With Imprisonment.* Beverly Hills, CA: Sage.

Skovron, Sandra Evans, Joseph E. Scott and Francis T. Cullen (1988). "Prison Crowding: Public Attitudes Toward Strategies of Population Control." *Journal of Research in Crime and Delinquency* 25(2):150-169.

Solicitor General of Canada (1981). *Solicitor General's Study of Conditional Release.* Ottawa, CAN: Minister of Supply and Services Canada.

Texas Criminal Justice Policy Council (1992). *Simulation of Impact: Abolishing Parole and Good Conduct Time.* Sentencing Dynamics Study, Report 3. Austin, TX: author.

Virginia State Crime Commission (1993). *Good Conduct Allowances for Prisoners in Local Correctional Facilities.* Richmond, VA: Commonwealth of Virginia.

Wagner, Dennis (1980). *Good Time Forfeiture Study.* Madison, WI: Wisconsin Bureau of Evaluation, Division of Policy and Budget (December).

Wasik, Martin (1992). "Arrangements for Early Release." *Criminal Law Review* (April):252-261.

Weisburd, David and Ellen F. Chayet (1989). "Good Time: An Agenda for Research." *Criminal Justice and Behavior* 16(2):183-195.

Winfree, L. Thomas Jr., John Wooldredge, Christine S. Sellers and Veronica Smith Ballard (1990a). "Parole Survival and Legislated Change: A Before/After Study of Parole Revocation Decision Making." *Justice Quarterly* 7(1):151-173.

—— Veronica Smith Ballard, Christine S. Sellers, and Roy R. Roberg (1990b). "Responding to a Legislated Change in Correctional Practices: A Quasi-Experimental Study of Revocation Hearings and Parole Board Actions." *Journal of Criminal Justice* 18:195-215.

Zimmerman, Sherwood E. (1982). *Potential Effect on Prison Populations of Crediting Good Time Against Minimum Sentences.* Albany, NY: New York State Division of Criminal Justice Services.

Patriarchy, Prisons, and Jails: A Critical Look at Trends in Women's Incarceration

**Meda Chesney-Lind*

Thinking about Decarceration: A Modest Proposal

Part of the challenge of doing feminist criminology is seeking ways to blend feminism, which in my view includes activism, with attempts to make sense of the law, crime, justice and the state. This orientation has led me, in the last few years, into work that lays the intellectual foundation for the decarceration of girls and women labeled as offenders. One reason I feel comfortable suggesting such a strategy on a national level is that I am living in a part of the United States that employed a non-incarcerative response to women's crime for many years.

Let me be specific. In 1973, I met and interviewed all of Hawaii's confined female felon population when I spoke with one woman. Her name was Yvonne "Thunder" Park, and she, like many low income women, died before her time. Her loss is regrettable; she was an artist, a prisoners' rights advocate, and someone who, had she lived, would have been able to make an even greater contribution to her community. I met her when I was helping volunteer attorneys from the American Civil Liberties Union in Hawaii in their work on her case, which contended that the transfer of female inmates to federal institutions in other states was unconstitutional. In those days, Hawaii had no facility for convicted women offenders; women were housed, short-term, in a portion of our jail, but women facing long sentences, like Thunder, were sent out of state.

In response to legal challenges, in 1976 the U.S. District Court in Hawaii concluded in *Park* v. *Thompson* that the transferring of women from Hawaii to California and then on to West Virginia constituted a "grievous loss and thus required procedural safeguards." At the time, this seemed to me to signal a major victory for women inmates, both in our state and in other states. No longer would women sentenced to prison in Hawaii be sent thousands of miles away from their families to do their time. Many legal experts concurred, and the case had national impact. (Pollack-Byrne, 1990).

In retrospect, I am not so confident that ultimately our work benefitted women inmates. Certainly it led to consequences that we did not anticipate. Reflections on my early experience in prison reform, as well as my involvement in two subsequent efforts to improve the situation for women inmates, frame this essay on trends in women's imprisonment. These reflections, combined with a startling increase in women's imprisonment, have convinced me that a feminist analysis of the ominous willingness of ths state to imprison women is essential and urgently needed —both to advance our understanding of the role of imprisonment in the maintenance of patriarchy and to develop the political strategy necessary to combat it.

***Meda Chesney-Lind is an Associate Professor in the Women's Study Program at the University of Hawaii at Manoa.** **She would like to acknowledge this article's origins in an earlier paper, "Women's Prisons: Overcrowded and Overused," by Russ Immarigeon and Meda Chesney-Lind, which is in press with the National Council on Crime and Delinquency. Continued discussions with Russ Immarigeon, Nicole Hahn Rafter, and Kathleen Daly on this topic have all informed the perspective and conclusions in this paper. The errors, of course, remain the author's own. This article was first prepared as a paper that was presented at the International Feminist Conference on Women, Law, and Social Control held in Mont Gabriel, Quebec in July of 1991.**

Analysis and action must be informed by the past. In the case of women's imprisonment, an understanding of the role of earlier reform efforts is essential. Reading the work of historians such as Nicole Hahn Rafter, I have discovered that my work on the *Park* case, and that of others who have worked much harder, was part of a larger effort at reform of women's prisons that emerged in the last three decades, an effort Rafter has dubbed the "parity movement." (Rafter 1990:185). In this instance, we sought to use constitutional language to argue that out-of-state transfers were an infringement on the rights of female prisoners, an infringement that made the conditions of their confinement more onerous than the confinement conditions of their male counterparts. In essence, we used the language of equity to argue for what we considered to be improvements in the conditions of confinement for women.

I suppose when one has lived long enough as both a feminist activist and academic, the ability to place biography into history becomes easier, although I am not at all sure that this sort of hindsight, which is always twenty/twenty, will stand me in good stead as I attempt to make sense of feminist prison reform movements of which I have been a part, and then seek to interpret what we should do next. As Barry Krisberg, President of the National Council of Crime and Delinquency, admonished those attending a meeting recently, "Worry about the current trend, it may be worse." Nonetheless, it is to the aim of examining the past as a guide for the future that this paper is being written; both as a cautionary tale and a call to action.

At the time I was working on the *Park* case, I was thinking about doing a dissertation on the fact that Hawaii did not have a women's prison. That we had crime by women was undeniable, but we had no women inmates. Thunder's case notwithstanding, we basically existed without a women's prison, and we were not alone. In 1973, only 28 states (including Puerto Rico and the District of Columbia) had separate institutions for women. Elsewhere, women either were housed in a portion of a male facility or, as in Hawaii, Rhode Island, and Vermont, convicted women were imprisoned in other states. (Singer 1973).

Even then I had a feeling that this was significant. Indeed, I felt that the official response to women's crime could be a model of decarceration for male offenders, since I knew that some women were, in fact, committing serious crimes. However, I believe that the reverse has happened and few have noticed. That is, the male model of incarceration increasingly has been used in response to women's offending. This increasingly punitive response to women's crime had been described by other observers as "equality with a vengeance" —the dark side of the equity or parity model of justice.

In retrospect, I can see that the parity movement played a role in this new orientation towards women's incarceration. Neither the *Park* case nor other cases that documented the deplorable conditions in women's prisons had the consequence of emptying the facilities, as many of the reformers involved in these cases (including me) might have hoped. Instead, as this paper will document, these court challenges increasingly have been used by correctional professionals to argue that equal treatment of women inmates requires the building of new, equal prisons for women. Moreover, even some of our allies in the parity reform movement are emerging supporters of this new approach to prison construction for women.

Before considering the theoretical implications of these developments as well as strategies to get beyond efforts to attain parity, the next section reviews two simple measures of the impact of this new willingness to utilize incarceration as a response to women's crime: data on the construction of women's prisons and data on the growth of women's prison populations.

Building Cells for Women

The United States has gone on a binge of building where women's prisons are concerned. Prison historian Nicole Hahn Rafter observes that between 1930 and 1950 roughly two or three prisons were built or created for women each decade. (It is important to note here that women's prisons are not always "constructed" but instead are created in a variety of ways. It is not uncommon for facilities designated for other purposes to be converted into a women's prison). In the 1960s, the pace of prison construction picked up slightly with seven units being opened, mostly in southern and western states. During the 1970s, 17 women's prisons opened, including units in states such as Rhode Island and Vermont that once relied on transferring women prisoners out of state. In the 1980s, 34 women's units or prisons were established; this figure is ten times larger than the figures for earlier decades. (see Figure 1).

Figure 1
Creation of State Prison Facilities for Women, 1930-1990

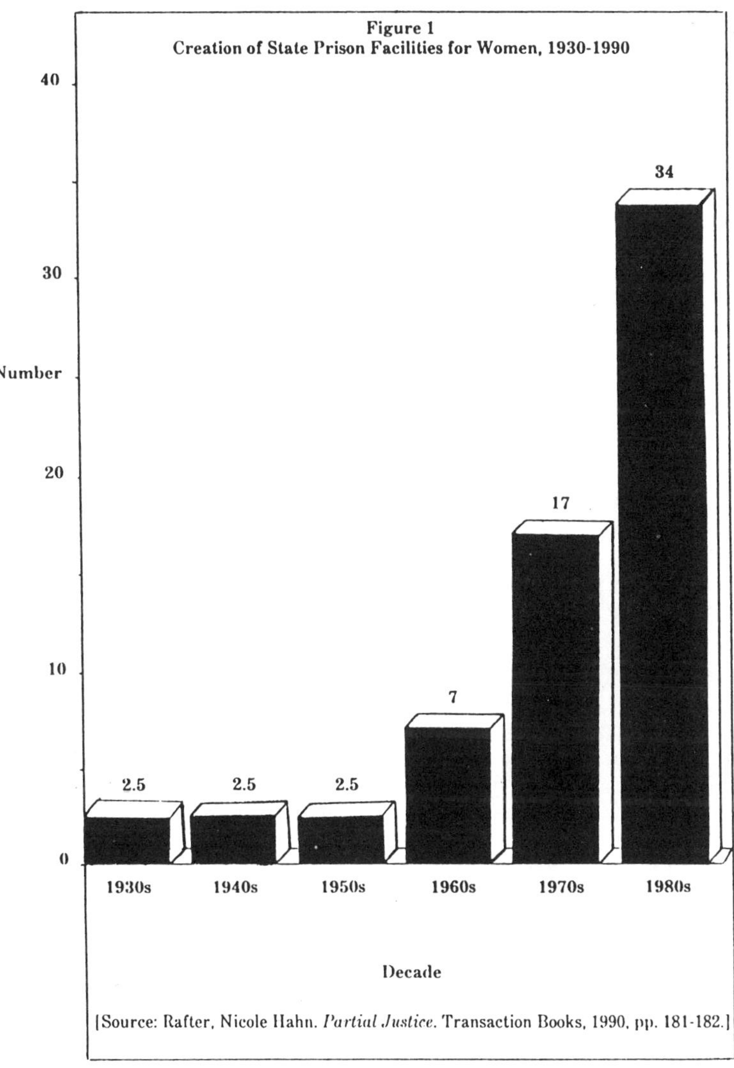

[Source: Rafter, Nicole Hahn. *Partial Justice*. Transaction Books, 1990, pp. 181-182.]

Moreover, this growth in prison facilities for women during the 1980s occurred with little thought or planning; rather it appeared to be a piecemeal response to the soaring number of women committed to prison. Commitments to women's prisons have more than tripled in the last decade, and few states were prepared for this. Instead of carefully reviewing which women required secure confinement and which could safely be housed in the community, women were placed almost anywhere —in abandoned hotels, motels, mental hospitals, nurses' dormitories, and youth training schools.

In the past decade, for example, Hawaii and Oklahoma have converted facilities formerly used for males or youths into women's prisons. In New Mexico, women began to be housed in a converted motel. In West Virginia, officials used a remodeled hospital to house women when the state's prison for women was closed because of fire and safety code violations. (DeConstanzo and Scholes 1988). California, Michigan, Minnesota, and Wyoming were among the states that built new prisons for women. In some cases, the costs of such expansion are known. In Hawaii, until political action stopped the building plan, the state was preparing to spend $200,000 per bed to build a "scaled down" facility of 96 beds for a total cost in excess of 22 million dollars. New York, a far larger state, doubled its capacity to imprison women in three years at a cost of 300 million dollars. (Huling 1991a).

The conditions in these makeshift and/or overcrowed women's prisons often are deplorable. In Massachusetts, cells meant for one person hold as many as eight. In Hawaii, over 100 women were crowded into a building designed to hold 36 juvenile females. (Chesney-Lind 1987). These conditions also brought legal challenges, a development whose impact will be explored later in this paper. This next section considers the source of this overcrowding and the resultant boom in construction of women's prisons —the soaring number of women sentenced to prison.

Imprisoning Women

The United States now imprisons more people than at any time in its history. More than 710,054 men and women are imprisoned in federal and state prisons, and local jails house at least 395,553 prisoners. (BJS 1990a; 1990b). According to a recent study by the Sentencing Project (Lafraniere 1991), the U.S. has the highest rate of incarceration in the world. Futhermore, the National Council on Crime and Delinquency estimates that the nation's prison population will grow by about 68 percent in the next five years. (Austin and McVey 1989).

Women have been hit hard by the increased willingness to incarcerate. The U.S. Bureau of Justice Statistics (BJS) reports that the average daily population of women confined in local jails rose by 95.3 percent between 1984 and 1989. By contrast, the number of men in jail increased by 50.9 percent during this period. (BJS 1990a:3). Stark increases also occurred in the number of women held in state and federal prisons. In 1980, there were 12,331 women in our nation's prisons. By 1989, that number had grown to 40,556, an increase of 230 percent. In 1980, there were 303,643 males in prison. This number grew to 669,498 in 1989, an increase of 120.5 percent. Indeed, increases in women's imprisonment surpassed increases experienced by men in every year after 1981. It must be recalled, however, that the male rate of incarceration is still substantially higher than that of women; in 1989, for example, the male incarceration rate was 531 per 100,000 compared to 29 per 100,000 for women. (BJS 1990a).

Some may suggest that the dramatic percentage increases in women's incarceration are simply an artifact of the smaller base numbers involved in women's imprisonment. For this reason, the increases in the jailing of women should be placed in historical context. Women made up four percent of the nation's imprisoned population shortly after the turn of the century. By 1970 the figure had dropped to three percent. By 1989, however, more than 5.7 percent of those incarcerated were women. In addition, the rate of women's imprisonment grew from six per 100,000 in 1925 to 29 per 100,000 in 1989. (Cahalan 1986; BJS 1990a:4). Finally, the base numbers involved in women's imprisonment are no longer small, and we are still seeing very large increases. In 1989, for example, the number of women incarcerated in federal and state prisons grew by 24.4 percent over the previous year (from 32,691 to 40,566). The number of men in prison increased by 12.5 percent.

By contrast, total arrests of women (which might be seen as a measure of women's criminal activity) increased by 65.6 percent between 1980 and 1989. The FBI reports that Part One arrests (including murder, rape, aggravated assault, burglary, larceny-theft, motor vehicle theft and arson) of women increased by about 51.5 percent during the same time period, while Part One arrests for men increased by about 32 percent. (F.B.I. 1989:173). While these trends in women's crime may sound serious, it should be noted that most of the increase in women's arrests is accounted for by more arrests of women for non-violent property offenses such as shoplifting, check forgery, and welfare fraud, as well as for offenses such as driving under the influence of alcohol and drugs.

Figures 2 and 3 show the disproportionate increase in both male and female jail and prison populations compared to the number of arrests during the same period. In one five year period (1985 to 1989), arrests of women increased about 24.1 percent while arrests of men increased by 15.2 percent. Arrests of women for Part One, or Crime Index offenses, showed a slightly smaller increase (22.5 percent), while male arrests for these offenses increased by 24.1 percent. (F.B.I. 1990:179). Jail populations for both men and women grew significantly during the same time —the women's jail population increased by 95.3 percent, while the men's grew by 50.9 percent. (BJS 1990b:2). The prison population grew by 89.5 percent for women and a lesser 45.9 percent for men. (BJS 1990). These figures suggest that increases in women's imprisonment cannot be explained simply by increases in women's crimes, at least as measured by arrests; they also show that the increases in women's imprisonment far outstrip those in the imprisonment of males.

Some would dispute this interpretation of the arrest data. Simon and Landis, for example, recently argued that changes in women's imprisonment are more or less in line with changes in women's arrests. In fact, they argue that "the [female] rate of commitment to prison did not keep up with the rate of female arrest from 1963 to 1987." (1991:78). However, their measure of this is essentially the proportion of women arrested for Part One offenses at two points in time: 1963 and 1987. They further disaggregate the commitments of women to state and federal facilities and conclude that "the rate at which [women] were sentenced to state prisons remained relatively stable." This is based on figures that show women as 4.7 percent of state prison populations in 1971 and 4.8 percent of those same populations in 1987; their figures, however, also show that women's share of the federal prison population increased dramatically during the same period from 3.7 percent to 6.3 percent; a trend they do not discuss.

Several comments must be made about the assertions Simon and Landis make —that women's share of serious crime has increased and that women's prison populations are in line with this trend. First, with reference to arrests, the greatest part of the early jump in women's share of Part One arrests was accounted for by increases in women's arrests for one offense —larceny theft. In 1953, for example, only one out of every twenty female arrests was for larceny theft; by 1972, it was one out of five. (Crites 1975:35). Even if Part One arrests are accepted as a measure of "serious" crime, women's share of these arrests over the last decade (1979-1983) rose from 20.5 percent of all arrests for these offenses to 22.1 percent —hardly anything to get excited about. If we examine the female share of violent crime, much the same pattern is seen. Women's share of arrests for violent offenses moved from 10.1 percent to 11.4 percent. (F.B.I. 1989:173). Indeed, women's proportional share of violent crime is remarkably stable and has stood at roughly 10 percent for years.

Figure 2
Percent Increase, Male & Female, 1985-1989

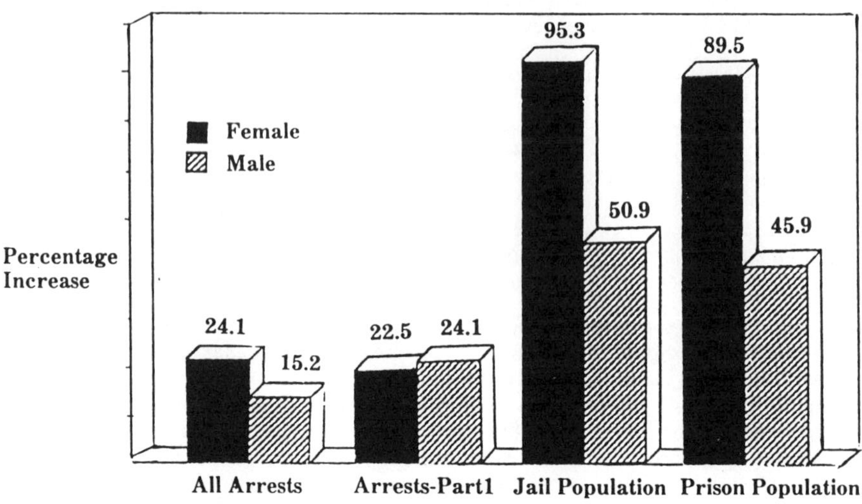

Figure 3
Percent Increase, Male & Female, 1980-1989

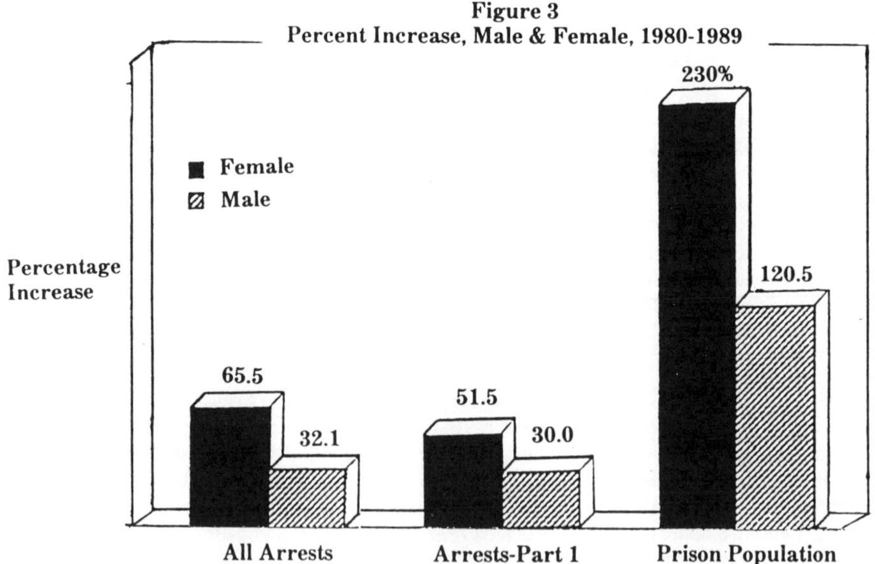

Turning now to Simon and Landis' minimization of the dramatic increase in women's imprisonment, even their own measure (incarceration of women in state institutions) showed a 23.1 percent increase in one year (between 1988 and 1989) and the increase of women in federal institutions was a startling 36.8 percent; women now make up 5.5 percent of those incarcerated in state prisons and 7.5 percent of those in federal facilities. (BJS 1990b:4). A look at national data on the characteristics of women in state prisons also supports a view that women are not being imprisoned because of a jump in the seriousness of their offenses. Indeed, the proportion of women imprisoned for violent offenses actually dropped during the 1980s; in 1979, nearly half (48.9 percent) of the women in prison were incarcerated for a violent offense; by 1986, this figure had fallen to 40.7 percent. By contrast, the number of women incarcerated for property offenses increased from 36.8 percent of women's commitments in 1979 to 41.2 percent in 1986, with most of the increase accounted for by a rise in the number of women committed for larceny/theft. Increases also were noted in the percentage of women imprisoned for public order offenses. Women also were slightly more likely to be incarcerated for drug offenses, but the Bureau of Justice Statistics reports that the increase was explained by a jump in the number of women incarcerated for possession of, rather that trafficking in, drugs. (BJS 1988).

More recent figures from certain states suggest, even more strongly, that the "war on drugs" has translated into a war on women. A study done by the Rhode Island Justice Alliance noted that in their state, which has had a 1000 percent increase in women's imprisonment in the last five years, 33 percent of the women were incarcerated for a drug crime. (Rhode Island Justice Alliance 1990). Research conducted by the Massachusetts Department of Corrections on women incarcerated in Massachusetts shows that fully 47 percent of the female state-sentenced offenders, but only 19 percent of the male offenders, were incarcerated for a drug offense in 1990. (LeClair 1990). Tracy Huling reports that in New York's prisons, only 23.3 percent of women inmates were incarcerated for drug offenses between 1980-1986. By February, 1991, that proportion has risen to 62 percent. (1991b). In my own state, Hawaii, 24 percent of the sentenced felons in 1987-1988 were doing time for a drug-related offense according to the official records; interviews with women in prison in Hawaii, however, put the figure far higher. (Nowak 1990). Finally, a study of women awaiting trial or sentenced in Connecticut compared the population in 1983 with that in 1986 and noted that in three years, the proportion of women incarcerated for drug sale or possession had increased from 13 percent to 22 percent. (Daly 1987:3).

Data on the characteristics of women in prison suggest that recent increases in women's imprisonment are a consequence of such factors as the "war on drugs" and changes in decision-making (not infrequently related to new sentencing guidelines) rather than a shift in the nature of crimes committed. Simply put, it appears that the criminal justice system now seems more willing to incarcerate women. Other evidence on the sentences women receive also suggests that this interpretation is correct. A recent California study found that the proportion of females who received prison sentences for the commission of felonies increased from 54 percent to 79 percent between 1978 and 1987. (California Department of Justice 1988). Earlier research had noted an increasing reliance on imprisonment in the sentencing of women received for murder and writing bad checks beginning in the 1970s. (Chapman 1980).

Another offense, that of Driving Under the Influence (DUI), recently has been the subject of much debate and penalties attached to it have escalated. Coles has reviewed arrest trends in one state, California, a state that now has the largest incarcerated female population in the world. She notes that California has seen a shift in women's arrests for DUI. Previously, women were rarely arrested for this offense unless the DUI involved a traffic accident or they physically or verbally abused an officer. Currently, that pattern appears to be shifting. Coles found that while misdemeanor DUI arrests of females have decreased, the felony arrest rate for this offense has increased. She also notes that women's share of these arrests appears to be increasing, at least in California. (Coles 1991). These figures suggest that women's traditional insulation from certain forms of arrest has been eroded in the wave of "get tough" legislation in the last ten years.

Explaining the Rise in Women's Prisons and Imprisonment

What has happened in the last decade? While explanations of this necessarily are speculative, some reasonable suggestions can be advanced. First, I think that mandatory sentencing for particular offenses at both state and federal levels has affected women's incarceration, particularly in the area of drug offenses. Sentencing "reform," especially the development of sentencing guidelines, also has been a problem. As noted earlier, in California this has resulted in increasing the number of prison sentences for women. (Blumstein *et al.* 1983). Sentencing reform has created problems in part because these reforms address problems that have developed in the handling of male offenders and are now being applied to women offenders. Blumstein *et al.* note, for example, that California's Uniform Determinate Sentencing Law "used the averaging approach, one consequence of which was to markedly increase the sentences of women —especially for violent offenses." (1983:114). Daly, in her review of this problem, reports that federal sentencing guidelines ordinarily do not permit a defendant's employment or family ties/familial responsibilities to be used as factors in sentencing. She states that these guidelines probably were intended to reduce class and race disparities in sentencing, but their impact on the sentencing of women likely was not considered. (Daly 1991).

Finally, the criminal justice system simply has gotten tougher at every level of decision-making. Langan (1991), for example, notes that the chances of a prison sentence following arrest have risen for all types of offenses (not simply those typically targeted by mandatory sentencing programs). Such a pattern is specifically relevant to women, since mandatory sentencing laws (with the exception of those regarding prostitution and drug offenses) typically have targeted predominantly male offenses such as sexual assault, murder, and weapons offenses. Langan's research confirms that the whole system simply is now "tougher" on all offenses, including those that women traditionally have committed. Thus, careful review of the evidence on the current surge in women's incarceration suggests that this explosion may have little to do with a major change in women's behavior. This stands in stark contrast to the earlier surges in women's imprisonment, particularly to the other great growth of women's incarceration at the turn of the century.

Historically, women prisoners were few in number and were an afterthought in a system devoted to the imprisonment of men. In fact, early women's facilities were often an outgrowth of men's prisons. In those days, women inmates were seen as "more depraved" than their male counterparts because they were acting in contradiction to their proper "moral organization." (Rafter 1990:13). The first large-scale and organized imprisonment of women occurred in the U.S. when many women's reformatories were established between 1870 and 1900. Women's imprisonment then was justified not because the women posed a public safety risk, but rather because they were seen to be in need of moral revision and protection. It is important to note, however, that the reformatory movement that resulted in the incarceration of large numbers of white working class girls and women, largely for non-criminal or deportment offenses, did not extend much to women of color. Instead, as Rafter has so carefully documented, African American women, particularly in the southern states, continued to be incarcerated in prisons where they were treated much like the male inmates. Not infrequently they ended up on chain gangs and suffered beatings if they did not keep up with the work.

(Rafter 1990:150-151). This racist legacy, the exclusion of black women from the "chivalry" accorded white women, should be kept in mind when the current explosion of the women's prison populations is considered.

The current binge in women's imprisonment seems to signal a return to older approaches to women offenders: women are once again an afterthought in a correctional process that is punitive rather than corrective. Women also are no longer being accorded the benefits, however dubious, of the chivalry that characterized earlier periods. Rather, they are increasingly likely to be incarcerated, not because the society has decided to crack down on women's crime specifically, but because women are being swept up in a societal move to "get tough on crime" that is driven by images of violent criminals (almost always male) "getting away with murder."

This public mood, coupled with a legal system that now espouses "equality" and rationality in sentencing, has resulted in a much greater use of imprisonment in response to women's crime. There also seems to be a willingness to return to an imagery of women's depravity from earlier periods —a peculiar view of women whose crimes put them outside of the ranks of "true womanhood." As evidence of this, consider the new hostility signaled by the bringing of child abuse charges against women who use drugs, even before the birth of their children. (Noble 1990; Chavkin 1990). The fact that, as we shall see, many of the women currently doing time in U.S. prisons are women of color further distances them from images of womanhood that require protection from prison life. All of this noted, it still seems that the escalation in women's imprisonment is largely the indirect and unanticipated consequence of a society bent on punishment.

Historically, the last surge of women's imprisonment was motivated by the special needs of women inmates. Although the reformatory system completely failed to address those needs —instead jailing countless women for offenses that were ignored in their male counterparts— returning to an appreciation of the differences between women and men prisoners and embracing the "separate spheres" notion offers a strategy for challenging the current pattern of incarceration. Using the special and unique needs of women offenders to argue against their imprisonment is the course I propose. This cause can be advanced by reviewing the backgrounds of women currently in prison. Such a review suggests why it has been easy for a society whose views of proper womanhood and good victims do not line up with the realities associated with the lives of young women of color existing on the economic margin to neglect the needs of incarcerated women.

The Women We Imprison

The American Correctional Association (ACA) recently conducted a national survey of imprisoned women in the U.S. and found that overwhelmingly they were young, women of color (57 percent), and mothers of children (75 percent), although only a third were married at the time of the survey. (ACA 1990). Their backgrounds as well as their current status clearly show the price these women have paid for being poor. About half of them ran away from home as youths, about a quarter of them had attempted suicide, and a sizeable number had serious drug problems. One-half of the women used cocaine; about a quarter of them used it daily. One-fifth said they used heroin daily. Indeed, about a quarter of the adult female offenders said they committed the crime for which they were incarcerated to pay for drugs.

The ACA survey found that over half of the women surveyed were victims of physical abuse and 36 percent had been sexually abused. (Another study of women in prison in Massachusetts suggests that, if anything, these figures are conservative. Mary Gilfus (1988) found that when childhood physical abuse, childhood sexual abuse, adult rape and battering were combined, fully 88 percent of her sample had experienced at least one major form of violent victimization). About one-third of the women in the ACA study never completed high school and a similar number quit because they were pregnant. Twenty-two percent had been unemployed in the three years before they went to prison. Just 29 percent had only one employer in that period. Generally, they had worked in traditional women's service, clerical, and sales jobs. Two-thirds had never earned more than $6.50 an hour for their labor.

Most of these women were first imprisoned for larceny-theft or drug offenses. At the time of the survey, they were serving time for drug offenses, murder, larceny-theft, and robbery. While these latter offenses sound serious, like all crimes they are heavily gendered. Research indicates, for example, that a considerable number of women convicted of murder or manslaughter had killed husbands or boyfriends who repeatedly and violently abused them. (Lindsey 1978). Recent statistics from New York reveal that of the women commmitted to the state's prisons for homicide in 1986, 49 percent had been the victims of abuse at some point in their lives and 59 percent of the women who killed someone close to them were being abused at the time of the offense. For half of the women committed for homicide, it was their first and only offense. (Huling 1991a). Studies of women charged with robbery often show that they were less active participants and non-initiators of these crimes. (Fenster 1977; Ward *et al.* 1968).

Profiles from smaller states suggest even more strongly that the surge in women's incarceration is not being fired by the appearance of a new, more serious women offender. In my own state of Hawaii, where until recently prison and jail inmates who were women were held in the same facility, women's imprisonment has soared. In 1975, we had an inmate population of 16. By 1985, it was more than 100. Looking at the profile of women offenders provides an idea of who is in jail and prison in my state. First, in 1987/1988, only 15.7 percent of incarcerated women were doing time for a violent crime. Forty-one percent were serving time for a property crime, and 24 percent were incarcerated on a drug-related offense. Looking at the data differently, during this period 33 percent of the women held in our facility were awaiting trial, guilty only of poverty.

A study done in Rhode Island (which also has seen an enormous jump in women's imprisonment —from 25 women incarcerated to 250 in five years) found that only 10 percent of the women are serving time for violent offenses, one-third of the women are incarcerated for prostitution or loitering and another third are confined for some form of drug offense. Two-thirds of the women are serving sentences of 18 months or less. (Rhode Island Justice Alliance 1990). In Connecticut, the proportion of women incarcerated for any sort of violent activity declined from 37 percent to 32 percent in the space of three years (1983-1987), while the proportion incarcerated for any sort of drug offense increased from 13 percent to 22 percent. In 1987, 26 percent of the women in Connecticut Correctional Institution at Niantic were convicted of drug violations. (Daly 1987:3 and personal communication to author).

In Massachusetts, the home of the stereotypical male killer, Willie Horton, only 22 percent of the women under the supervision of the Department of Corrections were incarcerated for violent offenses (the comparable figure for males was 48 percent). As noted earlier, a large percentage of women (37 percent) are incarcerated for drug offenses, compared to 19 percent of the men, and about a quarter of the women (26 percent) are doing time for property offenses. For state-sentenced offenders, the proportion of women incarcerated for violent offenses increases, but at 35 percent is still lower than the 49 percent of men held for such offenses. Finally, nearly half (47 percent) of the women held in Massachusetts prisons are there for drug offenses. (LeClair 1990). The profiles of women under lock and key suggest that crime among women has not gotten more serious. Rather, it appears —especially in small states— that what has happened is that incarceration is being used where other forms of non-incarcerative responses previously were utilized.

Talking Decarceration

We must begin to talk seriously about a moratorium on construction of women's prisons and the need to decarcerate women. The standard correctional response to an influx of new female inmates has been to crowd women into existing facilities and then to propose building out of the trouble. The construction response often follows from states being sued or threatened with litigation regarding the inadequacy of existing facilities. Consider again my own state of Hawaii. In 1982, the National Prison Project of the American Civil Liberties Union filed a suit about many problems with corrections in our state, including unconstitutional conditions at the Women's Prison. I welcomed the suit and assisted in any way that I could. The ACLU's primary concern was overcrowding, but when the consent decree ultimately was filed, many parity issues were addressed as well as issues about conditions. (*Spear* v. *Ariyoshi*, Consent Decree, Civil No. 84-1104, U.S. District Court, District of Hawaii, June 12, 1985).

As a result of a Consent Decree signed with the National Prison Project, conditions have improved for women offenders (particularly in the area of access to medical care and educational programming). (See "Implementation Plans Submitted to the Court for Approval and Incorporation into the Consent Decree," Civil No. 84-1104, filed January 11, 1986, and "Supplemental Agreement", Civil No. 84-1104, filed January 2, 1987). One immediate positive consequence of the suit was that a cap was set on the prison population. Thus, while arrests of women in Hawaii went up after the consent decree, the census at the facility remained more or less steady after having soared between 1975 and 1985, the decade prior to the consent decree's implementation. However, in the last few years Hawaii's Department of Public Safety (DPS) began to use the lawsuit to press the legislature for funds to construct a major new facility for women. Initially, state planners wanted to build a facility for 250 women (despite the fact that the current population at the women's prison is about 140). This was "scaled back" to 150 beds in response to considerable political pressure engineered by feminists in the community as well as legislators.

What was being proposed in this new design? The DPS proposal for "Phase One" of this facility came with three "housing units" (actually two rows of 24 single cells stacked on top of each other to total 48 cells each), two large program buildings, and additional facilities. These were to be surrounded by a "candy cane" security fence 12 feet high with a five foot diameter curve and "unclimbable mesh" and perimeter lighting involving thirty poles, each thirty feet high. As a result of community opposition, the DPS lowered the height of the light poles and assured the community that creative planting could obscure the impact of the fence line and perimeter road.

The cost to the taxpayers of even this "scaled down" prison remained extremely high —between 22 and 24 million dollars. The immediate question is why the costs still were so high. The first phase of planned construction at the new women's prison actually included the infrastructure for the 250 bed facility, a fact that only was discovered by pouring over design documents. Moreover, we determined that announced costs should be understood to represent only a down payment. In a public hearing on the facility, Vincent Schiraldi of the National Center on Institutions and Alternatives estimated that operating prisons over a thirty year time span costs 12 to 16 times the cost of construction. This meant that the new Hawaii women's prison could cost over $260 million over the the life of the facility. This translated to an annual cost of $8.8 million per year, or $59,000 per inmate each year.

In addition to testimony that conveyed this information, data I compiled on the characteristics of the women in Hawaii's prisons prompted state lawnmakers to ask the DPS to scale-back the size of its facility even further (to 96 beds). The cost per bed of this "scaled down" model was $200,000 per bed. This proposal was being aired and promoted by a state government that was simultaneously cutting hundreds of thousands of dollars from services to women —particularly for shelters and domestic violence programs. This same tradeoff has surfaced in other states as well. In New York State, a state that has just spent three hundred million dollars to build new prisons for women, 12,433 women and children were denied shelter in 1990 and nearly three quarters of these denials were because of a lack of space. (Huling 1991a:6).

Such skewed priorities are particularly ironic since the availability of shelters is clearly related to women's crime. An analysis of partner homicide in the United States from 1976 to 1984 revealed a "sharp decline" of 25 percent in the numbers of women killing male partners during that period; a decline linked by researchers to the passage of domestic violence legislation and the growth of legal resources for abused women. (Browne 1990). Every dollar that is spent locking women up could be spent far better on services that would prevent them from becoming so desperate that they resort to violence.

I have been attempting actively to alert policy makers to the fact that there are alternatives to the construction of the massive and intrusive women's "community correctional center" being planned for the lower slopes of Mount Olomana (which is currently conservation land). Simultaneously, I have been working with a coalition of Native Hawaiian activists, ecology groups, and women's groups to block the Department of Public Safety from obtaining the necessary permits to build the facility. Here, I have a few partial victories to report. In November, we were able to persuade the county planning committee to defer a decision to grant a necessary zoning variance. On January 30th, we got the City Planning Commission to vote five to one against the project (against the recommendation of their own professional staff). As a result of this victory, the DPS has decided to renovate existing buildings in a less ecologically-sensitive area in the same community. The taxpayers will save an estimated 13 to 15 million dollars, and the size of the facility will be "a maximum of 150 beds." (Dayton 1991a).

The Limits of Reform

Clearly, this victory is partial at best. In the view of many, this proposed facility is still far too large. Another perplexing challenge in this situation came from a different quarter. Notably, the Department of Public Safety, which very much wanted a much larger facility, was quite skillful in garnering at least partial support for their plans from an unlikely source —specifically the lawyers who originally sued over conditions in the current facility. Ironically, the National Prison Project of the American Civil Liberties Union, which had earlier been instrumental in blocking construction of another unnecessarily large youth institution, produced major problems for those of us attempting to block the unnecessarily large and security-oriented facility on the side of a local landmark. (In fairness, I should note that the ACLU was earlier instrumental in blocking construction of a very large youth training school and that Claudia Wright, then of the National Prison Project, also testified against the construction of a large new women's prison during the earlier legislative hearings). Al Bronstein, Executive Director of the National Prison Project, visited Hawaii twice between the first and second Planning Commission hearings (November 15, 1990 and January 30, 1991), and his visits were clearly welcomed by the Department of Public Safety, which made sure that they were heavily covered by the media.

The net result of Bronstein's visits was disturbing and demonstrates the limitations of the use of litigation as a strategy for those who oppose the building of more prisons. After Bronstein's visit, for example, a slew of articles and an editorial in one of the two major daily newspapers appeared —all building the case for immediate prison construction. On November 30, shortly after the first vote, Bronstein commented.

"Living there has got to stop." He also complained about the facility being "too spread out" and having "too few inmate programs." Finally, he said that, while he was "sensitive to community opposition", "there is a limit to how long we can wait." (Altonn 1990). On January 18, 1991, after Bronstein revisited the island a paper reported that: "The ACLU will go to court to force the dilapidated women's prison in Kailua to close next month if the state does not get moving on its long delayed plans to tear down the old facility and build a new one." The same article reported that in response to efforts to scale back and relocate the facility "Bronstein said yesterday he is unwilling to wait while the state ponders a new site or new design." He demanded a "clear mandate" to press ahead with the new prison and said he was "willing to return to federal court to have the old facility closed if the state waffles." (Dayton 1991). This ultimatum was followed by an editorial that stated simply: "Build a Women's Prison." The editorial cited ACLU's insistence that "the state cannot afford to drift in its plans to replace the women's prison, efforts to build a new facility must go forward in a hurry," and added that "those theorists who oppose confinement and the building of new prisons on principle must deliver a working alternative or get out of the way." (*Honolulu Star Bulletin* 1991).

Clearly the battle lines had been drawn, but what was troubling to me, and to many, was that those who brought suit on the grounds of conditions in the existing facility were now suddenly arm-in-arm with correctional officers in calling for new prison construction. It should be noted that Bronstein more recently has been discussing the abolition of women's prisons. (*Honolulu Star Bulletin* 1991:A-3). Clearly, however, this case study points to the limits of legal challenges and reminds us that those who seek to build prisons are quite adept at manipulating differences between allies. It also sharply illustrates the limits of the parity movement.

Lessons to be Learned

What are the lessons learned in this experiment in prison reform and from the growth in women's prisons and imprisonment in general? First, we should never underestimate the tenacity of correctional planners. The momentum to build prisons is strong and will out-wait much opposition. A good example of this can be found in Delaware, where early efforts by NCIA appeared to have blocked construction of a new women's prison, through advocacy for women inmates and the development of alternative sentencing and custody plans. Sadly, despite even the Governor's call for alternatives to women's incarceration, and many efforts to show that such a facility is not needed, Delaware is in the process of planning a 200 bed facility. (Hayes *et al.* 1989).

We must also be cautious about those within corrections who are simply seeking equality for women inmates. This sort of liberal feminist approach leads to the sort of logic I saw in a memo to our DPS by Jennie Lancaster, Female Command Manager, about women in prison in North Carolina. In responding to my published suggestion that alternatives to incarceration, such as Summit House in her state, be used instead of prisons, Ms. Lancaster wrote the following in a letter to prison planners in my state:

> "The North Carolina Department of Correction and the Governor's office are supportive of creative alternative programs. We have also concluded that North Carolina *must* have prison bed space available as an option to these alternatives to make these programs *viable*, [emphasis in original]. Our bed space need projections are based on a solid data base of the numbers of women and the "types" of women offenders we will be required to manage into the 21st century."

She went on to clarify that in her view, this means building more women's prisons. "Traditionally, states have addressed the capital improvement needs of the female offender as a 'last resort' item. Now we must build new prisons as a practical matter of addressing population growth and also to provide constitutional and reasonable resources that are necessary to effectively manage the women. I applaud your capital plan to provide new resources for your women offenders." (Lancaster memo 1990).

I find this sort of "equality" disturbing and precisely the sort of trap we enter when parity is our goal, either explicitly or implicitly, as feminists. But if not parity, then what? I would argue that we should demand a moratorium on construction of women's prisons in the United States with the ultimate goal of abolishing women's prisons. In order for this to occur, several steps must be taken.

First, we must begin to rebuild the literature on women's prisons. It is remarkably lean, particularly that literature that goes beyond profiles of offenders into the patterns of incarceration of women and their relation to patriarchy. The backgrounds of women offenders and the types of crimes that they commit, need to be reviewed with an eye toward the gendered nature of these women's lives, options, and crimes. Especially important is work that documents and explicates the role of class and race in women's lives. The literature available suggests that gender, race and class play special roles in the lives of women swept into the criminal justice system and that the lives of girls of color are filled with problems (e.g. physical and sexual abuse, poverty, and violence) that in many ways foreshadow their entry into the world of crime (see Arnold 1991). Such information will make the lives of women in prison more understandable to those we must reach to make decarceration thinkable. In the process of compiling this information, we must also be prepared to take issue with the logic of parity and move beyond it to a consideration of what constitutes a just, as opposed to equal, treatment of women who find their way into the criminal justice system. Women inmates are not identical to men and treating them as such is not only unjust, it is likely one of the major sources of the current surge in women's imprisonment.

Second, we need to become more current on the programmatic literature so that we can show policy makers that there are options other than incarceration. "Policy research" has always had very low status in a field that prides itself in the "creation of knowledge." We must challenge this sort of academic elitism, which both isolates us from the real world and makes us dependent on federal funding for research. In seeking to identify promising community initiatives in decarceration, we must make sure that these function as alternatives rather than as mechanisms to expand state control over the lives of women. (General Accounting Office 1990). Documenting the successes of grass roots programs is especially important, as is avoiding those programs that simply incarcerate women in homes and communities that are doing violence to them. In this work, we must create new networks for change, both locally and nationally. Our goal is to link women working on prison issues in different parts of the country and world. Often these women are outside the academic mainstream, but they are developing resources for women and doing research (some call it "fugitive research") that is extremely important. Indeed, I have been relying on some of this research in my paper (see Immarigeon and Chesney-Lind, forthcoming).

We must also begin to study those who lock women up. We must shift from simply studying the offender to studying the system. What role, for example, do political contributions play in the enthusiasm with which lawmakers embrace the building of prisons? In my own state, many of the companies and individuals who build prisons are also heavy contributors to political campaigns. Every year, the engineering firms and the architectural firms (who may get these "jobs" without even bidding) give the Governor and others in our state thousands of dollars. As the prison construction industry becomes a major component of many local economics, we must document its structure and policies.

Finally, we must be prepared to enter the political fray, something that academic criminologists often are loath to do because it jeopardizes their "objectivity", their access to funding, and ultimately even their careers. Feminist criminologists must be prepared to model a form of inquiry that is a marriage of thought and action —where the primary question is: how does this research inform political action? How does it improve women's lives? By this measure, research into the pattern of women's imprisonment and their relation to patriarchy must be high on every feminist scholar's intellectual agenda. Since the extraordinary increases in women's imprisonment have been a product of criminal justice policy shifts rather than significant changes in women's criminal behavior, equally dramatic reductions in women's prison populations ought to be within reach. Indeed, it has long been my belief that the decarceration of women might well be a model for reducing our reliance on imprisoning men as well, many of whom, contrary to public stereotypes, are property offenders or parole violators. (Garnett and Schiraldi 1991). In the process we will also rediscover the validity of some earlier feminist insights, among them, "free our sisters, free ourselves."

References

Altonn, Helen. "Progress at Two Prisons May Relax Monitoring." *Honolulu Star Bulletin* November 30: A-3(1990).

American Correctional Association. *The Female Offender: What Does the Future Hold?* Washington: St. Mary's Press (1990).

Arnold, Regina. "Processes of Victimization and Criminalization of Black Women." In Maxine Boca Zinn and Bonnie Thornton (eds.), *Women of Color in American Society* Philadelphia: Temple University Press (1991).

Austin, James and Aaron McVey. "The 1989 Prison Population Forecast: The Impact of the War on Drugs." San Francisco: National Council on Crime and Delinquency (1989).

Blumstein, Alfred, Jacqueline Cohen, Susan E. Martin, and Michael H. Tonry, eds. *Research on Sentencing: the Search for Reform.* Vols 1 and 2. Washington: National Academy Press (1983).

Browne, Angela. "Assaults Between Intimate Partners in the United States." Washington: Testimony before the United States Senate, Committee on the Judiciary. (December 11, 1990).

Bureau of Justice Statistics. "Profile of State Prison Inmates, 1986." Washington: U.S. Government Printing Office (1988).

____________. *Jail Inmates 1989.* Washington: U.S. Department of Justice (1990a).

____________. *Prisoners in 1989.* Washington: U.S. Department of Justice (1990b).

Cahalan, Margaret Werner. *Historical Correctional Statistics in the United States, 1950-1984.* Washington: Bureau of Justice Statistics (1986).

California Department of Justice. "Women in Crime: The Sentencing of Female Defendants." Sacramento: Bureau of Criminal Statistics (1988).

Chapman, Jane Roberts. *Economic Realities and the Female Offender.* Lexington, MA: D.C. Health and Company (1980).

Chavkin, Wendy. "Drug Addiction and Pregnancy: Policy Crossroads." *American Journal of Public Health* 80(4):483-87(1990).

Chesney-Lind, Meda. "Women's Prison Reform in Hawaii: Trouble in Paradise." *Jericho* 43 (Springs):6-7(1987).

Coles, Frances S. "Women, Alcohol and Automobiles: A Deadly Cocktail." Paper presented at the Western Society of Criminology Meetings, Berkeley, California, February (1991).

Crites, Laura, ed. *The Female Offender.* Massachusetts: Lexington Books (1975).

Daly, Kathleen. "Survey Results of the Niantic Interviews December 1983 and May 1986." (Mimeo, January 1987).

———. "Gender and Race in the Penal Process: Statistical Research, Interpretive Gaps, and the Multiple Meanings of Justice." (Mimeo, April 1991).

Dayton, Kevin. "ACLU Threatens to Have Women's Prison Shut Down." *Honolulu Advertiser* A-32 (January 18, 1991a).

———. "Officials Back Site Swap for Kailua Prisons." *Honolulu Advertiser* A-3 (March 1991b).

DeConstanzo, Elaine J. and Helen Scholes. "Women Behind Bars: Their Numbers Increase." *Corrections Today* 50(3):104-108(June 1988).

Federal Bureau of Investigation. *Uniform Crime Reports 1988.* Washington: D.C. (1989).

———. *Uniform Crime Reports 1989.* Washington: D.C. (1990).

Fenster, C. "Differential Dispositions: A Preliminary Study of Male-Female Partners in Crime." Unpublished paper presented to the annual meeting of the American Society of Criminology (1979).

Garnett, Rick and Vincent Schiraldi. "Concrete and Crowds: 100,000 Prisoners of the State." San Francisco: The Center on Juvenile and Criminal Justice (1991).

General Accounting Office. *Intermediate Sanctions: Their Impacts on Prison Crowding, Costs, and Recidivism are Still Unclear.* Washington: U.S. General Accounting Office (1990).

Gilfus, Mary E. *Seasoned by Violence/Tempered by Law: A Qualitative Study of Women and Crime.* Dissertation presented to Florence Heller School for Advanced Studies in Social Welfare, Brandeis University, Waltham, Mass. (1988).

Hayes, Linsey, et al. *The Female Offender in Delaware: Population Analysis and Assessment.* Alexandria: National Center on Institutions and Alternatives (1989).

Huling, Tracy. "New York Groups Call on State Lawmakers to Release Women in Prison." Correctional Association of New York. Press Release (March 4, 1991a).

———. "Breaking the Silence." Correctional Association of New York.(March 4, 1991b). mimeo.

Immarigeon, Russ and Meda Chesney-Lind. "Women's Prisons: Overcrowded and Overused." San Francisco: NCCD (forthcoming).

LaFraniere, Sharon. "U.S. Has Most Prisoners Per Capita in the World." Washington Post A-3 (January 5, 1991).

Lancaster, Jennie L. Memorandum. Department of Corrections, North Carolina, to Mr. John Borders, Department of Public Safety, State of Hawaii (March 12, 1990).

Langan, Patrick A. "America's Soaring Prison Population." *Science* 251:1569(March 29, 1991).

LeClair, Daniel. "The Incarcerated Female Offender: Victim or Villain?" Research Division, Massachusetts Division of Correction (October 1990).

Lindsey, Karen. "When Battered Women Strike Back: Murder or Self Defense?" *Viva* 58-59, 66, 74 (September 1978).

Noble, Amanda. "Criminalize or Medicalize: Social and Political Definitions of the Problem of Substance Use During Pregnancy." Report Prepared for the Maternal and Child Health Branch of the Department of Health Services (1988).

Nowak, Carol. "A Psychological Investigation of Women's Decisions to Participate in Criminal Activities." Dissertation submitted to Saybrook Institute, San Francisco (1990).

Pollack-Byrne, Joycelyn. *Women, Prison, and Crime.* Pacific Grove: Brooks/Cole (1990).

Rafter, Nicole Hahn. *Partial Justice: Women, Prisons and Social Control.* New Brunswick, NJ: Transaction Books (1990).

Rhode Island Justice Alliance. "Female Offender Survey, Rhode Island Adult Correctional Institution, Women's Division." (Mimeo, 1990).

Simon, Rita J. and Jean Landis. *The Crimes Women Commit, the Punishments They Receive.* Massachusetts: Lexington Books (1991).

Singer, Linda R. "Women and the Correctional Process." *American Criminal Law Review.* 11:295-308(1973).

Ward, David, et al. "Crimes of Violence by Women," in Mulvihil, Donald, J. et al., eds. *Crimes of Violence.* Vol. 13. Staff Report to the National Commission on the Causes and Prevention of Violence, Washington: U.S. Government Printing Office (1968).

Cases Cited

Park v. *Thompson*, 356 R. Supp. 783 (D. Hawaii 1976).

Spear v. *Ariyoshi*, Consent Decree, Civil No. 84-1104, U.S. District Court, District of Hawaii, June 12, 1985 and "Supplemental Agreement" Civil No. 84-1104, filed Jan. 2, 1987.

Volume 7 Number 3, Summer 1994

Critique: No Soul In The New Machine: Technofallacies In The Electronic Monitoring Movement

Ronald Corbett
Massachusetts Department of Probation

Gary T. Marx
Massachusetts Institute of Technology

"It's a remarkable piece of apparatus."
Opening line, The Penal Colony, by Franz Kafka

Since its legendary inception in the mind of a New Mexico judge inspired by *Spiderman* comics, the use of electronic monitoring as a correctional tool has grown in a manner most often described as "explosive" (U.S. Dept. of Justice 1990). From very isolated use in 1984, the use of electronic monitoring (hereafter EM) has expanded to at least 33 states (ACA 1989), with a three-fold increase during 1988 alone (Schmidt 1989).

Although hardly a mature industry, EM has attracted a growing number of manufacturers now totaling at least 14 (Tonry and Will 1989). For the last several years, exhibition areas at the annual conference of the American Probation and Parole Association have been occupied almost entirely by vendors of new technology, most of it EM equipment.

Clearly, EM has arrived on the correctional scene and has drawn much attention. Significant research findings regarding its impact recently have begun to come in. These studies have intensified the debate about the proper place of EM in criminal justice. In this paper we locate EM in the context of broader societal developments regarding surveillance, and we argue that unfortunately it has fallen prey to a series of technofallacies which undermine practice. Viewing the current electronic monitoring frenzy from the perspective of several decades of observing and participating in the correctional process, we have Yogi Berra's sense that "it's deja vu all over again," as yet another panacea is offered to criminal justice without adequate thought or preparation.

We address both academic and practitioner audiences. The former will recognize the sociological perspectives of unintended consequences, irony, and paradox (e.g., Marx 1981; Merton 1967; Seiber 1982) as applied to a new area. We hope that the latter— those who develop and administer policy—will gain from this presentation by seeing that innovations never stand alone and that avoidance of the fallacies identified here can mean improved practice.

THE NEW SURVEILLANCE

The development of EM in the 1980s not only is a

Inside This Issue

Critique: No Soul in the New Machine: Technofallacies in the Electronic Monitoring Movement 1
by Ronald Corbett and Gary T. Marx

Developing Drug Testing by Hair Analysis 16
by Bernard A. Gropper and Judy A. Reardon

Police Liability for Use of Wiretaps 20
by Michael S. Vaughn and Chad M. Laub

Legal Spotlight 9

Supervision -	Diaz v. Houck 632 A.2d 1081 (Pa.Cmwlth. 1993)
Drug Testing -	Vega v. Coughlin 609 N.Y.S.2d 262 (A.D.2 Dept. 1994)
EM Devices-	Bragado v. City of Zion/Police Dept. 839 F.Supp. 551 (N.D.Ill 1993)

 ISSN #1043-500X
Published by Alpha Enterprises, Post Office Box 326, Richmond, Kentucky 40476

response to specific factors (to be discussed below), but also reflects broader changes in surveillance. It must be viewed along with drug testing, video and audio surveillance, computer monitoring and dossiers, night vision technology, and a rich variety of other means that are changing the nature of watching.

Although these extractive technologies have unique elements, they also tend to share certain characteristics that set them apart from many traditional means. Some of the ethos and the information-gathering techniques found in the maximum-security prison are diffusing into the broader society. We appear to be moving toward, rather than away from, becoming a "maximum-security society."[1]

Such a society is transparent and porous. Information leakage is rampant. Barriers and boundaries—distance, darkness, time, walls, windows, and even skin, which have been fundamental to our conceptions of privacy, liberty, and individuality—give way.

Actions, as well as feelings, thoughts, pasts, and even futures are increasingly visible. The line between the public and the private is weakened; observations seem constant; more and more information goes on a permanent record, whether we will this or not, and even whether we know about it or not. Data in many different forms, from widely separated geographical areas, organizations, and time periods, can easily be merged and analyzed.

Surveillance becomes capital- rather than labor-intensive. Technical developments drastically alter the economics of surveillance such that it becomes much less expensive per unit watched. Aided by technology, a few persons can monitor many people and factors. The situation contrasts with the traditional gumshoe or guard watching a few persons and the almost exclusive reliance on firsthand information from the unenhanced senses.

One aspect of this efficiency, and the ultimate in decentralized control is self or participatory monitoring. Persons watched become active "partners" in their own monitoring. Surveillance systems may be triggered directly when a person walks, talks on the telephone, turns on a TV set, takes a magnetically marked item through a checkpoint, or enters or leaves a controlled area.

There is an emphasis on the engineering of control, whether by weakening the object of surveillance (as in the case of EM) or by hardening potential victims (as with access codes or better locks). Themes of prevention, soft control, and the replacement of people with machines are present. Where it is not possible to prevent violations physically, or when that process is too expensive, the system may be engineered so that profit from a violation cannot be enjoyed, or so that the violator is identified immediately.

As the technology becomes ever more penetrating and more intrusive, it becomes possible to gather information with laserlike specificity and spongelike absorbency. If we consider the information-gathering net as analogous to a fishing net, then, as Stanley Cohen (1985) suggests, the mesh of the net has become finer and the net wider.

Like the discovery of the atom or the unconscious, new techniques bring to the surface bits of reality that previously were hidden or did not contain informational clues. People, in a sense, are turned inside out; what was previously invisible or meaningless is made visible and meaningful. Electronic monitoring and the forms that increasingly accompany it, such as video identification and drug/alcohol testing, are part of this qualitative change i[n] monitoring. The home is opened u[p] as never before. In focusing on th[e] details, we must not forget that the[y] are part of a much broader group c[of] changes.

TEN TECHNOFALLACIES OF ELECTRONIC SALVATION

New public policies are base[d] partly on politics and interest[s], partly on empirical assessment, an[d] partly on values. Unfortunatel[y] wisdom too often plays only a mod[-] est role.

EM must be approached cau[-] tiously, or the stampeding her[d] may fall off the cliff. Before techn[o-] cal solutions such as monitoring ar[e] implemented, it is important to ex[-] amine the broader cultural climat[e], the rationales for action, and th[e] empirical and value assumption[s] on which they are based. Policy ana[-] lysts must offer not only theorie[s], concepts, methods, and data, bu[t] also—one hopes—wisdom. Part o[f] this wisdom consists of being ab[le] to identify and question the stru[c-] ture of tacit assumptions tha[t] undergird action.

In the analysis of new surveillan[ce] technologies, Marx (1990, fort[h-] coming) identifies a number of "ta[r-] nished silver bullet technofallaci[es"] that characterize many recent e[f-] forts to use technology to deal wi[th] social issues. Some of these apply [to] the case at hand. In critiquing th[e] EM movement, the following di[s-] cussion draws on and expands th[e] more general framework. We di[s-] cuss ten such fallacies:

1) The fallacy of explicit agendas;
2) The fallacy of novelty;
3) The fallacy of intuitive appeal o[r] surface plausibility;
4) The fallacy of the free lunch o[r] painless dentistry;
5) The fallacy of quantification;
6) The fallacy of ignoring the rece[nt] past;
7) The fallacy of technical neutra[l-] ity;

8) The fallacy of the 100% accurate or fail-safe system;
9) The fallacy of the sure shot;
10) The fallacy of assuming that if a critic questions the means, he or she must be opposed to the ends.

1. *The fallacy of explicit agendas.* This entails assuming that new programs are developed for their declared purpose and/or that there is a clearly developed purpose. It also assumes that the ostensible reasons for policy decisions are the real reasons rather than a mask for a decision based on other considerations (e.g., fiscal or political). In the case of EM the goals are varied, contradictory, and shifting, and sometimes hide other goals.

An important theme in contemporary corrections (Petersilla 1990; Tonry and Morris 1990) is the emphasis placed on proportionality or symmetry in sentencing. It is argued that traditionally, little in the way of penal sanctions "between probation and prison" has been available. No appropriate sanction exists for offenders who occupy the middle ground on a scale of severity of deserts. Liberals and conservatives alike have found appeal in this argument. A major rationale for EM is that it is an intermediate sanction which promises simultaneously to lighten onerous penalties and to increase lenient ones.

Nevertheless, EM has a number of other goals, sometimes acknowledged informally but rarely stated officially or in public. Policy disasters are more likely to occur when the declared purposes of a program are supplemented privately or eclipsed by additional, even contrary, objectives. With regard to EM, the foremost of these objectives is a powerful financial imperative.

In the late 1970s and early 1980s a "get tough" approach to sentencing offenders emerged from the presumed demise of the rehabilitative ideal. This was reflected first in the rhetoric of public officials and then in a spate of sentencing reform schemes, all pointing toward stricter and more certain punishment. Predictably enough, this approach put a tremendous strain on existing prison stock, and is an important cause of the decade-long prison overcrowding crisis.

Although building more prisons seemed the obvious solution, here again the agenda was by no means clear or uncomplicated. Prisons are very expensive institutions, averaging (in 1987 dollars) between $50,000 and $75,000 per new cell for construction and $14,000 for imprisoning one offender for a year (Petersilia 1987). "Get tough" suddenly meant "Go broke!" The goal of sentencing severity gave way fairly quickly to the goal of fiscal stability. As Petersilia reported, this financial concern became "the bottom line in deciding what to do with lawbreakers" (1987:xi).

Compounding the financial crisis was a nascent legal crisis of constitutional dimensions, brought on by overcrowded conditions in prisons. So serious was this situation that by 1987, 37 states were subject to judicial orders to address illegal conditions in their institutions (Petersilia 1987).

The conservative trend in sentencing philosophy potentially was jeopardized by an emerging legal/fiscal crisis. If these multiple and conflicting goals were to be served, clearly it would be necessary to develop a program that would sound tough while also reducing and relieving overcrowding. Thus were born "sentencing alternatives," which in time would be renamed "intermediate sanctions" and, most recently, "intermediate punishments," of which EM is perhaps the leading example. Pressure was put on probation to remake itself. State correctional administrators looked to the lower-cost option to bail them out. Offenders who might be incarcerated under the prevailing philosophy would now, of necessity, face technologically enhanced home imprisonment, which was believed to cost only one-third as much as prison.

Another equally powerful (if less noted) agenda item—a desire to enhance the public image of probation—was also present. Internally, the probation profession was feeling pressure to make itself more palatable in conservative times. Consequently the field adopted rhetoric that was, in Clear and Hardyman's view, unabashedly fierce," emphasizing qualities of toughness, strictness, and harshness (1990: 46). In the face of a public relations crisis, wherein probation was depicted as pathetically soft, it became politically wise to put on a meaner face and develop a more punitive approach. Probation would seek to pack the same punch as prison, minus the expensive bricks and mortar, by launching programs involving intensive supervision, boot camps, shock incarceration, and home confinement with electronic monitoring.

If EM has not worked in an empirical sense to date, as the incoming evidence suggests, that failure might be traced, at least in part, to this melange of shifting and conflicting goals.

2. *The fallacy of novelty.* This fallacy entails the assumption that new means are invariably better than the old. Decisions are often based on newness rather than on data suggesting that the new will work or that the old has failed. The symbolism of wanting to appear up-to-date is important.

The fallacy of novelty is related to a "vanguard" fallacy: "If the big guys are doing it, it must be good." Smaller organizations copy the actions of the larger or more prestigious organizations in an effort to appear modern.

The field of corrections often has been accused of being in constant thrall to fads and panaceas (Finckenauer 1982). Technofix attitudes unfortunately have become the kneejerk response of our society to complex issues whose causes are social, not technical. In a theme with solid roots in American history, newness is equated too quickly with goodness. New technology is inherently attractive to an industrial society. It's risky to be against new technology, however mysterious its operations or recondite its underlying engineering. Technical innovation becomes synonymous with progress. To be opposed to new technology is to be a heretic, to be old-fashioned, backwards, resistant to change, regressive, out of step. Reinecke observes sardonically, "To fall behind in the great technorace is to demonstrate a pathetic unwillingness to change with the times, to invite universal ridicule, and to write a receipt for economic disaster" (1982: 13).

Agency administrators become fond of the new and the original as a matter of careerism and survival. Fast-track reputations are more likely to be built on introducing new programs than on maintaining the old; few professionals want to be regarded as care takers. Invitations to speak at conferences, media coverage, job offers, and, most significantly, the availability of grant money depend on the implementation of novel approaches. Question about the fit of the innovation with the agency's mission and goal or about the existence of empirical support for the innovation will be considered mere details in the face of these forces. This point leads directly to our next fallacy.

3. *The fallacy of intuitive appeal or surface plausibility.* This entails the adoption of a policy because "it sure seems as if it would work." The emphasis is on commonsense "real-world" experience and a dash of wish fulfillment in approaching new programs. In this a historical and anti-empirical world, evaluative research has little currency.

The models for rational policy development taught in schools of public administration advance the notion that in the domain of social policy, research and evaluation determine policy. Unfortunately, these models usually bear little resemblance to actual occurrences in corrections practice. Finckenauer (1982) refers to a tendency for agencies to ignore evidence of program failure if the ideological "spin" is right. Clear and Hardyman (1990) speak of a rush to embrace intensive probation supervision when the evidence. Supporting such adoption is "weak." Tonry and Will cite administrators who proliferate programs and believe in their efficacy, even in the absence of careful evaluations. They note that "in a field (community corrections) . . . in which few rigorous evaluations have been conducted, the persuasive force of conventional but untested wisdom is great" (1990: 29).

Enthusiasm for EM programs runs high, even when data that call them into question are available. Petersilia's three-county random-assignment experiment involving EM in California found the following: "The highest technical violation and arrest rate occurred in the Electronic Monitoring Program in Los Angeles. About 35% of participants in the program had a technical violation, and 35% an arrest, after six months" (1990: 105). Probation with EM was found to result in rearrest rates identical to those of offenders under regular supervision.

An Indianapolis study released in 1990 compared the effectiveness of EM with that of human monitoring. No significant differences were found between the two methods. The study revealed, however, that nearly 44 percent of all participants "sneaked out" on the monitoring (Baumer and Mendelsohn 1990).

In Irwin's (1990) report on the use of EM in the Georgia IPS program, she concludes that it was a failure and that it seemed to exacerbate recidivism rates. Palumbo, Clifford, and Snyder-Joy (190) report that in an Arizona EM study concentrating on cost-effectiveness, the evidence suggests that EM did not reduce and might very well increase overall correctional costs due to net widening. Just as innovations are promoted without regard to supporting data, so can traditional approaches be abandoned casually with a lack of evidence. In the late 1970s and early 1980s it became the conventional wisdom that rehabilitation was a failure and that programs aimed at reforming offenders were bankrupt. EM and other "get tough" approaches to community corrections flourished in this environment, as the emphasis shifted toward punishment and deterrence.

Again, it is remarkable how little this conventional wisdom was supported by the available research. Byrne (1990), in an overview of intensive supervision programming, inveighs against systems that blindly negate or minimize the importance of treatment interventions and overestimate the impact of control-oriented interventions such as EM. Petersilia's methodologically rigorous study reports, as its only *positive* finding, that lower recidivism rates were found "among those ISP offenders who were fortunate enough to receive some rehabilitative programming" (1990: 3). In a major study of the effects of a sanctioning approach versus a treatment approach in reducing recidivism, Andrews and his colleagues (1990) found that across 80 different studies, criminal sanctioning without the provision of rehabilitative services did not work and that only programs incorporating principles of rehabilitation reduced recidivism significantly. They conclude, "There is a reasonably solid clinical and research basis for the political reaffirmation of rehabilitation" (384).

4. *The fallacy of the free lunch or painless dentistry.* This fallacy involves the belief that there are programs which will return only good results without any offsetting losses. It ignores the existence of low-visibility or longer-range collateral costs, and fails to recognize that any format or structure both channels and excludes.

In the making of public policy, new ideas all too often drive out old ideas, irrespective of their merit. New programs draw attention and resources away from the traditional efforts. This situation can entail significant opportunity costs. Personnel and other resources will be allocated to the innovation, often starving (or undernourishing) existing programs. Over time, the conventional ways of doing business may suffer from choked-off budgets and retention of less competent staff members who have been excluded from the new, high-priority program. Such persons also may be angry about not being included in the new programs.

Eventually this "Gresham"-style effect may develop a self-fulfilling quality. Whatever the merit of conventional programs, they become defenseless against the drain of resources into the innovation. Conversely, the innovation, whatever its merits, is provided with an introduction under the most favorable circumstances (ample start-up funds, generous publicity, an elite, hand-picked staff). This makes for an unrealistic test of its potential under normal non-"hallo" conditions.

The EM movement illustrates these dynamics nicely. Clear and his colleagues (1987), in their review of three intensive supervision projects, discuss the "secondary place" taken by treatment efforts when control is emphasized. Irwin, in discussing the use of EM in Georgia, observes that although the technology makes the control function easier, "at the same time [it] may make more difficult the part of the job that involves the motivation of offenders and gaining their cooperation" (1990: 73). Palumbo and colleagues conclude that because the program is sold on the basis of its capacity to control offenders, treatment becomes at best an "add-on": Under these conditions, there is likely to be little if any real treatment provided" (1990: 16).

5. *The fallacy of quantification.* When this fallacy is operating, costs and benefits and the value of goods and services are defined in a manner that gives priority to those things which can be measured easily. In a related fallacy, seemingly attractive means can serve to determine the end, rather than the reverse.

One potentially attractive feature of EM systems for administrators and line officers alike is its seeming operational simplicity. EM is a comparatively straightforward process, easy to learn, implement, and monitor. In this respect it stands in sharp contrast to the traditional "casework" approach to probation.

Traditional probation supervision might be characterized as counseling with an edge. It resembles social work plus the complications of coercion and involuntariness. Although offenders clearly prefer probation to prison, they could hardly be said to embrace the experience in the same way, for instance, as mental health "clients" may embrace therapy. Probation officers work in the shadow of the prison cell and can arrange for the imprisonment of intractable offenders. Simultaneously they are expected to remediate a range of profound personal difficulties (e.g., drug abuse, illiteracy, mental illness, joblessness) that are pushing the offender toward crime. Therefore, they are charged with hating the sin and loving the sinner. They have a dual role—cop and counselor—which is often misunderstood, if not resented, by offenders, who correctly sense the mixed message.

The complexity and the contradictory nature of the job are compounded by the "technical uncertainty" (Thompson 1967) inherent in the role. Traditional casework is assumed to be an imprecise science at best, even though a line of research by Andrews and colleagues (1980,1986,1990) has established a strong empirical foundation for effective supervision. Clear and Gallagher suggest that in the face of this technical uncertainty, "officers will tend to select conservative practices in offender management" (1985: 426)

The EM movement reconceptualizes the task before the probation officer as more mechanical and more concrete: install equipment, test, monitor, record, and respond. Redefining the goal as offender surveillance through technology eliminates the professional anxiety and guesswork endemic to the casework approach. EM minimizes, if it does not eliminate, the discretionary judgment and complex analysis required of the treatment model and replaces it with responsibilities akin to those of a clerk/technician.

EM also makes the manager's job less taxing. The traditional approach requires considerable investment in staff training in a variety of higher order skills (interpersonal communications, personality assessment, diagnostic protocols, crisis intervention, substance abuse assessment and referral). Supervising staff members with these responsibilities is difficult, as is the related task of setting performance criteria and organizational goals.

Small wonder, then, that organizations will find the relatively uncomplicated world of EM attractive. What had been nebulous and "soft" in casework systems becomes quantifiable and concrete with EM. If only it worked! A major change in the probation officer's job is being introduced without broad discussion, simply as an artifact of a seemingly simple technology.

6. *The fallacy of ignoring the recent past.* For the case at hand, this fallacy involves denying the possibility that EM might be just another corrections fad. Of course this characterizes nontechnical reforms as well. Yet whether from genuine enthusiasm or as a political strategy, those caught up in the excitement and the high stakes of promoting a reform often wear historical blinders. They do so at their peril.

The intense interest in EM has all the earmarks of a fad—broad media attention, quick, widespread adoption, rapid expansion and diversification of the product. Even a superficial familiarity with the recent history of community corrections should encourage a skeptical, or at least a go-slow, approach.

The history of the last 20 years of community corrections is punctuated at about five-year intervals by the appearance of new "panaceas" typically arriving suddenly and attracting enormous attention. The bad news is that they tend to disappear just as quickly. Examples include pretrial diversion in the late 1960s, mandatory sentencing in the mid-1970s, and intensive probation supervision (IPS) in the early 1980s. Their trajectory has been roughly similar: great early enthusiasm, widespread adoption, less-than-positive evaluations followed by disillusionment, and finally downscaling or elimination and receptiveness to the next panacea.

7. *The fallacy of technical neutrality.* This involves the assumption that technology per se is morally and ethically neutral; that any piece of machinery can have both good and bad implications, *depending on how it is used.* This fallacy can stop critical thought. It ignores the fact that the technology is always developed and applied in a social context which is never neutral..

EM technology is morally distinguishable from a microchip, for example. It is meant as a form of human restraint and tracking; with few exceptions, it has been used to incarcerate people in their own homes. Thus the moral rub.

In a democracy, the concept of "home" is a near-national icon; home represents a refuge, a sanctuary, the last bastion of privacy. The walls of a home have been thought to serve as an impermeable barrier, inviolate in defining the line between public and private domains. The Fourth Amendment incorporates this understanding into law: it admonishes the state that in a free society, it is to have little dominion over and very limited intrusion into the activities within a home.

With EM the home becomes deprivatized. The intrusion is telemetric and nearly invisible, and, as such, perhaps more insidious (Marx 1989). We have progressed from first-generation equipment that simply monitored physical presence, through emissions transmitted over telephone lines, to more recently manufactured equipment that allows for visual inspection and telemetric alcohol tests. Tonry and Will (1989) report that two-way video transmission soon will be cost-effective for use in home confinement programs.

The use of EM typifies trends toward decentralization of social control. Figuratively, prisons have been dismantled, and each individual cell has been reassembled in private homes. Once homes start to serve as modular prisons and bedrooms as cells, what will become of our cherished notion of "home"? If privacy is obliterated *legally* in prison and if EM provides the functional equivalent of prison at home, privacy rights for home confinees and family members are potentially jeopardized.

What price intermediate sanctions? In finding feasible alternatives to traditional incarceration, we might wish to preserve rather than dilute or corrode the time-honored distinctions between private and public realms. In Robert Frost's poem "The Hired Hand," we read:

> Home is the place that when you have to go there, they have to take you in.

The proliferation of EM programs may require that we update the poet as follows:

> In the late twentieth century, home is the place that when you want to leave there, they have to keep you in.

8. *The fallacy of the 100% accurate or fail-safe system.* The glamour surrounding sophisticated electronic technology may lead the uncritical to assume that its results are invariably reliable. In their enthusiasm vendors and program entrepreneurs may fail to acknowledge the technology's weaknesses. As an assessment of EM in Florida put it "the technology has proven both reliable and unreliable" (Papy and Nimer) 191. It may break or fail to work under certain conditions. The technology is also applied and interpreted by humans, with the possibility for errors and corruption.

There are many examples of technical failures: transmissions can be blocked or distorted by environmental conditions such as lightning, proximity to an FM radio station, the metal in mylar wallpaper and trailer walls, some house construction materials and water in a waterbed or bathtub (with some early versions participants even got electrical shocks while bathing). Poor telephone lines, wiring and equipment may transmit signals that cannot be accurately read. Power, telephone and computer failures may make it appear that a violation has occurred when it hasn't, or the reverse. The quality of telephone service required for confidence in the voice verification system is not available in many places Those monitoring the system to report violations can be compromised and with private contractors there may be less accountability than in the public sector. Of course in the adversarial context many participants will seek ways to neutralize the system and to exploit its ambiguities (at least four in ten do so according to research by Bauman and Mendelsohn 1990).

9. *The fallacy of the sure shot.* This fallacy assumes that technically based social interventions will reach their intended target with laser-like precision—the public policy equivalent of a surgical strike. There will be no impact on adjacent or unintended targets. Key participants are seen to be cooperative and of good will and to agree on the goal—rather than passively resisting or adhering to established customs and business-as-usual.

This fallacy encompasses "net widening" in the sense that programs may reach their intended target group and beyond. But it also includes the many criminal justice programs in which displacement occurs instead. Research on intermediate sanctions has frequently found that the intended target group is bypassed.

Highly independent judges may apply intermediate sanctions to an offender pool not envisioned by program planners. Judges may reduce their vulnerability by sentencing less risky clients to EM, even when the program is intended as an alternative to incarceration for more serious offenders. Morris and Tonry (1990) in a study of intermediate sanctions report, "when an intermediate choice is offered, it will tend to be filled more by those previously treated more leniently than by those previously treated more severely."

It is possible that the announced target is not the intended target. Intensive supervision programs such as EM are anxious to present themselves as directed at high-risk, prison bound offenders, since the expected savings of prison bed space and related expenses would otherwise not ensue. Hence, the publicized target group is variously described as "serious", "dangerous", and "recidivist".

However, the fine-print of selection criteria for program participants often incorporates exceptions and exclusions which minimize the possibility that truly serious offenders will participate. This lessens the stakes for administrators who naturally wish to decrease their exposure. Clear and Hardyman (1990) offer examples of the recruitment of comparatively low risk offenders for what was promoted as an intensive program aimed at high-risk offenders. Implementing the program with the original target group may come to be seen as practically or politically too difficult. Palumo et. al. (1990) report that in Arizona, where the legislature set definite criteria for participation in the EM program, the board of Pardons and Parole (BPP) was reluctant to utilize them, waiting five months to place the first inmate in the program. The BPP eventually came to substitute their own criteria—applying EM only to low-risk offenders who would ordinarily have received regular supervision, thereby undermining the intended cost-savings. Clear and Hardyman (1990) report on sites that had to repeatedly alter their eligibility requirements when insufficient referrals threatened the visibility of the programs.

Rather than the ready-aim-fire model of the traditional bureaucracy some of the initial experience with EM suggests that Peter Drucker's ready-fire-aim model may be more appropriate. One fires first and whatever is hit becomes the target.

10. *The fallacy of assuming that if a critic questions the means, he or she must be opposed to the ends.* This fallacy involves an attempt by technology's cheerleaders to meet any criticism of their means with the claim that the critics are really soft on, or opposed to, the end—in this case, alternatives to incarceration or enhanced forms of probation. This insinuation of bad faith is often a cheap shot. Nevertheless, critics have an obligation to acknowledge the decent intentions and real problems often associated with attempts at innovation.

And we do. To understand that policy experiments are often riddled with hidden, contradictory, ironic, and sometimes perverse consequences is not to suggest that they are inevitably doomed or necessarily directed toward the wrong goals. Awareness of technofallacies can sensitize policy makers to potential pitfalls, but it need not paralyze them. That which we distort through our eagerness to innovate and our infatuation with technical progress, we can correct in part through a growing policy "wisdom," sound program design, and sensitive and intelligent management.

We approach this topic not as Luddites who want to ban new technology, but in a spirit of responsible conservatism, which asks us to pause in the face of any proposed change and to consider its fit within the agency, the appropriateness of its possible latent agenda, alternative development scenarios, the costs of doing nothing, and its likely short- and long-range unintended consequences.

In Kafka's short story *The Penal Colony*, a correctional officer and his superior develop a complicated new machine capable of inflicting horrible mortal punishment on inmates. In the end, the officer who argued so proudly for the new technology is horrifically consumed by it. We don't suggest that anything like this will necessarily happen in corrections, but it is clear that innovations which are not thought out carefully and offered honestly and modestly run the risk of doing great damage. So far we have seen little theoretical or empirical support to justify the rush to EM.

REFERENCES

Andrews, D.A. and J.J. Kiessling (1980) "Program Structure and Effective Correctional Practice: A Summary of the CaVIC Research." In R.R. Ross and P. Gendreau (eds.), Effective Correctional Treatment. Toronto: Butterworth, pp. 441-63.

Andrews, D.A., J.J. Kiessling, D. Robinson, and S. Mickus (1986) "The Risk Principle of Case Classification: An Outcome Evaluation with Adult Probationers." *Canadian Journal of Criminology*. 28:377-96.

Andrews, D.A., Ivan Zinger, Robert D. Hoge, James Bonta, Paul Gendreau, and Francis T. Cullen (1990) "A Clinically Relevant and Psychologically Informed Meta-analysis." *Criminology* 28:369-97.

American Correctional Association (ACA) (1989) *Emerging Technologies and Community Corrections*. Laurel, MD.

Baumer, Terry L. and Robert L. Mendelsohn (1990) The Electronic Monitoring of Non-Violent Convicting Felons: An Experiment in Home Detention. Washington, DC: National Institute of Justice.

Bryne, James M. (1990) "The Future of Probation Supervision and New Intermediate Sanctions." *Crime and Delinquency* 36:6-41.

Clear, Todd R, Suzanne Flynn, and Carol Shapiro (1987) "Intensive Supervision in Probation: A Comparison of Three Projects." In B. McCarthy (ed.), *Intermediate Punishments: Intensive Supervision, Home Confinement, and Electronic Surveillance*. Monsey, NY: Willow Tree Press, pp. 31-50.

Clear, Todd R and Kenneth W. Gallagher (1985). "Probation and Parole Supervision: A Review of Current Classification Practices." *Crime and Delinquency* 31:423-44.

Clear, Todd R. and Patricia Hardyman (1990) "The New Intensive Supervision Movement." *Crime and Delinquency* 36:42-60.

Cohen, Stanley (1985) *Visions of Social Control*. Cambridge Engl: Polity.

Finckenauer, James O. (1982) *Sacred Straight and the Panacea Phenomenon*. Englewood Cliffs, NJ: Prentice-Hall.

Irwin, Billie (1990) "Old and New Tools for the Modern Probation Officer." *Crime and Delinquency* 36:61-74.

Lempert, Richard D. and Christy A. Visher, eds. (1987) "Randomized Field Experiments in Criminal Justice Agencies: A Summary of Workshop Proceedings." Washington, DC: National Research Council, Commission on Research on Law Enforcement and the Administration of Justice.

Marx, Gary T. (1981) "Ironies of Social Control: Authorities as Contributors to Deviance through Escalation, Nonenforcement and Covert Facilitation." *Social Problems* 28:222-46.

—(1988) *Undercover: Police Surveillance in America*. Berkeley: University of California Press.

—(1989) "Privacy and the Home: The King Doesn't Have to Enter Your Cottage to Invade Your Privacy." *Impact Assessment Bulletin* 7(1):31-59.

—(1990) "Privacy and Technology. *World & I* 3:523-541 (Sept.).

—(forthcoming) *Windows into the Sou Surveillance and Society in an Age High Technology*. Book based on th Jensen Lecture delivered to th American Sociological Associatio meetings, Cincinnati, 1991.

Merton, R. (1957) *Social Theory and Soci Structure*. Glencoe, IL: Free Pres.

Palumbo, Dennis J., Mary Clifford, an Zoann Snyder-Joy (1990) From N Widening to Intermediate San tions: The Transformation of Alte natives to Incarceration from M levolence to Benevolence." Pr pared for delivery at the meetings the American Criminological Ass ciation, Baltimore.

Papy, Joseph and Richard Nimer (199 "Electronic Monitoring in Florida *Federal Probation* 31-33.

Petersilia, Joan M. (1987) *Expandi Options for Criminal Sentencin* Santa Monica: RAND.

— (1990) "Officials Aim to Fill the G between Probation and Parole *Criminal Justice Newsletter*, Sept. 1 pp. 2-3.

Petersilia, Joan M. and Susan Turn (1990) "Comparing Intensive ar Regular Supervision for High-Ri Probationer: Early Results from Experiment in California." *Cri and Delinquency* 36:87-111.

Reinecke, Ian (1982) *Electronic Illusio* New York: Penguin.

Schmidt, Annesley K. (1989) "Ele tronic Monitoring of Offenders I creases." *NIJ Reports* no. 212 (Ja Feb).

Seiber, S. (1982) *Fatal Remedies*. Ne York Plenum.

Thompson, J.D. (1967) *Organizations Action*. New York: McGraw-Hill

Tonry, Michael and Norval Mor (1990) *Between Prison and Probati* New York: Oxford University Pre

Tonry, Michael and Richard Will (1990) *Intermediate Sanctions*. Washington, DC: Report to National Institute of Justice.

U.S. Department of Justice (1990) *Survey of Intermediate Sanctions*. Washington, DC: Dept. of Justice.

NOTES

· This section draws from G. Marx, 1988, *Undercover: Police Surveillance in America* (Berkeley: University of California Press); chps. 1 and 10.

An earlier version of this paper was presented at the Annual Meeting of the American Society of Criminology, Baltimore, 1990.

IS INCARCERATION REALLY WORSE? ANALYSIS OF OFFENDERS' PREFERENCES FOR PRISON OVER PROBATION*

BEN M. CROUCH
Texas A&M University

Recent correctional reforms have ameliorated the deprivations of prison and indirectly have caused states to toughen probation because many offenders must be diverted from incarceration to meet court-defined limits on prison crowding. These changes raise the possibility that offenders increasingly may view prison as easier or less punitive than probation. Using interview data from newly incarcerated Texas offenders, this analysis examines the extent to which offenders prefer incarceration when presented with choices between paired prison and probation sentences. Though a number of demographic and experiential variables are examined, multivariate analysis reveals that being African-American is the strongest predictor of a preference for prison. Implications of these results are discussed.

State penal codes, typically involving combinations of retributionist and utilitarian philosophies, represent society's hope of repaying offenders and of deterring crime (Hawkins and Alpert 1989: 86-90; Newman 1978: ch. 10). To these ends, penal codes reflect a hierarchy of punishments ranging downward from death through incarceration, probation, and fines. This hierarchy of sanctions not only is the basis for penal codes but also operates in the minds of citizens on juries or in voting booths and directly affects how prosecuting attorneys apply the law to offenders. Moreover, society holds a broad consensus regarding the correspondence between seriousness of crime and severity of punishment (Hamilton and Rytina 1980; Rossi, Simpson, and Miller 1985).

In this country imprisonment has been the preferred method of punishing serious offenders, and the use of the prison sanction recently has increased significantly. Through the 1980s, the number of persons incarcerated increased by 134 percent, and the

* The larger research project from which data for this analysis are taken was funded by the Texas Commission on Alcohol and Drug Abuse. Comments by Mark Fossett, Kelly Damphousse and three anonymous reviewers from *Justice Quarterly* significantly improved the manuscript and are gratefully acknowledged.

JUSTICE QUARTERLY, Vol. 10 No. 1, March 1993

rate of incarceration doubled (Dillingham 1991). Theoretically, if this extensive use of prisons is to have the punitive and deterrent effect on offenders that the public and officials desire, a fundamental assumption must consistently be met: that offenders generally share the state's punitiveness ranking of criminal sanctions. For example, offenders sentenced to prison should perceive that sanction as more punitive or more severe than probation.[1]

Recent correctional reforms, however, especially federal court-instigated reforms, (Jacobs 1980; Thomas 1988), may affect prisoners' perceptions of the relative severity of sanctions and in turn may challenge the validity of this basic assumption. Litigated reforms, for example, have heightened prisoners' access to courts, have curtailed extreme abuse by prison staff, and have improved living conditions (Crouch and Marquart 1990; Hawkins and Alpert 1989; Jacobs 1980). All of these changes translate into less capricious and less depriving institutions.

In addition, courts have proscribed overcrowding. To prevent prison populations from exceeding legal limits, state correctional officials often have taken the expensive but popular course of building new prisons to meet growing demands. Officials also have sought to control overcrowding by releasing many prisoners after only a short stay in prison to make room for more convicts and by diverting convicted felons from prison into community programs, especially probation (Morris and Tonry 1990). The public often objects to these latter strategies because they "put criminals back on the streets." Legislators typically have reacted to this objection by making nonincarceration sentences tougher. Intensive probation supervision (Clear and Hardyman 1990), for example, subjects offenders to routine reporting, probation fees, and the hassles of frequent drug tests and unannounced home visits.

Taken together, these correctional changes can make prisons less onerous (better conditions and possibly shorter stays) and probation more burdensome. These changes may lead some felons to define the "new," reformed prisons not only as less punitive than probation but even as preferable. Because prison and probation are the most widely used sanctions for serious crimes, such a shift in preference by offenders runs counter to society's hierarchy of sanctions. It tends to undermine the state's presumption that prison is "worse" than probation and thus a greater deterrent.

Evidence of such a shift in perceptions of sanctions is presented by Petersilia (1990) in a paper titled "When Probation

[1] See Hawkins and Alpert (1989) for a discussion of severity of sanctions.

Becomes More Dreaded than Prison." She cites a RAND Corporation study in which prison-bound felons were allowed to choose between staying in the community under intensive supervision by the probation department or going to prison. In the first year, one-third of those who initially had opted for probation changed their minds and asked to be sent to prison.

Similarly, in the late 1980s in Texas, probation officers and prosecuting attorneys began to note that prisoners increasingly were requesting prison and trying to avoid probation. One surprised Texas judge stated, "Not in my wildest six years on the bench has this ever come up before . . . I've had (offenders ask) for probation instead of prison, but I've never had one . . . ask me to do away with probation and go to prison" (Bryan-College Station Eagle 1991). Such preferences are surprising because at least through the mid-1980s, (Crouch and Marquart 1989) probation always was viewed as a break for the offender, especially in a state such as Texas, with its history of tough prisons.

Unfortunately, beyond these preliminary and anecdotal observations, little is known about how offenders today weigh the relative costs of prison and probation. Although considerable research has addressed perceptions of sanctions in relation to deterrent outcomes (see Hawkins and Alpert 1989:149-50 for review), the possibility that some offenders may prefer prison to probation has not been examined systematically. Yet a clearer understanding of these preferences is relevant to punishment theory as well as to policy; both would benefit from deeper insight into how offenders perceive our major sanctioning options, especially during a time of rapid change in American corrections. In this study I seek to fill a significant gap in the literature by examining perceptions of the relative punitiveness of prison and probation in a large sample of state offenders.

Determinants of Offenders' Perceptions of Sanctions

Although I know of no work beside Petersilia's (1990) thoughtful paper that bears directly on the questions raised here, several lines of research and theory suggest factors that may influence offenders' perceptions of sanctions. The first is a long tradition of research into prison subculture, which demonstrates that variations in experience with crime and the justice system cause offenders to perceive and cope with prison in different ways. Because of their greater involvement, "right guys," "thieves," and "convicts," (for example) would know more about the relative personal costs of various sanctions and thus would be less threatened by the prospect of prison than "square Johns" (Bowker 1977; Hawkins and Alpert 1989: chs. 7,8; Irwin and Cressey 1962). If prisons in some sense are becoming easier in relation to prison conditions of the past and to probation, experienced offenders should be more aware of these changes and should be inclined to introduce them into their calculations of sanction costs.

Factors not tied directly to offending or to experience with the justice system also may affect how offenders weigh sanctions. For example, it may be inferred from both social control theory (Hirschi 1969; Krohn 1990: 301-305) and the "underclass" argument (Jencks and Peterson 1991; Wilson 1987, 1991) that social and economic distance from conventional society may affect how offenders judge the relative punitiveness of probation and of prison.

Social control theory generally holds that weaker involvement in conventional social institutions translates into a greater likelihood of law violation. By extension, persons with weak ties to conventional institutions such as marriage and education might be more likely to reject the state's utilitarian hierarchy of punishment severity and to regard prison as a much less devastating personal experience than penal codes presume.

A similar inference emerges from the "underclass" thesis. Wilson (1987) argues that inner-city persons, especially members of minorities, have become increasingly disadvantaged as their environment has changed economically and technologically. Structural changes weaken both their families (Sampson 1987) and their labor force attachment; these circumstances exacerbate and promote economic marginality. Such changes also undermine the commitment of inner-city dwellers to conventional standards of law and commerce. As a result, they frequently turn to crime and drug sales (Sullivan 1989; Taylor 1990). If marginality results in limited access to and support of middle-class standards among underclass persons, it also may lead to a rejection of the conventional middle-class assumption that even a long probation is less severe than a year in prison.

Inner-city African-Americans are a specific focus in the underclass literature. As a group they are uniquely subject to the disadvantageous conditions caused by structural changes. Perhaps not surprisingly, this minority is incarcerated at a higher rate than other ethnic groups (Christianson 1991; Krisberg et al. 1987) and has constituted a steadily increasing proportion of prison populations for 50 years (Greenfeld and Langan 1987).

Some research suggests that African-Americans, once incarcerated, may adjust to prison more easily than other groups (Carroll 1982; Johnson 1976). Some observers offer a possible explanation for this differential pattern of adjustment: because so many of these inner-city males are imprisoned, they routinely find friends and even relatives already in prison who can provide information, protection, and material goods (Jacobs 1974; Rettig, Torres, and Garrett 1977).

A more fundamental explanation for racial differences in adjustment to prison is that the ghetto experience makes the potential violence and deprivation of a prison term seem less threatening to African-Americans (Carroll 1982; Johnson 1976). Because the ghettos from which many African-Americans come are often unpredictable and threatening environments, they learn to emphasize self-protection and to develop physical and psychological toughness. This toughness protects African-American prisoners and enables them to dominate others behind bars, especially whites. It is suggested that whites are targeted both because they often lack toughness and because they represent the society responsible for the disadvantages African-Americans have experienced (Carroll 1982; Lockwood 1980). This last argument, however, has not been supported consistently by research (Goodstein and McKenzie 1984). Wright (1989), for example, found that prison adjustment among African-Americans was related more strongly to economic marginality than to race.

Though Hispanics also may be affected by the underclass phenomenon (Tienda 1989), less research has concentrated on Hispanics' prison adjustment or perceptions of sanctions. Wright (1989), however, cites research suggesting that Hispanics, like whites, are less able than African-Americans to withstand the stress of incarceration. Though the available evidence is mixed and incomplete, it suggests that race and ethnicity may influence how offenders view the relative costs or punitiveness of criminal sanctions.

Finally, the broad reforms that have altered correctional practices and institutions over the past two decades (see Crouch and Marquart 1989; Jacobs 1977) also should affect offenders' perceptions of sanctions. In Texas, reforms clearly altered both prison and probation experiences. A survey of Texas prisoners in 1987 (Crouch and Marquart 1990) revealed that the litigated reform process made the state's prisons much less threatening than they had been in the late 1970s and early 1980s, expanded prisoners' rights, and reduced privations. At the same time, early release policies had to be instigated to meet court and legislative limits on crowding; the result was a reduction in actual time served. While prison time was becoming easier in many respects, correlated changes in probation were making community sanctions more onerous across the state. As a result of diversion programs rapidly developed to limit prison crowding, many offenders who would once have gone to prison remained in the community, typically under very close supervision.

Little is known about offenders' perceptions of the relative costs of prison and probation and about how these perceptions may vary. It is also unclear how the factors identified above contribute to this variation. Consequently this analysis addresses two questions: 1) How do felons today perceive the relative punitiveness of prison and of probation? 2) What accounts for variations in perception among offenders?

METHODS

Sample and Data Collection

The research reported here draws on a survey of 1,027 male[2] felons in Texas interviewed between mid-September and mid-December 1988. The respondents represent approximately a 10 percent random sample of all offenders sentenced to incarceration during this period. All interviews were conducted at the state prison's reception center, which processes all newly committed male prisoners. During the two days prisoners typically spend at this center, officials collect information on prisoners for classification and final assignment to a prison unit.

Each evening during the data collection phase, the lead interviewer drew a random sample of 15 names from the 150 to 175 prisoners who had just completed their second day of processing and would depart the next day for a prison unit. The interview team learned quickly that only about 11 or 12 interviews could be completed in an evening. A few more names were drawn daily, however, in case of refusals. Only 36 prisoners refused to be interviewed, and records maintained by the research team revealed no resultant sample bias. The final sample was representative of the population of felons sentenced to prison in Texas in 1988. The percentages of the sample and of the prison population were respectively white, 36 and 35; African-American, 41 and 43; Hispanic, 22 and 21.

A team of six well-trained criminal justice graduate students from San Houston State University conducted all interviews.[3] Interviewers began the lengthy instrument after each respondent

[2] Only male prisoners were interviewed in this study. Although females constitute less than 10 percent of the prison population, their presence in this research would have been valuable. Unfortunately, however, female prisoners are processed into the prison system at a site 175 miles away, and funds were not available to conduct research at both reception centers.

[3] The interview team included a native Spanish speaker who used, as required, a Spanish-language version of the interview schedule.

signed an informed consent form explaining that he would receive no payment, that all information given would be confidential, and that he could stop the interview with impunity at any time. All interviews were conducted in the reception center's visiting room, where interviewers and respondents were separated by a mesh screen (a standard security measure in Texas prisons). The setting was not crowded; thus respondents had enough distance from each other and from the lone security officer to facilitate a comfortable interview and to maintain confidentiality. Interviewers asked each question and recorded answers on the interview schedule, probing as required. Because the larger study from which these data come involved extensive information on drug use and criminality, the interviews often lasted between one and 1½ hours. So that the research would not conflict with normal activities in the reception center, all interviews took place after 5:30 pm, and virtually all were completed in one sitting.

Most of the data used in the analysis are self-reported. Some basic information obtained from respondents (e.g., age, race, offense) could have been verified through official records. Most of the information, however, could not be verified, either because that information is not maintained by prison officials or because much of the information which officials maintain and which is critical to this project came initially from prisoners' self-reports.

The Dependent Variable

Respondents cannot be asked to state a preference for prison or probation in the abstract. At the same time, there is an almost unlimited number of discrete prison and probation terms that respondents can be asked to weigh. Thus we developed a prison preference index, the dependent variable for this study.

In the survey, respondents were presented with 11 pairs of hypothetical criminal sanctions; each pair contained a specific probation term and a specific prison term. These pairs of sanctions, presented as years on probation versus years in prison, were 10 versus 1, 5 versus 1, 3 versus 1, 10 versus 2, 5 versus 2, 3 versus 2, 10 versus 3, 5 versus 3, 10 versus 4, 5 versus 4, 10 versus 5. In each pair, respondents were asked to indicate which sanction they would prefer to face personally.

Although the specific sanctions included in these pairs appear to be arbitrary gradations of sentences, several pairs reflect realistic possibilities in the Texas justice system from the late 1980s to the present. Because of limits on prison bed space, Texas offenders typically spend only about one calendar year in prison for each

10 years of their sentence. Thus, because the common prison sentences of 10, 15 and 20 years actually result in only about one, two, or three years behind bars, and because the most severe probation sentence in Texas is 10 years, the pairs of sanctions involving 10 years of probation and one, two, or even three years of prison reflect actual possibilities. We included other pairs, though less realistic in this sense, to ensure adequate variance in responses.

The final index was determined both empirically and logically. We ranked the pairs according to the proportion of respondents choosing prison over probation. For six of the 11 pairs, the proportion choosing prison was less than 16 percent. For the remaining five pairs, however, the proportion choosing prison ranged from 66 percent (10 vs. 1) to 25 percent (10 vs. 3). These five pairs also seemed to be logical choices in that they reflect most closely the actual sanctions that offenders might face in Texas, as noted above. For these reasons we included only five of the 11 pairs of sanctions in the final index.[4]

The following pairs of sanctions were included in the final index: 10 years' probation[5] versus one full year in prison,[6] five years' probation versus one year in prison, 10 years' probation versus two years in prison, three years' probation versus one year in prison, and 10 years' probation versus three years in prison. Probation choices were scored 0; prison choices, 1. I summed choices across

[4] To ensure that restriction of the prison preference index to five pairs of sanctions did not obscure some extreme patterns of choice or orientations of respondents, I regressed an index using all 11 pairs on the model examined here. Results (not reported) did not differ from those based on the five-pair index reported in this paper; signs and statistical significance patterns were virtually the same. Clearly, using the restricted index does not introduce bias into the results. At the same time, results are based on offenders' responses only to relatively realistic options.

I also explored another approach to the dependent variable, using two measures of preference for prison instead of the one reported here. The two measures were defined by dividing the five-item prison preference index into two separate indexes. The first of these indexes included those pairs of items in which a 10-year probation term was constant and was contrasted with prison terms of first one then two, then three years. The second index contained pairs in which the prison term was constant at one year and was contrasted with probation terms of first 10, then five, then three years. The purpose of examining two separate indexes was to assess the possibility that variations in terms may carry different meanings. That is, preferences for prison might take one pattern when the prison option is always a single year of incarceration and quite another when the prison term rises in relation to a constant probation term. Analysis showed that when these two different indexes were regressed on the model, results were very similar to those reported for the five-item prison preference index, but in several instances somewhat weaker. To maximize reliability and to simplify discussion, I used the five-item index in this analysis.

[5] I made no distinction between intensive supervision and regular probation.

[6] Interviews made clear that the year in prison was a full calendar year, not a one-year sentence reduced (as it frequently is) by parole.

the pairs to create the dependent variable. Scores on the preference index ranged from 0 (preferred probation regardless of prison options) to 5 (preferred prison regardless of probation options). See Table 1.) I did not weight choices in creating index scores.

Table 1. Coding of Variables

Prison Preference Index

In each of the five pairs of sanctions, probation choice=0 and prison choice=1. Index scores are determined by adding across choices; they range from 0 (never preferred prison) to 5 (always preferred prison).

Demographic Variables

Three race/ethnicity variables: 0=other, 1=African-American; 0=other, 1=Hispanic; 0=other, 1=white

Age: Actual age of respondent

Marital status: 0=not married; 1=married when locked up

Economic Marginality Variables

Occupational status: 0=not working; 1=working full-time

Education: 1=11 years or fewer; 2=12 years; 3=12 years or more

Criminal Experience Variables

Age at first arrest: 1=13 or under; 2=14 to 16; 3=17 to 18; 4=over 18

Self-reported criminal offenses: 1=fewer than 5 offenses; 2=5 to 10; 3=11 to 20; 4=21 to 75; 5=more than 75

Number of times in state prison: Self-reported

Present Sentence Variables

"Aggravated" sentence: 0=no; 1=yes

Current sentence: actual length of sentence

Perceptions of Key Elements of the System

Are "Texas offenders more likely to choose prison over probation today than in the early 1980s?" 0=no; 1=yes

"Probation has gotten much stricter." 4=strongly agree; 3=agree; 2=disagree; 1=strongly disagree

Preliminary analysis revealed marked consistency in patterns of choice: respondents who preferred one year in prison when the option was only three years' probation (3 vs. 1) virtually always also chose one year in prison when the options were 10 versus 1 and 5 versus 1. This consistency suggests that an additive variable adequately measures the strength of preference for prison.[7] Constructed in this way, intercorrelations ranging from .76 to .87 between the index and each pair also indicate considerable index validity.

[7] Though questions also were asked about perceptions of the justice system, these appeared in the instrument after the pairs of sanctions. Thus, the questions

The present analysis is not intended to discover the precise point at which offenders choose one sanction over another, nor does it aim at a fine-grained psychological mapping of attitudes toward particular punishments. In view of the limited amount of research devoted to offenders' perceptions of probation versus prison, the objective here is more modest: I wish to assess the extent of preferences for prison and then to ascertain the relationships between those preferences and relevant variables from existing theory and research. The dependent variable employed here seems appropriate to these tasks.

Other Variables

From the review of factors that may shape offenders' perceptions of criminal sanctions, I developed a number of variables. These variables, which constitute the model examined in this analysis, fall into five categories: demographics, economic marginality, involvement with crime and the justice system, nature of the present sentence, and perceptions of change in the justice system.

Demographic variables. These include race/ethnicity, age, and marital status before this incarceration. Because some research shows that some minorities may experience prison differently (Carroll 1982; Johnson 1976), I hypothesize that African-American offenders would choose prison more often than would other subgroups.

Two other demographic variables are age and marital status. Age is included as a measure of life experience and maturity. Here I assume that being older would be associated with a preference for probation. First, older offenders tend to mature out of crime, in part because of the personal costs of prison for them (Shover 1985). In addition, older offenders may wish to avoid an environment dominated by younger and often aggressive offenders (Alston 1986:218; Shover 1985). Marital status is taken as indicating not only ties to conventionality but also a reason to stay in the community on probation rather than opting for the isolation of prison. Being married should be related to a preference for probation.

Economic marginality. Because detailed data on economic marginality are lacking in this study, I rely on educational and occupational status before incarceration (Wright 1989). Offenders with

about changes in the justice system did not color responses regarding preference of sanction.

less education and those who were not working full-time are assumed to be more marginal. As indicators of underclass status, being poorly educated and lacking regular, legal employment should correspond to lower stakes in conformity. I hypothesize that marginality is associated with a greater likelihood of preferring prison.

Involvement with crime and the justice system. The hypothesis here is that greater experience with the justice system and with criminality will be associated positively with a preference for prison. Variables designed to measure involvement in crime are age at first arrest and prior incarcerations. An early beginning to a criminal career has been shown to predict a serious career in crime (Wolfgang, Thornberry, and Figlio 1987: ch. 5). Two additional indicators of involvement in the justice system are the number of times on probation and the number of times incarcerated in a state prison. I expect that as these formal exposures to the justice system increase, so will a tendency to prefer prison.

The final indicator of involvement in criminality is the amount of crime in which the respondent has engaged. The amount of personal crime is measured by self-reports of the number of times respondents committed (regardless of arrest) an array of crimes including breaking into a building or car to steal something, stealing without breaking and entering, using a weapon to get something desired, and physically hurting someone on purpose. I hypothesize that offenders with greater experience in crime will be more likely to prefer prison than will those with less crime experience.

Present sentence. These variables include the actual length of sentence and whether the respondent received an "aggravated" sentence. In Texas, an aggravated sentence requires an offender to serve one-fourth (by the calendar) of the assessed sentence before becoming eligible for parole consideration. I included these two variables to control for the possibility that the conditions of the sentence facing the respondent at the time of the interview could affect the choices of sanction.

Perceptions of change in the Justice System. These perceptions are assessed by two questions: "Do you think Texas offenders are more likely to choose prison over probation today than in the early 1980s?" and "Probation has gotten much stricter in recent years." In both questions, respondents weigh changes in prison and probation and state their own perceptions of current sanctions. The hypothesis here is that the greater the belief in changes in aspects of the correctional system (more people choosing prison; probation stricter), the greater the likelihood that respondents will indicate a preference for prison. A respondent need not have been on probation to have an opinion on its relative costs.

The model also includes two interaction terms involving race/ethnicity and crime involvement. These terms are included because prior research leaves unclear whether the experience of growing up African-American (or Hispanic) affects perceptions of prison or whether only minority males with long crime histories seem to adjust more easily to the prospect of prison. These interaction terms control statistically for the impact of crime experience combined with race, and thus allow the impact of race/ethnicity to emerge, net of crime experience.

Analysis

Ordinary least squares (OLS) regression is used here. Although respondents' choices in each pair yielded dichotomous data, the dependent variable is not dichotomous. Because the dependent variable is determined by summing responses across all five choices in the index, OLS is the appropriate technique. OLS regression permits us to assess the effects of each independent variable on responses regarding sanction preference while simultaneously holding constant the effect of other independent variables.

Limitations of the Research

Several qualifications should be noted in interpreting these findings. First, because the respondents' choices did not translate into a sanction they actually had experienced, the approach used here is artificial. Second, in a related vein, the fact that the respondents already were in prison when interviewed could have prompted them to choose prison more readily. There is no reason to expect, however, that the reality of incarceration affected respondents differentially or affected results significantly. Third, although statements regarding choices between prison and probation appear throughout the following discussion, this fact is not intended to convey categorical preference. That is, respondents weighed specific prison and probation terms rather than correctional alternatives in the abstract. Moreover, the prison terms in the choices were relatively short—never more than three years. Nonetheless, as indicated above, several of the choices approximate true alternatives that offenders in Texas and other states might face. Fourth, the research was conducted in only one state; thus the generalizability of findings to other offenders and other correctional systems is uncertain. Yet the diversity of crimes and ethnic groups in Texas, as well as the size of the state, argue that insights developed from offenders in Texas might well be paralleled in other states. Finally, although Texas offers much qualitative evidence that offenders' perceptions of prison and probation have been altered markedly by recent correctional reforms, no data are available on perceptions of sanctions before the reforms. Consequently the significance of the reforms for offenders' perceptions cannot be demonstrated directly here.

RESULTS

The first question addressed here concerns the extent to which offenders might prefer prison when asked to choose between various prison and probation terms. The responses (see Table 2) demonstrate clearly that prison is a relatively attractive option for many offenders: two-thirds of the respondents would choose one year in prison over 10 years on probation. Almost half still would opt for prison when the probation term is reduced to five years, and nearly one-third persist in preferring prison even when the alternatives are a seemingly light three years on probation and one year in prison. Even when the prison term rises to three full years against 10 on probation, one-quarter of the sample would choose prison. Thus it is evident that many Texas offenders would choose prison over probation, which society typically defines as less punitive.

Table 2. Offenders' Choices among Prison and Probation Terms

Choice of Sanction	Percentage Choosing Prison
1. 10 years probation 1 year prison	66
2. 5 years probation 1 year prison	49
3. 10 years probation 2 years prison	40
4. 3 years probation 1 year prison	32
5. 10 years probation 3 years prison	25

In an attempt to explain these patterns, I regressed preferences on a number of variables drawn from theory and prior research. Table 3 presents the results of zero-order correlations among the index and the variables used in the model; Table 4 displays the multivariate results.

Respondent's age is also significant; being older predicts a preference for prison. This finding is contrary to expectations. A

Table 3. Zero-Order Correlation Marix

	INDEX	AFROAMER	HISPANIC	WHITE	AGE	MARRIED	EDUCATN	WORKING	PROBATN	PRISONS	AGEARR	TOTCRIME	SENTENCE	AGGSENT	OTHRSPRF	AFRINTER	HISINTER	
index	1.0000																	
afroamer	0.0489*	1.0000																
hispanic	−0.0558*	−0.4440*	1.0000															
white	−0.0045*	−0.6695*	−0.3683*	1.0000														
age	0.1454*	−0.0368	−0.0158	0.0513*	1.0000													
married	−0.0751*	0.0083	0.0661*	−0.0634*	0.0838*	1.0000												
educatn	−0.0162	0.0756*	−0.1227*	0.0234	0.1514*	−0.0103	1.0000											
working	−0.0400	−0.1156*	0.0396	0.0871*	0.0149	0.1202*	0.0294	1.0000										
probatn	−0.0299	−0.0017*	−0.0103	0.0104	0.0216	−0.0410	−0.0040	−0.0367	1.0000									
prisons	0.1646*	0.0353	−0.1009*	0.0471	0.2412*	−0.0402	0.0175	−0.0858*	0.0333	1.0000								
agearr	−0.0365	0.1040*	0.0133	−0.1189*	0.2074*	0.0531*	0.1553*	0.0918*	−0.0392	−0.1810*	1.0000							
totcrime	0.0763	−0.1098*	−0.0516*	0.1568*	−0.1638*	0.0046	−0.0674*	−0.0885*	0.0048	0.2512*	−0.4506	1.0000						
sentence	0.1103*	0.0144	−0.0445	0.0219	0.0727*	0.0746*	−0.0277	−0.0034	−0.0431*	0.2014*	0.0394	0.1018*	1.0000					
aggsent	0.0448	−0.0473	0.0756*	−0.0136	0.0529	0.0220	−0.0505	0.0578	−0.0358	−0.0667*	−0.0089	−0.0433	0.2952*	1.0000				
probtuff	−0.0896*	0.0139	0.0416	−0.0489	0.0966*	−0.0101	0.0487	−0.0409	−0.0028	0.0602*	0.0130	−0.0127	0.0219	−0.0062	1.0000			
othrsprf	0.1921*	−0.0215	−0.0355	0.0517	−0.0634*	−0.0155	0.1079*	0.0281	0.0416	−0.0686*	0.0223	0.0752*	−0.0128	−0.0139	−0.1158	1.0000		
afrinter	0.0484*	0.8100*	−0.3597*	−0.5423*	−0.0669*	0.0216	0.0481	−0.1287*	−0.0109	0.1136*	0.0692*	0.3113*	0.0533	−0.0533	−0.0481	0.0274	1.0000	
hisinter	−0.0268	−0.3865*	0.8704*	−0.3206*	−0.0629*	0.0498	−0.1287*	0.0179	0.0092	−0.0433	−0.1009	0.1669*	−0.0259	0.0622	0.0388	−0.0074	−0.3130*	1.0000

*Significant at or beyond .05.

AGGARR=age 1st arrest; TOTCRIME=crime involvement; PROBATN=times on probation; PRISONS=times in prison; SENTENCE=sentence length; AGGSENT=aggravated sentence; PROBTUFF=probation tougher; OTHRSPRF=others are preferring prison; AFRINTER and HISINTER=interaction terms

Table 4. Coefficients for Regression of Prison Preference Index on Selected Independent Variables (Standard errors)

	Prison Preference Index	
Demographics		
Afroamer (a)	.784**	(.356)
Hispanic (a)	.204	(.437)
Age	.040***	(.009)
Married	−.361**	(.145)
Economic Marginality		
Education	−.163	(.105)
Working	−.071	(.136)
Crime Experience		
Age first arrest	−.039	(.064)
Prior Probations	−.025	(.017)
Prior Prisons	.176***	(.064)
Total crime	.145*	(.081)
Present Sentence		
Sentence Yrs.	.009*	(.005)
Aggravated	.193	(.234)
Justice System Views		
Probation tougher	.271**	(.110)
Others prefer prison	.424***	(.072)
Interaction Terms		
Af. Amer. x crime	−.161*	(.098)
Hisp. Amer x crime	−.051	(.125)

(a) Reference category is white.
Adjusted R square = .101
* $p<.10$ ** $p<.05$ *** $p<.01$

positive association between age and a preference for prison may reflect older offenders' desire to be cared for by a prison system which, through court order, recently has become more sensitive to prisoners' needs. Perhaps such offenders also have little community or family support; thus a few years in prison may be preferable, particularly if prison is no longer reputed to be so dangerous or so demanding.

Marital status, the final demographic variable, has a significant negative effect on preference for prison, as expected. Married men opt for probation, whereas unmarried men tend to choose prison. Being married seems to reflect both social and personal support in the community, which the isolation of prison threatens. Apparently the presence of a wife, who can offer at least some stability to a life frequently disrupted by brushes with the law, makes men wish to avoid prison.

I found only limited support, however, for the hypothesis that economic marginality is related positively to a preference for prison. I expected that full-time employment would give offenders a preference for a sanction that would let them remain in the community and allow them to avoid the disruption of prison. The results, however, show that although the sign is in the expected direction, working full-time does not significantly affect choice of sanction. One reason may be that for most of these men, full-time employment is often menial and short-term (Parker and Horwitz 1986:796). Thus even full-time jobs may not be sufficiently rewarding to affect offenders' choice of sanctions. Similar results obtain for the education variable. A higher level of education was taken to reflect a nonunderclass background and a desire to avoid not only the disruption but the stigma of prison. The analysis reveals that higher education is in the hypothesized direction, but the relationship is not statistically significant.

The third set of variables in the model measures commitment to criminality and experience with the justice system. Four variables—age at first arrest, prior probations, prior incarcerations, and the amount of crime reported by the respondent—were expected to give greater exposure to the street crime and to the personal cost of legal consequences today. Table 4 reveals that although age at first arrest is not related significantly to perceptions of sanctions, the total amount of crime reported by the offender is in the hypothesized direction and nears statistical significance ($p < .10$).

I found only partial support for the hypothesis that exposure to formal sanctions would be associated with a preference for prison. As expected, net of other effects, the frequency of incarceration in the past is associated positively and significantly with preferring prison to probation. Yet in the case of probation experience, although the sign surprisingly somewhat is negative (those most often on probation in the past tend to prefer it), the empirical relationship is not significant.

Interaction terms linking race/ethnicity with criminal involvement were included in the model to determine whether minority status combines with extensive criminality to affect perceptions. Theoretically the interaction terms reflect minority "heavies," offenders with a high frequency of crime commission. The analysis explores the possibility that a high percentage of minority heavy offenders might explain African-Americans' general preference for prison over probation. This possibility is reasonable because active African-American offenders may be more likely to be sent to prison, more familiar with what prison may hold in store, and more apt to find "homies" there (Jacobs 1974; also see Davidson 1974; Rettig 1977). Such circumstances would seem to make prison less threatening. Analysis reveals somewhat surprising results, however. First, the signs for both interaction terms are unexpectedly negative, and one interaction—African American by total crime—approaches statistical significance ($p<.10$). The negative sign hints at the intriguing possibility that because these offenders are heavies, they realize that their street activities are attractive and cannot be pursued as well in prison. Though prison is an expected occupational hazard for which they may be prepared, still it is an inconvenience to be avoided, and thus would not be preferred. This point is consistent with Irwin and Cressey's (1962) characterization of the "thief," but it is speculative. The important consideration is that even after controlling for crime involvement, the African-American status variable remains significant. This finding underscores the importance of racial status alone to perceptions of sanctions.

A fourth set of variables in the model involves characteristics of respondents' present sentence. These variables control for situational effects. Although all respondents already are in prison, nonetheless it seems reasonable that if respondents were beginning an "aggravated" or especially long sentence at the time of the interview, they might tend to choose probation. The results are mixed. Having an aggravated sentence has no effect on the choices examined here, but sentence length approaches significance ($p=.06$); respondents with longer sentences tend to prefer prison. Note, however, that although the coefficient is significant, it is relatively small. Therefore it appears that the attributes of respondents' sentences have a limited impact on choice.

The final set of variables in the model taps current offenders' perceptions of the Texas justice system and how offenders might react to it. The first variable, agreement that "probation has gotten much stricter in recent years," is associated positively and significantly with choice of sanction. The second, agreement with the question "Do you think Texas offenders are more likely to choose prison over probation today than in the early 1980s?," has an even more powerful effect on the dependent variable. The belief that other offenders are opting increasingly for prison apparently affects respondents' preferences for prison. This finding points not only to the impact of beliefs about others' sanction preferences, but also to the consequences of a widespread belief that choosing prison over probation is a wise and rational move in view of changes in the correctional system.

DISCUSSION

David Garland (1991) recently drew attention to the importance of the sociology (as opposed to the philosophy) of punishment. He states: "Properly done, the sociology of punishment should inform us about the social forces that condition penal processes and the various social consequences that these processes in turn produce" (Garland 1991:120). The analysis presented here contributes to a sociology of punishment by exploring how offenders judge the relative personal costs of probation and of prison.

In addition to demonstrating a frequent preference for prison, the analysis reveals offender characteristics that shape these preferences. Characteristics reflecting lifestyle, life course, or street experience are particularly important. That is, a preference for prison is more likely among offenders who are African-American, older, unmarried, and widely exposed to crime and institutional corrections, and who share beliefs that probation has grown stricter and that other offenders now prefer prison to probation.

Theoretically, these findings suggest that choosing prison may be related to offender characteristics that result in a relatively low personal cost for going to prison, at least for the terms examined here. If one has few ties either to the community or to the dominant conventionality, one has little to lose by being incarcerated. Older and unmarried men, for example, may risk few relationships by going to prison; in addition, prison offers a rather structured environment.

At the same time, the better-educated offenders tend to prefer probation, a pattern consistent with the notion of personal cost. Persons with more education presumably are more likely to be at risk of losing not only the time they spend in prison but their reputation and status as well. Remaining in the community on probation, where work and family can be maintained, permits a convicted felon to salvage more of a life than does going to prison.

Prison also is preferred by those who already are largely committed to a deviant lifestyle, with its attendant trips to jail and prison. For persons deeply involved "in the life," prison carried only the inconvenience of the sentence, not the added loss of reputation. Indeed, going to prison may even be a badge of honor for some offenders (Petersilia 1990:24). Moreover, as noted above, these would be the very persons to know that today's prisons are less like the isolated plantations or the forgotten warehouses of the past.

In addition, offenders with little to lose should be the most likely to learn through jail and street experience about the system designed to control them. The analysis showed that the presence of shared beliefs about the relative punitiveness of probation and incarceration is a strong predictor of a preference for prison. Community jails are places where these beliefs are shared. Jails routinely bring together experienced offenders, novices, and a full range of the community's "rabble" (Irwin 1985), who share information about crime and its current consequences. With the spread of the notion that prison is not as bad as probation and may not last as long as in the past, more offenders may wish to avoid probation and to opt for prison, if possible.

Finally, the analysis underscores the significance of race and ethnicity in understanding how offenders relate to the experience of incarceration. Results support the position that being African-American, as a proxy for a broad cultural experience, is singularly important in shaping offenders' views of sanctions (Carroll 1982; Johnson 1976). The significance of race is not weakened by economic marginality, as some research suggests (Wright 1989), or by criminal involvement. Possibly African-Americans tend strongly to feel that they will be subjected proportionately to harassment under strict probation supervision. Under such circumstances, prison may seem more attractive than the pressures of close supervision on probation. Indeed, many African-American offenders feel that because they are incarcerated so frequently, a probation term soon will lead anyway to revocation and a prison term. Thus, with little to lose but the hassles of probation, prison may be the lesser of two evils for many African-American offenders.

The model examined here certainly does not explain sanction preferences. Indeed, it accounts for only 10 percent of the variation in preferences. This finding is a clear indication that factors not included in the model are important. This research, however, sought primarily to determine the significance of variables that literature suggests are theoretically relevant rather than to maximize the percentage of variance explained. The results reflect the contribution of theoretically derived variables; at the same time, they point to a need for additional research on how these and other variables may affect offenders' perceptions of sanctions.

CONCLUSION

The present research bears on the assumption that offenders rather consistently will define prison as more punitive than probation. In view of the public's tendency to regard incarceration as the only means of "getting tough" on crime (Petersilia 1990; Sherman and Hawkins 1981; Zimring and Hawkins 1991), this assumption largely accounts for the importance of incarceration in

America's response to crime. As a corollary, citizens often are ambivalent about probation; they believe it allows offenders to avoid the presumed punitive and deterrent effects of prison. This public orientation also prompts resistance to the early release of prisoners and to other diversion programs used by state officials to relieve prison crowding. The present analysis, however, suggests that this assumption is frequently not met among offenders. Results show that many offenders define common prison terms as less punitive than even three or five years on probation. At least in part, this situation inverts the penal code's hierarchy of sanctions thought to control crime.

When this occurs, a fundamental irony emerges in our justice system. That is, the lawbreakers whom middle-class citizens are most likely to fear and want most to be locked away—members of minorities with limited ties to conventionality (see Anderson 1990), the disaffected, the disadvantaged, and the deviant in general—tend to be the very offenders who view prison terms of even two or three years as easier than probation and as preferable. To the extent that these views among offenders are widespread, the contemporary demand for extensive incarceration (but often for limited terms) may foster two unwanted outcomes: less deterrence and more prisoners.

It would be inappropriate to conclude that offenders view prison as pleasant; most probably would try to avoid a truly long stay. Nonetheless, the patterns of perceptions reported here suggest a need to rethink how sanctions affect those for whom they are designed. If offenders often regard probation as more difficult and more burdensome than the prison terms that many actually will face, citizens and legislators might be less inclined to view nonprison sanctions as barely acceptable options to be used only sparingly when prison beds cannot be found.

The results of this study thus encourage efforts to explore nonprison sanctions (Morris and Tonry 1990). If offenders often define probation to be as "tough" as prison, nonprison sanctions not only might meet public expectations (Petersilia 1990), but also might help to reduce the current staggering rate of imprisonment.

REFERENCES

Alston, L. (1986) *Crime and Older Americans.* Springfield, IL: Thomas.

Anderson, E. (199) *Streetwise: Race, Class and Change in an Urban Community.* Chicago: University of Chicago Press.

Bowker, L. (1977) *Prison Subcultures.* Lexington, MA: Heath.

Bryan-College Station Eagle 1991, "Man Picks Prison over Probation" (March 24. A-1)

Carroll, L. (1982) "Race, Ethnicity and the Social Order of the Prison." In R. Johnson and H. Toch (eds.), *Pains of Imprisonment*, pp. 181-203. Beverly Hills: Sage.

Christianson, P. (1991) "Our Black Prisons." In K. Haas and G. Alpert (eds.), *The Dilemmas of Corrections: Contemporary Readings*, pp. 64-76. Prospect Heights, IL: Waveland.

Clear, T. and P. Hardyman (1990) "The New Intensive Supervision Movement." (*Crime & Delinquency*) 36:42-60.

Crouch, B.M. and J. Marquart (1989) *An Appeal to Justice: Litigated Reform of Texas Prisons*. Austin: University of Texas Press.

——— (1990) "Resolving the Paradox of Reform: Litigation, Prisoner Violence and Perceptions of Risk." *Justice Quarterly* 7:103-24.

Davidson, T. (1974) *Chicano Prisoners: The Key to San Quentin*. New York: Holt, Rinehart and Winston.

Dillingham, S. (1991) *National Update*. Washington, DC: Bureau of Justice Statistics, Department of Justice.

Garland, D. (1991) "Sociological Perspectives on Punishment." In M. Tonry (ed.), *Crime and Justice: A Review of Research*, pp. 115-66 Chicago: University of Chicago Press.

Goodstein, L. and D. McKenzie (1984) "Racial Differences in Adjustment Patterns of Prison Inmates—Prisonization, Conflict, Stress and Control." In D. Georges-Abeyie (ed.), *The Criminal Justice System and Blacks*, pp. 271-306 New York: Clark Boardman.

Greenfeld, L. and P. Langan (1987) "Trends in Prison Populations." Paper presented at the National Conference on Punishment for Criminal Offenses, Ann Arbor.

Hamilton, V.L. and S. Rytina (1980) "Social Consensus on Norms of Justice: Should the Punishment Fit the Crime?" *American Journal of Sociology* 85:1117-44.

Hawkins, R. and G. Alpert (1989) *American Prison Systems: Punishment and Justice*. Englewood Cliffs, NJ: Prentice-Hall.

Hirschi, T. (1969) *Causes of Delinquency*. Berkeley: University of California Press.

Irwin, J. (1985) *The Jail*. Berkeley: University of California Press.

Irwin, J. and D. Cressey (1962) "Thieves, Convicts and the Inmate Culture. *Social Problems* 10:142-55.

Jacobs, J. (1974) "Street Gangs behind Bars." *Social Problems* 21:395-409.

——— (1977) *Stateville: The Prison in Mass Society*. Chicago: University of Chicago Press.

——— (1980) "The Prisoners' Rights Movement and Its Impacts 1960-1980." In N. Morris and M. Tonry (eds.), *Crime and Justice: An Annual Review of Research, Vol. 2*, pp. 429-70. Chicago: University of Chicago Press.

Jencks, C. and P. Peterson (1991) *The Urban Underclass*. Washington, DC: Brookings Institute.

Johnson, R. (1976) *Culture and Crisis in Confinement*. Lexington, MA: Lexington Books.

Krisberg, B., I.M. Swartz, G. Fishman, Z. Eisikovits, E. Guttman, and K. Joe. "The Incarceration of Minority Youth." *Crime and Delinquency* 33:173-205.

Krohn, M. (1990) "Control and Deterrence Theories." In J. Sheley (ed.), *Criminology: A Contemporary Handbook*, pp. 295-315. Belmont, CA: Wadsworth

Lockwood, D. (1980) *Prison Sexual Violence*. New York: Elsevier.

Morris, N. and M. Tonry (1990) *Between Prison and Probation: Intermediate Punishments in a Rational Sentencing System*. New York: Oxford University Press.

Newman, G. (1978) *The Punishment Response*. New York: Lippincott.

Parker, N. and A. Horwitz (1986) "Unemployment, Crime and Imprisonment: A Panel Approach." *Criminology* 24:751-73.

Petersilia, J. (1990) "When Probation Becomes More Dreaded Than Prison." *Federal Probation* (March):23-27.

Rettig, R., M. Torres, and G. Garret (1977) *Many: A Criminal Addict's Story*. Boston: Houghton Mifflin.

Rossi, P., J. Simpson, and J. Miller (1985) "Beyond Crime Seriousness: Fitting the Punishment to the Crime," *Journal of Quantitative Criminology* 1:59-90.

Sampson, R. (1987) "Urban Black Violence: The Effect of Male Joblessness and Family Disruption." *American Journal of Sociology* 93:348-82.
Sherman, M. and G. Hawkins (1981) *Imprisonment in America: Choosing the Future*. Chicago: University of Chicago Press.
Shover, N. (1985) *Aging Criminals*. Beverly Hills: Sage.
Sullivan, M. (1989) *Getting Paid: Youth Crime and Work in the Inner City*. Ithaca: Cornell University Press.
Taylor, C.S. (1990) *The Dangerous Society*. East Lansing: Michigan State University Press.
Thomas, J. (1988) *Prisoner Litigation: The Paradox of the Jailhouse Lawyer*. Totowa, NJ: Rowan & Littlefield, Publishers.
Tienda, M. (1989) "Puerto Ricans and the Underclass Debate." *Annals of the American Academy of Political and Social Sciences* 501:105-19.
Wilson, W.J. (1987) *The Truly Disadvantaged: The Inner City, The Underclass and Public Policy*. Chicago: University of Chicago Press.
——— (1991) "Studying Inner-City Social Dislocations: The Challenge of Public Agenda Research. *American Sociological Review* 56:1-14.
Wolfgang, M., T. Thornberry, and R. Figlio (1987) *From Boy to Man, from Delinquency to Crime*. Chicago: University of Chicago.
Wright, K. (1989) "Race and Economic Marginality in Explaining Prison Adjustment." *Journal of Research in Crime and Delinquency* 26:67-89.
Zimring, F. and G. Hawkins (1991) *The Scale of Imprisonment*. Chicago: University of Chicago Press.

COMMUNICATION POLICY CHANGES FROM 1971 TO 1991 IN STATE CORRECTIONAL FACILITIES FOR ADULT MALES IN THE UNITED STATES

GEORGE E. DICKINSON
College of Charleston

THOMAS W. SEAMAN
Lynchburg College

The objective of this research is to determine whether and how correctional institutions' policies on correspondence, visitation, and telephoning have changed between 1971 and 1991. Data were gathered in 1971, 1981, and 1991 from state correctional institutions for adult males in maximum and medium security facilities. The findings indicate to the authors that correctional institutions are making serious commitments to reduce the social isolation of inmates through more liberal communication policies. Implications for further research are suggested to determine the effects of inmates' increased contacts with the outside society through more liberal policies regarding correspondence, visitation, and telephoning.

Nearly a half century ago, Clemmer (1950) in his study of the prison community concluded that the lack of contact with the outside community contributed to the prisonization of inmates. He noted that prisonization was an adverse factor in rehabilitation. Today, there is increased attention to the impact of incarceration on the family unit and the problems families face in their efforts to maintain ties with imprisoned relatives. National conferences have explored family needs and problems, and several organizations have been formed to develop information networks for prisoners' families and those who assist them (Schafer, 1989).

Support from one's intimates, such as family and friends, is of major importance to those in stressful situations such as incarceration. The effects

The opinions expressed in this article are solely those of the authors and are not intended to represent the policies of the Federal Bureau of Prisons or the U.S. Department of Justice.

THE PRISON JOURNAL, Vol. 74 No. 3, September 1994 371-382

pointed out by Maguire and Flanagan (1991, p. 604): Between 1975 and 1989, the number of inmates held in state and federal penal institutions almost tripled, achieving a record number surpassing 680,000.

In the 1971 study, all but two states (Arkansas and Rhode Island) were represented; in 1981, two states (Alaska and Vermont) were not represented; and in 1991, New York was the only state not represented. Multiple state listings (from two to five correctional institutions per state in each survey) were found in 1971 and 1981 in California, Illinois, Maryland, Massachusetts, New Jersey, New York, Ohio, Oregon, Pennsylvania, South Carolina, Tennessee, and Wisconsin. Multiple listings in 1991 were found in California, Colorado, Connecticut, Florida, Georgia, Illinois, Indiana, Maryland, Michigan, Minnesota, Nebraska, Nevada, New Jersey, Ohio, Oregon, Pennsylvania, South Carolina, Tennessee, Texas, Washington, Wisconsin, and Virginia.

The 1971 and 1981 surveys were mailed to 69 institutions, and the 1991 survey was mailed to 112 facilities. Return rates were 93%, 96%, and 81%, respectively. None of the 11 New York facilities returned the survey in 1991 (without prior approval of the corrections commissioner, they would not respond), accounting for the overall lower return rate for 1991. The increased number of prisons included in the 1991 survey reflects the rapid expansion of correctional facilities in the United States during the 1980s. The 1971 questionnaire mailed to wardens in each of the 50 states was shortened for the 1981 and 1991 mailings (a copy of the questionnaire is in the Appendix) for the purpose of streamlining the survey. The 1981 and 1991 questionnaires had questions from the 1971 survey, simply fewer of them. For each of the surveys, one follow-up mailing sought responses from those not returning the initial questionnaire.

We did not sample the correctional institutions in the 50 states but mailed surveys to all maximum and medium security facilities in the United States. We feel that our return rate was high enough that the responses should be representative of the nation as a whole. We did not make comparisons between older and newer prisons or between individual prisons over the 20-year period. Responses varied within states; thus communication policies appear to be more institution-specific than statewide.

Information sought on inmate correspondence policies included the number of letters allowed to be written and received per week, whether or not incoming and outgoing mail was inspected, the manner of inspection, and payment for postage. Questions asked about visitation involved the number and length of visits allowed per month, visitation days, types of people allowed to visit, conditions of visitation, policy on physical contact, presence of a correctional officer, conjugal visitation, and changes regarding physical of isolation from family are particularly deleterious (Bukstel & Kilmann, 1980). Negative attitudes of significant others tend to produce negative effects on humans of all ages, whereas positive relations can help coping patterns during stressful periods. The prevailing argument is that maintaining positive relationships with family and friends will provide a valuable support system for the offender upon release.

The theoretical support for this point of view is found in social role theory and social support theory (Hairston, 1988). Social role theory suggests that visiting, along with other means of maintaining relationships with family and friends such as letters and phone calls, allows the prisoner to continue to maintain and function in desirable social roles—as a son, husband, father, brother, friend—making it more likely that he will be able to continue successfully these generally law-abiding roles upon release. Social role theory also asserts that when the desirable social roles are not maintained during incarceration, the ex-prisoner upon release is more likely to see himself and to be seen by others in one of the roles ascribed to "ex-cons." These "ex-con" roles are more likely to lead to renewed criminal behavior.

Social support theory argues that a social network that can be provided by family and friends and can be maintained in part through communication protects prisoners from stressful situations within prison as well as protecting the ex-prisoner from situations that might lead to recidivism upon release (Freedman & Rice, 1977; Glaser, 1964; Holt & Miller, 1972).

The primary objective of this study was to determine what changes, if any, had occurred between 1971 and 1991 regarding communication policies of state correctional institutions for adult males in maximum and medium security facilities with outsiders through correspondence, visitation, and telephoning. Consideration of changes in communication policies anticipated for the future was a secondary purpose of the surveys. Data were gathered from all the state correctional institutions for adult males in maximum and medium security facilities in 1971, from a follow-up of these same institutions in 1981, and from all additional new facilities in 1991 (addresses were obtained from the American Correctional Association's *Directory*). Selections were made according to the descriptions of the institutions in the *Directory* regarding the security levels of the prisons.

The same 69 institutions in 1971 and 1981 received the surveys except for two that had closed during those years; no effort was made to contact new prisons in 1981. Because of a rapid increase in the number of correctional institutions built in the 1980s, it was decided to include the new facilities in the mailing; thus 112 maximum and medium security institutions received a questionnaire in 1991. The need for these additional correctional facilities is

TABLE 1: Percentage of U.S. Prisons Participating in Selected Policies Governing Inmates' Communication With Outside Contacts in 1971, 1981, and 1991

Policy	*1971 (N = 64)*	*1981 (N = 66)*	*1991 (N = 91)*
Mail			
Incoming mail inspected	98	95	99
Outgoing mail inspected	89	40	45
Reading every letter	13	0	0
Scanning every letter	44	20	27
Spot-checking letters	43	20	27
Only looking for contraband	0	59	46
Visitation conditions[a]			
Open table	58	32	58
Sit in open area	19	63	38
Wire screen between	23	5	4
Physical facilities for visitation changed significantly in past 10 years	50	64	38
Anticipate changes in physical facilities in near future	44	39	18
Telephone calls			
Always monitored by a prison representative	60	10	9
Sometimes monitored by a representative	27	32	31
General			
Communication policies changed significantly in past 10 years	69	83	42
Changes had favorable effects.	82	84	81
Anticipate changes in communication policies in near future	50	20	20

a. Varies with classification of inmate. Some have "no contact" status; others needing high security talk via phone or glass barrier.

facilities for visitation. Information on telephone policies sought to determine the number and length of calls made and received per month, payment for calls, and whether or not calls were monitored. Findings of the surveys are discussed below, and selected results are summarized in Table 1.

CORRESPONDENCE

Institutional policies regarding letter writing varied over the years. In 1971, only 63% of institutions allowed inmates to write a maximum of "at least eight letters per week"; 97% and 99% allowed this in 1981 and 1991, respectively. Actually, the overwhelming majority currently have no maximum limit on the number of letters that can be written. The maximum number of letters allowed to be received per week hardly changed over the twenty years: 97%, 100%, and 99% allowed "at least eight letters per week," with the majority having no maximum.

Policies regarding authorization for a prison representative to open inmates' mail changed over the 20 years. In 1971, 67% of institutions asked inmates to sign such an authorization, yet only 23% and 14% required it in 1981 and 1991, respectively. Several of the institutions commented that notification of possible mail inspection was made clear at orientation. Incoming mail has been consistently inspected since 1971; however, inspection of outgoing mail has decreased since 1971 (see Table 1).

Procedures for inspecting mail have changed significantly over the two decades from an emphasis on reading or scanning each letter or spot-checking a limited number of letters to not reading but looking primarily for contraband (see Table 1).

Although institutional policies regarding letter writing have loosened up over the two decades, in actual practice the responses revealed that the number of letters sent and received per week has been up and down over the 20-year period: 3.5 in 1971, 5.6 in 1981, and 4.6 in 1991. The average number of letters sent and received per week per inmate was not known in some institutions. Reciprocity appeared to exist in correspondence—for each letter sent, a letter was received. Postage for outgoing mail was primarily shared by the inmate and the institution (53% in 1971, 73% in 1981, and 62% in 1991). In many states, the institutions did not share in the cost of postage and the inmate alone paid (33%, 23%, and 38% in 1971, 1981, and 1991, respectively).

VISITATION

Institutional policies regarding visitation changed over the 20-year period. The percentage of institutions permitting inmates more than four visits per month increased from 56% in 1971 to 75% and 76% in 1981 and 1991. The actual practice of visitation also changed over time: The average number of visits inmates received per month increased from 2.97 in 1971 to 5.12 in 1981, but dropped to 4.20 in 1991. Institutional policies regarding the length of time allowed for each visit also increased after 1971. In 1971, only 59% of institutions permitted visits of two hours or more, whereas in 1981 and 1991, 78% and 73%, respectively, allowed such lengthy visits.

Although more visitors came and stayed longer in 1981 and 1991 than in 1971, the policy regarding number of visitors an inmate could receive at a time changed over the two decades. Thirty-three percent had no limit on the number of visitors in 1971, whereas only 19% and 9% had no limit in 1981 and 1991, respectively. Yet in 1991, 55% permitted at least three visitors at a time, as compared to only 40% permitting at least three visitors at a time in 1971 and 1981. Some of the institutions noted that children were not counted in the number of visitors allowed at a time. A correctional officer continued always to be present in the majority of institutions: 97%, 98%, 97% in the three time periods.

Although institutional policies permitted visitation 365 days a year in approximately half of the institutions in 1971 and 1981 (48% and 55%, respectively), only 38% in 1991 allowed visitation every day of the year. The others allowed visitation on specific days of the week. All the institutions over the two decades limited visitors to anyone on an approved list of family, friends, and legal and spiritual advisors.

Conditions for visitation showed inconsistent patterns over the 20-year period. As noted in Table 1, open-table visitation was most popular in 1971 and 1991, whereas sitting together in an open area with no barriers was the most frequent way of visiting in 1981. A wire screen separating the inmate from visitors decreased after 1971 (see Table 1). Several institutions noted that restrictions for inmates in segregation/high security/no-contact status required different arrangements, such as a glass barrier with the individuals talking via telephone.

Regarding the intimacy of visits, the policy in the overwhelming majority of institutions (85%, 94%, and 95% in 1971, 1981, and 1991, respectively) allowed inmates and visitors to embrace. Conjugal visits were permitted in a minority of institutions: 6%, 18%, and 15% in 1971, 1981, and 1991, respectively. Perhaps they were not the cause, but following the 1988 national elections and the Republican advertisements about the furlough program in Massachusetts, the percentage of institutions in 1991 allowing furloughs reverted to the 1971 status (8% and 11% allowed furloughs in 1971 and 1991, respectively, whereas 32% of institutions allowed them in 1981).

Fifty percent or more of the institutions in 1971 and 1981 stated that physical facilities for visitation had changed significantly during the previous 10 years, yet only 38% stated such in 1991. Thus the changes were somewhat greater in the 1960s and 1970s than in the 1980s. In 1991, very few institutions anticipated changes in physical facilities for visitation in the near future, whereas over one third in 1971 and 1981 had anticipated such changes (see Table 1).

TELEPHONING

The number of telephone calls inmates were allowed to receive per month did not change significantly over the 20-year period: 62%, 56%, and 67% in

1971, 1981, and 1991, respectively, did not allow inmates to receive calls. The remaining institutions allowed calls to be received only in emergencies. On the other hand, policies regarding inmates' making calls have changed considerably since 1971. In 1971, 86% of institutions did not allow calls by inmates except in emergencies, and only 7% allowed more than three calls per inmate per month. In 1981 and 1991, however, only 6% and 10%, respectively, limited calls to emergency situations, and 66% and 86%, respectively, allowed more than three calls per month or an unlimited number of calls.

The length of time allowed per telephone call changed very little over the time period: 94% in 1981 and 1991 allowed inmates to talk longer than three minutes or had no time limit to the length of the calls, as compared to 87% allowing this in 1971. In 1981 and 1991, most telephone calls were either paid for by the inmate or made collect (87% and 100%, respectively), compared to 44% in 1971. An exception was sometimes made for emergency calls, which often were paid for by the institution. Paying for calls was shared as a general rule more by the institution and inmate in 1971 (56%) than in 1981 and 1991 (13% and 0%, respectively).

As is shown in Table 1, telephone conversations were "*always* monitored by a prison representative" much less in 1981 and 1991 than in 1971; in each of the time periods, some institutions noted that they "sometimes" listened in on calls but not always. Thus 87%, 42%, and 40% in 1971, 1981, and 1991, respectively, listened in on telephone conversations "sometimes" and/or "always."

COMMUNICATION POLICY CHANGES

Approximately three fourths of the respondents in 1971 and 1981 (69% and 83%, respectively) answered affirmatively to the questions "Have your communication policies changed significantly in the past 10 years?" and, if so, "Have these changes had favorable or unfavorable effects?" Less than half, however, in 1991 answered this question in the affirmative. Of those institutions reporting, over 80% in each of the three time periods stated that the changes had favorable effects (see Table 1).

Regarding changes in communication policies in the near future, half in 1971, as opposed to one fifth in 1981 and 1991, anticipated such changes (see Table 1). Thus the decades of the 1960s and 1970s were characterized by more anticipated and actual change in communication policies than the more recent decades of the 1980s and 1990s.

CONCLUSIONS

The data presented here suggest to us that a serious commitment has been made to reduce the social isolation of inmates through more liberal policies on correspondence, visiting, and telephoning. Compared to 1971, inmates today are allowed to write more letters, outgoing mail is inspected less, looking for contraband is emphasized more than reading letters, postage is shared more by inmates and the institution, and more mail is sent and received by inmates.

Prison visitation rules are more lenient today than they were in 1971. More visits per month are allowed, length of time for visits has increased, conditions for visitation allow more freedom, and institutions allowing conjugal visits have increased. Inmate telephone policies have become more liberal since 1971: More institutions allow inmates to make calls, and telephone conversations are monitored less.

The following are some of the favorable comments made by respondents regarding communication policy changes in recent years: collect call system for telephoning has permitted more calls by inmates; having more phones installed seems to have eased tensions; allowing collect calls has freed up time for counselors; inmate population is happier; inmate morale is improved; and the incidents of assault have been reduced. Other comments regarding changes in the physical facilities included the following: larger facilities allow for more visitation at a given time; more privacy allowed for visits because of improved facility, yet closer custody supervision; and morale improved with no significant sacrifice to security.

A need exists for further research to determine the effects of increased inmates' contacts with the outside society through more liberal correspondence policies, visitation rules, and telephone regulations; to determine whether less restricted correspondence and telephone policies aid in maintaining ties for inmates whose families and friends live far from the prison; and to determine whether inmates take advantage of more lenient restrictions to increase contraband and increase connections with past criminal contacts on the outside. Also, to what extent do less restraining communication policies contribute to inmate morale, inmate-staff interaction, and relations with family and friends? Finally, if a smoother transition to the outside society should in fact be evidenced from more lenient communication policies, what effect might this have on future recidivism rates?

APPENDIX
Survey of State Correctional Institutions' Policies Regarding Communication of Inmates With Persons Outside the Institution[a]

Communication Via Letters

1. The maximum number of letters an inmate is allowed to *write* per week is:
   _____a. 4 or fewer
   _____b. 5 to 8
   _____c. more than 8
   _____d. no maximum
   _____e. other, please specify ____________________

2. The maximum number of letters an inmate is allowed to *receive* per week is:
   _____a. 4 or fewer
   _____b. 5 to 8
   _____c. more than 8
   _____d. no maximum
   _____e. other, please specify ____________________

3. Upon admission to the institution each inmate is:
   _____a. asked to sign an authorization for the warden or his representative to open, read, and inspect mail
   _____b. asked to sign nothing regarding letter inspection
   _____c. other, please specify ____________________

4. *Incoming* mail: _____a. is inspected _____b. is not inspected

5. *Outgoing* mail: _____a. is inspected _____b. is not inspected

6. If mail is inspected, what procedure is used for the inspection?
   _____a. reading every letter
   _____b. scanning every letter
   _____c. spot-checking (reading or scanning a limited number of letters)
   _____d. other, please specify ____________________

7. What is the average number of letters *sent* per week per inmate? __________

8. What is the average number of letters *received* per week per inmate? _______

9. Postage for *outgoing* mail is paid:
   _____a. by the inmate
   _____b. by the institution
   _____c. a *and* b. Explain percentage paid by each ____________________
   _____d. other, please specify ____________________

Communication Via Visitation

10. The number of visits per month an inmate may have is:
    _____a. none
    _____b. one
    _____c. two
    _____d. three
    _____e. four
    _____f. more than four

11. The length of time for each visit is:
    _____a. under one hour
    _____b. one to two hours
    _____c. two hours
    _____d. more than two hours, please specify ____________________

(continued)

APPENDIX Continued

12. Visitation is permitted at your institution:
    _____a. 365 days per year
    _____b. only on week days
    _____c. only on weekends
    _____d. every day except holidays
    _____e. other, please specify ______________________________

13. Who is permitted to visit inmates?
    _____a. immediate family only
    _____b. friends and relatives only
    _____c. legal and spiritual advisor
    _____d. other, please specify ______________________________
    _____e. combination of a and c
    _____f. combination of b and c

14. Under what conditions is one allowed to visit an inmate?
    _____a. open table visitation
    _____b. wire screen separating the inmate and the visitor
    _____c. talk by telephone due to glass barrier separating the inmate and the visitor
    _____d. sit together in an open area
    _____e. other, please specify ______________________________

15. Is a guard present when a visit is being made?
    _____a. yes, always _____b. yes, sometimes _____c. no

16. Are the inmate and visitor(s) allowed to embrace?
    _____a. yes _____b. no

17. What is the average number of visits received per month per inmate? _______

18. An inmate is permitted to receive:
    _____a. one visitor at a time
    _____b. two visitors at a time
    _____c. three visitors at a time
    _____d. more than three visitors at a time, please specify _______________
    _____e. no limit on the number of visitors

19. Are private conjugal visits permitted?
    _____a. yes _____b. no _____c. no, but we have a temporary leave (furlough) program

Communication Via Telephone

20. How many telephone calls are inmates allowed to *make* per month?
    _____a. none
    _____b. one
    _____c. two
    _____d. three
    _____e. more than three, please specify ______________________________

APPENDIX Continued

21. How many telephone calls are inmates allowed to *receive* per month?
    _____a. none _____d. three
    _____b. one _____e. more than three, please specify _____________
    _____c. two _____f. only in emergencies

22. Telephone calls are paid for:
    _____a. by the inmate
    _____b. by the institution
    _____c. a *and* b. Explain percentage paid by each _________________
    _____d. collect calls
    _____e. combination of a and d
    _____f. other, please specify _________________________________

23. Are telephone conversations listened in on by a prison representative?
    _____a. yes, always _____b. yes, sometimes _____c. no

24. The length of time allowed per telephone call is:
    _____a. three minutes
    _____b. longer than 3 minutes, please specify length _________________
    _____c. no time limit

Communication Policy Changes

25. Have your communication policies changed significantly in the past ten years?
    _____a. yes _____b. no

    Have these changes had favorable or unfavorable effects? Explain: ________
    ____

26. Do you anticipate changes regarding your communication policies in the near future?
    _____a. yes _____b. no

27. Have your physical facilities for visitation changed significantly in the past ten years?
    _____a. yes _____b. no

    Have these changes had favorable or unfavorable effects? Explain: ________
    ____

28. Do you anticipate changes regarding your physical facilities for visitation in the near future?
    _____a. yes _____b. no

a. Although the 1971 survey was longer, the questions here were used in all three surveys.

REFERENCES

American Correctional Association. (1991). *Directory of Juvenile and Adult Correctional Departments, Institutions, Agencies and Paroling Authorities.* College Park, MD: Author.

Bukstel, L., & Kilmann, P. (1980). Psychological effects of imprisonment on confined individuals. *Psychological Bulletin, 88*, 469-493.

Clemmer, D. (1950). Observations on imprisonment as a source of criminality. *Journal of Criminal Law and Criminology, 41*, 311-319.

Freeman, B. J., & Rice, D. G. (1977). Marital therapy in prison: One partner "couple theory." *Federal Probation, 40*, 175-183.

Glaser, D. (1964). *The effectiveness of a prison and parole system.* Indianapolis: Bobbs-Merrill.

Hairston, C. F. (1988). Family ties during imprisonment: Do they influence future criminal activity? *Federal Probation, 52*, 48-52.

Holt, N., & Miller, D. (1972). *Explorations in inmate-family relations* (Research Report No. 46). Sacramento: California Department of Corrections.

Maguire, K., & Flanagan, T. J. (1991). *Sourcebook of criminal justice statistics 1990.* Washington, DC: U.S. Government Printing Office, U.S. Department of Justice, Bureau of Justice Statistics.

Schafer, N. E. (1989). Prison visiting: Is it time to review the rules? *Federal Probation, 53*, 25-30.

SAM HOUSTON STATE UNIVERSITY • CRIMINAL JUSTICE CENTER • HUNTSVILLE, TX 77341

CRIMINAL JUSTICE
Research Bulletin

Vol. 6 No. 2, 1991

The Privatization of Prisons in Historical Perspective

Malcolm M. Feeley
Center for the Study of Law and Society
University of California at Berkeley

This paper places the contemporary debate over privatization of corrections in historical perspective. In so doing, it shows that the debate ignores a central function of privatization, which is its potential to expand the state's capacity to punish. I demonstrate this in a three-part analysis. Part I traces the recent growth of privatization, examines the current debate over the relative efficiencies of private and public corrections, and then argues that this debate is misdirected. Part II develops this thesis by examining the consequences of earlier efforts at private penal administration. Part III assesses the implications of the current privatization movement in light of the lessons of history.

I. The Debate over Private Corrections

In recent years, there have been efforts to privatize significant segments of corrections (Savas, 1987:869; Logan, 1990; McDonald, 1990; and Ryan and Ward, 1989). Private entrepreneurs have begun to play a major role in financing and building correctional facilities, in suppling a variety of auxiliary services, and in obtaining contracts to operate and administer prisons and jails. Many private for-profit and nonprofit organizations also run programs for offenders who are released into their custody or who must participate as a condition of probation. These programs provide job training, drug treatment, educational services, and the like. The most controversial feature of the recent privatization movement, however, has been private companies assuming responsibilities for operating secure prisons and jails.

As of October 1988, more than 25 for-profit companies, many backed by venture capital, were competing for rights to build, own, and operate jails and prisons throughout the United States (Private Vendors in Corrections, 1988). Privatization in juvenile corrections has grown at an even faster pace. During the past thirty years, placements in private programs (e.g., training centers, residential treatment and counseling programs, foster care, and diversion programs) in lieu of state-run facilities has become quite common, and currently in the United States a substantial portion of all juveniles under court supervision are in the custody of privately operated programs. And in recent years jails, prisons, and juvenile facilities have also turned to private vendors to supply a host of services, including food, health, counseling, vocational training, education, and at times, administrative services (Hackett et al., 1987).

Furthermore, in recent years the private sector has also radically altered the ways correctional facilities are financed and built. Private lease-purchase arrangements are increasingly replacing government-issued bonds. Designed by such investment firms as E. F. Hutton, Merrill Lynch, Morgan Stanley and Company, and Shearson Lehman Brothers, lease-purchase agreements allow governments to make installment purchases of property which was privately financed and built (DeWitt, 1987; Chaiken and Mennemeyer, 1987).

Advocates of all these forms of privatization assert that they are efficient and cost effective. They claim that the private sector can finance, construct, service, and operate most types of correctional facilities more efficiently than can government. These claims are buttressed by a number of independent studies which conclude that private companies can finance new facilities without the need for voter-approved bond issues, and can construct them more quickly and cheaply than government (Chaiken and Mennemeyer, 1987:49). Other studies have found that private contractors, freed from cumbersome public personnel policies and unionized work forces, are able to run correctional institutions and related programs more efficiently and cheaply. Indeed, there is a widespread belief that privatization of a number of correctional functions, especially the new forms of financing and the new methods of providing services, is more effective and more efficient than long-standing conventional methods (Mullen, 1985).

Despite generally favorable reviews, correctional privatization has its critics who dismiss cost comparisons which show private enterprise to be more cost effective. The most substantial opposition, however, comes from those who raise principled objections to the idea of privatized corrections. For instance, John DiIulio (1987:79-80) draws on John Locke's *Treatise on Government* to argue that because punishment is one of the core functions of government, it should be administered by governmental agencies. "To remain legitimate and morally significant," DiIulio asserts, "the authority to govern behind bars, to deprive citizens of their liberty, to coerce (and even kill) them, must remain in the hands of government authorities."

As important as this debate over the efficiency, economy, and principle of privatized corrections is, it ignores other and, I believe, more important questions. For the most part, the debate assumes comparability of activities and asks simply, which sector--public or private--can perform them most efficiently? Even vigorous critics tend to frame issues this way. John DiIulio assumes that the central question is: Who should administer the prisons--the public or private sector? However, to frame the issues solely in terms of the substitution (of private for public functions) ignores another, more significant question: *To what extent does privatization expand and transform the state's capacity to punish?* This chapter argues that the most significant consequence of privatization historically has been the generation of new and expanded sanctions and forms of social control.

If I am correct, then the privatization movement should be assessed from a dynamic and historical perspective, one that can determine if and how privatization expands the sanctioning capacity of the state and how this expanded array of punishments is distributed across different sectors of society. These are obvious and important questions, but ones that are largely ignored in discussions of correctional privatization.

An examination of the questions will reveal that private corrections must be seen as a complement to and an expansion of public correctional programs.[1] This perspective is supported by a review of earlier efforts which relied on private entrepreneurs. Such an inquiry reveals that private entrepreneurs have generated new sanctions, which have been applied on those who otherwise would not have been sanctioned. The sanctioning and social control is both broader and deeper than what preceded it.

II. Private Corrections in History

The history of the development of the modern criminal justice system in Great Britain and the United States is a succession of piecemeal reforms brought about by pressures to expand the capacity and effectiveness of the criminal law. Many of the reforms were initiated by entrepreneurs who sought to accomplish what government could not or would not. Often, however, the two have gone hand in hand as entrepreneurs developed successful innovations that later were incorporated into the machinery of government.

Involvement of the private sector is found in all segments of the criminal justice process. No doubt, it stems in some part from the Anglo-American political culture which is skeptical of governmental authority and which promotes voluntary associations and private initiatives.[2] Whatever the precise reasons, it is clear the private initiatives have played an important role in shaping the modern criminal justice system. In England, privately run "prosecution societies" were the precursors of the modern, state-funded system of prosecution, and the modern police system has its origins in voluntary and private law enforcement schemes. Gaols in smaller communities throughout England, for centuries, were run as businesses by alehouse keepers, whose cellars doubled as gaols. From the Elizabethan era to the early twentieth century, English and American courts depended upon a type of private probation system to monitor petty offenders (Samaha, 1974).

The continued need to rely on the bail bondsmen is a modern example of this entrepreneurial heritage, but so too is the private corrections system. The private sector has played a crucial and innovative role in responding to demands to increase and expand sanctions in the face of rising crime and declining confidence in government. Current developments parallel earlier efforts, and so it is to the history that I now turn.

Transportation. Shortly after the first colonists arrived in Virginia in 1607, they were followed by a handful of convicted felons transported there as a condition of pardon to be sold into servitude. Thus was set into motion a new penal system, a system that operated successfully for nearly 250 years. For half of that period it constituted England's dominant mode of punishment for serious felons.

Emerging as a response to what was widely perceived as an ineffectual criminal justice system, transportation to the New World was a marriage of efficiency and effectiveness. Most of its costs were borne by profit-seeking merchants selling their human cargo and by planters who purchased it. It was effective in that it sanctioned thousands of offenders who otherwise would have gone unpunished.

During the long North American phase of transportation, some 50,000 convicts were shipped across the Atlantic, most notably to Virginia, the Carolinas, and Maryland where they were sold as agricultural laborers (Ekirch, 1987). Between the time the first convict ship sailed into Botany Bay in 1789 and the time transportation ended in 1868, over 100,000 convicts were put to work in Australia as agricultural workers, sheepherders, and manual laborers.

Why one form of punishment loses favor and another is instituted is not readily answerable. At any period, a number of alternatives may simultaneously be employed, and one may emerge to push others into the background. Banishment and forced labor, for instance, have been used as forms of punishment in diverse societies throughout history. Whatever the precise reasons for its emergence in seventeenth century England, transportation cannot be divorced from the rise of mercantilism and the British colonial experience.[3]

What underlay the entire administrative and economic structure of transportation was reliance upon private enterprise to effect the public policy. More precisely, transportation was an innovation promoted by mercantile interests which was only reluctantly embraced by public officials as they slowly came to appreciate its cost effectiveness. It began as an outgrowth of the trade in indentured servants. But the same social and economic conditions that induced people to settle in the New World also generated indentured servitude and, for that matter, transportation.

As it emerged first, in North America, transportation developed from a simple *ad hoc* arrangement to a sophisticated market, which allowed the state to sanction thousands of felons at little or no public cost, and which provided handsome returns to entrepreneurs. In the early days, arrangements for transportation were left to the offender, his or her family, or the county. But as business developed, shippers were guaranteed a steady supply of convicts, built specially designed ships to pack their human cargo tightly, and agreed--for a price--to take women, children, and the aged, as well as able-bodied male convicts.

The American Revolution called an abrupt halt to this lucrative and efficient regime of sanctioning, but not before convicts constituted a substantial portion of all immigrants to North America.[4] After prolonged consideration, Australia was selected as the site for a renewed and quite different type of policy of transportation. Despite its demise, the American policy of transportation more than justified the vision of its early supporters. For nearly 200 years it provided an extensive form of sanctioning at low- to no-cost to the state.

It is impossible to know who first seized upon the idea of transportation. Was it the entrepreneurs, experienced in the profitable trade in indentured servants and anxious to expand their markets? Or was it government officials desperate to find cheap ways to cope with the crisis of law and order? Whatever the precise history of its early years, transportation was an overwhelmingly successful innovation. In an era when strong government, and particularly a strong criminal justice apparatus, was anathema to large segments of the English population, the strategy of a decentralized, privately administered, low-cost penal system was a brilliant way to expand the state's capacity to sanction without having to expand its administrative structure. The policy of transportation multiplied the state's penal capacity and at low cost to the government. It expanded the reach and efficacy of the criminal sanction without the need for a centralized bureaucracy. From the vantage point of those who established it, the marriage of efficiency and economy, of penal policy and mercantilism, must be judged an enormous success.

The genius of this privately administered system of control may be appreciated more fully when one realizes that it was put into place and fully functioning one hundred years before the English Parliament first authorized the appointment of a full-time, paid judge, and nearly two hundred years before it established the first professional police force in London.

Transportation was not simply a substitute for the gallows. It was an innovation of gigantic proportions. It radically transformed the administration of criminal justice.[5] Although it was a merciful alternative to those few who otherwise would have been hanged, in terms of numbers it had its greatest impact on those who ran no risk of death. Those guilty of the worst offenses continued to be hanged, so that the punishment of transportation to North America had little or no impact on the use of capital punishment.[6] Rather, the new alternative swept up those who would have claimed benefit of clergy and escaped punishment altogether and those who otherwise would have received an unconditional pardon, a whipping, or a small fine. For still others, it increased the likelihood of prosecution, conviction, and punishment since victims were more willing to prosecute and juries were more willing to convict if they knew the offenders would not be hanged.

Transportation expanded the sanctioning power of the state enormously, which was precisely its intended effect. Unlike the quest of some contemporary reformers who seek alternatives that reduce reliance on the criminal sanction, transportation was designed as a sanction that would deter crime more efficiently than the threat of death and remove the criminal from society. It was motivated by a desire for more, not less, repression and it was successful.

The genius of this regime of sanctioning in an era when central government was weak and fiercely resisted was that responsibility for its administration and financing was wholly in the hands of entrepreneurs who operated it as a highly profitable business. In doing so, they succeeded beyond the wildest dreams of those who first embraced the idea.

Private prisons. Contemporary historians of the development of the modern prison in the eighteenth and early nineteenth centuries have emphasized theories of social control and reform that guided the early reformers. They have been intrigued with the theories of rehabilitation in the regime of solitary confinement in Philadelphia's Walnut Street Jail, and the system of silence in New York's Auburn Prison, as well as the importance these two institutions had in shaping American penal policy. By focusing on the theories of correction and discipline, and treating deviating practices as unintended consequences, these historians have ignored the economic factors that shaped early prisons.[7] From this perspective many of the early practices that appear to be failures in light of the idealists' theories can be reassessed more positively.[8] While they did not rehabilitate, some of these systems of punishment came close to paying for themselves. And certainly, one of their appeals was the claim of entrepreneurs that they could pay, at least partially, for themselves.

This section, then, argues that one of the reasons that the modern prison emerged as a viable alterative to transportation and the death penalty was that entrepreneurs successfully argued that it would increase the law's effectiveness at low or no cost to the state. I do not mean to argue that the idealism of early reformers who advocated imprisonment as an effective and more humane means of dealing with criminals was unimportant. Clearly it was.

Indeed, the idealists and entrepreneurs were often one and the same, as will be seen in the discussion of Jeremy Bentham's involvement in English prison policy. To wrench David Rothman's (1980) phrase out of context, prison policy in both England and the United States was, from the outset, a marriage of "conscience and convenience." Entrepreneurial reformers promised a modern form of punishment that was at once more humane and cost-effective. Private contractors could manage prisons and employ convicts in labor which would be both morally uplifting and rehabilitative as well as financially rewarding. Plans took various forms: locating private businesses in public prisons, privately operating prisons, locating state-run businesses within the institutions, leasing convicts to private contractors, or using convicts on public works projects in lieu of contract labor.

In England the leading proponent for privately managed factory-prisons was Jeremy Bentham. Well-known for his efforts to rationalize and codify the criminal law and for his design of the Panopticon, Bentham also developed detailed plans for a private contractor to run the Panopticon once it was built.[9] Indeed, he (1834:iv) campaigned tirelessly to obtain this contract for himself, believing that it would make him a wealthy man. Those commentators who have focused on this little known interest of Bentham characterize it as an obsession that lasted more than twenty years. Although Bentham lost his bid to become England's private corrections czar, his views and efforts led to the belief that public services can be provided more efficiently by private contractors than by government agents.

Working with his brother, Samuel, Jeremy designed and aggressively promoted his design for the Panopticon, a prison of efficient design which would allow maximum surveillance at minimum cost. From the early 1780s until the early 1800s, he was obsessed with this idea. He invested thousands of pounds of his own money in efforts to acquire a site and to develop a prototype of the Panopticon.

Bentham lost his bid to build and manage a private prison and eventually he turned to pursue other interests. But his plans were published and widely circulated and continued to influence the development of prisons. Throughout the nineteenth century in both France and the United States, his ideas for delegating prison services to private contractors were put into effect.

In the United States a version of Bentham's plans was promoted by one of his great admirers, Edward Livingston of Louisiana. In his proposed "Code of Reform and Prison Discipline," Livingston (1873:590-4) covered in Bentham-like detail every minute facet of prison design and management, including a provision that the warden's pay was to be determined in part by a "percent of the gross amount of sales . . . of the articles manufactured in their prisons . . . and also [a] percent on the amount of sums paid for the labour of the convicts by manufacturers." In France the government also came to rely on private contractors to operate prisons (O'Brien, 1982).

Contemporary historians have tended to dismiss as naive the plans of officials for economic viability of prisons during the early years of their development. But in so doing they have ignored the importance of labor and private contractors in the early prisons. Even the celebrated "reformatories" in Pennsylvania and New York, although built, owned, and operated by government, originally relied on private contractors to use convict labor to offset a large share of the costs. The importance of such ideas, as we have seen, is suggested by Livingston's elaborate plans which, among other things, linked the income of the warden to the productivity of prison labor. Indeed, in a number of states contractors paid the prison a fee or a percentage of their profits for the right to employ convicts. Although many quickly came to find that a prison could not be run as a business and that it was likely to be a drain on the state, some states, particularly those with limited resources and rapidly growing populations, came to depend heavily on private contractors. More generally, the belief that it was possible was one of the reasons why officials selected imprisonment as their punishment of choice.

The first state to rely upon a private contractor to run the entire prison system as a business was Kentucky. Frustrated by the high cost of running an inefficient and costly prison, in 1825 the legislature leased the entire prison and its population to an enterprising businessman (Lewis, 1922:257). The agreement called for the contractor, Joel Scott, to clothe, house, and feed the prisoners, maintain the buildings, and pay the state $1000 plus one-half his net profits. In return, he could employ the convicts at hard labor, and in lieu of salary keep the other half of the net profits from their labor. By several accounts, Scott was successful in running the operation. Kentucky's leasing system continued for some years, and only came to an end in the 1880s when workers succeeded in getting the legislature to pass a law restricting the "unfair competition" of prison labor.

Kentucky's lease system also served as a model for other states. In Tennessee and some other states contractors used convict labor in coal mines. Elsewhere convicts were employed in small-scale manufacturing. And in the late nineteenth century, the convict lease system provided labor for road and railway construction (Lewis, 1922; McKelvey, 1977; Wines, 1880:106-16; 161-211; Cable, 1883:296).

The southern convict lease system was especially successful. Despite economic dislocations of the Civil War, southern states were able to accommodate the increased number of criminal offenders that resulted from the shattered economy and the abolition of slavery. And widespread reliance on the criminal sanction and convict labor served as a means to control the black population. Indeed, by relying on convict lease systems, southern states were more efficient than the more wealthy states in the northeast; they were able to incarcerate a higher proportion of offenders and impose longer average sentences than states in other regions of the country (Cable, 1883:297). Furthermore, they were able to accomplish all this at a cost well below that of other states (Cable, 1883-297; Martin and Ekland-Olson, 1987). In short, reliance on private contractors facilitated the expansion of the capacity of the criminal justice system at a time when state governments could not easily afford to provide such services themselves.

Similarly, privatization was an efficient solution for rapidly growing western states. Post Civil War governments in Nebraska, Kansas, Oklahoma, and Oregon all leased their prisons and prisoners to contractors who, for a small fee and the right to use convict labor, agreed to assume responsibility for them (McKelvey, 1977:227).

California embraced private prisons in the 1850s as a response to the dramatic increase in demand for services brought about by the rapid influx of people at the outset of the gold rush. Here too demand outstripped the capacity of the fledgling state government, and in the first decade after statehood it had to turn to private contractors to house convicts in surplus ships in San Francisco Bay and to build and operate the prison at San Quentin.

From the outset there was strong opposition to the contract and convict lease systems, and by the middle of the twentieth century, it was strong enough to end them. Several factors led to their demise: (1) the success of a coalition of labor, manufacturers, and farmers who opposed unfair competition and pressed for legislation restricting the use of convict labor and the sale of convict-made goods; (2) the efforts of reformers who mobilized public opposition to the scandalous conditions in many of the privately run facilities and lease systems; and (3) the growth of the modern welfare state, which increased the capacity of governments to manage large-scale institutions.[10]

This brief history of the earlier experience with privatization in prisons reveals just how intimately the origins of the modern prison are bound up with the efforts of private entrepreneurs and the appeal of privatization. To a considerable extent, the modern prison is an invention of entrepreneurs who convinced government officials that they could create and maintain an extensive penal system at little or no cost when the state lacked the administrative capacity. Although the entrepreneurs were in retrospect wrong, they nevertheless were convincing enough at the time to have played an important role in formulating a policy of heavy reliance on imprisonment and to have created the expectation that its costs could be offset by running prisons according to business principles.

More generally, this brief history suggests that when the state is faced with demands it cannot meet, entrepreneurs can and do help develop a response, ultimately enlarging the state's capacities. As with transportation, early private prison contractors responded to a widely-felt crisis, developed innovative solutions and quickly implemented them. That their inventions were later modified or absorbed by the state does not indicate failure but success. Merchants responded to the crisis of law and order in the eighteenth century by developing a market in convict labor and developed the system of transportation. When this policy faced problems, shrewd businessmen saw the value of putting surplus naval vessels to good use. As transportation waned and the United States grew, enterprising businessmen and planners responded to the crisis of law and order by exploiting convict labor in the American South and West. Each of these policies represents an extension and an expansion of penal policy--entrepreneurs inventing new forms to respond to immediate crises which, in turn, were incorporated into the fabric of an expanded and more effective criminal justice system.

III. The Lessons of History

Despite its awesome powers, the modern criminal justice system remains something of a clumsy giant; it can impose terror through the death penalty and lengthy prison terms, and it can slap offenders on the wrist with fines and suspended sentences. But it has limited capacity to do much in between. In the twentieth century, probation and parole emerged as such intermediate forms of sentencing and control. They are important additions to the state's capacity to sanction, and have grown rapidly. Still, there is a widespread belief that probation is ineffective and that new forms of intermediate sanctions are needed. Sensing this, private entrepreneurs have taken a lead in developing and promoting a new array of intermediate sanctions.

Just as entrepreneurs in the eighteenth century pioneered in the development of transportation as intermediate punishment, entrepreneurs today have pioneered in the development of three new forms of intermediate penalties. Most of them involve expanding the functions of probation and creating new conditions to be imposed. They include: (1) treatment programs; (2) supervised release for parolees and "pre-parolees" employing new forms of low-security custody; and (3) sophisticated technologies for surveillance of probationers. Each of these new forms merges rehabilitative and punitive philosophies, just as the concepts of surveillance, custody, incarceration and liberty begin to merge at times. It is the involvement of private contractors with these forms of intermediate punishments, and not the operation of private high-security custodial facilities, that constitute the greatest growth area of private corrections.[11]

Private sector treatment programs. Supervised treatment programs, usually imposed as a condition of probation, include drug and alcohol abuse treatment, and job training programs. Virtually nonexistent thirty years ago, they are now commonplace components of the criminal justice system. Almost all are private and many are run for profit, deriving both their clients and their income 'rom contracts with local governments. Some are lesigned as long-term, residential facilities and others as out-patient clinics. Program philosophies vary widely; some are organized with strict, military-ike discipline; others are based upon religious beliefs; some are devoted to group therapy; others stress rugged individualism and self-reliance. The growing desire to respond to the widespread use of drugs has rekindled interest in these types of programs, and we can expect their numbers to ncrease.

These programs handle a large number of criminal offenders. For every offender housed in a privately managed jail or prison, there are hundreds n privately operated noncustodial treatment programs operating on contracts with state and local governments. Despite their numbers and importance, hese private programs are largely ignored in discussions of privatization in corrections. This may be because such programs are regarded as merely service providers rather than penal programs. Or it nay be because their role as agents of state control is obscured because participation is voluntary. But if we broaden our frame of reference and consider them as forms of punishment (or substitutes for ncarceration), we must realize that these new reatment programs are also integral components of he penal system that extend the reach of the criminal sanction and expand the array of penalties the state can impose. As such, they are part of a much expanded repertoire of punishments which can be used in concert with each other. In the aggregate they also constitute an impressive extension of state control which is often exempted from due process standards required of public agencies.

Low-security custodial programs. Another mportant development in corrections in recent years has been the growth of low-security custodial facilities. Many of the most innovative types of low-security custody have been developed by advocates of privatization, and many of the most successful such institutions are operated by private contractors. Today this form of custody constitutes one of the fastest growing areas of corrections and the most mportant segment of the business of private for-profit contractors.

The juvenile justice system, in particular, has come to rely on private contractors to provide such ow-security custodial facilities (Cohen, 1985:64). This in turn has increased its flexibility in dealing with juveniles and expanded its capacity to commit hem into custody. California, Florida, Massachusetts, Michigan, Pennsylvania, Rhode Island, and Washington, among others, all rely extensively on private contractors to care for their wards. In a number of states placement in private out-of-home settings constitutes a major component of the state's juvenile corrections policy; in some, private placements outnumber placements in public facilities. It must be stressed that these private custodial placements in California, Massachusetts, and elsewhere are not simply more efficient versions of state-run programs. Although they have redirected some juveniles who otherwise would have been detained in secure public institutions, they also target groups that once would not have been placed in custody at all. In short, they add a new intermediate level of sanctioning to the state's repertoire.

Private contractors have played a similar role in developing low-security facilities for adult offenders and there is a growing differentiation between what the private and public sector facilities offer. The private sector is developing more facilities at the low end of the security spectrum, such as community work-release centers, work camps, pre-release centers, short-term detention facilities, restitution centers, return-to-custody facilities, residential treatment programs, and the like.

Community corrections also has clearly had the effect of expanding penal options through the involvement of the private sector. Connecticut law, for example, provides for a network of public and private agencies to offer services--including custody at the local level--for offenders who otherwise would be imprisoned. Colorado has come to depend on an extensive network of private vendors to provide minimum security facilities. Maryland law provides state funding for local community corrections centers, which, in some locations, are run by private contractors. Private-sector involvement in community corrections is increasing, and there are indications that it will continue to grow, especially as prison populations exceed capacity highs and pressures mount to increase alternatives that are more flexible and less costly.

New technologies for surveillance and control. New technologies are still another response to the growing concern with crime. Only a few years ago, for example, chemical testing was performed by state laboratories in a costly and time-consuming manner. Now private drug testing companies can offer fast, cheap, and reliable tests to detect a large variety of illegal substances. But expanded use of cheap and reliable drug tests has increased the likelihood of detection, which in turn has raised the number of parole and probation violations. This has transformed probation and parole officers from social workers to law enforcement officials. The upsurge in the numbers returned to custody has in turn generated demands for specialized low security custodial facilities and new forms of confinement. In short, new technology has placed burdens on the correctional system and affected traditional rules.

Private contractors have also introduced a variety of electronic devices which monitor the movement of people. These devices can be used for surveillance and offer the possibility of confinement without custody. Developed by specialized security firms and still in its infancy, electronic monitoring has a vast potential as an effective and inexpensive intermediate form of punishment. For instance, it can easily replace work-release facilities and be used to confine drunk drivers to their homes or places of work.

Conclusion

Let me return to the question posed at the outset: Are private prisons more efficient and effective than public prisons? I have argued that this is not the most important question to ask. My excursion into the history of privatization suggests that the most significant feature of private involvement in corrections is the capacity of the private sector to promote new forms of penalty which expand the capacity of the state to apply the criminal sanction.

Similarly, current privatization efforts may be producing equally significant changes. In recent years the private sector has played a major role in promoting new forms of intermediate level control and new technologies for surveillance and control. In so doing it has helped to expand the reach of the criminal sanction. Indeed these developments suggest that traditional categories and concepts of punishment are insufficient to describe new forms of control, forms that blur the distinction between law enforcement and corrections, punishment and surveillance, custody and liberty.

REFERENCES

Babcock, William (1985). "Corrections and Privatization: An Overview," Prison Journal LXV (2).

Branch-Johnson, W. (1957). The English Prison Hulks. London: Christopher Johnson.

Beattie, John M. (1986). Crime and Courts in England: 1660-1800. Princeton: Princeton University Press. 2 (2): 1-49.

Cable, George W. (1883). Proceedings of the Tenth Annual Conference of Charities and Corrections, pp. 296-7.

Camp, Camille and George Camp (1985). "Correctional Privatization in Perspective," Prison Journal 65:14-31.

Chaiken, Jan and Stephen Mennemeyer (1987). Lease-Purchase Financing of Prison and Jail Construction. Washington, D.C.: National Institute of Justice and U.S. Department of Justice, November.

Cohen, Stanley (1985). Visions of Social Control: Crime, Punishment and Classification. Oxford: Polity Press.

DeWitt, Charles B. (1987). Building on Experience: A Case Study of Advanced Construction and Financing Methods for Corrections. Washington, D.C.: National Institute for Corrections and National Institute of Justice, U.S. Department of Justice, June.

Dickey, Walter (1987). Panel on Corrections Policy. La Follette Institute Conference on Privatization in a Federal System. Wingspread: November 5-7.

DiIulio, John J. (1987). "What's Wrong with Private Prisons," Public Interest, 79-81.

DiIulio, John J. (n.d.). "Private Prisons," Crime File. Washington, D.C.: National Institute of Justice and U.S. Department of Justice.

Ekirch, A. Roger (1987). Bound for America: The Transportation of British Convicts to the Colonies, 1718-1775. Oxford: Clarendon Press.

Elton, G. R. (1953). The Tudor Revolution. Cambridge: Cambridge University Press.

Flanagan, Timothy J. and Katherine M. Jamieson (eds.) (1988). Sourcebook of Criminal Justice Statistics--1987. Washington, D.C.: U.S. Department of Justice.

Foucault, Michael (1979). Discipline and Punish. New York: Vintage Books.

Garland, David (1985). Punishment and Welfare. London: Gower.

Himmelfarb, Gertrude (1968). "The Haunted House of Jeremy Bentham," Victorian Minds. New York: Alfred A. Knopf.

Howard, John [1792] (1929). The State of Prisons. London: J. M. Dent.

Hume, L. J. (1973). "Bentham's Panopticon: An Administrative History--I," Historical Studies XV:703-21.

natieff, Michael (1978). A Just Measure of Pain. London: MacMillan.

risberg, Barry (1989). Presentation at the Center for the Study of Law and Society, University of California, Berkeley, April 17.

:wis, Orlando (1922). The Development of American Prisons and Prison Customs: 1779-1845. Albany, N.Y.: Prison Association of New York.

ivingston, Edward (1873). "Title V" of "A Code of Reform and Prison Discipline," in The Complete Works of Edward Livingston on Criminal Jurisprudence, Vol. II, pp. 590-594. New York: National Prison Association.

ɔgan, Charles H. (1990). Private Prisons: Cons and Pros. New York: Oxford University Press.

:artin, Steve and Sheldon Ekland-Olson (1987). The Walls Came Tumbling Down. Austin, TX: Texas Monthly Press.

acDonald, Douglas (Forthcoming). Prisons for Profits: The Privatization of Corrections.

icAfee. Ward M. (1987). "Tennessee's Private Prison Act of 1986: An Historical Perspective with Special Attention to California's Experience," Vanderbilt Law Review 40:851-865.

[cConville, Sean (1981). A History of Prison Administration, Vol. I, 1750-1877. London: Routledge and Kegan Paul.

[cKelvey, Blake (1977). American Prisons: A History of Good Intentions. Montclair, N.J.: Patterson Smith.

[elossi, Dario and Massimo Pavarini (1981). The Prison and the Factory: Origins of the Penitentiary System. New York: Barnes and Noble.

[ullen, Joan (1985). Corrections and the Private Sector. Washington, D.C.: National Institute of Justice, SNI 191.

'Brien, Patricia (1982). The Promise of Punishment: Prisons in Nineteenth Century France. Princeton: Princeton University Press.

ldham, Wilfred (1933). The Administration of the System of Transportation of British Convicts, 1763-93. Ph.D. Dissertation, University of London.

rivate Vendors in Corrections (1988). National Criminal Justice Reference Service, October 6 (on file with the author).

Radzinowitz, Sir Leon (1968). A History of English Criminal Law and its Administration from 1750. London: Stevens and Sons.

Reports on the General Treatment and Conditions of Convicts in the Hulks at Woolwich with Minutes of Evidence Appendices and Index [1847] (1970). Shannon, Ireland: Irish University Press.

Robbins, Ira P. (1988). The Legal Dimensions of Private Incarceration. Washington, D.C.: Criminal Justice Section, American Bar Association.

Rothman, David (1980). Conscience and Convenience: The Asylum and its Alternatives in Progressive America. Boston: Little Brown.

Rusche, George and Otto Kirchheimer [1939] (1968). Punishment and Social Structure. New York: Russell and Russell.

Ryan, M. and T. Ward (1989). Privatization and the Penal System. Open University Press.

Samaha, Joel (1974). Law and Order in Historical Perspective: The Case of Elizabethan England. New York: Academic Press.

Savas, E. S. (1987). "Privatization and Prisons." Vanderbilt Law Review 40:868-899.

Shearing, C. D. and P. C. Stenning (1983). Private Security and Private Justice. Montreal: Institute for Research on Public Policy.

Smith, Abbott Emerson [1947] (1965). Colonists in Bondage: White Servitude and Convict Labor in America, 1607-1776. Glouster, Mass.: Peter Smith; originally published by University of North Carolina Press.

Spierenburg, P. (1987). "From Amsterdam to Auburn: An Explanation for the Rise of the Prison in 17th Century Holland and 19th Century America," Journal of Social History 4.

Tocqueville, Alexis de. [1836] (1945). Democracy in America. New York: Vintage Books.

Webb, Sidney and Beatrice Webb (1922). English Prisons under Local Government.

Webb, Sidney and Beatrice Webb (1927). English Poor Law History, Part I: The Old Poor Law.

Webb, Sidney and Beatrice Webb (1929). English Poor Law History, Part II.

Wines, E. C. (1880). The State of Prisons and Child Saving Institutions. Cambridge: Cambridge University Press.

NOTES

1. Most of the literature and debate about privatization is framed in terms of whether privatized corrections is marginally more efficient than publicly managed corrections.
2. This tendency is a distinguishing feature of America government, and has been commented on frequently since Tocqueville published his celebrated Democracy in America ([1836] 1961). See, e.g., Walter Dickey (1987).
3. For an excellent overview of the rise of this form of punishment and a description of how it fits within the larger system of punishments of the times, see John M. Beattie (1986:445-519).
4. Smith ([1947] 1965:336) estimates that excluding the Puritan migrations of the 1630s, as many as one-half to two-thirds of all immigrants to the American colonies were indentured servants or transported convicts.
5. In making the claim that transportation expanded the power of the state before it possessed a large administrative apparatus of its own, I do not wish to enter into the controversy over the origins of the modern administrative state. See, e.g., G. R. Elton (1957) who argues that the Tudors developed a relatively sophisticated governmental administration, and Sidney and Beatrice Webb (1922; 1927; 1929) who argue that the administrative state was a product of the nineteenth century. In contrast I simply want to emphasize that with the institution of transportation the state expanded significantly its capacity to punish, and this development in the seventeenth century preceded by many years the expansion of the state's judicial and policing capacities. Although not quite expressed this way, this is one of the main themes of John M. Beattie's (1986) monumental study of English criminal courts in the seventeenth and eighteenth centuries.
6. John Howard ([17992] 1929:289-90] reports the following figures on executions and transportation ordered at London's Old Bailey: 1749-55: 306 executions; 1756-63 (wartime): 139 executions; 1764-71: 233. During this same period, the court ordered over 5,600 offenders to be transported. Howard attributes the decline in capital punishment during this middle period to war, which redirected some offenders who otherwise might have been hanged into naval service. Even though transportation came to be used more frequently towards the end of this period, there was no corresponding decrease in executions. Nor was the level of executions prior to the introduction of transportation anywhere near he level that it was once transportation was embraced. In short, transportation did much more than provide an alternative for capital punishment, it significantly expanded the repertoire of sanctions available to the government. See Howard ([1792] 1929:289-290).
7. There are notable exceptions. See e.g., Melossi and Pavarini (1981); Ignatieff (1978); Rusche and Kirchheimer ([1939] 1968); and Spierenburg (1987).
8. History is, of course, usually written from a winner's perspective. This may account for the fact that contemporary historians have taken the rehabilitative ideal of the early reformers so seriously. However, with the loss of salience of the rehabilitative ideal, if not its demise, and the recent increase of interest in privatization, it is possible to reassess the early experience with prisons. Those early prison policies which contemporary historians have judged failures for their inability to rehabilitate may yet be seen more positively, as successful efforts to design and administer cost-effective institutions.
9. For a sustained discussion of Bentham's plans for Panopticon, see Himmelfarb's chapter entitled "The Haunted House of Jeremy Bentham" (1968) and L. J. Hume (1973:703-21).
10. For an interesting study which shows the intimate connection between the rise of the modern welfare system and the rise of modern penal policies, see Garland (1985).
11. Camp and Camp (1985) identify only a handful of private companies running institutions. In contrast they identify hundreds of private vendors who contract to provide treatment programs for offenders.

ABOUT THE AUTHOR

Malcolm Feeley, B.A., Austin College, M.A., Ph.D. (Political Science), University of Minnesota. Professor Feeley was formerly Professor of Political Science at the University of Wisconsin. He has also held appointments at New York University and Yale. His research interests include the impact of court decisions, the administration of criminal justice and sociological theory. He is the author of *The Process Is The Punishment, Court Reform on Trial,* and *The Policy Dilemma* (with Austin Sarat). In addition he has co-edited and contributed to several major studies of law and social policy, including *Affirmative School Integration* and *The Impact of Supreme Court Decisions*. His current research focuses on the history and antecedents of plea bargaining, court orders affecting conditions in prisons, and a historical study of women and crime.

REAFFIRMING REHABILITATION IN JUVENILE JUSTICE

DAN MACALLAIR
Center on Juvenile and Criminal Justice, San Francisco

This article examines the decline of rehabilitation in juvenile justice throughout much of the United States over the past 20 years. This decline was facilitated by the progressive community's abandonment of rehabilitation and their acceptance of the justice model as a means to restrict the growing number of youths in correctional institutions. The justice model was conceived as a means to impose confinement limitations through standardized sentencing while accommodating conservative demands for retribution and punishment. However, contrary to expectations, the justice model promoted an unprecedented rise in the number of incarcerated youths and a deterioration in institutional conditions. This was occurring despite mounting evidence demonstrating the superior effectiveness of rehabilitation models in altering patterns of delinquency. Conclusions were based on an analysis of juvenile correction systems in California, Massachusetts, Utah, and Washington. The evidence shows that rehabilitation should be reaffirmed as the foundation for a progressive agenda in juvenile justice.

REHABILITATION AND THE JUVENILE JUSTICE SYSTEM

For the past 20 years, the juvenile justice system in the United States has been the subject of the most intensive policy debates in its history. These debates were the result of a number of studies conducted during the 1970s that concluded that most correctional rehabilitation programs had little impact on the offender's postrelease behavior. The most infamous of these studies was the Lipton,

YOUTH & SOCIETY, Vol. 25 No. 1, September 1993 104-125

Martinson, and Wilks (1975) report. After examining 231 evaluation studies of correctional treatment programs, the authors concluded, "With few and isolated exceptions, the rehabilitative efforts that have been reported so far have no appreciable effect on recidivism" (p. 25).

This statement, interpreted as "nothing works," resounded through correctional bureaucracies, legislatures, and the media. The Lipton et al. (1975) report was published at a time when crime rates were on the rise (Krisberg, Schwartz, Litsky, & Austin, 1986). Many viewed this trend as indicative of both a breakdown in the moral and social order and the leniency of the criminal courts.

The indictment of the rehabilitative model, along with growing public concern over crime, propelled a search for an alternative. Conservatives traditionally viewed the philosophy of rehabilitation with derision because it conflicted with their notion of deterrence and reciprocity through punishment. Liberals, lamenting the juvenile justice system's historic emphasis on custody and control, abandoned their traditional support for rehabilitation as impractical. As a result of this dissension, rehabilitation experienced a precipitous decline throughout most of the United States during the 1980s (Greenwood, 1986).

The concept of rehabilitation in juvenile justice was based on the belief that childhood and adolescence are periods of growth and development. Because patterns of proper behavior evolve from nurturing, the goal of benign intervention was to serve the best interests of the child. With the state assuming the role of parent, formal legal procedures and protections were shunned in favor of an informal decision process (Empey, 1982).

For most of the 19th and 20th centuries, youths under the age of 18 were sent to institutions, also known as reform schools or training schools, for offenses such as stubbornness, thievery, truancy, assault, and lewdness. The institution's purpose was to provide a strict and isolated environment far from urban corruption where youths could be imbued with proper work habits and moral fortitude (Empey, 1982).

However, it was soon recognized that involuntary confinement in these institutions bred the worst aspects of human behavior. As a result, staff became obsessed with maintaining order and security. As living conditions grew more restrictive and oppressive, youths became more recalcitrant and the institutional environment became the antithesis of humane individualized care. After reviewing the history of the Massachusetts State Reform School at Westborough, Lief (1988) noted that despite continual attempts to "reconstruct architecture, secularize the curriculum, revise the roles of personnel, rename philosophical objectives, and modify systems of punishment and control . . . it is striking how little the daily experiences of inmates and keepers changed over a period of 128 years" (p. 1).

Under the institutional system, the goal of rehabilitation became subordinate to organizational demands and political expediency. Policymakers, needing a convenient response to crime and poverty issues, continued to expand the number of public training schools throughout the 19th and 20th centuries. By 1960, the position of institutions as the foundation for the juvenile correctional system stood unchallenged.

DIVERSION AND DEINSTITUTIONALIZATION

During the 1960s, the efficacy of correctional institutions came under increasing assault (President's Commission on Law Enforcement and Administration of Justice, 1967a, 1967b). In response, reformers designed new strategies to reduce the number of institutionalized youths. Two primary reforms emerged from these efforts: diversion and deinstitutionalization.

Diversion was designed to encourage police, prosecutors, and probation officers to refer youths to community programs as an alternative to arrest and formal judicial processing. However, later evaluations revealed that diversion was practiced on youths who previously would have been released at the time of intake and not formally processed. In addition, youths who were not deemed eligible for diversion were subjected to harsher treatment and more severe sanctions (Palmer, Bohnstedt, & Lewis, 1978). This situation led researchers to conclude that diversion was actually extending systems of social control (Krisberg & Austin, 1978).

Deinstitutionalization was intended to divert youths from correctional institutions once they were formally processed and committed. One of the most widely reviewed experiments of deinstitutionalization was carried out by the California Youth Authority (CYA) during the 1960s. In an effort to slow its institutional population growth, the CYA, through state legislation, initiated a probation subsidy program to encourage counties to retain youths at the local level. Although its purpose was to reduce commitments to the state juvenile correctional system, it was never intended to replace or supplant the CYA's institutional system. Later studies revealed that throughout the period of probation subsidy institutional expansion in California continued. Although the rate of commitments declined, periods of confinement within CYA institutions were steadily increased to maintain a consistent population. In addition, counties began expanding local training schools and secure detention facilities. The proportion of institutionalized youths throughout California remained unchanged during the period of probation subsidy (Lerman, 1975).

THE ASCENDANCY OF THE JUSTICE MODEL

Disillusioned with the failed efforts of diversion and deinstitutionalization, progressive reformers sought to reconcile their strategies to the institutional system's realities. To reach a compromise with conservative constituencies, many juvenile justice reformers embraced the justice or "just deserts" model of corrections (Castellano, 1986; Cullen & Gilbert, 1982).

First promulgated in the 1970s, the justice model is founded on the concept of fixed and uniform degrees of punishment for specific crimes. Its intent is to inject certainty and consistency into the sentencing process by limiting the discretion of judges and correctional personnel in determining lengths of incarceration. Under this scheme, correctional administrators are no longer expected to pursue rehabilitation or other forms of individualized intervention. Their main function is to administer punishments in a fair and humane manner (Fogel, 1975).

Contrary to the expectations of its proponents, the justice model strengthened the institutional system and left progressive advocates without a compelling alternative. In their critique of the justice model, researchers Cullen and Gilbert (1982) identified three primary failures of this strategy as a basis for progressive reform:

> First, in basing punishment strictly on the crime and not the criminal, implicit in the determinate sentencing paradigm is the assumption that the state not only has no right but also no obligation to do anything about the condition or needs of an offender. Yet, we may ask, is a philosophy that gives legitimacy to state neglect of individual needs likely to be more benevolent than one that mandates, however imperfectly, state concern? Second, it is highly ironic that those who mistrust the state to administer criminal justice rehabilitation in a just and humane manner are now placing their total faith in the state (the legislature in particular) to punish justly and humanely. We have searched in vain to discover the basis for this faith. And third, in the past, the failure of treatment programs has invariably evoked a plea among liberal reformers that inmates receive more and not less rehabilitation. When the new agenda for punishment fails to reduce crime at some point in the future, what will the call be for then? Less punishment—or more? (pp. 19-20)

The reality of Cullen and Gilbert's warnings was quickly manifested. The justice model facilitated unprecedented increases in institutional populations and an accompanying deterioration in confinement conditions.

THE IMPACT OF THE JUSTICE MODEL ON JUVENILE CORRECTIONAL SYSTEMS

The states of Washington and California adopted the justice model through different approaches. However, both approaches had a profound effect on institutional populations.

Washington, in 1977, implemented a comprehensive justice model when the state legislature established mandatory sentencing standards requiring all adjudicated juvenile offenders between the ages of 8 and 17 to serve specified time periods in a correctional institution for specific offenses (Siegel & Senna, 1985).

Within 5 years, the number of institutionalized youths in the state of Washington swelled while confinement conditions deteriorated (Castellano, 1986; Corsaletti, 1991a, 1991b). Although the average length of stay in secure custody initially declined, a higher percentage of youths were committed to state correctional institutions. Since 1984, the average length of stay has increased every year. Currently, the three main facilities are operating at 112% of capacity (Children's Alliance, 1991).

The Washington juvenile correctional system is now the subject of a possible lawsuit over institutional conditions. After touring the state's juvenile training schools, attorneys from the National Center for Youth Law and the Youth Law Center noted that they were all in a state of decay. Programming was compromised for security concerns, and violence and abuse was pervasive. Staff maintain order through the use of police riot equipment, which includes a pepper-based eye spray that incapacitates disruptive youths. Washington's Department of Juvenile Rehabilitation consulting physician, Dr. James Owens, concluded that the product could cause permanent eye damage (D. Lambert, National Center for Youth Law, personal interview, August 1991; C. Wright, Youth Law Center, personal interview, May 1991).

One rationale underlying the Washington State reforms was the belief that recidivism would be lowered by increasing the certainty of punishment. In her study on the effects of Washington's mandatory sentencing guidelines on juvenile recidivism, Schneider (1984) found that the new law had little impact on postrelease behavior and that in urban counties delinquent activity actually increased. This led Castellano (1986) to conclude from his review of the Washington system that "there is no evidence to suggest that the adoption of a 'just deserts' approach to juvenile offending has reduced juvenile delinquency" (p. 502).

In California, uniform confinement guidelines were adopted by the Youthful Offender Parole Board (YOPB) in 1978 following the implementation of the adult determinate sentencing act. The YOPB, composed of gubernatorial appointees, establishes confinement lengths for all youths committed to the California Youth Authority (CYA) by the juvenile courts. Similar to the adult sentencing laws, the YOPB guidelines have been revised upward on three occasions over the past 13 years. According to a recent report by the YOBP,

> the accompanying time intervals were established to be consistent with the time-setting intent described by the Legislature when mandatory sentences for adults committed to State prison were adopted. A still existing correlation was thus established between parole consideration dates and what was then the newly established determinate sentencing law. It was at that time that seven offense categories were identified and an appropriate time interval for each category was assigned. (California Youth Authority, 1988)

The YOPB uses seven categories to designate lengths of institutional stay based on the seriousness of the crime and the youth's prior record.

Although California ostensibly maintains rehabilitation as a guiding principle, the state legislature amended the juvenile court statutes in 1982 to include punishment as a disposition goal:

> Minors under the jurisdiction of the juvenile court as a consequence of delinquent conduct shall, in conformity with the interests of public safety and protection, receive care, treatment and guidance which is consistent with their best interest, which holds them accountable for their behavior, and which is appropriate for their circumstances. . . . Such guidance may include punishment that is consistent with the rehabilitative objectives of this chapter. . . .
>
> (e) As used in this chapter, "punishment" means the imposition of sanctions which include the following:
>
> (1) Payment of a fine by the minor.
> (2) Rendering of compulsory service without compensation performed for the benefit of the community by the minor.
> (3) Limitations on the minor's liberty imposed as a condition of probation or parole.
> (4) Commitment of the minor to a local detention or treatment facility, such as a juvenile hall, camp, or ranch.
> (5) Commitment of the minor to the Department of the Youth Authority (California Welfare and Institutions Code, Section 202).

This amendment legitimized the punitive nature of the California system and provided further impetus toward longer and more severe periods of incarceration.

Within 12 years of the adoption of parole guidelines, the CYA population went from approximately 4,707 to 7,032 (California Youth Authority, Information Services, personal correspondence, September 24, 1991). The absence of a rehabilitative emphasis is evidenced by the large prison design and congregate dormitories. Like the reform schools of the past century, daily conditions in the CYA's 16 juvenile institutions are characterized by extreme degrees of violence, intimidation, and idleness. Little meaningful intervention occurs as youths vie for dominance within a traditional prison subculture (Lerner, 1986).

The increase in incarceration was followed by a corresponding rise in recidivism rates. A study by the National Council on Crime and Delinquency (NCCD) found an alarming 84% rearrest rate for CYA parolees within 3 years of release. In addition, a study by the CYA's own research division cited a rise in recidivism among parolees as periods of institutionalized confinement increased (California Youth Authority, 1988) (see Figures 1 and 2).

The expansion of the CYA population was unrelated to any increase in the crime rate or its severity. In 1988, the CYA was incarcerating a higher degree of less serious delinquent youths than they were in 1977 (see Figures 3 and 4). The justice model's vulnerability to political manipulation and meddling was evident from the start. Because just punishment is a subjective judgment, calls for harsher sentences are easily accommodated within a punitive oriented system (Cullen & Gilbert, 1982). Despite its past limitations, rehabilitation challenged the propriety of conditions within institutions and offered a basis for the development of noninstitutional alternatives. When this expectation was removed, the incentive among correctional bureaucracies to improve conditions or maintain treatment was eliminated.

REHABILITATION AND ORGANIZATIONAL COMMITMENT

While California and Washington were abandoning rehabilitation, Massachusetts and Utah were reconfirming it. Recognizing the failure of the institutional model, Massachusetts, in 1971, under

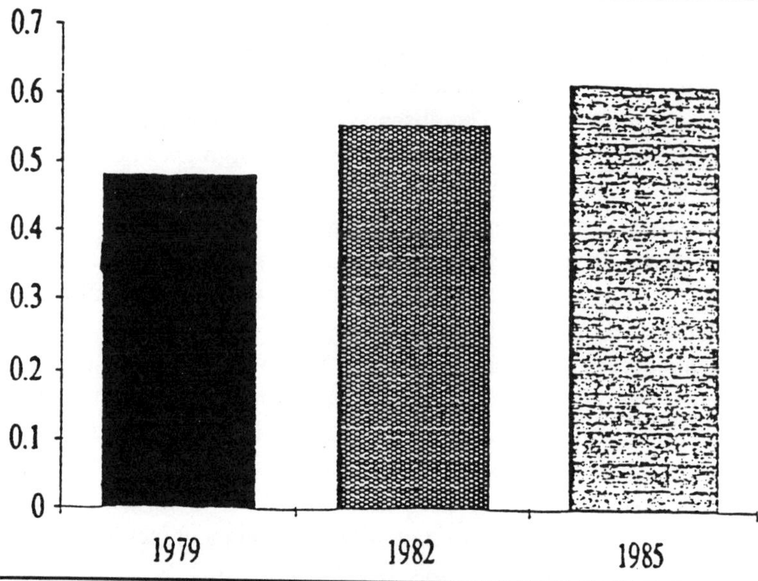

Figure 1: Percentage of People Unsuccessfully Terminated From Parole
Note: 1979, 48.5%; 1982, 55.7%; 1985, 61.8%.
Source: California Youth Authority.

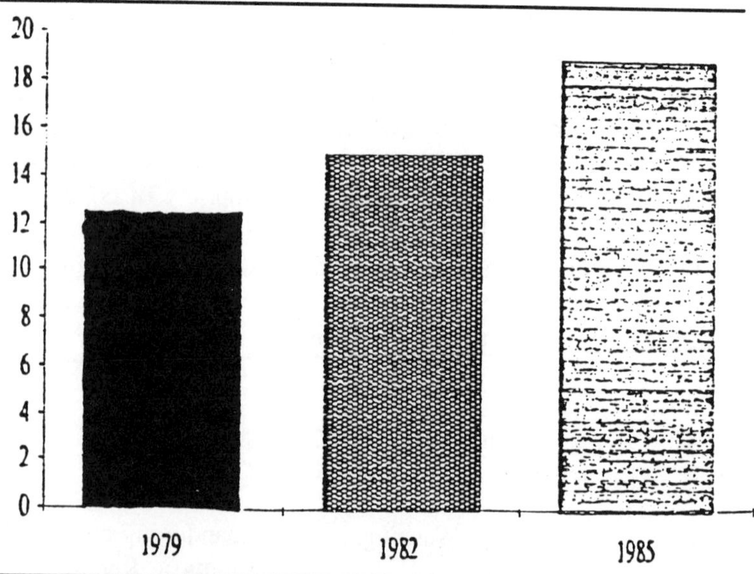

Figure 2: Average Length of Stay at Release for First Commitments (in months)
Note: 1979, 12.6; 1982, 15.0; 1985, 19.1.
Source: California Youth Authority.

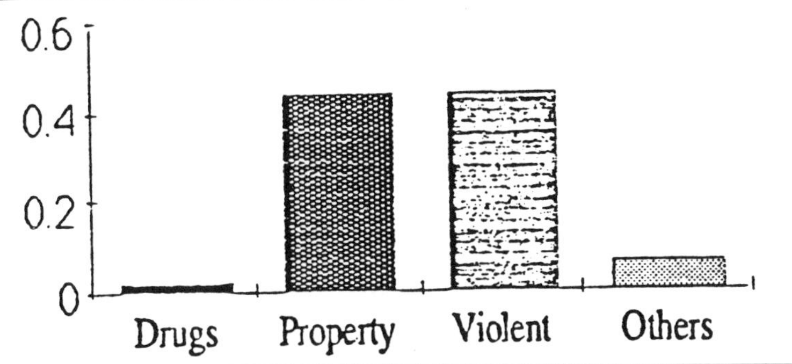

Figure 3: Type of Crime—Offenses Committed by Those Entering CYA Institutions for the First Time (1977)
Note: Drugs, 2.5%; property, 45.3%; violent, 45.1%; others, 7.1%.

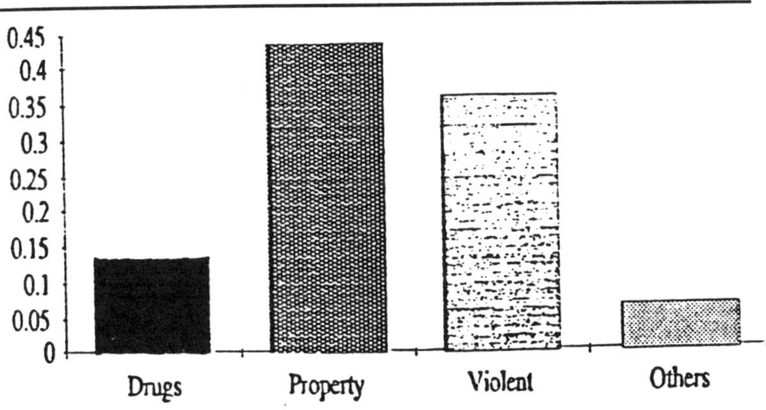

Figure 4: Type of Crime—Offenses Committed by Those Entering CYA Institutions for the First Time (1988)
Note: Drugs, 14%; property, 43.6%; violent, 36.1%; others, 6.3%.
Source: California Youth Authority, California Legislative Analyst.

the leadership of Commissioner Jerome G. Miller, closed its five juvenile correctional training schools (Bakal & Polsky, 1979; Coates, Miller, & Ohlin, 1978; Rutherford, 1974).

Rather than abandon rehabilitation, Miller, on his own initiative, sought to redress the contradictions of the institutional system. He determined that the only way to eliminate institutional violence and abuses was to abolish the training school system. Between 1971 and 1973 all five of the Massachusetts training schools were closed. They were replaced by a network of small community-based programs operating in neighborhoods throughout the state. These reforms were the most dramatic in the history of corrections in America. Never had an established correctional bureaucracy been so completely altered and recast. Miller envisioned that the closing of the institutions would allow the juvenile justice system to finally pursue its original goal of humane individualized treatment (Bakal & Polsky, 1978; Coates et al., 1978; Rutherford, 1974).

Although the initial disruptions and uncertainties resulted in a political backlash and the eventual departure of Commissioner Miller, the closing of the institutions was irreversible. As Miller's successors consolidated the reforms, a consensus developed reinforcing the propriety of the changes (Bakal & Polsky, 1978; Coates et al., 1978; Rutherford, 1974).

Following the Massachusetts example, Utah, in 1980, closed its one 450-bed training school and shifted youths to community-based programs. As in Massachusetts, money that formerly was spent maintaining institutions went toward contracting with private agencies in local communities and neighborhoods. Services were designed to meet the demands of youths with diverse needs and circumstances. For the few youths who required secure confinement, Utah maintains two 35-bed intensive treatment programs (Van Fleet, Rutherford, & Schwartz, 1987).

With a flexible range of programs, the state was able to invest heavily in providing high-quality treatment services for its chronic and violent offenders in secure confinement. What distinguishes these programs from the past large congregate institutions is the absence of a prison subculture. Treatment is comprehensive and individualized. For those youths requiring nonsecure custody, intensive outreach and tracking programs are provided in their home and neighborhoods. This treatment is offered at a fraction of the cost of secure residential treatment or confinement (Krisberg, Austin, Joe, & Steele, 1988).

A study by the National Council on Crime and Delinquency (NCCD) found a 66% decline in the frequency of subsequent arrests for youths released from Utah's juvenile correctional programs during a 12-month follow-up. This "suppression effect" led NCCD researchers to conclude that

> the recidivism data for Youth Corrections offenders strongly indicate that the imposition of appropriate community-based controls on highly active serious and chronic juvenile offenders is consistent with public protection goals. The well-structured community-based programs of Utah's Division of Youth Corrections may well constitute an important new range of dispositional options for handling serious and chronic juvenile offenders. (Krisberg et al., 1988, p. 147)

COMPARING REHABILITATION MODELS WITH JUSTICE MODELS

Of the 1,600 youths committed to the Massachusetts Department of Youth Services in 1990, only 15% are confined in locked secure-treatment programs. The majority of the committed population is spread throughout a variety of residential and nonresidential programs. Approximately 65% of these youths are maintained in their homes with supportive services (Loughran, 1987). The programs used in Massachusetts and Utah include day treatment, temporary care shelter, intensive outreach and tracking, specialized foster care, wilderness adventure, group care, and secure residential (Lerner, 1990).

By contrast, 100% of first commitments to the California Youth Authority (CYA) and 90% of the committed population to the Washington Division of Juvenile Rehabilitation (DJR) are confined in secure correctional institutions. In addition, the average length of confinement in a CYA training school is now 24.7 months, whereas in Massachusetts the average period of time in a secure program is 7.3 months. The vulnerability of justice models to consistent increases in periods of incarceration is reflected in Figure 5. Between 1982 and 1990, the average length of institutional confinement in Washington and California steadily increased; however, it remained relatively stable in Utah. In addition, although yearly figures were not available for Massachusetts, the state's Department of Youth Service (DYS) officials assert that the average

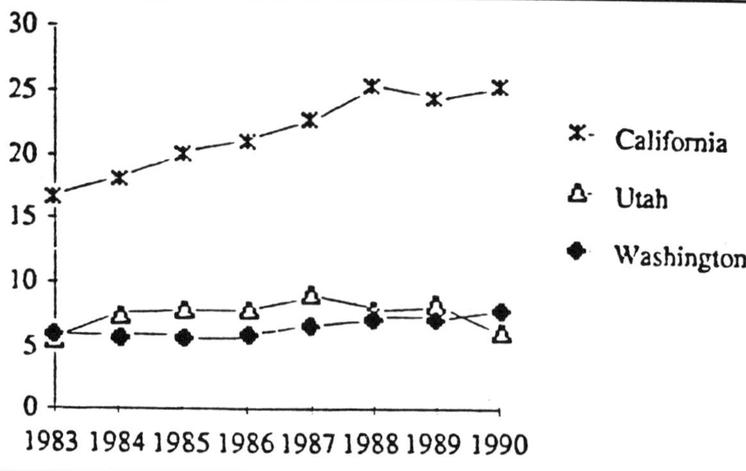

Figure 5: Average Length of Stay in Secure Custody (in months)

length of stay has remained constant (Executive Assistant to the Commissioner, DYS, personal interview, September 1991).

By correctional standards, conditions of confinement in secure facilities in Utah and Massachusetts are considered models of humane treatment, whereas youth correctional institutions in California and Washington are riddled by violence and decay (Corsaletti, 1991a, 1991b; Lerner, 1986, 1990). In addition, a recent study concluded that

> California now incarcerates a higher percentage of its youth for longer periods of time in larger and more secure facilities than any other major state in the nation. Rates of incarceration at local and state levels are twice the national average. (DeMuro, DeMuro, & Lerner, 1988, p. 15)

The differences in the four states is even more startling when census figures from the Office of Juvenile Justice and Delinquency Prevention (OJJDP) on youths in public custody facilities is examined (see Table 1). According to OJJDP researchers Thornberry, Tolnay, Flanagan, and Glynn (1991), public facilities, "whether short-term or long-term, were much more likely to be institutional" (p. 16). Additionally, there are extreme differences between states in the

TABLE 1
Youths in Public Custody Facilities, per 100,000

	1987	*1989*
National average	208	221
California*	496	535
Massachusetts	42	48
Utah	88	85
Washington*	229	236

Source: Office of Juvenile Justice and Delinquency Prevention.
*California has the highest rate among all states, whereas Washington ranks eighth.

TABLE 2
Secure Custody Comparisons, 1990

	Average Daily Population in Secure Confinement	*Percentage of First-Time Commitments in Secure Custody*	*Average Length of Stay in Secure Confinement (in months)*	*Average Number of Prior Sustained Petitions for Youth in Secure Custody*
California	8,209	100	24.7	2.9
Massachusetts	172	15	8.0	N/A
Utah	70	26	7.5	9.0
Washington	587	90	6.3	N/A

Sources: California Youth Authority, Information Services; Massachusetts Department of Youth Services, Executive Assistant to the Commissioner; Utah Division of Youth Corrections, Research Analyst; State of Utah, Administrative Office of the Courts; and Washington Division of Rehabilitative Services, Information Systems Coordinator.

number and type of committed youths placed in institutional confinement (see Table 2).

RECONSIDERING REHABILITATION

The decline of rehabilitation was partly attributed to the perceived failure of researchers to demonstrate clearly that rehabilitation fostered lower rates of recidivism. According to Cullen and Gendreau (1989), “A reality has been constructed and legitimized by many criminologists that rehabilitation is a failed policy that the public will no longer tolerate" (p. 38). As a result of this pervasive perception, tougher sentencing and waivers to adult court became the dominant juvenile justice reform in the majority of states (Greenwood, 1986).

However, during the 1980s new evidence emerged suggesting that the demise of rehabilitation was premature. A growing number of studies indicate that rehabilitative intervention is effective in de-escalating criminal behavior (Gendreau & Ross, 1987; Krisberg et al., 1988). Various well-designed interventions reduce the severity and frequency of delinquency and alter the cycle that leads to adult crime.

Studies have noted that approximately 40% of adult prison populations are graduates of institution-based juvenile justice systems (Rivers & Trotti, 1989). This finding is consistent with reviews of the adult prison population in Massachusetts prior to 1971. According to evaluations, since the reforms of 20 years ago, the number of youths graduating to the adult criminal justice system in Massachusetts has fallen to 15% (Loughran, 1987).

A 1987 evaluation of the Massachusetts juvenile justice system by the NCCD revealed a recidivism rate of 42%, as measured by the number of youths reconvicted of an offense after 1 year. When compared to four other states, Massachusetts had the lowest rates. In contrast, California, the most extreme example of a punitive institutional model, recorded a reconviction rate of 53% (see Figure 6). Finally, only 23% of Massachusetts youths were reincarcerated after 36 months compared to California's rate of 62% (Krisberg, Austin, & Steele, 1989) (see Figure 7).

Well-developed and properly implemented rehabilitative programs are demonstrating tangible evidence of altering delinquent behavior and arrest patterns. For example, the Violent Juvenile Offender (VJO) Program was an experimental project designed to test the effectiveness of intensive programming for chronic and violent juvenile offenders. Services were provided along a continuum starting with secure care and then progressing to community reintegration through intensive case management. The project was tested in four cities around the country. When recidivism results

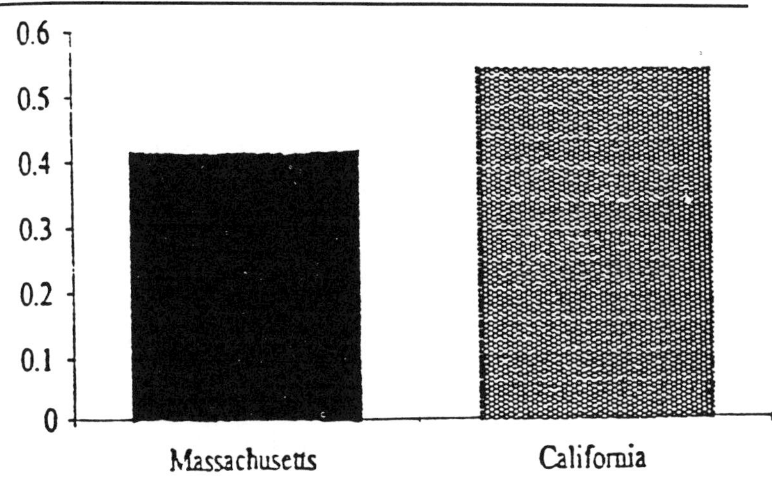

Figure 6: Percentage of Parolees Reconvicted
Note: Massachusetts, 42%; California, 55%.
Source: National Council of Crime and Delinquency.

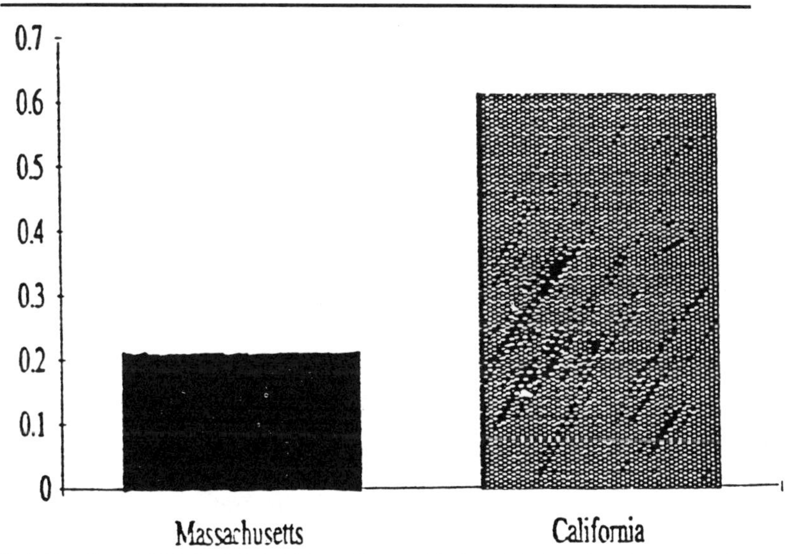

Figure 7: Percentage of Parolees Reincarcerated Within 36 Months of Release
Note: California, 62%; Massachusetts, 22%.
Source: National Council of Crime and Delinquency.

strongly favored the experimental group, researcher Jeffrey Fagan (1990) concluded that

> the VJO Program tested a central proposition: carefully implemented and well-managed programs, rooted in sound theory and advanced practice, can effectively control violent juvenile crime and return offenders to their communities without risking community safety. The well-implemented programs resulted in significant reductions in the number and severity of arrests for experimental youths, as well as in significantly greater time until rearrest. The delays in return to crime for experimental youths during the critical first year following release suggest that the reintegration strategy also may be effective crime control. (p. 258)

The positive effect of other well-designed and implemented intervention models continues to be recognized. A RAND Corporation evaluation of Vision Quest, an experiential education program, showed substantially lower rates of recidivism among Vision Quest graduates, compared to a matched sample of youthful offenders from a county training school in California. The lower recidivism occurred despite the fact that Vision Quest youths had considerably longer and more serious histories of delinquency. After a 1-year follow-up, Vision Quest youths had a recidivism rate of 55%, compared to 71% for the training school youths. In addition, a smaller matched sample of CYA youths recorded a recidivism rate of 88%. Recidivism was measured by new arrests (Greenwood, 1987).

Another study conducted by the Oregon Social Learning Center tested the effectiveness of specialized foster care (SFC) for chronic delinquent youths who were diverted from state correctional institutions. Youths in the experimental group were placed in specialized foster homes and provided with highly individualized treatment. Youths in the comparison group were placed in traditional residential programs or facilities. One year after completing the program, experimental youths had dramatically lower reoffense rates, as measured by subsequent reincarceration. According to Chamberlain (1988),

> During the first year of follow-up post-treatment, 6 of 16 adolescents in the experimental group (38%) and 14 of 16 in the control group (88%) were reinstitutionalized. (p. 10)

> The results presented in this report provide preliminary support for the efficacy of applications of the SFC model. (p. 13)

A study by Palmer and Wedge (1989) on county camps and ranches in California found that smaller individualized programs had rates of recidivism 18% lower than those with more traditional congregate institutional designs and practices. These differences were maintained even among youths with longer and more severe delinquent histories.

The value of intensive case management was demonstrated in 1988 when the State of Maryland closed one of its two training schools by contracting with the National Center on Institutions and Alternatives (NCIA). Under the plan, the state provided funding for the purchase of services on a case-by-case basis. Individualized service plans were implemented for 117 of the institution's most intractable youths. Case managers worked closely with youths to develop trust and understanding, and services were purchased from private sector vendors according to each youth's circumstances and needs. A follow-up evaluation found that after 1 year only 35 youths were rearrested. Of those 35, 1 had committed a violent offense and only 6 were reincarcerated (Lerner, 1990).

Similar results were recorded by NCIA's Hawaii Youth Advocacy Project. NCIA was contracted by the Hawaii Department of Corrections to initiate the process of deinstitutionalization through the closing of Hawaii's youth correctional facility. Through intensive case management, 26 of the total population of 75 youths were returned to the community within a 6-month period. A follow-up evaluation found that only 4 of those 26 were rearrested. This led criminologist Andrew Rutherford (1990) to conclude,

> As only 4 of the 26 releasees have been rearrested for further offenses (for which charges were still pending and none of which involved violence), it is reasonable to conclude that the project was conducted without undue threat to public safety. Indeed, the results strongly suggest that the project has provided enhanced public protection through the new services provided during the three month follow-up period. (p. 19)

The NCIA programs demonstrated the effectiveness of an intensive personalized approach to providing services to the juvenile justice system's most troubled youths. The vital element in achieving success was the programs' vigorous advocacy and the ability of staff to form bonds with youths (Macallair, 1990).

The positive results of the NCIA programs was supported by Lipsey's (1990) meta-analysis of 443 juvenile correctional treatment programs. His analysis showed modest but positive results overall. However, when various types of approaches were examined, dramatic results were observed. For example, Lipsey found that programs employing case work approaches could reduce recidivism by 10% to 20%. In contrast, programs administered by juvenile justice bureaucracies yielded the least favorable results. Programs that used deterrence strategies, such as shock incarceration and "scared straight" approaches, tended to escalate delinquent behavior.

In their comprehensive review of the research on rehabilitation, Gendreau and Ross (1987) concluded that, contrary to popular assumptions, the evidence overwhelmingly indicates that rehabilitation programs work. Although rehabilitation does not eliminate recidivism, it is more effective than correctional institutions in reducing the rate and seriousness of criminal behavior.

CONCLUSION

An examination of juvenile justice in much of the United States reveals a system dominated by archaic 19th-century correctional models and theories. Despite the doctrine of rehabilitation, the institution-based system is an unequivocal failure. As former Office of Juvenile Justice and Delinquency Prevention Director Ira Schwartz (1989) notes, "All large training schools should be closed. These institutions are expensive to operate and difficult to manage, and they simply don't work. They have no place in an enlightened and cost effective youth correctional system" (p. 169).

Due to their past inabilities to alter institutional conditions, reformers have been rendered frustrated and disheartened. This situation led many to resign themselves to the institutional system and embrace the justice model in hopes of at least limiting periods of confinement. However, by abandoning rehabilitation, progressive advocates effectively disarmed themselves in the battle over juvenile justice policy. Legislative and bureaucratic debates came to center on degrees of punishment rather than its legitimacy. Under these conditions, conservatives were able to pursue their agenda of harsher punishments with little opposition.

The acceptance of the justice model by the progressive community proved disastrous. Instead of reining in the power of the institutional system, it served to augment it. To regain the political momentum, reformers must reembrace rehabilitation. Rehabilitation enjoys broad public support as demonstrated in a recent California poll. In contrast to its current public policies, 82% of California residents voiced their belief that the purpose of the juvenile justice system should be the pursuit of rehabilitation (Wallace, 1988).

A commitment to rehabilitation will reignite efforts to dismantle the institution-based system. Those states and jurisdictions that have implemented effective rehabilitation programs provide models on which to build a new reinvigorated progressive agenda. However, a new commitment to rehabilitation will require a resurgence of activism within the progressive community. A return to rehabilitation is presently the only viable strategy for achieving reduction in custodial confinement and promoting the humane and effective treatment of troubled youths.

REFERENCES

Bakal, Y., & Polsky, H. W. (1979). *Reforming corrections for juvenile offenders*. Lexington, MA: Lexington Books.

California Youth Authority, Youthful Offender Parole Board. (1988). *Youth Authority institutional length of stay and recidivism, California juvenile arrest rates, and guidelines for parole consideration dates*. Sacramento: State of California.

Castellano, T. C. (1986). The justice model in the juvenile justice system: Washington State's experience. *Law and Policy, 8*, 479-506.

Chamberlain, P. (1988). *Treatment of chronic delinquents in specialized foster care: A matched comparison study*. Eugene: Oregon Social Learning Center.

Children's Alliance. (1991). *The state of the child: A selected statistical overview*. Seattle, WA: Author.

Coates, R. B., Miller, A. D., & Ohlin, L. E. (1978). *Diversity in a youth correctional system*. Cambridge, MA: Ballinger.

Corsaletti, L. T. (1991a, July 16). Overcrowding at Echo Glen: New urgency to old lawsuit. *Seattle Times*, pp. 1-2.

Corsaletti, L. T. (1991b, August 2). Youth center's staff swamped: State panel told of attacks, stress. *Seattle Times*, p. 10.

Cullen, F. T., & Gendreau, P. (1989). The effectiveness of correctional rehabilitation: Reconsidering the "nothing works" debate. In L. Goodstein & D. L. Mackenzie (Eds.), *The American prison: Issues in research and policy*. New York: Plenum.

Cullen, F. T., & Gilbert, K. E. (1982). *Reaffirming rehabilitation*. Cincinnati, OH: Anderson.

DeMuro, P., DeMuro, A., & Lerner, S. (1988). *Reforming the CYA: How to end crowding and diversify treatment and protect the public without spending more money*. Bolinas, CA: Commonweal Research Institute.

Empey, L. (1982). *American delinquency: Its meaning and construction*. Homewood, IL: Dorsey Press.

Fagan, J. A. (1990). Treatment and reintegration of violent juvenile offenders: Experimental results. *Justice Quarterly*, *7*, 233-263.

Fogel, D. (1975). *We are the living proof . . . ? The justice model for corrections*. Cincinnati, OH: Anderson.

Gendreau, P., & Ross, R. R. (1987). Revivification of rehabilitation: Evidence from the 1980's. *Justice Quarterly*, *4*, 249-407.

Greenwood, P. (1986). *Juvenile offenders*. Washington, DC: U. S. Department of Justice, National Institute of Corrections.

Greenwood, P. (1987). *An evaluation of the Vision Quest Program*. Santa Monica, CA: RAND.

Krisberg, B., & Austin, J. (1978). *The children of Ishmael*. Palo Alto, CA: Mayfield.

Krisberg, B., Austin, J., Joe, K., & Steele, P. (1988). *The impact of juvenile court sanctions*. San Francisco: National Council on Crime and Delinquency.

Krisberg, B., Austin, J., & Steele, P. A. (1989). *Unlocking juvenile corrections: Evaluating the Massachusetts Department of Youth Services*. San Francisco: National Council on Crime and Delinquency.

Krisberg, B., Schwartz, I. M., Litsky, P., & Austin, J. (1986). The watershed of juvenile justice reform. *Crime & Delinquency*, *32*, 5-37.

Lerman, P. (1975). *Community treatment and social control: A critical analysis of juvenile correctional policy*. Chicago: University of Chicago Press.

Lerner, S. (1986). *Bodily harm: The pattern of fear and violence at the California Youth Authority*. Bolinas, CA: Commonweal Research Institute.

Lerner, S. (1990). *The good news about juvenile justice: The movement away from large institutions and toward community-based services*. Bolinas, CA: Commonweal Research Press.

Lief, J. G. (1988). *A history of the internal organization of the State Reform School for Boys at Westborough, Massachusetts (1846-1974)*. Unpublished doctoral dissertation, Harvard University.

Lipsey, M. W. (1990). *Juvenile delinquency treatment: A meta-analytic inquiry into the variability of effect*. Unpublished manuscript, Claremont Graduate School, Claremont, CA.

Lipton, D., Martinson, R., & Wilks, J. (1975). *The effectiveness of correctional treatment: A survey of treatment evaluation studies*. New York: Praeger.

Loughran, E. (1987). Juvenile corrections: The Massachusetts experience. In L. Edison (Ed.), *Reinvesting youth corrections resources: A tale of three states*. Ann Arbor: University of Michigan, Center for the Study of Youth Policy.

Macallair, D. (1990, Spring). ACLU's demands trigger change in Hawaii's juvenile justice system. *National Prison Project Journal*, pp. 5-6.

Palmer, T., Bohnstedt, M., & Lewis, R. (1978). *The evaluation of juvenile diversion projects: Final report*. Sacramento: California Youth Authority.

Palmer, T., & Wedge, R. (1989). California's juvenile probation camps: Findings and implications. *Crime & Delinquency, 35*, 234-253.

President's Commission on Law Enforcement and Administration of Justice. (1967a). *The challenge of crime in a free society*. Washington, DC: U.S. Government Printing Office.

President's Commission on Law Enforcement and Administration of Justice. (1967b). *Task Force report: Juvenile delinquency and youth crime*. Washington, DC: U.S. Government Printing Office.

Rivers, J., & Trotti, T. (1989). *South Carolina delinquent males: A follow-up into adult corrections*. Columbia: South Carolina Department of Youth Services.

Rutherford, A. (1974). *The dissolution of the training schools in Massachusetts*. Columbus, OH: Academy of Contemporary Problems.

Rutherford, A. (1990). *Assessment of the Hawaii Youth Advocacy Project*. Southampton, England: University of Southampton.

Schneider, A. L. (1984). Sentencing guidelines and recidivism rates of juvenile offenders. *Justice Quarterly, 1*(1), 107-124.

Schwartz, I. M. (1989). *(In)justice for juveniles: Rethinking the best interests of the child*. Lexington, MA: Lexington Books.

Siegel, L. J., & Senna, J. J. (1985). *Juvenile delinquency: Theory, practice, and law*. St. Paul, MN: West.

Thornberry, T., Tolnay, S. E., Flanagan, T. J., & Glynn, P. (1991). *Children in custody, 1987: A comparison of public and private juvenile custody facilities*. Washington, DC: Office of Juvenile Justice and Delinquency Prevention.

Van Fleet, R., Rutherford, A., & Schwartz, I. M. (1987). Reinvesting in youth corrections resources in Utah. In L. Edison (Ed.), *Reinvesting youth corrections resources: A tale of three states*. Ann Arbor: University of Michigan, Center for the Study of Youth Policy.

Wallace, B. (1988, December 13). Big majority opposes jailing juveniles. *San Francisco Chronicle*, p. 1.

Dan Macallair is currently the director of juvenile justice projects for the Center on Juvenile and Criminal Justice in San Francisco. His expertise is in the development of placement options for youthful offenders and designing strategies for systems reform. He has been a featured speaker at a number of national and regional conferences on issues of juvenile justice policy. He has published articles and provided testimony to state and county legislative committees. Prior to joining CJCJ, he was the education director of the Homeward Bound program of the Massachusetts Department of Youth Services. He holds a master's degree in public administration with a concentration in juvenile justice and community-based corrections.

PROBATION AND PAROLE: PUBLIC RISK AND THE FUTURE OF INCARCERATION ALTERNATIVES*

MICHAEL R. GEERKEN
HENNESSEY D. HAYES
The Orleans Parish Criminal Sheriff's Office and Tulane University

Jail and prison populations in the United States have continued to grow unabated during the past two decades but crime rates have not declined. Partly in response to the pressures caused by burgeoning correctional populations, the use of alternatives to incarceration has expanded. An ongoing debate centers on the effectiveness of these alternatives. Many criminal justice professionals and some researchers question whether such alternatives seriously restrict the criminal justice system's ability to incapacitate the active offender. This study deals specifically with two alternatives to incarceration: probation and parole. We examine offender recidivism for a sample of probationers and parolees active in New Orleans, Louisiana, and offer a new approach to addressing the effectiveness issue. Past research has evaluated the effectiveness of alternatives by examining failure rates of diverted offenders. High failure rates, we argue, do not necessarily imply a significant loss of the incapacitative effects of imprisonment. We suggest that a more appropriate measure of the loss of incapacitative effect is the proportion of all offenses committed by persons on probation or parole. Our results suggest that such losses are surprisingly low. The policy implications of our findings are discussed.

The use of alternatives to incarceration has become very controversial in recent years. Rapidly increasing jail and prison populations have led to calls for increasing the use of alternatives, while continued high crime rates have led to demands for reductions in their use through mandatory sentencing and tough sentencing guidelines.

The contradictory pressures of jail and prison overcrowding and high crime rates have resulted in a heated debate over the continued use of alternatives to incarceration. Proponents of alternatives believe that diversion from

* This research was supported by the National Institute of Justice, U.S. Department of Justice, grants 86–IJ–CX–0021 and 90–IJ–CX–0019. Contents of this document do not necessarily reflect the views or policies of the National Institute of Justice or the U.S. Department of Justice. We would like to thank Sheriff Charles C. Foti, Jr., for his invaluable cooperation and support of this project, as well as James D. Wright, Joseph Sheley, and several anonymous reviewers for their helpful comments on earlier versions of this paper.

incarceration serves the interests of the criminal justice system and the offender. Alternatives help to lessen the administrative pressures of increasing jail and prison populations and they facilitate the reform efforts of offenders. On the other hand, those who are skeptical about the effectiveness of alternatives argue that offenders rarely reform on release from custody, and that a significant percentage of all offenders released through some form of incarceration alternative continue to commit crimes. Those offenders are responsible, they argue, for a significant amount of all reported crime. For example, Petersilia et al. (1985) reported that approximately two-thirds of a sample of felony probationers in California were rearrested during a 40-month follow-up period. The results of this study received a great deal of attention, and the effectiveness of felony probation was seriously questioned.

Other research on probation, however, has shown that the results of Petersilia et al.'s (1985) study may be unique to felons in California. Vito (1986), who followed a sample of felony probationers in Kentucky for 36 months, found that only 22% were rearrested. Likewise, McGaha et al. (1987) followed a sample of felony probationers in Missouri for 40 months and found that only 22% were rearrested. These authors concluded that probation for felony offenders is relatively effective and that failure rates of 22% do not warrant abolishment of probation as a sentencing alternative.

In addition to these studies, Petersilia et al. (1986) reevaluated their sample of felony probationers. In the second study probationers were matched with a sample of prison releasees, and the recidivism rates of both groups were compared. The authors found that those released from prison recidivated at higher rates than did the probationers.

Petersilia et al.'s 1986 findings raise questions about the effects of incarceration on postrelease offending and arrest; that is, whether jail and prison actually contribute to a greater likelihood of postrelease offending and whether this effect cancels out the loss in incapacitative effect caused by use of probation. They concluded that probationers still committed a marginally higher number of crimes during the study period. Unfortunately, however, there remains a shortage of reliable evidence regarding the effects of incarceration on the likelihood of postrelease offending and arrest. Nevertheless, it is known that probationers' offenses are more likely to be detected merely by virtue of their supervision (Turner et al., 1992).

Yet, there remains a degree of skepticism among some criminal justice professionals and researchers about the effectiveness of alternatives to incarceration for felony offenders. In fact, our own informal discussions with a number of criminologists convince us that it is commonly believed that probationers and parolees, in particular, are responsible for a significant percentage of crime. In this paper we examine the evidence on which this belief is based.

We begin by summarizing the literature on probation and parole effectiveness and then we add results from our study of a sample of probated and paroled offenders arrested for burglary or armed robbery in New Orleans, Louisiana. While these results are indicative of the effectiveness of specific incarceration alternatives for the offender, they offer little information about the impact these alternatives have on the incapacitative effect of the criminal justice system.

In this paper we argue that measures of crimes committed while under alternative forms of supervision do not provide an appropriate basis for making policy recommendations about the use of such alternatives. Instead, the *contribution* of these crimes to the overall crime rate is the proper framework within which to formulate policy and provides an upper limit to the impact any restriction in the use of alternatives can have. Thus, we estimate the percentage of crime committed by persons on probation or parole to obtain a more valid estimate of the loss of incapacitative effect caused by continued use of these alternatives.

RESEARCH ON PROBATION AND PAROLE EFFECTIVENESS

A relatively recent review of research on probation prior to the 1980s shows that the percentage of probationers who "fail" (defined in various ways across studies) ranges anywhere from 16% to 55% (Allen et al., 1985; see Table 1). Studies that defined failure as a reconviction yielded the lowest failure rates because probationers are more likely to avoid reconviction than rearrest (Sutherland et al., 1992:460).

A more recent study conducted by the Rand Corporation examined the success or failure rates of a sample of 1,672 offenders convicted of felonies in Los Angeles and Alameda counties, California (Petersilia, 1985a, 1985b; Petersilia et al., 1985). They found that approximately two-thirds (65%) of the offenders were arrested before their probation period expired. In addition, 51% of the sample members were reconvicted and 34% were reincarcerated. The authors concluded that use of probation as a sentencing alternative should perhaps be reduced for felony offenders and that perhaps one viable alternative sentence for felony offenders would be the increased use of intensive supervision (ISP), a form of probation requiring several contact visits and, in most cases, ongoing drug testing. They cautioned however, that ISP programs should be sufficiently evaluated before their use is promoted for all felony offenders.[1]

1. Turner et al. (1992) subsequently conducted an evaluation of several ISP programs involving probated drug offenders. Their results indicated that ISP programs did not significantly reduce the likelihood of rearrest. In fact, the number of offenders in ISP programs arrested on technical violations increased. This finding was partly due to the

In a study released by the Bureau of Justice Statistics (Langan and Cunniff, 1992) on the recidivism rates of probated felons, the authors reported that, of approximately 79,000 felons sentenced to probation in state courts in 32 U.S. counties, 43% were rearrested for a felony within three years of sentencing.

Whitehead (1991) examined the effectiveness of probation for a sample of New Jersey probationers. Unlike the studies reviewed by Allen et al. (1985), Whitehead varied his measure of recidivism and noted the effects on failure rates. When the measure was rearrest, 36% of probationers failed. However, when the measure was incarceration, the failure rate dropped to 15%. These rates were observed after three years of follow-up. After four years of follow-up, 40% were rearrested, but only 17% were reincarcerated.

The use of parole for the serious offender raises similar concerns about recidivism and public safety. Based on figures provided in the Uniform Parole Reports, Allen et al. (1985) reported that for 1979 approximately 25% of all felons released on parole were rearrested before the expiration of their term. They noted, however, that some of the failures were due to violations of the conditions of parole. In a more recent study, conducted by the Attorney General's Office for the state of Hawaii, researchers found that, of 366 offenders (approximately 68% of whom were arrested for an index offense) released on parole, approximately 46% were rearrested before their term expired (Attorney General's Office, 1989). In an even more recent study, Gould et al. (1991) followed a sample of 102 nonviolent offenders released on parole from the Louisiana Department of Public Safety and Corrections for 12 months. They found that, when failure was defined as "revocation of the parole status" (p. 11), the failure rate observed was approximately 25%.

We have calculated failure rates, for probation and parole, for a group of burglary and armed robbery offenders whose 1974–1986 criminal justice records were assembled for the New Orleans Offender Study (Geerken et al., 1993, see Table 2). We selected the 4,160 terms of probation and the 327 terms of parole that began for sample members between January 1, 1974 and December 31, 1981.[2] Fifty percent of the probationers and 46% of the parolees were rearrested for an index offense during their period of supervision.

The results of the studies we reviewed along with the results from our sample indicate that there is a great deal of inconsistency in the degree of failure observed across samples and jurisdictions. Including more recent studies of probation effectiveness and the probation effectiveness observed for our sample with those reviewed by Allen et al. (1985; see Table 1), the range of failure

strict nature of the surveillance for offenders in the ISP program. Nevertheless, ISP programs resulted in increased program costs without concomitant reductions in offending by program participants.

2. We did this to reduce right censoring and, in fact, 97% of these terms expired or were completed by reincarceration before the end of the measurement period.

rates is 12% to 65%. The failure rates reported in Table 1 are inconsistent for a variety of reasons. First, researchers still have not arrived at a consensus on what the definition of probation failure should be. Second, the follow-up periods are markedly dissimilar across studies. Third, offender populations and data collection and recordkeeping methods vary significantly across jurisdictions.

Allen et al. (1985) noted that "while most [researchers] agree that recidivism should be a primary performance measure, there is no agreement on its definition nor on the indicators to be used for its measurement" (p. 249). It is apparent from the New Orleans Offender Study results that the failure rate is quite sensitive to failure criterion. Failure rates for offenders in our study ranged from 31% to 71% for probation and from 21% to 65% for parole. If we compare studies with similar failure criteria, however, the range narrows. Although rearrest rates range from 12% to 65%, 7 of the 11 studies fall in the 33% to 65% range.[3] Reconviction rates range from 16% to 55%, although if the two studies of white-collar crimes from the 1950s (Caldwell, 1951; England, 1955; see Table 1) are eliminated, the remaining four failure rates range from 30% to 55%.[4]

Comparing the studies conducted on parole success yields similar inconsistencies. The failure (defined as rearrest) rates for parolees reported in the studies we reviewed along with the rate observed for our own sample range from 25% to 46%. However, comparisons of reported parole effectiveness are also suspect because offenders, follow-up periods, jurisdictions, failure criteria, and sentencing policies vary markedly across studies.

Regardless of the degree of inconsistency in reported success or failure of probation and parole across studies, one general conclusion emerges: if the criterion for failure is rearrest, a significant proportion of offenders placed on probation or parole will recidivate before their term expires. Including results obtained from our own data, from one-third to two-thirds of all probationers were rearrested, and from one-quarter to one-half of all parolees were rearrested.

These failure rates are substantial enough to warrant concern over the future use of probation and parole. Given the high failure rates and large number of offenders under probation or parole supervision,[5] it can be argued

3. From Table 1, these studies are Clarke et al. (1988), Geerken and Hayes (1993), Irish (1972), Jones (1991), Langan and Cunniff (1992), and Whitehead (1991).

4. From Table 1, these studies are Comptroller General (1976), Irish (1972), Missouri Division of Probation and Parole (1976), and Whitehead (1991).

5. In recent years the number of convicted offenders released on probation has continued to rise. In 1983 the rate per 100,000 U.S. adult residents at which offenders were placed under probationary supervision was 897; in 1990 this rate was 1,443 (Flanagan and Maguire, 1991; Flanagan and McGarrell, 1985). Greenfeld (1987) reported that approximately 60% of all convicted felons are placed on probation in a given year. The parole

that the elimination of these alternatives would result in a significant decrease in crime. Indeed, the potential effect on the crime rate of reducing the use of probation and parole—and substituting imprisionment—is important for policy. But the proper measure of this effect is not the probation or parole failure rate, regardless of the criterion one uses to measure failure. Instead, the percentage of all crimes committed by persons on probation or parole provides an estimate of the potential effect on the crime rate of replacing these forms of supervision with imprisonment and, therefore, of the incapacitative effect lost through these alternatives. To our knowledge, such a calculation has not been made.

Below, we attempt to answer the following question: What reduction in crime might be achieved through a reduction in the use of probation and parole? This question has not been addressed by researchers on alterntives to incarceration. The answer to the question is both relevant and important if informed decisions are to be made about the future of sentencing alternatives for serious offenders.

DATA

The official record data base of the New Orleans Offender Study contains the 1974–1986 arrest, incarceration, and probation and parole supervision histories of the 22,497 individuals who were arrested for burglary or armed robbery in New Orleans from 1973 through 1986.[6] The data base was compiled from the following criminal justice data bases (Geerken and Hayes, 1992; Geerken et al., 1993):

1. the New Orleans jail information management system (STARS) for 1981 through 1986;
2. the New Orleans Police Department's arrest history system (MOTION) for 1973 through 1986;
3. the Louisiana adult penitentiary and probation/parole information system (CAJUN) for 1974 through 1986;
4. the Louisiana juvenile corrections information system (JIRMS) for 1974 through 1986; and
5. the Louisiana criminal history system (FINDEX) for 1974 through 1986, which includes information on out-of-state arrests maintained by the Federal Bureau of Investigation on individuals arrested for serious offenses in Louisiana.

---

population has also increased markedly between 1983 and 1990. The rate per 100,000 U.S. adult residents under parole supervision was 147 in 1983 and 287 in 1990 (Flanagan and Maguire, 1991; Flanagan and McGarrell, 1985).

6. Actually, 22,561 offenders originally met these criteria, but 64 offenders had to be removed because of identification or unsolvable coding problems.

Table 1. Studies Reporting Recidivism Rates for Probationers

Study	Instant Offense	Follow-up Period	Failure Criterion	Failure Rate (%)
Caldwell (1951)	Internal Revenue Laws (72%)	Postprobation: 5½–11½ years	Conviction	16.4
Davis (1964)	Burglary; forgery and checks	To termination: 4–7 years	2 or more violations/ revocations (technical and new offenses)	30.2
England (1955)	Bootlegging (48%) and forgery	Postprobation: 6–12 years	Conviction	17.7
Frease (1964)		On probation: 18–30 months	Inactive letter, bench warrant, revocation	20.2
Landis (1969)	Auto theft, forgery and checks	To termination	Revocation (technical and new offenses)	52.5
Irish (1972)	Larceny and burglary	Postprobation: minimum of 4 years	Arrest or conviction	41.5
Comptroller General (1976)		Postprobation: 20-month average	Revocation and postrelease conviction	55.0
Kusuda (1976)	Property	To termination: 1–2 years	Revocation	18.3
Missouri Division of Probation and Parole (1976)	Burglary, larceny, and vehicle theft	Postprobation: 6 months–7 years	Arrest and conviction	30.0
Irish (1977)	Property	Postprobation: 3–4 years	Arrest	29.6
Petersilia (1985a)[a]	Felonies	40 months from term initiation	Rearrest	65
Vito (1986)[a]	Felonies	36 months from term initiation	Rearrest	22
McGaha et al. (1987)[a]	Felonies	40 months from term initiation	Rearrest	22
Clarke et al. (1988)[a]	Felonies	3 years from term initiation	Rearrest	33
Irish (1989)[a]	Felonies	5 years from term initiation	Rearrest Violations Rearrests and violations	12 6 26
Jones (1991)[a]	Felonies and misdemeanors	From term initiation to 5-1-87 (median 3.4 years at risk)	Rearrest	39
Whitehead (1991)[a]	Felonies	3 and 4 years from term initiation	Rearrest Reconvicted Incarcerated Imprisoned	3 & 4 yrs. 36, 40 31, 35 15, 17 9, 11
Langan and Cunniff (1992)[a]	Felonies	3 years from term initiation	Rearrest	43
Geerken and Hayes (1993)[b]	Index offenses	To term expiration	Rearrest	50

SOURCE: Harry E. Allen et al. (1979:35).

[a] These studies do not appear in the original table but are included here to provide more recent information on probation effectiveness.

[b] Result extracted from Table 2 of this paper.

Table 2. Probation and Parole Failure Rates, by Failure Criterion, for Persons Placed on Probation, 1974 through 1986

	Probation (N = 4,160)			Parole (N = 327)		
Failure Criterion	Percent Failed	Number Failed	Mean Days To Failure	Percent Failed	Number Failed	Mean Days To Failure
Reincarceration in Penitentiary	31.0	1,291	617	20.8	68	579
Violent Index Arrest	38.7	1,611	395	34.3	112	409
Any Index Arrest	50.0	2,081	356	45.6	149	362
Any Index or Drug Arrest	55.5	2,309	343	49.9	163	338
Any Arrest Except Alcohol-related and Traffic	65.6	2,731	315	60.9	199	319
Any Arrest Except Traffic	69.8	2,902	300	63.3	207	301
Any Non-traffic Arrest Including Technical Violations	70.5	2,932	299	64.5	211	299

METHOD

To determine the impact that probated or paroled offenders have on the burglary and armed robbery rate, we examined the percentage of all burglary and armed robbery arrests between 1974 and 1986 that involved persons on probation or parole at the time. The New Orleans Offender Study data base is uniquely suited to making this calculation because it includes every arrest for burglary and every arrest for armed robbery in New Orleans during the study period and the supervision status of the arrestee.

Note that we can determine the probation and parole status of the offender only for arrests rather than crimes. In this analysis we assume, therefore, that the probability of arrest after commission of a crime is no different for probationers/parolees than for nonprobationers/nonparolees. Evidence suggests, however, that probationers' offenses are more likely to be detected (MacKenzie, 1991; Turner et al., 1992).

RESULTS

Table 3 indicates that only about 8% of adult arrests for burglary or armed robbery involved offenders on probation. Between 1% and 2% of all adult arrests for these crimes involved offenders on parole.

Table 3. Percentage of Burglary and Armed Robbery Arrests Between 1974 and 1986 for Persons on Probation and Parole

Index Offense	Percent Arrests of Persons on Probation (*N*)	Percent Arrests of Persons on Parole (*N*)	Total Arrests
Burglary	8.1 (1,981)	1.3 (320)	24,520
Armed Robbery	8.4 (1,100)	1.8 (233)	13,020

These percentages are contrary to expectation and surprisingly low. They suggest that even the complete elimination of probation and parole would have a very negligible effect on the burglary and armed robbery rates since more than 90 percent of all burglaries and armed robberies were committed by persons *not* on probation or parole at the time of their arrest. We draw no conclusion about the frequency of criminal activity of probationers or parolees compared with other groups of offenders. We argue only that since a low percentage of all burglary and armed robbery arrests are of persons on probation or parole at the time, policy changes tightening or eliminating these forms of supervision can affect only a small percentage of these crimes. Specifically, we argue that even complete abolishment of probation and parole would not affect the crime rate by more than 10 percent for either burglary or armed robbery. Note that these results measure the percentage of *adult* arrests involving persons under probation or parole supervision. The percentage of *all* arrests that could be affected by adult probation/parole policy is about 6%.[7]

The percentage of all index charges for the study population while on adult probation is 6.3%; on adult parole, 0.9%. Since we do not have a complete count of all index arrests—only those for this population—the results for index crimes other than burglary and armed robbery must be interpreted with caution. Nevertheless, it is likely that policy changes tightening probation and parole would have a minimal effect on other index offenses as well.

We note that even these low increases in the incapacitative effect that could be achieved by eliminating probation and parole are probably exaggerated, for a number of reasons, and that the true improvement in incapacitative effect would be even lower. If probation was eliminated as an alternative

7. Our data base does not include information on juvenile probation.

option, for example, many guilty pleas now obtained through plea bargaining would not be secured, and many more cases would go to trial (Champion, 1988b:45–48; Champion, 1988a). In a certain percentage of these cases, the defendant would be found not guilty and, therefore, not incarcerated. In addition, it is not clear that "mandatory" sentencing guidelines can, in fact, be enforced. Tonry (1992) points out that many judges and prosecutors attempt to secure guilty pleas by ignoring mandatory sentencing guidelines and imposing or seeking probation, and that judges may be more inclined to dismiss cases for which probation would have served as an appropriate sentence rather than follow mandatory guidelines. Finally, as noted, we assume that the probability of arrest for a crime is the same for those under probation or parole supervision as for those who are not. It has been argued, however, that supervision increases the chance of arrest for a crime (MacKenzie, 1991:218; Turner et al., 1992). If this is so, the percentage of *arrests* while under supervision will provide an overestimate of the percentage of crimes committed while under supervision.

The reason the high failure rates for these alternatives do not translate into a comparable effect on the crime rate can be illustrated by an example. We selected the 1957 birth cohort from our sample (ages 17–29 during 1974–1986) for detailed analysis.[8] This cohort ($N = 1{,}293$) had a 49% failure rate for its 604 terms of probation (failure defined as any index arrest). Yet, only 8.9% of all index arrests occurred while on probation for this cohort during these ages. The reason can be simply explained. Only 41% of the cohort had any probation terms. Of those who had probation terms, only 20% of their 13 young-adult years was spent on probation. From these two figures, alone, one can expect that only 8% (20% of 41%) of arrests would occur during probation terms, assuming that arrest rates during probation are the same as arrest rates for periods not on probation.

Some critics might argue that our findings concerning probation are probably the result of probation policies specific to New Orleans or Louisiana and other "tough" sentencing states. That is, it might be argued that finding such a low loss of incapacitative effect for probation is due to the nature of a probation policy in Louisiana, and New Orleans in particular, that reserves probation for the mild, less serious offender. The evidence, however, is that the opposite may be true.

A study of sentencing practices in 18 U.S. municipalities (Cunniff, 1984:25) shows that 34% of all convicted serious offenders in New Orleans were placed on probation for an average term of 2.72 years (see Table 4). Moreover, the second highest rate of probation disposition (55%) among the 18

8. We selected these ages because 87% of all probation terms occur at these ages.

cities was observed for Jefferson Parish, Louisiana, which borders New Orleans.[9] Of all 18 cities examined, New Orleans ranked seventh in the percentage of all serious offenders placed on probation. It is clear, therefore, that the probation policies affecting the New Orleans Offender Study population are no more selective than those of other large U.S. cities, and perhaps less so.

Table 4. Percentage of All Sentences Involving Straight Probation Terms in Selected Municipalities

Municipality	Percent	Average Term in Years
Denver	58	2.31
Jefferson Parish	*55*	*2.08*
Maricopa County	45	2.97
Riverside County	43	3.07
Baltimore County	39	2.85
Oklahoma County	37	2.86
New Orleans	*34*	*2.72*
Jefferson County	33	4.79
Baltimore City	32	3.75
Milwaukee County	32	2.53
Philadelphia	31	3.46
Lucas County	26	2.93
Lancaster County	25	2.14
Davidson County	22	3.48
Hennepin County	17	3.81
Kane County	12	1.64
Dade County	9	4.65
Los Angeles County	9	3.23

SOURCE: Cunniff (1984).

A better indication that local probation and parole policies are typical of other jurisdictions is the failure rates observed for this sample. Recall that offenders in our study failed at rates at least as high as those reported in most other studies on probation and parole effectiveness (see Table 2; cf. Table 1). Table 2 indicates that when the failure criterion is arrest for "any index offense," 50% of the probationers and 46% of the parolees failed. Table 2 also indicates that, regardless of the criterion one uses for program failure,

9. Of the 51,739 index arrests in the study data base that occurred from 1980 through 1986, 86% (43,196) occurred in New Orleans and 9% (4,749) occurred in Jefferson Parish. Thus, this study of sentencing practices is directly applicable to about 93% of the arrests for our study population.

probationers and parolees in our sample failed at fairly similar rates, but parolees are uniformly less likely to fail.

Thus, it seems that the offenders followed in this study tended to recidivate at rates at least as high as offenders examined in most other jurisdictions, and that probation was used as a sentencing option as often in New Orleans as in most other cities. The findings reported in Table 2 are, therefore, indicative of the ineffectiveness of probation and parole for burglary and armed robbery offenders in New Orleans and demonstrate that probated and paroled offenders are as criminally active as those in other studies. The limited negative effect probation and parole have on the incapacitative effect of the criminal justice system in New Orleans, therefore, can be generalized to other jurisdictions.

THE LIMITS OF "GET TOUGH" POLICY

We acknowledge that caution must be exercised whenever one considers the results of a study limited in offender type and jurisdiction. Our purpose here has not been a complete evaluation of probation and parole policies in New Orleans,[10] but rather a determination of the impact that elimination of these alternatives would have on the incapacitative effect of the criminal justice system. While the failure rates for the New Orleans Offender Study sample add to the body of literature on probation and parole effectiveness, our focus is primarily on the finding that these high failure rates for burglary and armed robbery are coupled with a minimal loss of incapacitative effect for these offenses.

This finding, that the incapacitative effects of probation and parole elimination are minimal, is both surprising and important.[11] These results do not provide the means to make precise estimates of the effect of changes in probation and parole policy. They do, however, provide an upper limit of the effect any *tightening* of probation and parole policies would have on the crime rate through an increase in incapacitation—almost certainly less than 10%. This is true both for a serious property crime—burglary—and the most frequent violent crime—armed robbery.

---

10. We have ignored, for example, general and special deterrent effects of probation and parole.

11. The effect is "minimal" relative to our, and we suspect, other researchers' expectations. It is also minimal relative to the usual year-to-year fluctuations in the rates of these crimes. For example, year-to-year changes in robbery rates in New Orleans exceeded 10% in 6 of the 10 years of the 1980s. Finally, it is minimal compared with the enormous costs imprisonment of these offenders would impose on society. In an absolute sense, however, 10% of burglaries and armed robberies is a large number of crimes and a lot of victims. In New Orleans, this would amount to almost 2,000 additional *reported* burglaries and armed robberies per year, and about 514,800 burglary victimizations and approximately 57,500 robbery victimizations in the United States each year (U.S. Department of Justice, 1992).

It is clear that the additional facility and operating costs needed to house current probationers and parolees would not translate into a similar decline in the crime rate. For instance, as of 1988 there were 2,356,483 offenders on probation and 404,977 offenders on parole in the United States. If probation and parole had been eliminated and these offenders returned to jail or prison, the secure correctional population would have increased by approximately 390% (Bureau of Justice Statistics, 1991). Yet the abolishment of probation and parole can effect no more than a 10% reduction in crime from increases in the incapacitative effect. In addition, if prison in itself is criminogenic, either by increasing offenders' rate of offending after release or pushing back the termination date of their "careers," the replacement of probation and parole with imprisonment would have an even weaker effect on the overall crime rate. Petersilia et al.'s (1986) research offers some support for this view, but additional research is needed to make a more definitive conclusion.

Any restriction in probation and parole policy short of elimination, therefore, can have only a very minimal effect on the crime rate. Suggestions, for example, that alternatives to incarceration be reserved for less violent, property offenders (Steffensmeier, 1992) or that probationers be supervised more intensively (Turner et al., 1992) can therefore also have little effect.

Our results, however, should not be interpreted to mean that a significant *expansion* in the use of probation or parole would have no significant effects on the crime rate. The criminal justice system is intended by judges, prosecutors, and law enforcement officers to be selective, that is, to keep the most dangerous and active offenders behind bars. To some extent, the system succeeds, although how well it succeeds is a matter of much debate. If those offenders now incarcerated are in fact more dangerous and would in fact commit more crime if released than current probationers and parolees, sharp expansion of the use of probation and parole might cause substantial increases in the crime rate.

In summary, the results of this study cannot be construed either as support for the abolishment of probation or parole or the increased use of these alternatives. The results do, however, dispel a commonly held belief among many criminal justice professionals and some researchers, that is, that probationers and parolees are responsible for a large percentage of crime.

REFERENCES

Allen, H.E., E.W. Carlson, and E.C. Parks
1979 Critical Issues in Adult Probation. Washington, D.C.: Law Enforcement Assistance Administration.

Allen, Harry E., Chris W. Eskridge, Edward J. Latessa, and Gennaro F. Vito
1985 Probation and parole effectiveness. In Harry E. Allen, Chris W. Eskridge, Edward J. Latessa, and Gennaro F. Vito (eds.) Probation and Parole in America. New York: Free Press.

Attorney General's Office, State of Hawaii

1989 Parole and Recidivism. Honolulu: Hawaii Criminal Justice Data Center.

Bureau of Justice Statistics

1991 Correctional Populations in the United States, 1988. Washington, D.C.: U.S. Department of Justice.

Caldwell, Morris G.

1951 Review of a new type of probation study made in Alabama. Federal Probation 15:3–11.

Champion, Dean J.

1988a Felony plea bargaining and probation: A growing judicial and prosecutorial dilemma. Journal of Criminal Justice 16:291–301.

1988b Felony Probation: Problems and Prospects. New York: Praeger.

Clarke, Stevens H., Yuan–Huei W. Lin, and W. LeAnn Wallace

1988 Probationer recidivism in North Carolina: Measurement and classification of risk. Institute of Government, University of North Carolina at Chapel Hill.

Comptroller General of the United States

1976 State and County Probation: Systems in Crisis, Report to the Congress of the United States. Government Printing Office, Washington, D.C.

Cunniff, Mark

1984 The Scales of Justice: Sentencing Practices in 18 Felony Courts. Bureau of Justice Statistics Statistical Series Project. National Association of Criminal Justice Planners, Washington, D.C.

Davis, George F.

1964 A study of adult probation violation rates by means of the cohort approach. Journal of Criminal Law, Criminology and Police Science 55:70–85.

England, Ralph W.

1955 A study of postprobation recidivism among five hundred federal offenders. Federal Probation 19:10–16.

Flanagan, Timothy J. and Kathleen Maguire (eds.)

1991 Sourcebook of Criminal Justice Statistics—1990. Bureau of Justice Statistics. Washington, D.C.: U.S. Department of Justice.

Flanagan, Timothy J. and Edmund F. McGarrell (eds.)

1986 Sourcebook of Criminal Justice Statistics—1985. Bureau of Justice Statistics. Washington, D.C.: U.S. Department of Justice.

Frease, Dean E.

1964 Factors Related To Probation Outcome. Olympia, Washington: Department of Institutions, Board of Prison Terms and Paroles, Section on Research and Program Analysis.

Geerken, Michael and Hennessey D. Hayes

1992 The New Orleans Offender Study: Codebook for official criminal history datasets. National Institute of Justice, Washington, D.C.

Geerken, Michael, Alfred Miranne, and Mary Baldwin Kennedy

1993 The New Orleans Offender Study: Development of official record databases. Report to the National Institute of Justice. Washington, D.C.

Greenfeld, Lawrence A.
1987 Probation and Parole, 1985. Bureau of Justice Statistics. Washington, D.C.: U.S. Department of Justice.

Gould, Larry A., Doris Layton MacKenzie, and William Bankston
1991 A comparison of models of parole outcome. Paper presented at the Annual Meeting of the American Society of Criminology, San Francisco.

Irish, James F.
1972 Probation and its Effect on Recidivism: An Evaluative Research Study of Probation in Nassau County, New York. Nassau County Probation Department, Mineola, New York.
1979 Probation and Recidivism. Nassau County Probation Department, Mineola, New York.
1989 Probation and recidivism: A study of probation adjustment and its relationship to post-probation outcome for adult criminal offenders. Nassau County Probation Department, Mineola, New York.

Jones, Peter R.
1991 The risk of recidivism: Evaluating the public-safety of a community corrections program. Journal of Criminal Justice 19:49–66.

Judge, Frank T. III
1982 Relief for prison overcrowding: Evaluating Michigan's accelerated parole statute. University of Michigan Journal of Law Reform 15:547–576.

Kusuda, Paul H.
1976 1974 Probation and Parole Terminations. Division of Corrections, Madison, Wisconsin.

Landis, Judson R., James K. Mercer, and Carole E. Wolff
1969 Success and failure of adult probationers in California. Journal of Research in Crime and Delinquency 6:34–40.

Langan, Patrick A. and Mark A. Cunniff
1992 Recidivism of Felons on Probation, 1986–1989. Bureau of Justice Statistics Special Report. Washington, D.C.: U.S. Department of Justice.

MacKenzie, Doris Layton
1991 The parole performance of offenders released from shock incarceration (boot camp prisons): A survival time analysis. Journal of Quantitative Criminology 7:213–236.

McGaha, Johnny, Michael Fichter, and Peter Hirschburg
1987 Felony probation: A re-examination of public risk. American Journal of Criminal Justice 11:1–9.

Missouri Division of Probation and Parole
1976 Probation in Missouri, July 1, 1968 to June 30, 1970: Characteristics, Performance, and Criminal Reinvolvement. Division of Probation and Parole, Jefferson City, Missouri.

Petersilia, Joan
1985a Community Supervision: Trends and Critical Issues. Crime and Delinquency 31:339–347.
1985b Probation and felony offenders. Federal Probation 49:4–9.

Petersilia, Joan, Susan Turner, James Kahan, and Joyce Peterson
1985 Executive summary of Rand's study, "Granting Felons Probation: Public Risks and Alternatives." Crime and Delinquency 31:379–392.

Petersilia, Joan and Susan Turner, with Joyce Peterson
1986 Prison versus Probation in California: Implications for Crime and Offender Recidivism. R–3323–NIJ. Santa Monica, Calif.: Rand Corporation.

Steffensmeier, Darrell
1992 Incarceration and Crime: Facing Fiscal Realities in Pennsylvania. Center for the Study of Law and Society. University Park: Pennsylvania State University.

Sutherland, Edwin H., Donald R. Cressey, and David F. Luckenbill
1992 Principles of Criminology. 11th ed. New York: General Hall.

Tonry, Michael
1992 Mandatory penalties. In Michael Tonry (ed.), Crime and Justice: A Review of Research. Vol. 16. Chicago: University of Chicago Press.

Turner, Susan, Joan Petersilia, and Elizabeth Piper Deschenes
1992 Evaluating intensive supervision probation/parole (ISP) for drug offenders. Crime and Delinquency 38:539–556.

U.S. Department of Justice
1992 Criminal Victimization in the United States, 1990. Washington, D.C.: U.S. Department of Justice.

Vito, Gennaro F.
1986 Felony probation and recidivism: Replication and response. Federal Probation 50:17–25.

Whitehead, John T.
1991 The effectiveness of felony probation: Results from an eastern state. Justice Quarterly 8:525–543.

Michael R. Geerken is Chief Administrative Officer for the Orleans Parish Criminal Sheriff's Office and Adjunct Associate Professor of Sociology at Tulane University. He has published in the areas of deterrence theory, incapacitation, geographical mobility, the psychological effects of sex and marital roles, drug use, survey methodology, and the uses of official crime statistics.

Hennessey D. Hayes is a research analyst at the Orleans Parish Criminal Sheriff's Office and a Ph.D. candidate, Department of Sociology, Tulane University. He has recently published work on federal civil procedure. His current research areas are juvenile justice policy, inmate classification, and juvenile delinquency causation.

THE RESPONSE OF THE CRIMINAL JUSTICE SYSTEM TO PRISON OVERCROWDING: RECIDIVISM PATTERNS AMONG FOUR SUCCESSIVE PAROLEE COHORTS

WILLIAM R. KELLY
SHELDON EKLAND-OLSON

Over the past decade crowded prison conditions became the subject for lawsuits across the country, resulting in restrictions on the "capacity" of prison systems in a number of states. These restrictions produced pressures throughout the criminal justice system, from arrest to release on parole. The question addressed in this research is whether these restrictions and pressures affected the probability and pattern of return to prison among parolees. Data were collected at yearly intervals from four successive cohorts of parolees in Texas. Each cohort was followed for thirty-six months to determine the pattern and probability of returning to prison. Four alternative explanations for shifts in recidivism probabilities are explored using "survival analysis" techniques. Evidence is found for reduced deterrence in addition to effects from cohort composition and administrative discretion.

INTRODUCTION

In the early 1980s, prison crowding was flagged as "the most critical administrative problem facing the United States criminal justice system" (Blumstein 1983:229). While debates emerged as the decade unfolded over what criteria should be used to document the meaning of "crowding" (Sherman and Hawkins 1981; Gaes 1985), concern with crowded conditions occupied more policymaking time for the criminal justice system than any other single issue in the 1980s. By mid-decade, all but eleven states had at least one prison considered "overcrowded" by some court-defined standard. California embarked on a crash construction program that dwarfed all previous efforts (Zimring 1990). In the closing years of the decade, under substantial court pressure, Texas enacted sweeping

This research was supported by a grant from the National Institute of Justice. We would like to thank Hee Jong Joo, Michael Eisenberg, Jeff Olbrich, Pablo Martinez, and Eve Van Cleve for their assistance throughout the project.

LAW & SOCIETY REVIEW, Volume 25, Number 3 (1991)

criminal justice reform legislation, including a statewide restructuring of administrative control and a large-scale construction effort (Ekland-Olson and Kelly 1989). Parallel efforts occurred nationwide.

Faced with burgeoning prison populations and limited resources, states increasingly turned to the "backdoor" solution of parole release. Between 1977 and 1988, supervised releases from state prisons increased by 183 percent, from 89,636 in 1977 to 253,646 in 1988 (Bureau of Justice Statistics 1990). This dramatic rise in parole releases significantly increased the parole population. In the last half of the 1980s alone, the number of persons under parole supervision in the United States increased by 52 percent, from 300,203 to 456,797 (ibid.).

Like other major shifts in criminal justice policy, this large-scale rapid transformation of criminal justice may have been responsible for a variety of unanticipated consequences (e.g., Merton 1936; Hegel 1953; Schneider 1971). In particular, we consider how the changes in imprisonment and release patterns affected the rate at which persons return to prison once they are released on parole.

THE TEXAS PRISON CROWDING CRISIS

The growth in the prison population in the Texas Department of Corrections (TDC) exemplifies the national trend. In the early to mid-1970s, the prison population hovered between 16,000 and 20,000. By 1981, it had increased to more than 30,000, and by 1989, even with stringent population "caps" in place, it was just over 40,000. Texas also followed the national trend of increasing parole releases. Between 1980 and 1989, parole and mandatory supervision releases increased by 320 percent, from 7,180 in 1980 to 30,102 in 1989 (Texas Department of Corrections 1988). Increases in admissions to TDC were in part a function of rising crime. Total index crimes increased by nearly 175 percent during the 1970s and 1980s. Predictably, arrests also rose, by about 70 percent. Convictions were up as well (by about 57 percent) but not at the same rate as arrests (see Ekland-Olson and Kelly (in press) for a more detailed discussion of the evolution of the crowding problem at TDC).

In addition to the increased demands placed on the prison system from rising crime, arrests, and convictions, there was a higher likelihood that, once convicted, individuals would be sentenced to prison. Between 1976 and 1989, the ratio of incarcerations to convictions rose by more than 35 percent. Moreover, between 1976 and 1989, the percentage of those with no prior confinement in TDC rose from 76 percent to 85 percent (Texas Department of Corrections, various years). Thus, an increasingly prevalent "get tough policy" contributed to the prison population problem. The result was that the primary source of the rise in the on-hand prison population during the 1980s was increased admissions (see Table 1), indicated by the ratio of new admissions to the total on-hand population, which rose from a low of .47 in 1973 to a high of .94 in 1990.

In summary, the prison crowding problem in Texas began with increasing crime. It was exacerbated by the increased tendency to sentence convicted offenders to prison, including those with no prior prison time in TDC. As the prison population began to climb, the courts began to intervene in prison conditions cases, in Texas as well as elsewhere.

Table 1. Total On-Hand Prison Population and the Ratio of Total Received to Total On-Hand Population; Texas, 1972–1990

Year	Total On-Hand Population	No. Received	Ratio
1972	16,171	7,725	.48
1973	16,689	7,780	.47
1974	16,956	8,217	.49
1975	18,151	9,358	.52
1976	20,976	10,554	.50
1977	20,862	11,077	.53
1978	24,615	12,894	.52
1979	25,164	13,041	.52
1980	28,543	14,176	.50
1981	30,315	15,702	.52
1982	34,393	18,837	.55
1983	36,769	22,870	.62
1984	35,772	23,058	.64
1985	37,320	25,365	.68
1986	38,246	30,471	.80
1987	39,652	35,007	.88
1988	39,664	33,816	.85
1989	41,626	33,303	.80
1990	49,157	46,290	.94

SOURCE: Texas Department of Corrections, *Fiscal Year Statistical Report* 1972–89.

In *Ruiz v. Estelle* (1980), the federal court held that the entire Texas prison system was unconstitutional, due primarily to crowded conditions. (See Martin and Ekland-Olson 1987 and Ekland-Olson and Kelly 1989 for detailed discussions of the *Ruiz* case.) Beginning in 1981, court-imposed population "caps" were placed on the TDC. These restrictions forced the state to develop solutions to the prison population crisis.

The legislature responded to the *Ruiz* decision by implementing expanded good-time allowances and passing, in 1983, the Prison Management Act (PMA), which effectively shifted the responsibility for managing the prison population to the Board of Pardons and Paroles. Among other things, the PMA clarified the capacity standard by which the state was in violation of the *Ruiz* decision, defining the system's capacity in terms of space and facilities available and setting the upper limit at 95 percent of capacity. When the inmate population reached 95 percent of capacity, the PMA triggered the application of more liberal good-time allowances as well as the advancement of parole eligibility in thirty-day increments, up to a total of ninety days.

The impact of this legislation was immediate. In 1980, 7,180 inmates were released with continued supervision. In 1985, this figure had risen to 21,192. In 1989, it reached 30,102. The dramatic rise in parole release was accomplished through an equally dramatic increase in the percentage of parolees released after their initial parole hearing. In 1983, about 40 percent of inmates were released on parole after their first hearing. By the end of the decade, this had increased to nearly 80 percent (see Fig. 1).

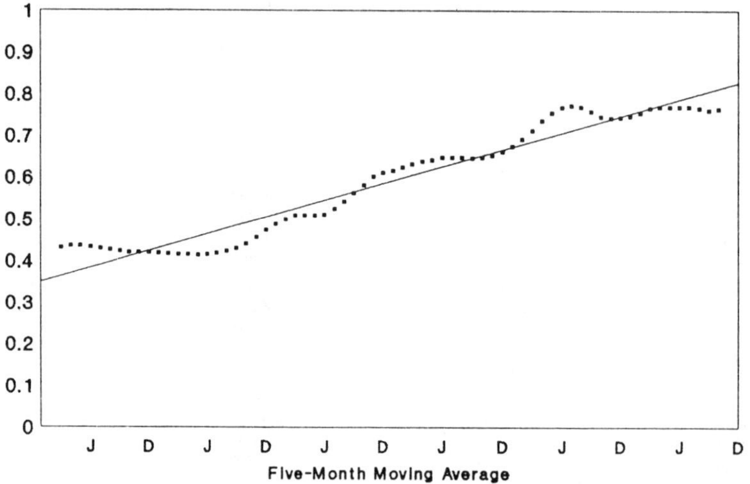

Figure 1. Proportion of parolees released at initial hearing, January 1983–December 1988

One important consequence of this increasing reliance on parole release was a significant decline in the proportion of sentences served by TDC inmates. In 1980 (pre-*Ruiz*) the typical inmate served 37 percent of his/her sentence, for an average length of incarceration of 2.39 years. By 1989, the average percentage of sentence served dropped to 21 percent and the average length of incarceration dropped to 1.70 years.

Another consequence of rising parole releases was the increase in the relative size of the parole population compared to the total adult population. Table 2 presents the rate of parolees per 100,000 population for Texas and the nation as a whole for the years 1983–89. In every year, Texas ranked second in the nation in terms of the relative size of the parole population, second only to Washington D.C. But even more telling is the comparison of the relative increase in the Texas rate and the national rate over this five-year period. Between 1983 and 1988, the national parole rate increased by 84 percent, to 248 per 100,000 population. The rate for Texas increased by 160 percent, to 758 per 100,000 adults.

Table 2. Number of Parolees Per 100,000 Adult Population, 1983–1989

Year	U.S.	Texas
1983	135	290
1984	155	362
1985	158	410
1986	184	489
1987	201	570
1988	213	657
1989	248	758

SOURCE: U.S. Department of Justice, Bureau of Justice Statistics, *Source Book of Criminal Justice Statistics.*

These dramatic changes show a prison system in conflict over enforcement demands and due process constraints. In this research we examine recidivism probabilities and patterns among parolees to assess the consequences of these major transformations for crime control. Our primary analytic strategy is to compare the three-year survival patterns (i.e., 1 minus the reincarceration rates) of four parole cohorts released from the TDC between 1984 and 1987. The design is longitudinal, providing for the evaluation over time of inmates released in a given year as well as the assessment of changes across cohorts of parolees. Thus, our focus is on both the shifting patterns and overall probabilities (levels) of reincarceration during this period of rapid change in the criminal justice system in Texas. Because, as we have shown elsewhere (Ekland-Olson and Kelly in press), the patterns of recidivism for 1984 and 1985 are similar to the patterns found nationally for 1983, we will use 1984 and 1985 as a baseline against which to examine changes in the patterns for the 1986 and 1987 cohorts.

At least four mechanisms have been suggested to explain how the increasing use of parole to regulate the prison population might affect reincarceration. The first is a "composition" explanation. As parole releases increase, the composition of the parole eligible population may change. For example, the pool of parolees may become increasingly "high risk," primarily due to the high volume of release. This change alone could produce an increase in the probability of returning to prison. The second is the "strained resources" argument. The volume of parole release may affect the ability of the parole officers to monitor releasees, producing a decrease in detection of violations and/or an increase in violations due to reduced monitoring. For example, in 1982, the average caseload per parole officer was 67. By 1986, it had risen to 93 parolees per officer, and then declined to 90 in 1987 and 74 in 1988. The third explanation is a reduced deterrence effect. Fear of punishment, the central variable in deterrence theory, is linked to the perceived certainty and severity of punishment (Gibbs 1975; Ekland-Olson, Lieb, and Zurcher 1984). As prisons become crowded and prison officials become more liberal in awarding good-time credits, and as parole boards become increasingly likely to release inmates, the perception of the severity and certainty of imprisonment may decline, and with it the deterrent effect of punishment.

Finally, there is what might be called the "administrative discretion" influence. Reincarceration rates may reflect changing practices on the part of the parole board and parole officers. The decision whether to revoke parole for a technical violation gives the parole officer wide discretion. It is reasonable to assume that technical parole violation revocations are most likely to be used on releasees with the most serious criminal records, providing a way to keep high-risk offenders off the streets without a large investment in court time. Pressure from the media and/or the legislature may have altered the parole officers' revocation practices by providing a quick and procedurally simpler means for controlling the parole population. As a result, as the proportion of high-risk parolees increases, we might expect to observe increases in technical violation revocations.

DATA AND RESEARCH DESIGN

Records provided by the Texas Board of Pardons and Paroles, the Texas Department of Public Safety, and the Texas Department of Corrections were used to compile data on four cohorts of parolees released in February 1984, 1985, 1986, and 1987. The 1984 cohort consists of 1,435 parolees, the 1985 cohort contains 1,119, the 1986 cohort consists of 1,671 parolees, and the 1987 cohort contains 2,063. The design allows for a thirty-six-month follow-up on all four cohorts as well as a monthly tracking of these parolees to determine not only if they were reincarcerated but if so, how long after release they were returned to prison.

Data on the parolees' characteristics include prior incarceration offense (release offense), age, gender, race/ethnicity, assessed risk, and reincarceration offense (return offense). Prior incarceration offense and reincarceration offense categories consist of murder, sexual assault, robbery, burglary, larceny/theft, motor vehicle theft, fraud/forgery, drug offenses, assault, and traffic/DWI. For return offenses we also coded technical violations. Age is categorized into 18–22, 23–27, 28–32, 33–37, 38–42, and 43+ years. Race/ethnicity includes Anglo, Black, and Hispanic. Assessed risk, based on the multidimensional Salient Factor Score (see Appendix A), was collapsed into high (scores of 0–4), medium (5–10), and low (11–15). This scale was used by the parole board to assess the likelihood that parolees would return to prison.

We use survival analysis (Brown et al. 1979) to assess changes across cohorts because the variable of interest is the time interval between an initial event (in this case, release from prison) and a subsequent, terminal event (reincarceration). Survival times are measured in monthly intervals, permitting the computation of monthly survival trajectories for each cohort. Two related survival functions are used. The first is the survival probability, which is the cumulative proportion surviving at the end of a specified time interval. It is 1 minus the proportion who have been reincarcerated by that time, that is, 1 minus the recidivism rate. The second is the hazard rate, which is the probability that a person not reincarcerated at the beginning of a specified time interval (month) will be reincarcerated during that interval.

Trends in Reincarceration

Figure 2 presents the monthly survival probabilities for the thirty-six-month follow-up periods for the four cohorts. Two parallel yet distinct trends are evident: The 1984 and 1985 cohorts are virtually identical. The trends in the survival probabilities for the 1986 and 1987 cohorts are nearly parallel to the two previous years but show a lower rate of survival and differ in some important ways in the follow-up periods. Approximately five months following release, parolees in the 1986 cohort have somewhat lower survival probabilities. This trend continues until about the thirteenth month of release. Thereafter, parolees in the 1987 cohort have slightly lower survival probabilities.

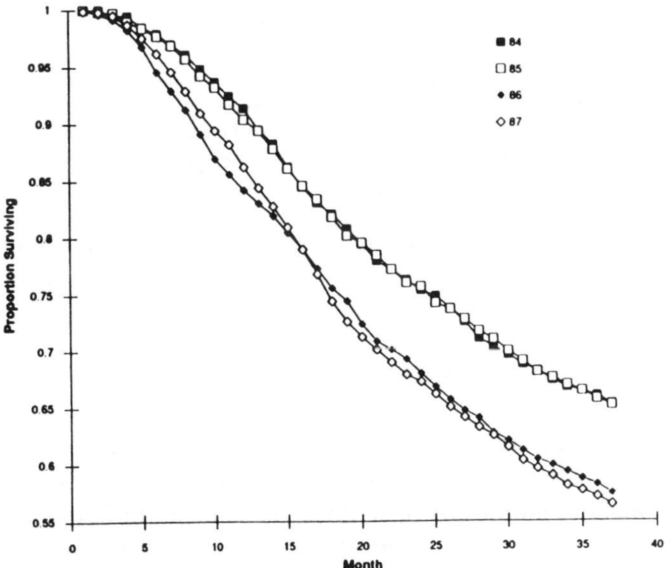

Figure 2. Cumulative proportion surviving for the 1984–1987 cohorts

Table 3 presents the cumulative percentage surviving in each cohort at twelve-, twenty-four-, and thirty-six-month intervals. After twelve months the proportions surviving among all parolees in the 1984 and 1985 cohorts were identical—89.5 and 89.4, respectively. Members of the 1986 and 1987 cohorts were less likely to survive to the end of the first year—83.1 percent and 84.4 percent, respectively.

The survival rates after twenty-four months demonstrate a similar pattern. The 1984 and 1985 cohorts had survival rates that again are virtually identical—74.9 and 74.3. Consistent with the pattern for the first twelve months of release, the 1986 and 1987 cohorts exhibit a lower survival rate. As a whole, about one-third of 1986 and 1987 parolees were reincarcerated after twenty-four months, compared to about 25 percent for the 1984 and 1985 cohorts.

These trends continue during the third year of release. The percentage surviving from the 1984 and 1985 cohorts is essentially identical (about one-third were returned to TDC by the end of the third year). The rates for the 1986 and 1987 cohorts are quite similar as well, although the failure rate is considerably higher in these later cohorts (about 44 percent were returned after thirty-six months).

The differences across cohorts become clearer when we examine the six-month moving average for monthly hazard rates in Figure 3. Moving averages were computed to obtain a trend undistorted by month-to-month fluctuations. The data indicate quite similar rates for the first two cohorts, with an increase in the first twelve months, a leveling off at the maximum rates for a period of a few months, a gradual decline, and then a second leveling off.

In comparison, the hazard rates for the 1986 cohort increased faster and peaked sooner than those for the other cohorts. There was then a decline and a second increase at about fifteen months, tracking the peak for the earlier cohorts. Thus, not only is the overall *level* of reincarceration higher for the 1986 cohort, but this cohort also exhibits a distinctive *pattern* of reincarceration. Note that level and pattern differences do not reflect precisely the same underlying phenomena. Fluctuations in the *pattern*, what has been called the basic "transition curve," seem to be most directly linked with administrative actions and plea-bargain decisions. At least some shifts in the *level* of reincarceration appear to reflect a reduced deterrent effect. Supporting data follow.

The hazard rate trends for the 1987 cohort are different from the trends for the other cohorts. The patterns for the 1984, 1985, and 1987 parolees all show rates that increase monotonically up to about the twelfth to fourteenth month and then gradually decline as the release period increases. What distinguishes the 1987 cohort from the rest is the level of the probability that persons would be returned to prison within a given time frame. The peak rates for

Table 3. Survival Probabilities by Selected Characteristics for the 1984–1987 Release Cohorts

	12 Months				24 Months				36 Months			
	1984	1985	1986	1987	1984	1985	1986	1987	1984	1985	1986	1987
Total	89.5	89.4	83.1	84.4	74.9	74.3	66.9	66.2	65.3	65.2	57.5	56.4
Release offense												
Murder	93.2	90.4	94.4	89.5	86.4	78.9	86.1	75.0	77.7	75.0	81.9	63.0
Rape	100.0	81.0	72.4	70.6	76.3	76.2	51.7	41.2	63.2	57.1	48.3	35.3
Robbery	89.1	92.3	84.2	82.1	75.5	72.1	66.5	62.5	64.1	59.7	53.1	47.8
Burglary	85.3	85.2	76.2	82.3	67.4	65.4	57.6	63.6	57.1	56.2	48.9	54.4
Larceny	88.1	90.7	85.2	88.1	75.7	79.0	66.4	66.6	64.5	71.6	59.2	54.7
MVT	84.1	83.0	79.0	77.5	61.9	64.2	61.8	53.9	47.6	52.8	51.3	42.2
Forgery	90.2	93.2	87.0	81.8	77.7	78.4	74.8	62.5	72.3	67.1	60.0	55.7
Drug	98.5	95.7	88.4	87.7	89.3	81.7	75.7	71.3	77.1	71.3	64.7	63.7
Assault	92.0	91.8	85.0	82.5	74.0	81.6	65.0	63.8	68.0	79.3	60.0	63.7
Traffic/DWI	88.9	90.9	88.8	83.8	72.2	85.5	73.8	76.3	63.9	78.2	66.3	71.3
Gender												
Male	89.2	88.7	82.7	83.7	74.2	73.4	66.0	65.1	64.2	63.8	56.8	55.5
Female	92.7	98.7	88.6	91.1	83.6	87.0	78.7	76.8	78.2	84.4	66.7	65.3
Age												
18–22	83.9	86.4	75.9	74.1	65.1	66.9	57.7	54.2	55.4	56.5	51.4	43.9
23–27	89.0	88.3	79.5	82.1	74.4	74.1	64.5	64.1	65.1	64.5	53.4	52.4
28–32	92.4	90.9	84.9	85.4	76.0	71.5	68.7	63.3	63.9	61.6	56.9	54.5
33–37	91.4	89.1	83.8	87.8	79.2	75.6	65.8	71.4	72.4	65.4	55.8	61.8
38–42	91.1	92.3	91.2	93.6	74.2	76.9	74.8	77.6	61.3	71.4	68.7	71.8
43+	88.2	90.8	89.8	90.9	80.9	85.5	74.9	78.9	73.7	79.4	69.5	69.7
Race/Ethnicity												
White	91.3	90.6	86.8	86.5	77.6	79.3	71.3	69.3	70.2	72.0	67.5	62.0
Black	88.0	86.7	82.3	81.5	72.0	69.1	65.6	60.9	61.8	58.6	54.1	48.5
Hispanic	88.7	91.9	76.7	85.4	75.3	73.3	60.1	69.3	61.8	63.3	54.0	59.2
Assessed Risk												
High	78.4	83.5	74.1	77.7	62.1	59.0	53.7	53.4	48.4	51.8	43.1	42.2
Medium	89.1	88.4	82.1	83.0	73.3	73.0	66.4	63.4	63.0	62.9	56.9	53.1
Low	94.7	94.5	92.4	91.4	83.6	84.6	78.1	79.4	77.0	76.8	69.7	71.9

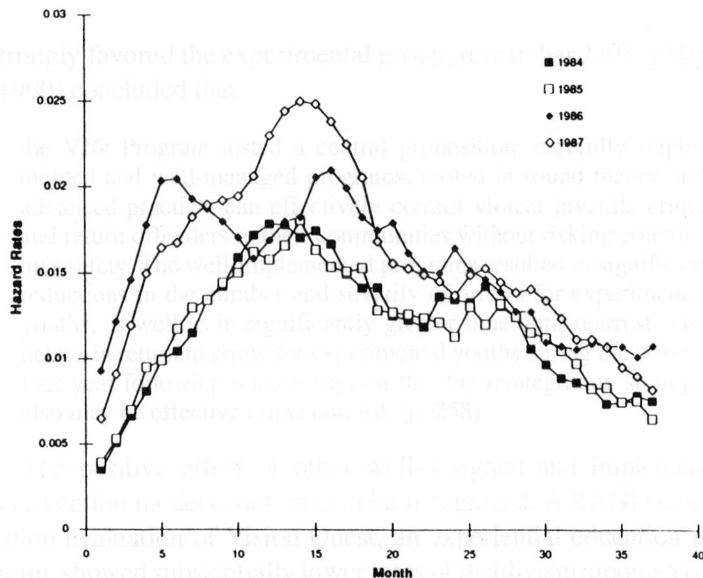

Figure 3. Hazard rates for the 1984–1987 cohorts

the 1987 cohort, while occurring at about the same time as the other cohorts, are considerably higher than the others.

It is clear that the 1986 and 1987 cohorts depart from the 1984–85 baseline, but in different ways. The 1986 cohort produced the early peak in the hazard rates, followed by a decline and then a second peak. In contrast, the pattern of hazard rates for the 1987 cohort followed the 1984 and 1985 pattern, but the level was considerably higher. These departures from the baseline years of 1984 and 1985 provide evidence that the changes occurring in the administration of criminal justice during these years were, indeed, associated with shifts in both the pattern and level of reincarceration among those released on parole in 1986 and 1987. We now evaluate the potential explanations for these trends.

CORRELATES OF RECIDIVISM DIFFERENCES ACROSS COHORTS

Our central question here is whether the large-scale, rapid change in the criminal justice system produced changes in the patterns and probabilities that persons would end up back in prison after being released on parole. For persons released in the early years (1984 and 1985), the answer to this question is a clear no. In both years, the three-year patterns of return reflect the often-noted "transition curve" (e.g., Irwin 1970; Minor and Courlander 1979; Rossi, Berk, and Lenihan 1980; Ekland-Olson, Supancic, Campbell, and Lenihan 1983). These patterns are quite consistent with national data for the same time frame (Ekland-Olson and Kelly 1989). In this sense, it can be said that the broad-based changes in the criminal justice system, precipitated by the federal court intervention in *Ruiz*, had little if any impact on recidivism among these parolees.

In contrast, persons released on parole in 1986 and 1987 had higher return rates. The 1986 cohort also departed from the basic transition curve with a bimodal distribution and an accelerated return early in the release period.

We have suggested several potential explanations for these patterns. Of these explanations, the administrative discretion and compositional change alternatives appear most likely to explain the unique pattern of return in the 1986 cohort. On the other hand, an altered deterrent effect from the criminal sanctioning process and administrative discretion appear as more likely explanations for the 1987 pattern.

We first consider the extent to which the 1986 cohort differs compositionally from the prior cohorts and thus the extent to which such differences may account for its distinctive survival and hazard rate trends. Table 4 presents the percentage distributions for each cohort, broken down by prior incarceration offense, gender, age, race/ethnicity and assessed risk.[1]

While there are some relatively minor differences between the 1986 and earlier cohorts (e.g., a higher percentage of parolees with a prior incarceration offense of burglary), the most important compositional shift is the increase in 1986 in the proportion of parolees assessed as high risk. It is quite likely that the increase in high-risk parolees contributed to the overall lower survival rates for the 1986 cohort (see Table 3). However, this cannot be the entire explanation. If the lower survival probabilities and higher hazard rates for the 1986 cohort are solely due to compositional shifts, we would not expect to see lower survival probabilities *within* risk categories. That is, the fact that high-risk parolees in 1986 experienced lower survival rates compared to 1984 and 1985 is not due to the compositional changes evident in Table 4.

It is possible that another, more subtle, compositional change occurred. Those within the high-risk category in the 1986 cohort may have been riskier than their counterparts in other cohorts. To assess this possibility, we computed mean risk scores for each category of assessed risk for each cohort and found essentially no difference. Thus, on balance, we conclude that the trends in survival and hazard rates for 1986 are only in part a function of the increased proportion of high-risk parolees.

In the case of the 1987 cohort, the compositional explanation

---

[1] Region of the state to which persons were paroled was also examined but made no discernable difference, and was therefore not included in further analyses.

Table 4. Percentage Distributions by Selected Characteristics for the 1984–1987 Cohorts

	Cohorts			
	1984 (N=1,435)	1985 (N=1,119)	1986 (N=1,671)	1987 (N=2,073)
Release offense				
Murder	7.2	4.6	4.3	3.7
Rape	2.6	1.9	1.7	0.8
Robbery	13.4	11.5	9.8	8.9
Burglary	29.9	30.2	32.9	27.6
Larceny	14.6	14.5	13.3	13.4
MVT	4.4	4.7	4.5	4.9
Forgery	7.8	7.9	6.9	8.5
Drug	9.1	10.3	11.8	17.7
Assault	3.5	4.4	3.6	3.9
Traffic/DWI	2.5	4.8	4.8	3.9
Gender				
Male	92.3	93.1	93.2	90.8
Female	7.7	6.9	6.8	9.2
Age				
18–23	13.0	13.8	13.2	14.6
24–27	32.3	30.0	29.1	26.9
28–32	20.1	23.5	23.3	24.3
33–37	15.4	13.9	14.4	16.6
38–42	8.6	8.1	8.8	7.6
43+	10.6	11.7	11.2	10.1
Ethnicity/race				
White	41.7	42.7	40.7	41.7
Black	39.0	38.4	40.2	37.6
Hispanic	19.2	18.8	18.7	20.1
Assessed risk				
High	10.7	12.4	16.4	12.1
Medium	61.7	61.4	61.5	62.8
Low	27.6	26.1	22.1	25.1

fails almost entirely. Table 4 indicates that on most dimensions, the 1987 cohort was quite similar to the 1985 cohort. Moreover, based on the differential distribution of other characteristics in the 1987 cohort, we would expect that the survival probabilities would, if anything, be lower for the 1987 cohort. Specifically, compared to the 1985 cohort, the 1987 cohort had proportionally fewer parolees with incarceration offenses of burglary and larceny; had relatively more parolees with a prior incarceration offense involving drug trafficking; had relatively more females; was relatively older; and had proportionately fewer high-risk parolees.

Turning to the administrative discretion explanation, we note that during the time frame of this research the parole system found itself in a double bind. On the one hand, there was pressure to manage the crowding-induced crisis in the Texas prison system. This meant that prison beds and parole revocations had to be treated like precious resources. On the other hand, there was what came to be known as the "Willie Horton" factor in the national presidential campaign of 1987 and 1988. In Texas, as elsewhere, there was increased media attention and consequent political pressure and public concern over the release of dangerous felons and more generally over the "revolving prison door." In Texas, instead of the weekend furlough of Willie Horton, newspapers carried stories about the early release of the "Choker Rapist" and "Animal."

As discussed elsewhere (Ekland-Olson and Kelly in press), publicity and political pressure surrounding the release of convicted felons reached a peak in 1986 and 1987. It was also during this basic time frame that the number of persons released from TDC increased by about 40 percent (from 23,333 in 1985 to 33,370 in 1987). The resulting political and administrative pressures corresponded to the months of heightened "hazard rates" among members of the 1986 parole cohort. It is plausible, therefore, that the early peak in hazard rates for members of the 1986 cohort resulted when parole officers responded to the heightened public concern through increased use of technical violations when parolees appeared to be getting into trouble or committing new offenses.

Some evidence suggests that this was indeed the case. Among persons paroled in the 1986 cohort, 20 percent of those revoked on technical grounds returned to prison within the first six months. The corresponding percentages for the 1984 and 1985 cohorts were 5 and 6 percent, respectively, or about one quarter of the first-six-month rate of the 1986 cohort.

While technical violations are a more efficient way to return persons to prison, they are also more likely to fill the prison to capacity, producing a double bind for the parole system. Legislation responding to the impact of parole decisions on the prison crowding side of the double bind came in 1985 (Senate Bill 1167) and took effect just prior to the release of the persons included in our 1986 cohort. The explicit purpose of S.B. 1167 was to reduce prison crowding due to violations of the administrative conditions of parole. In particular, it allowed prison officials to reinstate "good-time" credits (after ninety days of satisfactory institutional adjustment) accumulated during the returning individual's previous stay in prison. This resulted in substantially shortened lengths of stay for those returned for "technical" reasons. Thus, for the parolee who had committed a new crime, there were benefits in securing a technical revocation rather than a new conviction. In the process, the legislative intent of reducing prison crowding resulted in aggravation of what came to be called the revolving door of release and return.

The patterns of technical violations reveal the use of selective discretion by parole officers. As political pressures rose to get high-profile persons off the streets, the proportion of technical parole violations rose. When concerns about crowded cellblocks took over and convicted felons began backing up in local jails, technical violations began to fall. This roller-coaster pattern is evidenced by the finding that technical violations were more likely to be used early in the 1986 cohort, but over the total period of the study they were less likely to be applied than in the 1985 cohort. By the time the 1987 cohort had been in the community for three years, the rate of technical violations had returned to the level of the 1984 cohort.

To explore the extent to which the early use of technical violations in the 1986 cohort might explain the differences between reincarceration rates across cohorts, we removed from each cohort those parolees who were returned to prison during the first six months of release for a technical violation and recomputed hazard rate curves. These are presented in Figure 4. As is readily apparent, early technical revocations alone do not explain the noted differences across cohorts.

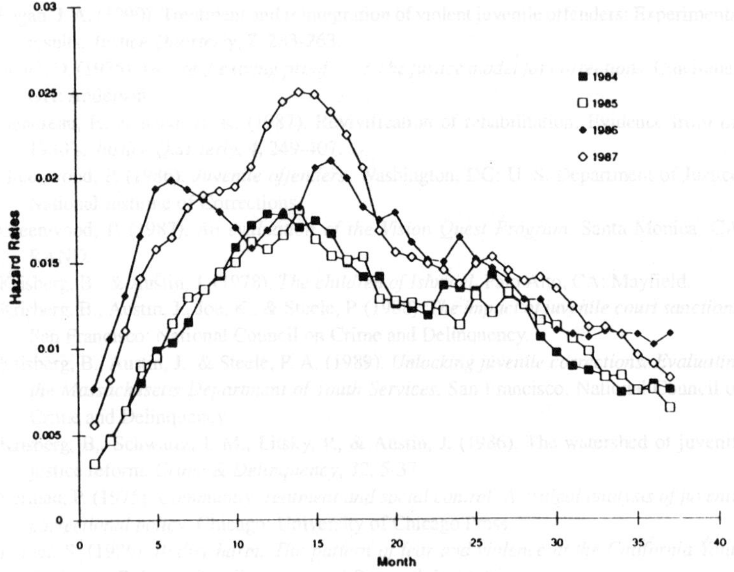

Figure 4. Hazard rates for the 1984–1987 cohorts, omitting early technical revocations

While the curves become somewhat more parallel, they do not begin to overlap. "Technicalities" alone do not generally send persons back to prison, especially when the receiving prisons are already full. Rather, technical revocations are generally used for more expeditious handling of high-profile cases where the person charged is suspected of committing another crime and where the parole offense is more serious than the new charge.

A technical revocation is the major tool parole officers have for controlling potentially high-profile cases. Thus, among those who returned to prison, persons on parole for murder, sexual assault, and assault charges were the most likely to receive a technical revocation. In the 1986 cohort, 40 percent of those on parole for a sentence of murder who returned to prison were returned on a technical revocation. The comparable percentage for sexual assault and assault offenders was 30 percent. By contrast, only 13 percent of the recidivist burglars returned to prison following a technical revocation. This basic pattern held across cohorts.

This difference, as illustrated in Table 4, may be due to an overall higher rate of reincarceration among these individuals in the 1986 and 1987 cohorts. The most dramatic difference in characteristic-specific survival patterns across cohorts is among those released on parole after serving time for sexual assault (rape). At the end of thirty-six months, in the 1986 and 1987 cohorts, only 48 and 35 percent of these parolees, respectively, were still in the community. This is the lowest three-year survival percentage of any category.

The question becomes whether this increased recidivism was due to a rise in criminal activity (possibly a reduced deterrent effect) or to heightened administrative sensitivity to these high-profile offenders. The possibility of a reduced deterrent effect among this subcategory of parolees is made less likely, though not eliminated, by the finding that the percentage returning for reconviction on repeat violent offense charges remained at a relatively constant 35–40 percent across the four cohorts. This does not suggest a reduced deterrent effect. This pattern of repetitious offending patterns is not the same across other types of offenses.

A contrasting pattern is found in the *overall* tendency between 1984 and 1987 for persons who were returned to prison to come back for the same crime for which they were released. This is evidenced in Table 5. When specific crime categories are compared, the percentage of persons returning to prison for the same crime (e.g., released after serving a sentence for robbery and returned for another robbery conviction) rose from 27 to 40 percent. Aggregated percentages of those who returned to prison for their release offense (e.g., released property offenders returned for another property offense) rose from 45 to 58 percent, comparing the 1984 and 1987 cohorts.

This pattern of increased repetitious offending is most evident among property offenders and, in particular, the chances that recidivist burglars returned to prison on a new burglary charge. Among persons returning to prison for repetitious burglary convictions, the percentage with new burglary or larceny/stolen property offenses rose from 39 percent to 49 percent between 1984 and 1986. This, then is the first evidence we find indicating a possible reduction in the deterrent influence (defined by repetitious offenses) from an overburdened criminal justice system.

Given these findings, we decided to remove from each of the cohorts early-returning (within the first nine months) technical violators, as well as those on parole for sexual assault and burglary.

Table 5. Cross-Tabulation of Prior Incarceration Offense by Return Offense by Release Cohort

Prior Incarceration Offense	Return Offense: Violent	Property	Drug
		1984	
Violent	35%	23%	9%
Property	15	52	8
Drug	23	20	30
		1985	
Violent	36%	26%	7%
Property	12	60	9
Drug	22	24	46
		1986	
Violent	40%	25%	5%
Property	13	59	14
Drug	8	23	53
		1987	
Violent	36%	33%	11%
Property	10	70	10
Drug	5	33	54

By so doing we hoped to assess the most obvious combined effects of administrative decision, composition, and possibly reduced deterrence across cohorts. The resulting hazard rate curves for each cohort are presented in Figure 5.

As is apparent, the variation in the *pattern* of return across cohorts is thereby greatly reduced, although the increased *level* of return is not totally eliminated. It is also apparent that as members of the 1985 cohort entered the middle of their second year of release, the months corresponding to the heightened return rates in the 1986 cohort, the probability of persons returning to prison began to rise. This further underscores the already-noted administrative effect stemming from heightened public and political concern during these months. Thus, it appears that the differential timing of return to prison, characteristic of the 1986 cohort, was primarily a function of administrative action combined with the sentence benefits of S.B. 1167 for defendants, cohort composition, and perhaps the reduced deterrent effect among property offenders.

This leaves the reincarceration patterns for the 1987 cohort. We have already seen that compositional differences do not account for the heightened recidivism among these individuals. There is little evidence to suggest that the administrative-discre-

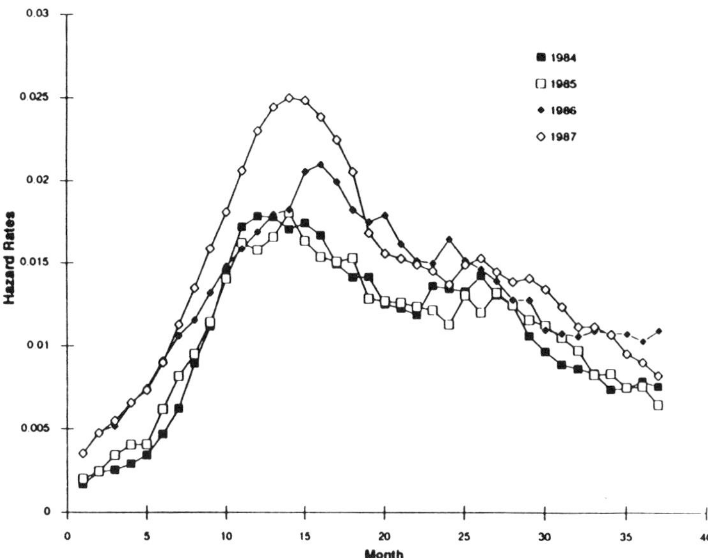

Figure 5. Hazard rates for the 1984–1987 cohorts, omitting parolees with technical violations, sexual assaults, and burglary offenses who returned within the first nine months.

tion/sentence-benefits explanation is as relevant as it was for the 1986 cohort. Figures 3 and 4 indicate that the pattern of return among those released in 1987 is essentially unaffected by the adjustments for early technical revocations, property offenses, and sexual assault incarceration offenses.

Nor does the "strained resources" explanation appear to account for the 1987 patterns. Data from the Texas Board of Pardons and Paroles (various years) indicate that parole officer caseloads were in fact declining in 1987 and 1988. The ratio of parolees to officers was considerably lower in 1988 (74:1) than in 1984 (81:1), 1985 (92:1), 1986 (93:1), and 1987 (90:1).

What we are left with, then, is how changes taking place in the administration of criminal justice during these years might have affected the estimates of the certainty and severity of punishment among offenders. While we do not have direct perceptual measures, and are thus unable to test the strict versions of the deterrence doctrine (Gibbs 1975), we do find evidence across cohorts that persons released on parole returned to prison on charges close or identical to their earlier offense.

As is clear from Table 5, this increase over previous cohorts is most marked among property offenders. This pattern, of course, is consistent with the idea that property offenses, more than other crimes, are linked to the rational calculations implied by deterrence explanations of crime. The same pattern occurred among persons released and then reconvicted on drug trafficking charges. In the 1984 cohort, 30 percent of those released after serving a sentence for a drug-trafficking charge returned after a conviction for a similar offense. This return rate rose to 54 percent in 1987, an 80 percent increase. While this increase in repetitions offending, especially among property offenders, is intriguing, it occurred in the context of a sharp downturn in the state's economy (Ekland-Olson and Kelly in press) and thus, as always, we are left with some empirical loose ends to be tied up in subsequent research.

SUMMARY AND CONCLUSIONS

During the 1980s the administration of criminal justice in Texas, like many other states, underwent dramatic restructuring, due largely to pressure from the federal court. It was widely charged that this restructuring resulted in a seriously flawed criminal justice system. Allegedly, those making sentencing decisions were reacting to crowded conditions in the prisons rather than to the nature of the offense charged. Likewise, it was noted that due to variation in sentencing and release decisions over the years, dangerous and otherwise high-risk individuals were being released before their time and then returning through revolving prison doors.

Attempts to reform the criminal justice system may have produced the ironic consequence of heightened return rates to prison. This, of course, would not be the first time that unintended consequences have emerged from actions taken by judicial and legislative policymakers. For example, it was Hegel (1953:35) who wrote, "human actions in history produce additional results, beyond their immediate knowledge and desire." Indeed, such ironies have been noted over several decades in the social science literature (e.g., Merton 1936; Schneider 1971). The research we have reported was designed to evaluate policy shifts in light of offender behavior based on data collected from four successive cohorts of parolees in Texas. There is some indication that the composition of these cohorts did change over the time period covered. Proportionately more parolees assessed as high risk in terms of their likelihood of returning to prison were released. There is also evidence that recidivism rates rose in the 1986 and 1987 cohorts.

We first suspected that the unique pattern of hazard rates for the 1986 cohort was due primarily to high-risk offenders and those reincarcerated for technical violations. However, when these subgroups were omitted from the samples, the early "spike" remained.

We then plotted the hazard rates for specific prior incarceration offenses and discovered that the offense categories contributing most were burglary (about one-third of the sample) and sexual assault (a small number but very high early hazard rates). Other offense categories had hazard-rate trends consistent with the earlier overall patterns. When the cohorts were equated in terms of early-returning burglary, sexual assault, high-risk, and technical revocations, the survival curves and hazard-rate *patterns* came closer together, but the 1986 and 1987 cohorts remained more likely to return to prison than those in the earlier years.

Parolees with new offenses cannot be processed through the system and return to prison in five to six months if a trial is held. Thus, the most plausible explanation for these early returns is that these parolees, rather than being processed through the court system, elected to plead guilty to a technical violation. Why? First, the courts were crowded. Thus, prosecutors and judges were motivated to accept such pleas. Second, in 1985, the Texas legislature passed legislation giving parolees returned to TDC on a technical violation the good time they had accumulated during their prior incarceration. Thus, parolees could plead guilty to a technical violation and begin their sentence with a dramatic head start on when he or she would be released.

The consequence of this law, designed to accelerate the release time of those with prior incarcerations, actually fed the prison-crowding problem as well as the administrative burden of prison officials by encouraging the quick return of offenders and reducing the amount of time between admission and release. This also may have produced a reduced deterrent effect. S.B. 1167 may very well have reduced the deterrent effect of reincarceration by reducing or minimizing the punishment associated with the commission of a new offense. Evidence for this possibility comes from heightened rates of repetitious offending, especially among property and drug offenders. The remaining competing explanation is whether this increased repetitious offending was influenced by economic changes taking place in the state at this same time (e.g., Ekland-Olson and Kelly in press).

What produced the decreased survival rates in the 1986 and 1987 cohorts? It appears that it was the commingling of several factors, all simultaneous responses to prison crowding, affecting not only the pattern of reincarceration but also the overall level of return. These factors include changes in the composition of the parole cohorts, public pressure that encouraged the early revocation of parole, and legislation that unintentionally increased the incentives for "technical" revocations and a possible reduction in deterrence. Combined, these factors ironically contributed to increased reincarceration rates at a time of maximum pressure on the capacity of the Texas Department of Corrections.

REFERENCES

BLUMSTEIN, Alfred (1983) "Prisons: Population, Capacity and Alternatives," in J. Q. Wilson (ed.), *Crime and Public Policy*. San Francisco: ICS Press.

BROWN, B. W., H. WALKER, M. SCHIMEK, and P. T. WRIGHT (1979) "A Life Table Package for SPSS," 33 *American Sociological Review* 225.

BUREAU OF JUSTICE STATISTICS (1990) "Probation and Parole 1989," *Bureau of Justice Statistics Bulletin* (U.S. Department of Justice).

EKLAND-OLSON, Sheldon, Michael SUPANCIC, James CAMPBELL, and Kenneth LENIHAN (1983) "Post Release Depression and the Importance of Familial Support," 21 *Criminology* 253.

EKLAND-OLSON, Sheldon, and William KELLY (1989) "Justice under Pressure: Implications for Deterrence." Presented at American Society of Criminology meetings, Reno, Nevada, 9–10 Nov.

——— (in press) *Justice under Pressure*. New York: Springer-Verlag.

EKLAND-OLSON, Sheldon, John LIEB, and Louis ZURCHER (1984) "The Paradoxical Impact of Criminal Sanctions: Some Microstructural Findings," 18 *Law & Society Review* 159.

GAES, Gerald (1985) "The Effects of Overcrowding in Prison," in M. Tonry and N. Morris (eds.), *Crime and Justice: Annual Review of Research*. Chicago: University of Chicago Press.

GIBBS, Jack P. (1975) *Crime, Punishment, and Deterrence*. New York: Elsevier.

HEGEL, G. W. F. (1953) *Reason in History* New York: Liberal Arts Press.

IRWIN, John (1970) *The Felon*. Englewood Cliffs, NJ: Prentice-Hall.

MARTIN, Steve J., and Sheldon EKLAND-OLSON (1987) *Texas Prisons*. Austin: Texas Monthly Press.

MERTON, Robert K. (1936) "The Unanticipted Consequences of Purposive Social Action," 1 *American Sociological Review* 894.

MINOR, W. W., and M. COURLANDER (1979) "The Post-Release Trauma Thesis: A Reconsideration of the Rise of Early Parole Failure," 16 *Journal of Research in Crime and Delinquency* 273.

ROSSI, Peter H., Richard A. BERK, and Kenneth J. LENIHAN (1980) *Money, Work, and Crime: Experimental Evidence*. New York: Academic Press.

SCHNEIDER, Louis (1971) "Dialectic in Sociology," 36 *American Sociological Review* 667.

SHERMAN, Michael, and Gordon HAWKINS (1981) *Imprisonment in America: Choosing the Future*. Chicago: University of Chicago Press.

TEXAS BOARD OF PARDONS AND PAROLES (Various Years) "Annual Statistical Report." Austin: Texas Board of Pardons and Paroles.

TEXAS DEPARTMENT OF CORRECTIONS (Various Years) "Fiscal Year Statistical Report." Austin: Texas Department of Corrections.

ZIMRING, Franklin E. (1990) "Correctional Growth in Context." Presented at Growth and Its Influence on Correctional Policy—Perspectives on the Report of the Blue Ribbon Commission, Clark Kerr Campus, University of California, Berkeley, 10–11 May.

CASE CITED

Ruiz v. Estelle, 503 F.Supp. 1265 (1980)

STATUTES CITED

Restoration of Good Conduct Time, Tex. Crim. Proc. sec. 497.004(d) (1985).

Texas Prison Management Act, Tex. Rev. Civ. Stat. Ann. art. 6184 (Vernon 1983).

The Meaning of Correctional Crowding: Steps Toward an Index of Severity

John M. Klofas
Stan Stojkovic
David A. Kalinich

Correctional crowding remains an ill-defined and poorly measured concept, particularly at the institutional level. Its usefulness for research and management is limited because measures do not facilitate comparisons over time or across facilities. To address this problem, a focus group was used to identify variables for an index of the severity of jail crowding. Group members described a comprehensive model of jail crowding in which severity is a function of population factors, facilities, and management practices. The participants also drew on a theoretical approach to understanding institutions that has received little attention in the study of prison or jail crowding.

There is little doubt about the significance of correctional crowding for criminal justice policymakers and researchers during the 1980s. Surveys of police managers, prosecutors, and corrections administrators found the crowding of correctional facilities to be among the two or three most important problems that faced criminal justice (Gibbs 1983; Guynes 1988). Researchers worked to improve the accuracy of models of the criminal justice system (see Rhodes 1990), studied case flow (Hall, Henry, Perlstein, and Smith 1985) and assessed the costs and impact of alternatives to traditional policies of confinement (Harris 1987). Correctional crowding changed the practice of criminal justice through the development of alternatives to incarceration, the occasional use of emergency release mechanisms, and by dramatic increases in prison and jail capacity.

Despite the attention and ameliorative efforts, population increases have continued to outpace capacity. From 1982 to 1989 inmate populations grew by 114%. In 1990 the prison population was still growing at a rate of 8% a

---

JOHN M. KLOFAS: Associate Professor of Criminal Justice, Rochester Institute of Technology, **STAN STOJKOVIC:** Associate Professor of Criminal Justice, University of Wisconsin – Milwaukee. **DAVID A. KALINICH:** Professor of Criminal Justice, Northern Michigan University.

The authors wish to express their appreciation to the focus group participants and to the American Jail Association.

CRIME & DELINQUENCY, Vol. 38 No. 2, April 1992 171-188

year (Bureau of Justice Statistics 1991). The consistency in population growth, however, does not imply that the crowding problem has remained the same. Although the statistics used to measure crowding have shown little change, there have been important changes in the analysis and discussion. New perspectives are challenging our basic understanding of the phenomenon of correctional crowding.

These developments raise questions about the value of the concept of correctional crowding for describing or explaining conditions in prisons and jails. It is, therefore, an appropriate time to assess its uses and to consider whether correctional crowding can be defined and, ultimately, measured in more useful ways. In this article we will describe the results of a focus group in which corrections administrators developed a model of jail crowding. Their efforts provide a foundation for assessing crowding levels and systematically describing conditions in correctional facilities.

THE CHANGING DISCUSSION

Until recently there was considerable consensus in the way prison and jail crowding were viewed and understood. The consensus is evident in the language used in discussions of the subject. That crowding has been a "problem" (see, for example, Government Accounting Office 1990) appears to have been universally accepted and the term "crisis" was widely adopted (see Gottfredson and McConville 1987). Further, policymakers and researchers often spoke in terms of solutions by "relieving" or "alleviating" crowding (see Hall et al. 1985; Blumstein 1988). Although there was disagreement over the best strategy – whether it was controlling population growth by diverting people from corrections and shortening sentence lengths or whether it was by increasing capacity, there was agreement that the problem could be resolved. Differences in perspective seemed to be overshadowed by the common notion of crisis.

Perceptions of correctional crowding are undergoing substantial revision in the 1990s. One sign of this is the decline in the number of crowding articles appearing in the academic literature. One indexing service, Criminal Justice Abstracts, lists only half as many articles on crowding in 1990 as it did in 1985. A second indication can be found in the nature of the discussions that remain. Overcrowding is likely to be discussed as a chronic condition to be managed rather than an acute problem to be resolved (Camp and Camp 1989; Klofas 1990a). Although such reports may not clearly portend significant change, there is other evidence of fundamental shifts in thinking.

Two examples illustrate the new approaches to understanding prison and jail crowding. The first reflects the influence of largely unsuccessful efforts to explain the size of correctional populations in the United States. In a recent book, for example, Zimring and Hawkins (1991) found little relationship over time or across the states between the size of the prison population and a host of variables including crime rates, drug use and enforcement, and demographic or economic variables. The failure of aggregate measures to explain the size of the prison or jail population has forced consideration of basic questions about the nature and causes of crowding. Zimring and Hawkins have, thus, been prompted to address the question of whether crowding has become a constant condition unaffected by the expansion of prison and jail capacity and independent of the use of alternatives to confinement. This question is related to more familiar, and still unresolved, arguments over the extent to which the size of the prison and jail population is determined by available capacity (see Blumstein 1988; Klofas 1990b). The concern, however, has been extended significantly from the question "if you build will you fill it?" to the question of "if you build will you overfill it?"

Although the inevitability of crowding is rejected by Zimring and Hawkins, their attention to the argument reflects a shift in the nature of the discussion. Until recently it seemed clear that the term "crowding" referred to a condition in which institutions were regarded as populated to a point beyond what is normal or desirable. If overcrowding has become the norm, however, it is clear that the literal definition is not sufficient. Should Zimring and Hawkins be mistaken and the ratio of prison population to capacity has risen to some new stable level, crowding may be such a generic condition that it loses any value as a descriptor.

In the second example, a more radical perspective on overcrowding completely rejects any traditional understanding of the term. Bleich (1989) argues that many of those concerned with the topic have had an interest in maintaining the perception of correctional crowding. For prison administrators, crowding has meant increases in budgets and in the powers available for exercising control. For reformers, crowding has been the foundation for advocating policies of decarceration and humanitarian reform. Prisoners have used crowding to make a case for early release and alternative sentences. All of this has been possible, Bleich argues, because crowding has become detached from any objective analysis of prison conditions. Bleich goes further, however, and suggests that an objective use of the term may be impossible. He argues that correctional crowding is a social construction that cannot be defined in a moral or political vacuum.

Arguments about the possible inevitability of crowding or about the politics of crowding illustrate changes in understanding and approach from the 1980s. They suggest that prison and jail crowding may increasingly be regarded as imprecise terms that provide little or no information about conditions in corrections facilities. As such, they will inevitably drift out of the lexicon of terms relevant to social science research or to management in corrections. In the 1990s, a potentially useful concept is in danger of degenerating to a point of having no scientific value.

THE MEASUREMENT PROBLEM

The problem, of course, is not with the concept itself but rather in its use in the field of criminal justice. Significant psychological research has focused on the causes and effects of crowding in a wide variety of settings (see Sundstrum 1978). Within the large body of crowding research, a comparatively small number of the studies have involved correctional facilities. That research has also been widely criticized. For example, Gaes (1985, p. 69) has summarized the corrections research by saying: "Unfortunately, while deeply held views about the effects of crowding are common, the core scientific knowledge on which informed opinion must be based is small and is constrained by methodological limitations that caution against generalizing from it."

Ruback and Innes have questioned the value of the research for other reasons. As they describe the studies (1988, p. 687); "The psychological research on prison crowding has focused, as one would expect, on individual's reactions (e.g., felt crowding, perceived control) rather than on aspects of the system and its operation." This, they argue, has contributed to the perception of crowding research as irrelevant in criminal justice. Using their model of the policy relevance of psychological research, Ruback and Innes point out that the crowding research fails because it does not deal with variables that are easily manipulated by policy. Although there is evidence that perceptions of crowding and responses to crowding can be influenced by a variety of policies including those dealing with housing design (Schaeffer, Baum, Paulus and Gaes 1988), information about environments (Wener and Kaminoff 1983), and social supports (Evans, Pulsane, Lepore, and Martin 1989; Toch 1985), it is true that the analyses often do not make policy implications clear.

Another way of describing the research and assessing its usefulness for policy may be to focus on the unit of analysis in crowding studies. Two levels of measurement are common in the literature (see Gaes 1985). At the individual level, crowding is assessed through such measures as spatial or social density, personal space, and perceived crowding. Aggregate level measures have combined capacity with social or spatial density to characterize crowding levels in particular institutions or parts of institutions. These latter measures may be the most significant for criminal justice policy because they purport to describe crowding in ways that permit comparisons at the institutional level. The problem with them, however, is that they depend on assessments of capacity and there seems to be little agreement on how many prisoners a particular institution should hold.

The most common approaches to capacity are known as "design" and "rated" capacity. Design capacity refers to the number of inmates that architects planned to house in a facility. It is generally defined by square footage. Rated capacity reflects the number of inmates that can be housed safely in a facility. That is determined by facility staff or corrections standards enforcement agencies and is based on square footage along with other design issues.

These capacity measures provide little information about conditions within facilities and are susceptible to wide interpretation and manipulation. As Bleich (1989, p. 1131) has stated "Whether a prison can accommodate an increase in its population cannot be determined simply by counting floor tiles or beds. Rather the answer may depend in large part on the configuration of the sleeping units, the composition of the population, the types of programs provided, and the levels of staffing." As early as 1937 the Bureau of the Census abandoned the use of capacity measures in assessments of crowding because of the difficulty in determining the "normal capacity" of prisons and jails (see Bleich 1989, p. 1141).

The limitations of the measures used to assess crowding at the institutional level are also illustrated by current court decisions. In cases dealing with jail and prison crowding, the Supreme Court has recognized the complexity of institutional crowding and has rejected approaches based solely on capacity. In *Bell v. Wolfish* (1979) the Court ruled on, among other things, the constitutionality of the "double bunking" of pretrial detainees. The decision focused on the absence of punitive intent by officials, and the Court also considered the fact that inmates were provided adequate room for sleeping, were detained for relatively short terms, and were allowed out of their cells for substantial periods each day.

In *Rhodes v. Chapman* (1981) the Supreme Court considered the double bunking of prison inmates. For crowding to result in constitutionally prohibited cruel and unusual punishment, conditions would need to "involve the wanton and unnecessary infliction of pain" or "be grossly disproportionate to the severity of the crime warranting imprisonment." As Justice Brennan described in a concurring opinion, the Court used a "totality of circumstances test" and found no constitutional violation. Among the factors considered by the Court in *Rhodes* were the amount of time inmates spent out of cells, the quality of food, ventilation, programming, and inmate safety.

In decisions before and after *Bell* and *Rhodes*, lower courts have found constitutional violations in some crowded institutions. Plaintiffs in these cases delineated, with varying degrees of specificity, the harmful effects of crowding in their particular institutions (see Thornberry and Call 1983). Although remedies have often been linked to capacity by requiring reductions in prison or jail populations, the cases make it clear that measures of crowding based solely on capacity are of very limited value. And, the problem is not only that judicial perspectives on crowding are not adequately reflected in measures of crowding. As the Director of the Jails Division of the National Institute of Corrections, Michael O'Toole, has noted (personal communication, March 16, 1990), it is common wisdom among corrections professionals that two institutions may be filled equally beyond their design or rated capacities and still be very different places in which to work or live.

From a measurement perspective, the problem with the capacity-based operational definitions of crowding is that they fail to adequately represent the conceptualization of the phenomenon (see Babbie 1983, p. 109) as suggested in the court cases and comments of corrections experts. Crowding, as an attribute of institutions, is a complex phenomenon that includes but is not limited to concerns with population and space. If correctional crowding is to be a useful social science and management concept there is a need to develop standard measures that more completely reflect the richness and complexity of a shared conceptualization of the phenomenon. This is not to argue that some quantification of a legal test of "totality of circumstances" is possible or even desirable. Describing crowding and deciding the constitutionality of conditions that are described are different tasks and the latter may be accomplished best through the detailed analyses advocated by Justice Brennan in the *Rhodes* case. Without measures that reflect the complex understanding of crowding, however, it is impossible to make meaningful comparisons either across institutions or across time, comparisons that are necessary for progress in research and useful in directing and assessing policy interventions. The first step toward developing more useful measures is to specify precisely the dimensions that compose the concept of crowding.

METHODOLOGY

The problems of measuring complex phenomenon are certainly not unique to the study of correctional crowding. One area in which considerable progress has been made, and that may provide a model methodology for corrections research, is in the development of indices of disease severity in medicine. These indices combine measures of symptoms with patient characteristics and medical history to produce a numerical score reflecting the severity of disease. The measures are designed to allow physicians to discriminate among degrees and kinds of illnesses. Their primary use has been as decision support systems for helping direct patient care. They have also been used to stratify patients into comparable groups for evaluations of the use of hospital resources and to compare the efficacy of treatments in different hospitals over time (see Knaus, Wagner, and Draper 1989). Indices that have achieved some degree of acceptance in emergency room medicine include the Reaction Level Scale (RLS85) and the Glasgow Comma Scale for neurosurgical patients (see Starmark, Stalhammar, Holmgren, and Rosander 1988), and the more general Acute Physiology and Chronic Health Evaluation (APACHE) scales (see Knaus, Draper, Wagner, and Zimmerman 1985).

An extensive review of the methodology for developing indices of disease severity was conducted by Gustafson et al. (1986). The authors favor the use of expert judgmental models that incorporate group processes. They argue that severity is a judgmental phenomenon that must be defined by experts whose views can later be validated empirically. The focus group process (see Morgan 1988; Krueger 1988) is used to identify the necessary components of additive multiattribute models. These suggestions for methodology formed the foundation of an effort to develop a model of the severity of jail crowding. The goal of the project was to identify the institutional attributes which define different levels of crowding and to begin to operationalize an index of severity which would reflect the complexity of jail crowding as it is understood by experts.

A focus group was conducted at the annual meeting of the American Jail Association in May 1991 in Atlanta. Under the session title, "Developing an Index for Measuring Jail Crowding," jail administrators from across the country met for the purpose of exchanging information on what overcrowding means. Twenty people participated in the 4-hour session, including Sheriffs, jail administrators, a police commander, jail inspector, a program specialist from the National Institute of Corrections, and a compliance consultant. The participants averaged 20 years experience in criminal justice and 4.4 years in management. The 15 jail managers worked in institutions with populations ranging from 26 to 1,400. The average jail population for the group was 425. Two participants worked in jails with a population of fewer than 100 inmates. Participants were nearly split in representing "new generation" jails and traditional linear intermittent supervision facilities.

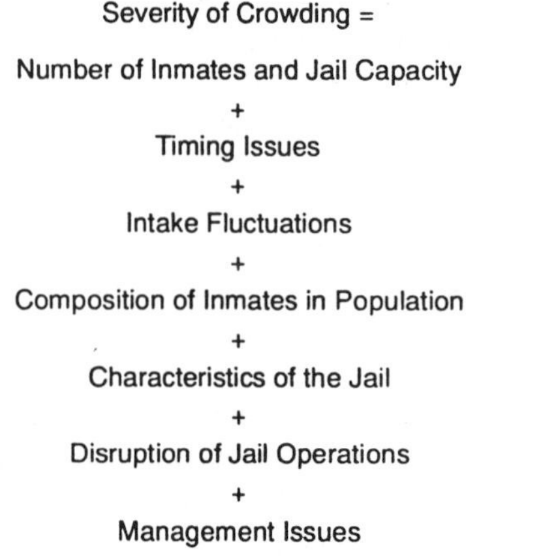

Figure 1: A Model of the Severity of Jail Crowding

A MODEL OF JAIL CROWDING

After instructions and discussion of the project, the focus group began by addressing the general question: "What do administrators mean when they say a jail is crowded?" As the medical researchers suggest, a tentative model was used to help structure the discussion. Group members were asked to discuss issues dealing with the number of inmates, types of inmates, and features of facilities. The expert participants refined, revised, and explicated the ideas in developing a final multidimensional additive model of jail crowding. The group members described the following elements of the model (See Figure 1).

Number of Inmates and Jail Capacity

The group first turned to the question of how many inmates it takes for a jail to be crowded. The ratio of inmates to design capacity was discussed and there was consensus that the effects of crowding could begin to be seen when a jail was filled beyond 80% of capacity. Group members were aware of the limitations of the capacity measures, however, and made two significant additional points. First, the 80% benchmark is important because, they argued, it is at that point that administrative flexibility begins to be reduced. It is, therefore, also useful to measure loss of flexibility in areas such as inmate classification and movement and not just the number of inmates. Second, when using the inmates-to-capacity ratio, not only is the capacity measure a problem but so is the count of inmates. For example, counting work release inmates, inmates being transported, or inmates being booked but released in short order illustrate differences in procedure that must be taken into account.

In summary, the participants agreed that understanding jail overcrowding requires more than a simple inmate-to-capacity ratio but that this measure could not be eliminated. They cautioned against over-reliance on the statistic and indicated a need to consider a variety of institutional characteristics and to include measures of the disruption of normal operations. Those issues surfaced repeatedly in the focus group discussion.

Timing Issues

The expert participants next addressed the question: "Are there certain times of the year, week, or day when crowding is worse than at other times?" The point is that crowding may be cyclic or transitory and that when it is measured may be important.

The participants confirmed and explained temporal patterns in crowding. After holidays, they argued, it is common for jails to experience a sudden influx of inmates. Judges, it seems, often postpone sentencing, causing a post holiday jam. Unexpectedly, participants also reported that the inmate population fell during the summer months and increased again during the fall. This was especially true in counties with universities or colleges.

As expected, day of the week is also significant. Inmates arrested over the weekend often remain in jail until they are processed by the courts on Monday. For some jails, the number of inmates falls early in the week, whereas on Thursdays and Fridays, the number of admissions rises. To facilitate comparisons, it may be useful to control for these fluctuations by measuring crowding mid-week. Increased bookings can also result from special events such as rock concerts and political protests. One administrator, for example, stated that his jail could count on an increase in bookings whenever the Chicago White Sox played in his town. Tactical activity by the police, such as prostitution sweeps, large drug arrests, and antigang sweeps, can also create sudden increases in jail admissions. A jail administrator from a popular resort town reported that jail admissions increased at the peak of the business season when "street sweeps" in tourist areas led to the arrests of large numbers of people on prostitution, loitering, and other similar charges.

The participants agreed that there were regular time periods and unique events that were associated with changes in the number of jail admissions and the size of the jail population. Group members also pointed out the implications of the temporal changes. The patterns mean that the crisis is not uniform. Instead, critical periods rise and fall and their predictability creates opportunities for management. In an argument that would surface several times, the administrators pointed out that productive relationships with the police, the courts, and other local criminal justice organizations often allowed them to smooth out peaks and valleys and to better manage their resources.

Intake Fluctuations

Next, the group focused on the intake process and the problems posed by the admission of certain kinds of inmates. Intake was regarded as dealing with a distinct set of resources and thus was addressed separately from concerns surrounding inmates in the jail population. Participants were most concerned with managing inmates with health problems, including those with communicable diseases, intravenous drug users, and mentally ill or physically handicapped inmates.

Offenders who need some form of protection from the general inmate population were also identified as a potential source of strain as a jail's population increased. This group includes inmates charged with particular kinds of crimes such as child molesting, or those testifying as special witnesses for the state, or co-conspirators who require separation. In addition, people arrested in connection with political protests, sporting events, or rock concerts may have special difficulties adjusting to confinement and may be vulnerable to more experienced inmates.

Whereas some inmates may require protection others will pose problems due to their aggressiveness. The participants reported that concerns about violence were most frequent with youthful inmates, especially known gang members who may require separation from some inmates. Other inmates may also require special resources on admission. Several participants reported that non-English-speaking or illiterate inmates created an extra burden for their jail personnel.

Unexpected increases in the admissions of any of these inmates can strain jail resources. But here, too, problems could be minimized by aggressive jail management. Adequate screening and intake classification, a staff trained to deal with unusual circumstances, as well as good working relationships with police and medical and psychiatric services could reduce problems even under crowded conditions. Measuring crowding will require information about the distribution of inmates admitted in a given period as well as the resources available for dealing with special needs admissions.

Composition of Inmates in Population

The intake of special needs inmates can require skills and resources similar to those found in hospital emergency rooms. When jails are unable to direct those resources appropriately, the severity of overcrowding increases. The focus group members distinguished between the potential problems associated with intake and the more prolonged drain on resources associated with special needs inmates within the jail population.

Participants again reported that inmates with medical or mental health problems strained jail resources. Substance abusers, pregnant inmates, and suicidal inmates exacerbated crowding. Inmates who are small in stature, homosexual, or known to be HIV infected may require extra care and supervision and possibly protective segregation. Elderly inmates and members of some religious groups might need protection, special privileges, or special medical care. Sentenced inmates waiting to be transferred to the state correctional system were considered a problem as they had little incentive to conform to jail rules and regulations.

In summary, participants identified a number of categories of special needs inmates within jail populations who may also tax resources more than their numbers would suggest. Overcrowding can be made more severe by the management and supervision requirements of these groups and an assessment of crowding levels must take into account the mix of inmates in the population and the ability to address special needs.

Characteristics of the Jail

In the administrators' approach to overcrowding, the number and types of inmates combine with available resources to increase or diminish problems. To the group members, one of the most important resources is the structure of the jail facility itself. The participants described features of jails that contribute to problems when the number of inmates in a facility increases. They agreed that architecture makes a difference and that "new generation" jails provide more flexibility for improvising housing and make supervision easier than do traditional linear jails. Another issue related to architecture dealt with inmate movement. Overpopulated jails are likely to have more problems if inmates must be supervised during movement and if separate dining or visiting facilities are used.

Increases in the number of inmates can also interact with specific areas of the jail in significant ways. The ability of the kitchen and laundry facilities to take on additional burdens is important. The property room was seen as a place important to understanding crowding levels. Inmate property gets lost or misfiled when space is inadequate, resulting in increased tensions and grievances as well as other problems.

A final characteristic of the setting received considerable attention. Population increases tax an institution's infrastructure. Plumbing, heating, electrical, and other mechanical systems can become overloaded and break down. Assessment of crowding levels, then, must also take into account features of the physical environment and their capacity to accommodate increases in inmates.

Disruption of Jail Operations

As the participants identified relevant features of the jail environment, it became clear that their concerns extended beyond physical characteristics to include jail operations. They agreed that the extent of disruption of normal jail operations was an important element to consider in assessing the severity of crowding. The group participants delineated significant elements of jail operations that might be influenced or altered by increases in the number of inmates.

Among the experts' greatest concerns were programming and supervision issues. Classification and the planned separation of inmates can be problematic as space becomes inadequate. Adjustments to or near abandonment of classification systems can be indications of serious crowding. Likewise, the supervision of inmates is made more difficult when staff are stretched too thinly or when inmates are housed in areas intended for other purposes. Security routines may also be upset due to worn or inoperable devices.

Another significant indicator may be found in changes in scheduling of routine activities. As a jail's population increases, recreation and other programs may need to be limited or scheduled at unusual hours. Finally, administrators returned to a concern with institutional infrastructure by arguing that disruption of routine maintenance schedules can provide insight into the degree of crowding. They suggested operationalizing the issue by measuring how long it takes to fix broken toilets or by how long it has been since housing units had been painted.

In short, many aspects of the normal routine of jail operations can be disrupted by increases in the number of inmates and the extent of disruption offers one indicator of the degree of crowding. The participants argued, however, that the disruption was not inevitable and there were opportunities for management to intervene to mitigate the adverse effects of population increases.

Management Issues

The session participants also addressed the impact of management more directly when they described the resources whose availability could diminish or exacerbate crowding problems. The group members supported inclusion of management issues in an index of crowding severity. They argued, for example, that the ability to use overtime without limitations could be valuable in coping with crowding but that problems also arose when officers worked "too many" hours. Stress created by working long hours under adverse conditions could lead to absenteeism, turnover, and conflict among staff.

Another cluster of management concerns centered on hiring and training issues. A high proportion of officers with little experience or seniority was viewed as a potential contributor to crowding problems. Reductions in the amount of time spent in preservice and inservice training were viewed similarly.

A third set of concerns among the experts returned to a theme already mentioned several times. Population increases can limit the ability to manage proactively. The need to continually respond to crises can inhibit long-term planning and reduce the ability to analyze problems and take corrective action. The frequency of development of new policies and procedures, particularly those not related to population pressures, may provide some evidence of crowding severity.

Relationships With Outside Agencies and Organizations

The comments of group members emphasized another issue that was not part of the original, tentative model of crowding. The experts felt strongly that the problems associated with crowding were also related to the jail's contacts with outside organizations. Not only are the causes of crowding to be found with the police, the courts, and other criminal justice agencies that control the flow of cases, but the management of the problem also depends on the quality of ties to those and other organizations. The focus group members stressed the importance of including an assessment of those links in a measure of crowding severity.

The experts felt that the ability to negotiate with criminal justice agencies was important and that participation in local coordinating efforts was valuable. Specifically, effective jail management could depend on working with judges to postpone admitting some sentenced inmates until there was space available, or on working with police to increase the use of citation release. Additionally, the participants felt that a good working relationship with public interest groups, like the American Civil Liberties Union (ACLU), supports sound jail management. Pressure from those groups and the threat of legal action can help direct resources toward the jail.

DISCUSSION

The primary task of the focus group was to explicate a model of jail crowding that reflects expert opinion and is capable of describing variations in severity. The group members finished the session by discussing outcome variables that they expect to be useful in validating their crowding model. Their list included increases in violence, disciplinary problems, staff grievances and turnover as well as other variables. The findings of research that has examined the effects of crowding on these variables, and has used the common capacity measures, have been inconclusive (see Gaes 1985). The group discussion, however, demonstrated the members' confidence in crowding as a useful concept with implications for management and for research.

The elaboration of a model of crowding is a step toward the development of an index of severity. A national survey of jails is planned in order to complete the empirical procedures necessary for constructing the measure. The completed additive index will be composed of subscales representing each concept in the model. The subscales will contain variables that the survey indicates are capable of discriminating among jails and that accurately represent the experts' view of crowding. A multidimensional index that meets those criteria has the potential to advance understanding. An additional goal, however, involves validation of the index to an external criterion, namely the crowding-related problems described by group participants. Multivariate analyses can provide a basis for assigning weights to the components of the model and can be used to examine the ability of the index to predict the crowding problems.

A parsimonious index of severity can have implications for practice as well as for research. Used regularly and with a data base of information on a large number of jails, a severity index can serve as a decision support system (see Heymann and Bloom 1978; Alter 1980) to assist in jail policy development and evaluation. Viewing the project most optimistically, one can image conversations among jail management staff that might include statements like; "This month our overall crowding level was about the same as last year and is average for jails this size. However, we score worse than other jails with regard to fluctuations in intake and relationships with outside agencies. We need to contact other jails to see how they manage admissions and we need to better train our staff to deal with the unusual admissions cases. We also need to work more closely with judges and to re-examine these areas next month."

Along with such practical consequences, this approach to measuring crowding also suggests directions for other research. Besides attempting to improve the predictive power of the measure and pursuing comparative studies, other perspectives and other goals should be considered. It is likely that the components of prison crowding will differ substantially from those discussed here. A similar process might be used to describe those factors and to develop measures of prison crowding. Further, the meaning of crowding for central office administrators, correctional officers and inmates should also be examined. Those studies may provide insight regarding common elements as well as differences in perspective resulting from differences in role within correctional organizations.

Two additional and related issues regarding the model described by the jail experts are worthy of further discussion. First, the dimensions and the variables noted by the participants all seem eminently sensible. This is not to say, however, that the focus group has not added to the body of information on the subject. The benefit of their effort lies in the systematic organization of the concept of crowding that emerged from the group process. That the elements of the model are easy to accept is testament to the face validity of the participants' ideas.

The second issue concerns the administrators' theoretical approach to understanding correctional crowding. Correctional environments have been described from a variety of theoretical perspectives. Phenomenological perspectives, for example, are concerned with individuals' perceptions of environmental characteristics, including crowding (see, Toch 1977). Social climate perspectives assume that measurable characteristics of social settings emerge from interactions of individuals and their organizational or institutional environments (see, Moos 1975; Wright and Boudaris 1982). Although the crowding model may contain few surprises, a theoretical perspective that has not been common to crowding research is evident in the administrators' analysis.

The participants brought to the focus group session a perspective that assumes that management can play a central role in determining the characteristics of institutions. For the group members, conditions within jails are not determined by uncontrollable forces and managers are not the passive recipients of crowding problems. Crowding severity is determined by the interaction of population (both number and mix of inmates), the features of facilities, and a range of administration or management practices that can adjust for and accommodate the other variables. Within this perspective, institutions that strive to maintain normal operations, that work with relevant outside agencies, and that hold to a variety of other describable management practices, are less crowded than other institutions that may have the same inmate-to-capacity ratio. They are, thus, expected to have fewer crowding related problems. At first consideration this may appear to confuse cause and effect. For example, the disruption of operations could be viewed as an effect of crowding rather than as an indicator and, therefore, a cause of crowding related problems. But that would not be consistent with the participants' perspective. In their approach, failure to maintain the facility, for example, is not the inevitable effect of increases in population but instead reflects administrative priorities and decisions made when population is just one of many possible considerations.

The theoretical perspective implicit in the focus group participants' analysis of crowding is a managerial perspective. It is consistent with an extensive body of management literature that advocates aggressive management that is responsible for accomplishing specific outcomes (see, for example, Drucker 1973). Until recently, the perspective has received little attention among social scientists studying corrections. In a comparison of Texas, California, and Michigan systems, however, DiIulio (1987, 1991) has begun to articulate a "governmental perspective" that he describes as a way of thinking about and studying prisons in which administrators are key actors in determining the quality and character of correctional environments. That view comes through clearly in the group members' understanding of jail crowding.

Although it is possible that anything can be measured (see Babbie 1983, p. 101), the focus group process makes clear the importance of the theoretical understanding that is brought to the task (see Peak 1966). The ease with which the jail experts described how they think crowding should be measured illustrates the value of their implicit theory. That, in turn, suggests that the failure to develop more useful, policy-relevant measures of crowding may not be the result of a problem of measurement but rather of the failure of social scientists to elaborate a theoretical understanding of crowding at the institutional level. This supports the need for improved collaboration between practitioners and academics and supports the use of expert judgmental approaches to crowding that can be subjected to empirical testing.

REFERENCES

Alter, Steven. 1980. *Decision Support Systems: Current Practice and Continuing Challenges.* Reading, MA: Addison-Wesley.

Babbie, Earl. 1983. *The Practice of Social Research* 3rd ed. New York: Wiley.

Bell v. Wolfish, 441 U.S. 520 (1979).

Bleich, Jeff. 1989. "The Politics of Prison Crowding." *California Law Review* 77:1125-80.

Blumstein, Alfred. 1988. "Prison Populations: A System Out of Control?" Pp.231-66 in *Crime and Justice: An Annual Review of Research* Vol. 10, edited by M. Tonry and N. Morris. Chicago: University of Chicago Press.

Bureau of Justice Statistics. 1991. *National Update* 1:7-8.

Camp, George and Camille Camp. 1989. *Managing Crowded Prisons.* Washington, DC: National Institute of Justice.

DiIulio, John J. 1987. *Governing Prisons: A Comparative Study of Correctional Management.* New York: Free Press.

———. 1991. *No Escape: The Future of American Corrections.* New York: Basic Books.

Drucker, Peter F. 1973. *Management: Tasks, Responsibilities, Practices.* New York: Harper & Row.

Evans, Gary, M. N. Pulsane, Sephen J. Lepore, and Janea Martin. 1989. "Residential Density and Psychological Health: The Mediating Effects of Social Support." *Journal of Personality and Social Behavior* 6:994-99.

Gaes, Gerald G. 1985. "The Effects of Overcrowding in Prison." Pp. 95-106 in *Crime and Justice: An Annual Review of Research* Vol. 6, edited by M. Tonry and N. Morris. Chicago: University of Chicago Press.

Gibbs, John J. 1983. "Problems and Priorities: Perceptions of Jail Custodians and Social Providers." *Journal of Criminal Justice* 11:327-38.

Gottfredson, Stephen and Sean McConville, eds. 1987. *America's Correctional Crisis: Prison Populations and Public Policy.* Westport, CT: Greenwood.

Government Accounting Office, 1990. *Prison Crowding: Issues Facing the Nation's Prison Systems.* Washington, DC: U.S. Government Accounting Office.

Gustafson, David H., Dennis G. Fryback, Jerry H. Rose, Victor Yick, Constance T. Prokop, Don E. Detmer, and Jennifer Moore. 1986. "A Decision Theoretic Methodology for Severity Index Development." *Medical Decision Making* 6:27-35.

Guynes, Randall. 1988. "Nation's Jail Managers Assess Their Needs." *National Institute of Justice, Research in Brief,* August.

Hall, Andy, D. Alan Henry, Jolanta Perlstein, and Walter F. Smith. 1985. *Alleviating Jail Crowding: A Systems Perspective.* Washington, DC: National Institute of Justice.

Harris, M. Kay. 1987. "A Brief for De-escalating Criminal Sanctions." Pp. 205-20 in *America's Correctional Crisis: Prison Populations and Public Policy,* edited by S. Gottfredson and S. McConville. Westport, CT: Greenwood.

Heymann, H. G. and Robert Bloom. 1978. *Decision Support Systems in Finance and Accounting.* New York: Quorum.

Klofas, John. 1990a. "The Jail and the Community." *Justice Quarterly* 7:69-102.

———. 1990b. "Measuring Jail Use: A Comparative Analysis of Local Corrections." *Journal of Research in Crime and Delinquency* 27:295-317.

Knaus, William, Elizabeth Draper, Douglas Wagner, and Jack Zimmerman. 1985. "APACHE II: A Severity of Disease Classification System." *Critical Care Medicine* 13:818-29.

Knaus, William, Douglas Wagner, and Elizabeth Draper. 1989. "Implications." *Critical Care Medicine* 17:219-21.

Krueger, Richard A. 1988. *Focus Groups: A Practical Guide for Applied Research*, Newbury Park, CA: Sage.

Moos, Rudolf H. 1975. *Evaluating Correctional and Community Settings*. New York: Wiley.

Morgan, David L. 1988. *Focus Groups as Qualitative Research*. Newbury Park, CA: Sage.

Peak, Helen. 1966. "Problems of Objective Observation." Pp. 243-99 in *Research Methods in the Behavioral Sciences*, edited by L. Festinger and D. Katz. New York: Holt, Rinehart & Winston.

Rhodes, William. 1990. *Models of the Criminal Justice System: A Review of Existing Impact Models*. Washington, DC: Bureau of Justice Statistics.

Rhodes v. Chapman, 452 U.S. 347 (1981).

Ruback, R. Barry and Christopher A. Innes. 1988. "The Relevance and Irrelevance of Psychological Research: The Example of Prison Crowding." *American Psychologist* 43:683-96.

Schaeffer, Marc A., Andrew Baum, Paul B. Paulus, and Gerald G. Gaes. 1988. "Architecturally Mediated Effects of Social Density in Prison." *Environment and Behavior* 20:3-19.

Starmark, Jan-Erik, Daniel Stalhammar, Eddy Holmgren, and Bjorn Rosander. 1988. "A Comparison of the Glasgow Coma Scale and the Reaction Level Scale." *Journal of Neurosurgery* 69:699-706.

Sundstrum, Eric. 1978. "Crowding as a Sequential Process: Review of Research on the Harmful Effects of Population Density on Humans." Pp. 31-116 in *Human Response to Crowding*, edited by A. Baum and Y. M. Epstein. New York: Wiley.

Thornberry, Terence P. and Jack E. Call. 1983. "Constitutional Challenges to Prison Crowding: The Scientific Evidence of Harmful Effects." *The Hastings Law Journal* 35:313-51.

Toch, Hans. 1977. *Living in Prison: The Ecology of Survival*. New York: Free Press.

———. 1985. "Warehouses for People?" *Annals of the American Academy of Political and Social Science* 478:58-72.

Wener, Richard E. and Robert D. Kaminoff. 1983. "Improving Environmental Information: Effects of Signs on Perceived Crowding and Behavior." *Environment and Behavior* 15:3-20.

Wright, Kevin and James Boudaris. 1982. "An Assessment of the Moos Correctional Institutions Environment Scale." *Journal of Research in Crime and Delinquency* 19:255-76.

Zimring, Franklin E. and Gordon Hawkins. 1991. *The Scale of Imprisonment*. Chicago: University of Chicago Press.

The Impact of Shock Incarceration Programs on Prison Crowding

Doris Layton MacKenzie
Alex Piquero

The impact of shock incarceration programs on prison crowding in five states was examined using a model to estimate bed space loss or savings. Recidivism rates, duration of imprisonment, dismissal rates, and program capacity were used to estimate the programs' impact if the probabilities that the offenders would have been in prison or on probation were varied. Results indicated that if the goal of a short-term incarceration program is to reduce prison crowding, it must be carefully designed and monitored with this purpose in mind.

From 1980 to 1990, state and federal prison populations rose 134% to a record 771,243 inmates. By 1990, prisons were operating between 18% and 29% in excess of capacity (Greenfeld 1992). Faced with this crisis in prison crowding, states searched for ways to alleviate the pressure on prisons. Intermediate sanctions were viewed by many as a viable method of addressing the problem. Although originally designed and supported as a method of helping offenders become law-abiding citizens, many intermediate sanctions are currently being promoted and developed with the express purpose of reducing prison crowding (Palumbo and Snyder-Joy 1992). As such, they are expected to provide alternatives to incarceration and lead to a reduction in the number of offenders in prison.

DORIS LAYTON MACKENZIE: Research Scholar, Department of Criminal Justice and Criminology, University of Maryland. **ALEX PIQUERO:** Graduate Research Assistant, Department of Criminal Justice and Criminology, University of Maryland.

This article was originally presented as a paper at the Annual Meeting of ASC, October 1993, Phoenix, Arizona. This investigation was supported in part by grant #90-DD-CX-0061 from the National Institute of Justice, Office of Justice Programs, U.S. Department of Justice to the University of Maryland. Points of view in this article are those of the authors and do not necessarily represent the official position of the U.S. Department of Justice. Thanks are expressed to all those who have worked on the multisite study. Requests for copies should be sent to the senior author at the University of Maryland, Department of Criminal Justice and Criminology, 2220 LeFrak Hall, College Park, MD 20742. Telephone 301-405-3008.

CRIME & DELINQUENCY, Vol. 40 No. 2, April 1994 222-249

However, in many situations, the goal of reducing prison crowding goes unrealized because intermediate sanctions that were designed as alternatives to incarceration have actually been used for offenders who would otherwise have received a lesser, not a more punitive sentence (Austin and Krisberg 1981; Morris and Tonry 1990). In fact, in a study of community correctional programs, Hylton (1980) found that instead of reducing prison populations, as they were designed to do, the programs actually tripled the proportion of persons under state control. In other words, these programs not only strengthened the net, they also created new nets in the form of community corrections to control more offenders.

In another study, Palumbo and Snyder-Joy (1992) examined the effect of a home arrest program in Arizona. Not only was the program not cost-effective, but there were actually increased rates of technical violations for those in the house arrest program compared to those supervised on regular parole. Furthermore, the house arrest program resulted in placing inmates in house arrest who would have otherwise been on regular probation, thereby widening the net of control. Similar net widening has also been found in juvenile arbitration procedures (Ezell 1989), in the Japanese juvenile justice system (Yokoyama 1986, 1989), and in a study of electronic monitoring in British Columbia, Canada (Mainprize 1992).

Not everyone considers net widening to be a disadvantage of intermediate sanctions; some argue for deterrence, just deserts, and more punishment. In their opinion, the only way we can keep our streets safe is by increasing social control, and this means increasing the number of prison beds. Conservative legislators often support intermediate sanctions in the belief that they will both reduce costs and, at the same time, provide greater control over offenders who might be given probation. From this perspective, any reduction in prison crowding will occur because offenders will be deterred from committing new criminal activities and, therefore, the crime rate will be reduced.

In contrast, those who advocate increased diversion, decriminalization, due process, and decarceration to shrink the net argue that the United States has the highest national incarceration rate and, furthermore, that we can no longer afford to build prisons and keep prisoners locked up for lengthy periods of time. In their opinion, most offenders will eventually be returned to the street and the prison is not the best way to change offenders so that they will not return to criminal activities when they are released. Intermediate sanctions provide a reasonable alternative to incarceration for those who would otherwise be imprisoned.

In their recent book, Morris and Tonry (1990) argued that a reasonable system of sanctions may increase control over some offenders and decrease it over others. Judges are frequently forced to choose between nominal supervision in the community versus a traditional prison sentence. In many cases, offenders are given the benefit of the doubt and receive probation. However, if an intermediate punishment is entered into the equation, judges tend to sentence to the intermediate punishment those offenders formerly treated more leniently rather than those who would otherwise receive a prison sentence. From a judge's perspective, there is often a need for more restrictive punishments than probation for more serious probationers. Thus, although some individuals involved in developing intermediate sanctions may have expected these programs to reduce prison crowding, reducing crowding may not be the highest priority for all decision makers. Rather, the goals of different decision makers may actually conflict.

Although many studies have found that intermediate sanctions may increase the net of control, there is evidence that some of them have the desired effect of reducing prison populations. For example, in a study of community corrections in Colorado counties, Covey and Menard (1984) found that offenders in the diversion program more closely resembled incarcerated offenders than they did those placed on probation. They concluded that, although this was not true of all counties, in many, the diversion program did appear to reduce prison commitment rates.

After a similar study examining the impact of community corrections programs in four Kansas counties, Jones (1990) concluded that without them, the prison system in Kansas would be facing far worse problems than its present crowding crisis. However, he did find differences among the four counties studied. Using a time series analysis of monthly prison admissions of program-eligible offenders in each county, he found that in two of them, the community corrections programs had indeed drawn participants from the prison-bound population; in the other two counties they had not. He emphasized that net widening is not an inevitable by-product of community-based alternative programs and under some circumstances, programs designed as alternatives to incarceration can achieve their goals.

Boot Camp Prisons

One intermediate sanction, which has become increasingly popular in the past decade, is boot camp prisons. The number and size of these prisons for adult felons have been rapidly escalating. Since boot camps first began in Georgia and Oklahoma in 1983, 29 states and the Federal Bureau of Prisons have opened 46 boot camps. The original camps were small in size, but by 1993 there were over 7,500 prison beds in adult correctional systems devoted to boot camp programs.

There are many reasons for the rapid growth of boot camp prisons. Politicians and policymakers, fearful of a "Willie Horton problem," can appear to be tough on crime by supporting boot camps (MacKenzie and Parent 1991). They, as well as the public, seem to think that boot camps address the lack of discipline and self-control, which they believe are characteristic of young, nonviolent offenders. Correction officials, in contrast, emphasize the importance of these programs in rehabilitating offenders, reducing recidivism, and providing drug education (MacKenzie and Souryal 1991).

Almost everyone expects the boot camps to reduce prison crowding. They differ, however, in how they expect this reduction to occur. Some believe that crowding will be reduced by lowering recidivism rates because fewer offenders will be arrested, convicted, and returned to prison. Thus fewer prisoners will enter prison and the need for prison beds will be reduced.

However, there are different opinions about the mechanisms that initiate these changes in individual offenders. Some argue that recidivism will be reduced because offenders will be deterred from committing new crimes; others argue that the programs will rehabilitate offenders so they will not return to criminal activities once they have been released. In both of these situations, offenders are expected to change as a result of the programs and, therefore, they are expected to have lower rates of recidivism.

Another way boot camp prisons may affect prison crowding is by reducing the time offenders spend in prison. An offender who receives a 5-year sentence to a traditional prison might be eligible for parole after serving one third of the sentence and, with additional time off for good behavior, might be paroled from prison after serving 2 years. In contrast, an offender who completes a boot camp program may be eligible for parole after serving a much shorter time. For instance, an offender with the same 5-year sentence might complete a 3-month boot camp program and be eligible for release after serving only 3 months. In the former case, a prison bed would be needed for 24 months, whereas the boot camp bed would be needed for only 3 months—a difference of 21 months. The boot camp may, in such cases, represent a method for some offenders to earn their way out of prison earlier than they would otherwise be released.

To have an impact on prison crowding, there must be a sufficient number of eligible inmates who successfully complete the program in a shorter time than they would have served in prison. Many shock programs have rigid eligibility criteria that will severely restrict the type of offender who will be considered acceptable for the program. Furthermore, if the program is lengthy or if there is a long wait between entering prison and entry to the program, the net reduction in days served may be minimal. There is evidence from previous studies that offenders with shorter sentences will not volunteer or will drop out of a shock program (MacKenzie, Shaw, and Gowdy 1993). They seem to use a rational decision-making model by weighing the choice of doing "tough time" in the boot camp versus easier but longer time in a traditional prison.

Along with a reduction in recidivism rates and shortening of time in prison, there are other factors that will influence the potential of boot camps to have an impact on prison crowding. One factor that is vitally important is whether offenders are drawn from those who under other circumstances would be incarcerated. If they are not, and the incarceration net is widened by selecting offenders who would otherwise have been on probation or in some other program (e.g., diversion), then the boot camp would increase the number of offenders in prison.

The present study examined five boot camp prisons and explored their potential for reducing prison crowding in the state correctional system. Five states, Florida, Georgia, Louisiana, New York, and South Carolina, participated in an evaluation (MacKenzie 1990). The study had three major components: (a) a process evaluation, (b) a study of offender changes, and (c) an examination of the potential impact of the programs on prison crowding, the focus of this article. The process evaluation included a description of the development and implementation of the boot camp prisons in each site. Interviews were conducted with participants, staff, and administrators, and written reports, policies and procedures, and program documentation were examined. The goals of each program were identified in this process. Consistent with the development of other intermediate sanctions (Morris and Tonry 1990), the two major goals of all five boot camp prisons were (a) changing offenders, and (b) reducing prison crowding (MacKenzie and Souryal 1993). The latter, however, was not a primary goal of many of the individuals interviewed. Many of those working directly with inmates in the shock program emphasized its importance in having an impact on the lives of individual offenders and were not as concerned about reducing prison crowding. However, in almost all of the states, prison crowding had provided a major impetus for developing the boot camp prison.

THE FIVE BOOT CAMP PROGRAMS

Offenders incarcerated in each of the five boot camp prisons were separated from general population inmates in a military-like atmosphere emphasizing strict rules and discipline and were required to participate in drill and physical training. Beyond this common core, there were many differences among programs.[1] Some emphasized treatment, such as education, counseling, or vocational training during the time offenders are incarcerated. For example, inmates in Louisiana and New York boot camp prisons spent 3.5 hours and more than 5 hours per day, respectively, in treatment and education programs. In contrast, inmates in Georgia spent a very short period of time per day in rehabilitative type activities.

Different Program Models

Of particular importance to this study were the differences among sites in entry and exit decision making. To examine differences among programs, we constructed flow charts for each site to describe the process of selection, rejection, dismissal, and completion for each shock program.

A comparison of two flow charts, New York and Georgia, highlights some of the major differences in decision-making processes. In New York, the offenders were sentenced to a term of imprisonment under the supervision of the department of corrections. The department screened the offenders; those who were evaluated as eligible and suitable for the shock incarceration program were given the opportunity to volunteer (Figure 1). If they successfully completed the program, they served 180 days in prison. If they left for any reason, they were required to return to prison and to serve until they were paroled. The only change in this procedure is that there are now some additional restrictions for offenders who are between 26 and 29 years of age.[2]

As can be seen in the flow chart in Figure 2, the decision-making process was very different in Georgia. The chief probation officer determined whether the offender was eligible for the program. A contact was made with the shock staff for verbal confirmation of acceptance to the program and if the answer was "yes," the probation chief certified to the court that the offender had been accepted into the program. The court could then sentence the offender to the program as a condition of probation. The court retained responsibility over the offender if there were any changes in status (whether they were rejected by the department of corrections (DOC), dismissed from the program, or their probation was revoked).

When the flow charts from the five shock programs were compared, large differences among programs in the process of entry and exit decision making became evident. There were two basic variants in the selection procedure. In the first, the sentencing judge placed the offender in the program and maintained decision-making authority over him or her until release from the

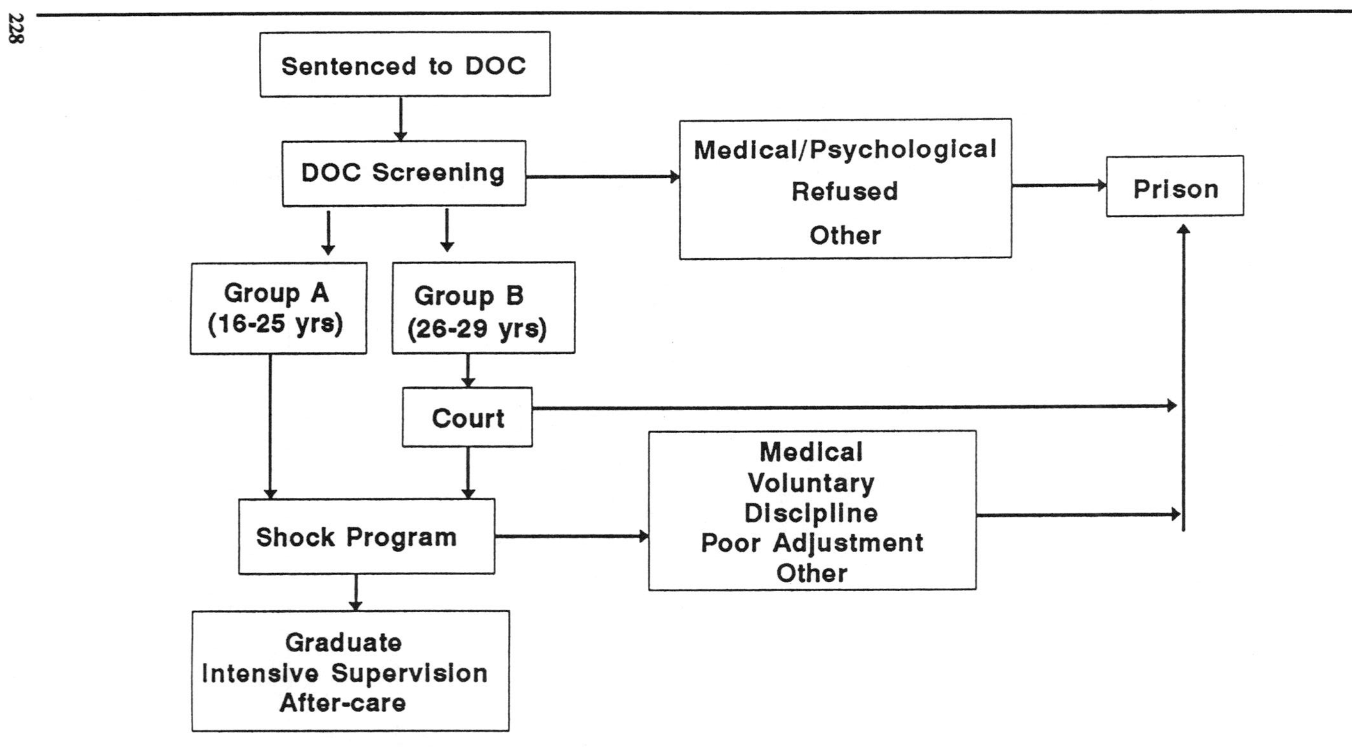

Figure 1: Flowchart Showing Entry and Exit Decision Making for the New York Boot Camp Prison, 1990

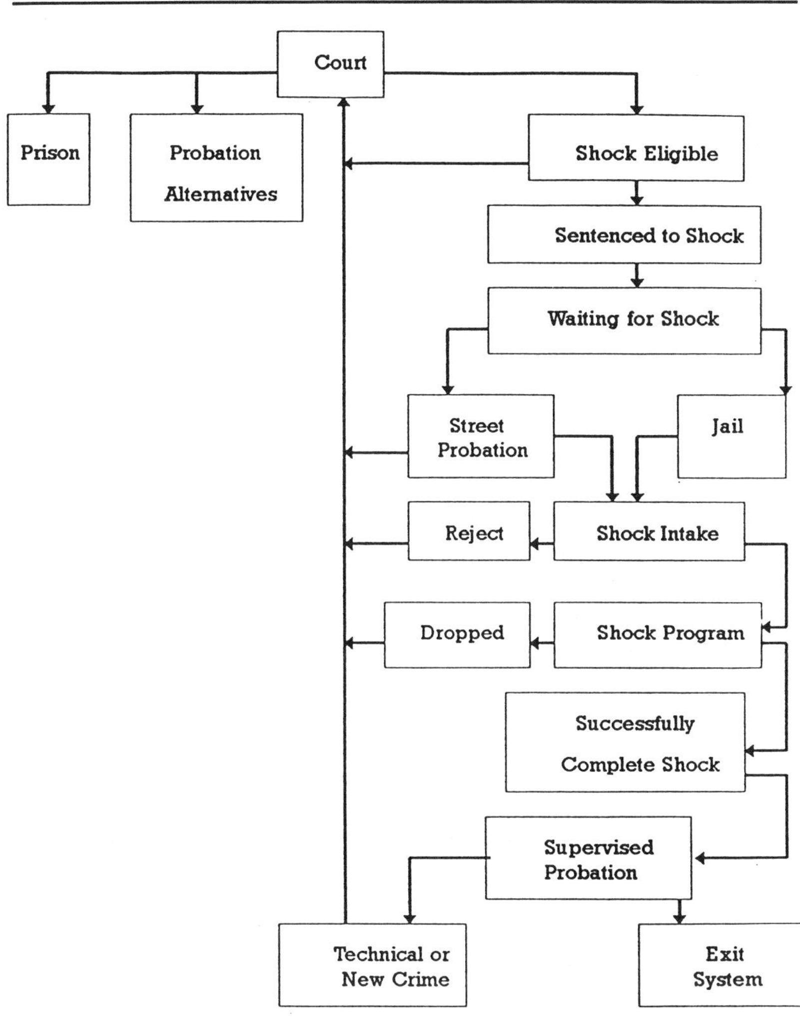

Figure 2: Flowchart Showing Entry and Exit Decision Making for the Georgia Boot Camp Prison, 1989

program. At the other extreme, the DOC had complete control over offenders who entered the program. Those who were dismissed before completing the program in this model were sent to prison.

Differences in entry decision-making can easily affect the impact of the shock program on the larger correctional system. As Morris and Tonry (1990) argued: when the court has placement control, the shock program may be more likely to be used as an alternative to probation. If, on the other hand, the DOC has control over who enters the program, there is a higher probability that offenders entering the program would have otherwise spent time in prison.

When we examined the process evaluations of the five sites, we identified at least three variations in placement decision making:

- Judge places in shock and maintains full control over offenders: Georgia, South Carolina.
- DOC selects for shock, judge approves: New York (ages 26-29), Florida.
- DOC has full control over who enters and judge has little or no control: New York (ages 16-25), Louisiana.

Judges had full control over sentencing offenders to shock in both Georgia and South Carolina. In South Carolina, as in Georgia, the judge sentenced offenders to the shock program and offenders remained under the jurisdiction of the court for 90 days. After at least 75 but no more than 90 days, the sentencing judge had the option to either place a shock inmate on probation or convert the offender to the general prison population. Completion of the shock program, therefore, did not ensure release to probation. Offenders who were not placed on probation prior to the 91st day were automatically converted to general population status. Preliminary data from the program indicated that approximately 6% of the offenders who completed the program were converted to the general prison population.

A major issue in South Carolina and Georgia is whether judges used the program as an alternative to probation. If this is the case, they may have sentenced offenders to the program who would have otherwise simply received probation. This is not an unreasonable use of the program because in many cases a judge may believe an offender needs a more restrictive sanction than probation, but something less than a long term of incarceration. At the same time, this practice clashes with the stated goal of reducing crowding.

In the remaining types of entry, the DOC selected offenders and the judge had varying levels of influence over placement. In these states, the possibility of net widening should be less of a concern. In Florida, the DOC selected offenders for the shock program, although the judge must have approved the selection. Similarly, offenders aged 26-29 in New York, who the DOC selected as candidates for the program, must also have had the judge's approval before actually entering. Decisions regarding entry to shock incarceration were the responsibility of the DOC in Louisiana and New York (ages

16-25), although the judge must have recommended it for offenders in Louisiana. In both states, offenders who were not admitted to shock were sent to a traditional prison.

States that place prison-bound offenders in shock incarceration may face other problems in seeking to reduce prison crowding. Most sites have fairly restrictive criteria for inmates who are permitted to enter the program. In such situations, one danger may be that the number of offenders considered appropriate may be less than the number of beds. Rather than increasing the number of probation-type offenders entering the program, the problem here would be one of too few offenders entering. In other words, the number of participants might be insufficient to fill the allocated beds or to have an impact on crowding.

Characteristics of Offender Participants: Eligibility and Suitability Criteria

To have an impact on crowding, a sufficient number of offenders must enter the shock program. Prior to entry, offenders are evaluated for "appropriateness" for shock. All states have legal mandates that restrict participation to certain classes of offenders. Most states also have additional criteria—which we call suitability criteria—that are consistently used to make decisions regarding qualifications for entry into the shock program. The reasons for the development of suitability criteria vary. For example, in Louisiana, offenders over the age of 39 were considered unsuitable, due to the medical evaluation teams' recommendation that if individuals 40 or older were going to participate in the rigorous physical activity required by the program, additional medical tests would be necessary. Considering the small number of legally eligible offenders over 40, the DOC decided that the cost of such tests would be prohibitive.

Another suitability criterion adopted in Louisiana was a restriction on the entry of offenders with a history of sex offenses. The sex offender prohibition arose early during the operation of the shock program when an offender who had done well in it was denied parole by the board because he had been convicted of a sex offense. The DOC felt strongly that all offenders who successfully completed the program should be released, but the parole board refused to release certain offenders. To avert future problems such as this one, the department in conjunction with the parole board developed a list of "types" of offenders who might be accepted for the program, but not necessarily be paroled; those judged unsuitable were not admitted.

Although the suitability criteria differed among states, all states had some criteria that were consistently used to limit entry to the program. Most programs were designed for youthful offenders. Indeed, Georgia and New York had legislative mandates that limited the age of participants. South Carolina restricted the age further to a maximum of age 24. Florida had no legislative maximum; however, the department set a maximum age of 25 as one of its suitability criteria. Like Florida, Louisiana had no legislative maximum; however, the DOC set a maximum age of 39 as one of its suitability criteria.

In addition to the age requirement, three states had a legislative mandate that offenders not have any mental or physical impairment that would prevent them from participating in a rigorous shock program (e.g., Georgia, Florida, South Carolina). In Louisiana and New York, the DOC has added this requirement to its list of suitability criteria. Also related to the health of offenders, Georgia and South Carolina specify that offenders must be free of any contagious or communicable diseases.

The second basic characteristic of offenders entering the shock programs is that, as compared to prison-bound offenders, in general they tended to be lower-risk offenders. This is ensured by various legislative restrictions on sentence length, types of sentence, types of offenses, and criminal histories of offenders. When considering criminal history, Florida and Georgia require that the offender be convicted of a first felony and Florida specifies no previous incarceration; others, such as Louisiana, permit an offender convicted of a second felony to enter if there has been no previous incarceration in a state prison.

Georgia and South Carolina do not statutorily restrict offenders who previously have been incarcerated, but in these states the DOC imposes the condition that the offender have no previous incarcerations as a suitability criterion. In some states, the DOC is even more restrictive regarding criminal history. For example, Louisiana and New York require that offenders have no history of any serious sex offense, and Louisiana and New York will not permit an offender who has a history of assaultive or violent behavior to enter the program. New York requires that offenders have not been convicted of any abscond or escape offense, and the Florida DOC requires that offenders be classified as either medium or minimum security.

In addition to restrictions on criminal history, some states have restrictions on current offense. Most states make the assumption that eligible offenders will be convicted of nonviolent offenses, but New York and South Carolina make this explicit. In contrast, Florida only stipulates that offenders not be convicted of a capital or life felony crime.

A final restriction on offender eligibility is on type and length of sentence. Although there is some variation in the legislative technicalities of these requirements, this is probably due more to variation in sentencing across states rather than to types of offenders eligible. New York requires only that offenders be sentenced to an indeterminate term of imprisonment; however, offenders must be parole eligible within 3 years. More restrictive in its guidelines, South Carolina requires that offenders be convicted of an offense that carries at least a 5-year prison sentence. In Louisiana, offenders must be sentenced to 7 years or less and they must be parole eligible. Similarly, offenders must be sentenced to 6 years or less in Florida and also be parole eligible. As noted above, Florida permits some offenders convicted of violent offenses to enter the program; however, the restriction on sentence length and security classification would limit the seriousness of eligible offenders. At the other extreme, offenders in Georgia must be sentenced to 1 to 5 years of probation, with shock incarceration being a special condition of their probated sentence.

If the program is considered to be an early release from prison (important if the program is expected to reduce crowding), the legal eligibility criteria were most likely developed to limit the severity of the current offense and the past criminal history of offenders who would be eligible for the program and hence early release. The dilemma is that a sufficient pool of offenders who are judged eligible and suitable must be available to enter the program.

Thus, in the majority of states, eligible offenders generally must be young, physically and mentally healthy, and serving short sentences. They cannot have had a very serious past history of crime; in all sites a previous incarceration disqualified an offender from entry. Such severe restrictions on entrants may limit the pool of eligible offenders, and this may be a particular problem in states that select participants from prison-bound offenders. The problem is that there may be too few offenders evaluated as appropriate (eligible and suitable) for entry and, therefore, the number of participants may be insufficient to have an impact on crowding.

Program Characteristics, Capacities, and Completion Rates

As shown in Table 1, these five state programs differ in program capacity, program length, percentage of entrants dismissed prior to graduation, voluntary entry and exit, and the placement authority.[3] In Georgia and South Carolina, the judge has the responsibility for entry decisions, and offenders who are evaluated as unsuitable or who drop out of the program are returned to the court for resentencing. In contrast, in Florida, Louisiana, and New York, offenders are first sentenced to prison and are then selected for program participation by the DOC. If inmates in these states are dismissed from the program or if they voluntarily drop out, they serve the remainder of their sentence in prison. Programs also differ in whether offenders volunteer to participate or whether they can drop out voluntarily. In two states (Florida and South Carolina) offenders do not volunteer to enter and they cannot voluntarily leave. On the other hand, in Louisiana and New York, offenders volunteer to enter and can voluntarily leave. The Georgia program permits voluntary entrance but offenders cannot leave voluntarily.

New York had by far the largest capacity (500), and by 1991 this capacity had been increased to 1,500. Georgia's capacity was much smaller (250); however, approximately the same number of offenders completed the Georgia program in a 1-year period, 932 versus 953 in New York. This shows the influence of both length of time offenders spend in the program and the number of participants who do not complete. Offenders in the Georgia program spend an average of only 89 days in the program and only 9% were dismissed prior to completing the program. In New York these numbers are very different. New York has the largest number of offenders in shock, but the program has the longest duration (180 days). In addition, a substantial number of the entrants do not complete the program (31%).

In the two states (Georgia and South Carolina) where the judge has the most authority over placement in the programs, the largest number of entrants complete shock (8.9% and 16% dismissal rates, respectively). In the other three states, the DOC has control and the noncompletion rates are much higher (ranging from 31.3% to 51.5%).

A relatively high percentage of noncompleters in the two states where judges have authority over offenders are dismissed from shock for medical reasons. In Florida, New York, and Louisiana, the sites where the DOC has authority over decisions after offenders are dismissed from shock, offenders leave either voluntarily or for disciplinary reasons. Offenders in the Florida program cannot leave voluntarily, so the majority of those who leave do so for disciplinary reasons. In New York and Louisiana, offenders can voluntarily exit, but surprisingly, the rates of disciplinary dismissals are high in New York, whereas voluntary exit is high in Louisiana.

Thus the biggest differences in dismissal rates are between the sites where the judge has authority over the offender after dismissal and the sites where the DOC has authority. The DOC-authority sites have much higher dismissal rates. Furthermore, in the DOC-authority sites, offenders leave for reasons that are more under their own control (poor behavior or volunteering out) whereas judge-authority dismissals are more often for medical reasons.

METHODOLOGY

The model used to estimate bed space needs was based on one developed by MacKenzie and Parent (1991) to estimate the impact of the Louisiana boot

TABLE 1: Program Characteristics and Capacity for Five State Shock Programs Showing Graduation and Dismissal Rates for a 1-Year Period

	Placement Authority				
	Florida: DOC	*Georgia: Judge*	*Louisiana: DOC*	*New York: DOC*	*South Carolina: Judge*
Voluntary					
Entrance	no	yes	yes	yes	no
Exit	no	no	yes	yes	no
Capacity (beds)	100	250	120	500/1,500	120
Total exits (date)	329.5[a]	932 (1989)	298 (1987)	953 (1988)/ 2,993 (1990)	470 (1989)
Graduated					
n	159.7	849[b]	169	743	395
Percentage	48.5	91.1	56.7	68.7/ 1,907 63.7	84.0
Time in days	100.5	89	125.7	180	84.2
Dismissed, percentage	51.5	9.0	43.3	31.1/36.3	16.0
Reasons for dismissal, percentage					
Discipline	39.9	3.3	7.4	16.8/7.3	8.3
Medical	8.6	5.7	3.7	1.3/1.3	7.6
Voluntary	—	—	27.5	7.9/12.3	—
Other	3.1	—	4.7	5.1/15.3	—

NOTE: DOC = department of corrections. Values are given for 2 years for New York, 1988 and 1990, when the capacity had greatly increased. If the values did not differ, only one value is given.
a. This value was calculated as the average from 10/87 to 1/91.
b. These estimates were based on percentages from actual data for 1984 to 1989.

camp program on the prison beds needed to accommodate the inmates entering prison. The model estimates the total person-months of confinement saved by determining the difference between the average prison term and the average shock incarceration duration, and multiplying that difference times the program capacity (or the actual number admitted in a year). The initial months saved are then discounted by (a) the probability that the persons would not have been confined (they would have been on probation) and (b) the time served by those who drop out, "wash out," or who are revoked. The model calculates the impact of the program on prison beds and on person-months of confinement.

The variables used in these analyses were program capacity, annual shock capacity, probabilities of washing out and dropping out, probability of imprisonment for washouts, probability of imprisonment for voluntary dropouts, revocation rates for shock graduates, probability of revocation for probationers, average term of imprisonment for shock-eligible offenders, average shock duration, duration of imprisonment for shock dropouts, duration of imprisonment for shock washouts, duration of imprisonment for shock graduates who were revoked, duration of imprisonment for shock-eligible offenders who were revoked on probation (see appendix for definitions of data). Data were obtained from official records and from the results of studies examining each program.[4] Shown in Table 2 are the data for each boot camp program.

ESTIMATING BED SPACE NEEDS

No data were available on the probability that these offenders would be in prison versus probation.[5] Therefore, we employed different models to examine the impact of the shock program on prison crowding if 0%, 25%, 50%, 75%, or 100% of the shock entrants were taken from prison-bound entrants (Table 3). The other variables were the best available estimates of probabilities and durations. By varying the estimates, we could examine the potential these programs had for influencing the need for prison beds.

The bed space model examined the net change in prison beds needed per year as a result of a shock incarceration program.[6] We calculated the person-months of confinement saved by the program and then reduced this by the person-months lost because of the dropouts, the washouts, and the revocations. The resulting estimate of the person-months of confinement was then changed to the number of beds saved (or lost) in a 1-year period as a result of the boot camp program.

For example, Florida's boot camp program had an annual capacity of 363.63. If 50% of these offenders would have been prison bound (and, conversely, the remaining 50% would have been probationers), the program would have saved approximately 336 person-months of confinement. However, the program lost 1,396 person-months of confinement due to washouts and revocations (there were no dropouts in Florida) for a net loss in person-months (336 minus 1,396 or –1,067 person-months). This translates to the need for an additional 88 prison beds per year (–1,067 person-months/12 months) because of the boot camp prison.

TABLE 2: Summary of Variables Used In Bed Space Model for Five State Boot Camp Prisons

	Florida	*Georgia*	*Louisiana*	*New York*[a]	*South Carolina*
Capacity					
Beds available	100	250	120	500/1,500	120
Total annual capacity (beds/year)	363.6	1,000	360	1,000/3,000	480
Actual yearly completions	329.5	932	298	953/2,993	470
Probability					
Offender would be imprisoned					
Offender would be on probation					
Imprisonment for dropout	0	0	1	1	0
Imprisonment for washout	1	.37	1	1	1
Voluntary dropout	0	0	.28	.08/.12	0
Nonvoluntary removal (washout)	.52	.09	.16	.23/.24	.16
Revocation shock graduate	.16	.27	.17	.16/.09	.24
Revocation probationer	.29	.16	.10	.15/.14	.31
Durations of imprisonment					
Shock duration (months)	3.3	3.0	4.0	6.0	3.0
Shock dropout (months)	0	0	13.7	18.1	0
Shock washout (months)	9.5	2.6	14.5	20.4	12.0
Shock-eligible prisoners (months)	8.5	9.6	20.5	17.9	12.4
Shock graduates revoked (months)	13.4	13.4	10.7	20.6	13.2
Shock-eligible probationer (months)	14.5	22.6	12.0	18.6	10.4

a. Values for 2 years are given for New York, 1988 followed by 1990, when the capacity had been increased.

TABLE 3: Results of Five Different Models Used to Estimate Beds Saved (+) or Needed (–) by Five State Prison Systems as a Result of the Boot Camp Prison Showing Differences as a Function of the Probability That the Offenders Would Have Been Prison Bound if the Boot Camp Prison Had Not Existed

	Probability of Imprisonment				
Models	*0%*	*25%*	*50%*	*75%*	*100%*
Standard model					
Florida	–153	–121	–88	–56	–24
Georgia	–230	–106	18	143	267
Louisiana	–277	–133	12	156	300
New York	–2,807	–1,846	–885	76	1,037
South Carolina	–174	–84	7	97	188
Actual completions					
Florida	–139	–109	–80	–51	–22
Georgia	–214	–99	17	133	249
Louisiana	–229	–110	10	129	249
New York	–2,801	–1,842	–883	75	1,034
South Carolina	–171	–82	7	95	184
Reduced recidivism					
Florida	–137	–105	–73	–40	–8
Georgia	–93	31	156	280	404
Louisiana	–261	–117	28	172	316
New York	–2,653	–1,692	–731	230	1,191
South Carolina	–121	–30	60	151	241
Reduced washouts					
Florida	–95	–63	–31	1	34
Georgia	–240	–116	8	133	257
Louisiana	–257	–112	32	177	321
New York	–2,329	–1,368	–407	554	1,515
South Carolina	–146	–56	35	125	216
Saving prison revocations (parole)					
Florida	–153	–89	–25	39	103
Georgia	–230	–30	169	369	568
Louisiana	–277	–123	30	184	338
New York	–2,807	–1,689	–570	549	1,668
South Carolina	–174	–52	71	194	317

NOTE: Calculations for New York are based on 1990 data from Table 2.

RESULTS

It was clearly evident from the process evaluation of these boot camp prisons that a major goal of all of them was to reduce prison crowding. The bed space analysis examined the effect on need for prison beds depending on whether the entrants to the boot camp prisons were chosen from those who would otherwise be prison-bound offenders or probation bound. Five different variants of the model were examined to inspect how these changed the beds needed. The first model (standard model) examined the changes in bed space when the total annual capacity was used for annual capacity in the model. The second model changed the value for the annual capacity to the number of actual completions in the year (see Table 2). Model 3 examined the effect on bed space by reducing the recidivism rate by 50%. The fourth model reduced the washout rate by 50%, and the fifth model included a term in the calculations to account for additional beds saved due to the parolee return to prison rates.

As expected, as the percentage of prison-bound offenders in the boot camp declined (and conversely probationers increased), the need for prison beds increased. The larger the percentage of the offenders who would otherwise have been in prison, the larger the impact on beds needed, or conversely saved (Table 3). Figure 3 shows the change in estimated bed space savings for four states using the standard model. As the probability that these offenders would have been imprisoned increased to 100%, instead of needing additional beds (indicated by "–" in Table 3) there were beds saved in all systems except in Florida. Even when all of the offenders would have been prison bound, the Florida system would need an additional 24 beds to accommodate the boot camp program.

What is evident from these models is that the predominant factor driving the need for beds is whether the program is used for prisoners or probationers. Widening the net to include a large percentage of probationers means an increased need for prison beds. However, the design and operation of the specific program also had a significant impact on the number of beds needed. A comparatively long program like New York (6 months), which devoted a large number of beds to boot camp offenders, could have had a major impact on prison crowding. Furthermore, changing the parameters in the model also created considerable differences in the estimated need for prison beds in New York (Figure 4). For example, if all entrants are prisoners (e.g., probability of imprisonment = 100%), reducing the washout rate led to an increased savings of 478 beds (1,515 compared to 1,037 at the current washout rate).

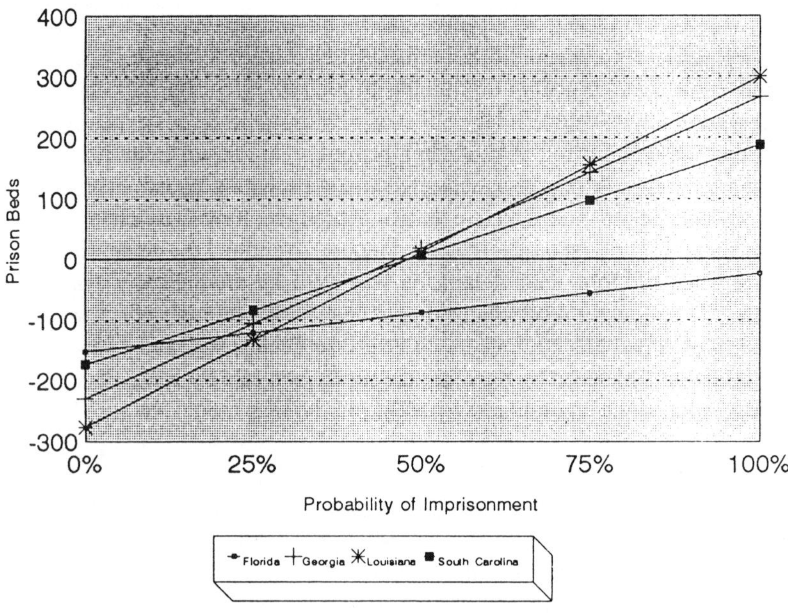

Figure 3: Estimates of Bed Space Needs and Savings for Four States Showing Changes as a Function of the Probability That Entrants Would Have Been Imprisoned if the Boot Camp Programs Did Not Exist

The third model we examined for all five states changed the recidivism rates for the shock graduates. This analysis addressed the issue of the short-term impact on prison beds if the recidivism rates of those who successfully completed the shock program were cut in half. Recidivism rates in Georgia (27%), and South Carolina (24%) were high, and reduction of them did increase the bed space savings (or reduced the loss). This was particularly noticeable in Georgia where the estimate was that 404 beds (a difference of 137 beds) would be saved by the program if all of those admitted to the program were prison bound and the recidivism rate was cut in half.

The results from the model reducing the washouts was similar to the results from the recidivism model. When the washout rates were cut in half, the states with the highest washout rates saved the most beds. This made a difference of 478 beds in New York (1,515 compared to 1,037).

A fifth model was developed to reflect the impact of the program if the savings from parolees were incorporated into the model. The original model

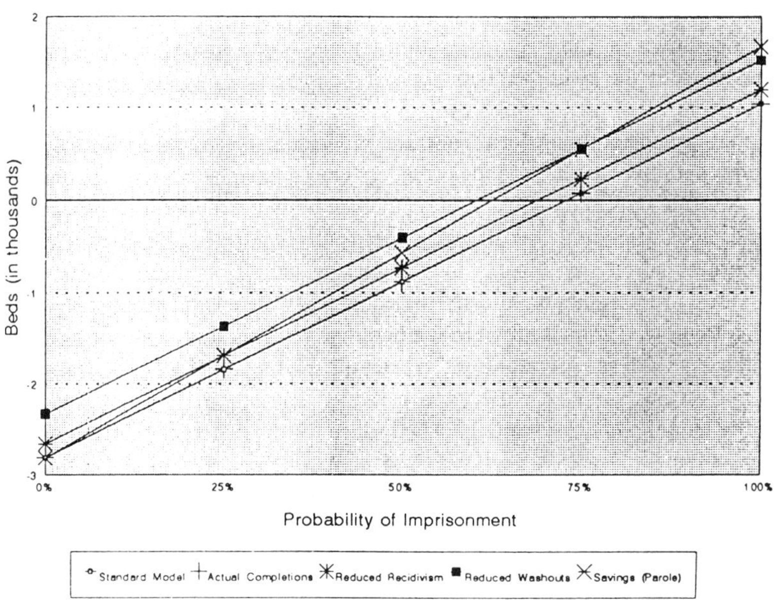

Figure 4: Estimates of Five Different Bed Space Models for New York Showing the Changes That Occur as a Function of Changes in the Probability of Imprisonment and Program Characteristics

developed by MacKenzie and Parent (1991) did not include time estimates for parolees. In a review of the current article, Aziz and Korotkin (personal communication 1993) argued that the recidivism rates and duration of imprisonment for shock-eligible parolees should be added to the person-months of confinement saved by the program. Model 5 gives the bed space loss or savings when we added the person-months of confinement saved because prison parolees who are revoked will be returned to prison to serve time (see Table 3).

This model could prove to be controversial because it assumes that if the capacity (annual capacity) for shock was used for prisoners, these prisoners would also be released at some point and some proportion of them would be revoked. Thus, in the model, the time they spend in prison after revocation (the duration) is added to the time saved by the shock program because these offenders would now be shock offenders and not prison parolees. Because the prisoners who are shock eligible would spend between 8.4 and 20.5

months in prison (Table 2), any impact on prison beds would not occur until much later.

As shown in Table 3, adding this savings to the model created a major difference in the estimated bed space. If the programs targeted prison-bound offenders, all of them would result in saving beds. The number of beds saved would be substantial in New York, and in Florida, this model predicted a bed savings if 75% to 100% of the offenders would have been prison bound.

Another important consideration in improving the model is to include the time shock offenders have to wait prior to entering the shock program. Many programs admit participants in platoons or squads. If there are stringent eligibility requirements, offenders may have to wait several months in prison or jail before being admitted to the boot camp.[7] This time was not included in the early release calculations. To examine the impact of a 2-month waiting period on the demand for bed space, we added 2 months to the shock durations in the model and recalculated the bed space for the different probabilities of imprisonment. At 75% probability of imprisonment, this model estimated that the states would save 21 beds (Florida), 202 beds (Georgia), 124 beds (Louisiana), 49 beds (New York), and 114 beds (South Carolina), a fairly substantial reduction from the original estimates in the model (see Table 3).

DISCUSSION

After reviewing the decision making (see flow charts) and examining the program characteristics, we conclude that there is every reason to believe that the models that most appropriately represented the situation in Florida, Louisiana, and New York were those that are based on 75% to 100% of the shock entrants being prison bound. In all three of these states, the boot camp entrants had been sentenced to prison. Furthermore, those who were judged to be ineligible or unsuitable or who leave the program after entry must complete their sentence in a traditional prison. Although there may have been some who plea bargained or who were sent to prison by the judge because there was a boot camp, in the vast majority of cases we believe that they would have been prison bound had the boot camp not existed. If this assumption is correct, then the most appropriate estimates from the models for these states are the columns representing 75% to 100% probability of imprisonment.

At 100% probability of imprisonment, the different Louisiana models varied from a low of 249 to a high of 338; at 75% probability of imprisonment, these values varied from 129 to 184. If most of the offenders had been in prison and the size of the program stayed the same, changes in the characteristics of the program in the models would not have a major impact on the prison system. Thus, if Louisiana wants to have an impact on prison crowding, it will be important to insure that the participants are selected from those who would otherwise be in prison.

These results are very different for the New York program. First of all, the size of the program means that it could have a significant impact on the prison system. If all of the participants were prison bound, 1,037 to 1,668 beds could be saved by the shock program. However, when only 75% of the participants would be prisoners, only 76 to 549 beds would be saved. Thus even small changes in the percentage of offenders who are prison bound could have a major impact on the prison system. However, the bed savings also depend on other characteristics of the program. If all of the inmates would have been prison bound, as few as 1,037 beds would be saved by the program if the actual completion rates are used to estimate bed space savings. Changes in actual completions or recidivism rates would have a minimal effect on bed space. A much larger impact comes from the model that reduces the number of washouts.

Florida presents a very different picture from the other states. As noted, after examining the program we believe that a large share of these participants would have been prison bound if the program did not exist. Therefore, we focused on the estimates of beds needed or saved if 75% or 100% of the offenders were prisoners. As shown in Table 3, three of the models predict that the program will result in an overall need for prison beds, although the need will be small (ranging from a need for 8 to 56 additional beds). The results seem to be driven by the high washout rate and the small difference between the time served in shock and the time served in prison by those who were shock eligible but did not go to shock.[8] When the washout rate in Florida was reduced, there were bed savings, although this was only 34 beds. However, in the new model adding in the savings due to parolee revocations and their time in prison, 230 beds were saved. It may be reasonable to use this model to estimate bed space savings in Florida because shock-eligible prisoners spent a relatively short period of time in prison. In any case, even if all of the offenders were prison bound, the shock program would have had a minimum effect on prison beds given the overall size of the Florida prison population and therefore, the program has not accomplished the goal of reducing prison crowding. The Florida example demonstrates how important it is to design an intermediate sanction with the program goals clearly recognized. Furthermore, even a program that targets prison-bound offenders may have trouble reducing prison crowding if other aspects of the program are not carefully planned.

After reviewing the decision-making process, we concluded that many of the offenders in boot camps in Georgia and South Carolina would have been given probation if the boot camp had not existed. It this is true, the boot camps in these two states would have increased the demand for prison beds.

Incarcerating offenders is expensive. Per day costs for incarcerating offenders in the boot camp programs vary greatly among states. In reports describing the programs, South Carolina, New York, and Georgia reported per day costs of $34.22, $68.50, and $44.58, respectively. There may be many hidden costs to boot camps that are not reflected in the per diem costs and these estimates do not include capital outlay costs. However, these can be used as rough estimates to convert the bed space estimates to costs. Using the 75% probability of imprisonment as a conservative estimate, the predicted savings from the new model (model 5) and the average per diem cost of incarcerating an offender ($49.10), Florida, Louisiana and New York would save an estimated $698,939, $3,297,556, and $9,838,904, respectively, per year because of the boot camp prisons. On the other hand, Georgia and South Carolina, at the time of this study, were probably taking many offenders who otherwise would have been on probation. If the same model and the same cost estimates are used, but the probability of imprisonment is reduced to 25% (i.e., 75% would have been on probation), the model estimates that programs in Georgia and South Carolina would cost the states, $537,645 and $931,918, respectively, per year.

Boot camp prisons have attracted the attention of correctional professionals and politicians. Many people believe that one benefit of these programs will be a reduction in prison crowding. Although an intermediate sanction like boot camp may increase the net of correctional control, this is not necessarily always the case. The analyses completed in this article demonstrate how important program design is if the goal of an intermediate sanction is to reduce the prison population. The programs have the potential for reducing prison crowding; however, they also have the potential for substantially increasing the number of offenders in prison. The major factor that will make the difference will be the degree to which the participants would otherwise have been imprisoned. The larger the program, the more important this will be because even if 50% of the offenders were prison bound, the program could result in the need for a considerable number of additional beds. If the goal of a boot camp prison is to reduce prison crowding, a jurisdiction designing a boot camp prison must insure that offender-participants are those who would otherwise be sent to prison.

There are other factors that will influence the number of beds needed by the prison system. Reducing recidivism rates and lowering the dropout and washout rates will also result in bed savings. Even what appears to be a small change in the prison situation, such as increasing the waiting time between entry to prison and admittance to the boot camp, can have a substantial impact on the need for prison beds. However, these will not overcome the influence of net widening. There is no support for the position that boot camp prisons will significantly impact prison crowding by reducing recidivism rates unless they are combined with a program that shortens the prison term of offenders who would otherwise be in prison.

Although many people argue that intermediate sanctions automatically widen the net of control, we argue that widening the net is not an automatic effect of all intermediate sanctions. Determining the impact of such sanctions is an empirical question that can be answered using appropriate data. The model proposed in this article can be used to determine the potential of an intermediate sanction for reducing or increasing the need for prison beds.

APPENDIX

Program capacity of each shock program was based on the number of beds available at the time of the data collection for the study (see Table 1).

Annual shock capacity represents the number of offenders who could complete the program in a 1-year period considering the number of beds available.

Probabilities of washout and dropout. The probabilities for nonvoluntary removal or washout (disciplinary, psychological, medical, or other) and voluntary removal or dropouts (inmate voluntarily drops), were based on 1-year dropout and washout rates. New York and Louisiana were the only two states that allowed offenders to drop out of the program voluntarily. The probability of dropping out was set to 0 for the programs that did not allow offenders to drop out.

Probability of imprisonment for washouts. In Florida, New York, and Louisiana, offenders were under supervision of the DOC and those who were dismissed were sent to prison to serve the remainder of their sentence; therefore the probability was set to 1.

In Georgia and South Carolina, offenders were returned to the court and the court decided on the sentence. We had data from a small sample of cases in Georgia indicating that 36.8% of the dismissals were sent to prison and therefore the probability of imprisonment for dropouts in Georgia was set at .368. These 36.8% had been dismissed from the programs for disciplinary reasons. The remaining 63.2% were dismissed for medical reasons and were given probation.

Data indicating the time served in prison for those who washed out of the South Carolina program and interviews with program staff suggested that almost all of those who washed out were sent to prison. Therefore, the probability of imprisonment for

(continued)

APPENDIX Continued

washouts in South Carolina was set to 1. This may overestimate the number sent to prison. However, the impact on the bed space model would be minimal because the washout rate was low (approximately 16%).

Probability of imprisonment for voluntary dropouts. In Florida, Georgia, and South Carolina, inmates were not allowed to voluntarily drop out of the shock program; therefore, the probability of imprisonment for a dropout was set at 0. Conversely, in the two states that allow inmates to voluntarily drop out (New York and Louisiana) the probability of imprisonment for a shock dropout was set to 1 because, in both of these states, inmates who drop out of shock must finish the remainder of their sentence in prison.

Revocation rates for shock graduates from Florida, Georgia, and South Carolina represented estimates from survival analyses examining the performance of offenders during 1 year of community supervision (Souryal and MacKenzie 1993). Revocation rates for New York (New York State Department of Correctional Services 1993) and Louisiana (MacKenzie and Parent 1991) were taken from previously completed work. Revocation rates for shock graduates varied between 9% for New York (in 1990) and 27% for Georgia.

Probabilities of revocation for probationers were taken from data estimating recidivism rates for samples of probationers who would have been eligible for the shock program but were instead given a sentence of probation. These are either estimates from survival analyses (Souryal and MacKenzie 1993) or they were taken from the same agency reports or publications as the revocation rates for the shock graduates (referenced above).

Average terms of imprisonment for shock eligible offenders were calculated for a sample of offenders within each state who had been eligible for the boot camp program but had served time in traditional prisons.

Average shock durations in months were obtained from each site for a sample of offenders. Average shock durations varied from state to state, usually between 3 and 6 months. Note that this does not include possible waiting time in prison before being admitted to the boot camp program.

Durations of imprisonment for shock dropouts were calculated to be a number other than 0 only for Louisiana and New York, which were the two states that allowed offenders to drop out. The durations were obtained from previously reported data (MacKenzie and Parent 1991; New York State Department of Correctional Services 1990). For the other sites, the probability of a voluntary dropout was set to 0 and, therefore, the duration of imprisonment for a shock dropout was set at 0 because this would not be used in the calculations of the model.

APPENDIX Continued

Durations of imprisonment for shock washouts were calculated from small samples of offenders who were released from prison after serving time in traditional prisons following their dismissal from the shock program. Only a limited number of cases were identified for the duration of imprisonment for the Georgia shock washouts and shock-eligible probationers, and thus these numbers should be interpreted with caution. In Georgia the average number of months served by shock washouts was less than the shock program because 63.2% were placed on probation after the dismissal and, therefore, served less time than they would have in the shock program.

Durations of imprisonment for shock graduates who were revoked were obtained from the samples of shock graduates who had been revoked after being released from the shock program. This was the average time they spent in prison after being revoked. In Florida, Georgia, and South Carolina, the durations of imprisonment for the shock graduates and shock-eligible probationers who were revoked were truncated because some of the offenders were still in prison at the time of data collection. Therefore, this estimate is shorter than would otherwise be the case. The majority of the shock-eligible probationers in Georgia had absconded while on probation, and therefore the number of offenders who were imprisoned was quite small.

Durations of imprisonment for shock-eligible offenders who were revoked on probation were calculated in the same manner as was the duration for the shock graduates who were revoked.

NOTES

1. For a more complete description of the programs, see MacKenzie and Souryal 1993. The data for this study were collected in 1990, and program descriptions are based on the characteristics of the programs at the time of data collection. Since that time, there have been substantial changes in many of the programs. For instance, Georgia has made substantial changes in all aspects of its program (Flowers, Carr, and Ruback 1991). South Carolina changed from being the responsibility of the department of probation to being the responsibility of the department of corrections. The express purpose of this change was to maximize the shock program's ability to reduce prison crowding by insuring that the offenders participating in the program were prison bound.

2. In 1988 New York permitted offenders up to but not including 26 years of age to enter the program. This was amended in 1989 when inmates age 26 through 29 were admitted to the program with some additional restrictions. By 1992, the age limit was again increased (to 35 years) and the additional requirements for older inmates were eliminated.

3. The capacity of New York's program was greatly increased in 1990 and therefore the values shown in the table include both the 1988 and 1990 values.

4. The numbers and probabilities for Louisiana were taken from the previously published report that was used as a model for this study (see MacKenzie and Parent 1991).

5. In a survey, researchers in New York (New York State Department of Correctional Services 1991) asked judges if they had changed their sentencing practices as a result of the shock program. Only 5% responded that they had sentenced nonviolent felons to prison rather than jail or probation because of the shock program. Another 5% said that they gave longer sentences to insure that offenders would not be eligible for shock, and 14% said that they gave shorter sentences to assure that offenders would be eligible for the shock program. This suggests that only a small percentage of the judges are using the program as an option for offenders who would otherwise be on probation.

6. A detailed description of the formula for calculating bed space estimates is given in MacKenzie and Parent (1991).

7. In examining their early boot camp, New York researchers found that inmates had served an average of 57 days in prison or jail before being admitted to the boot camp. Additionally, during interviews with program officials and inmates in many states, mention was made of a long waiting period between the time of entering prison (or volunteering for the boot camp) and admittance to the program.

8. The amount of time the boot camp participants served was not that much different than the time they would have to spend in a traditional prison. This small difference in time may also account, in part, for the high washout rate in Florida.

REFERENCES

Austin, James and Barry Krisberg. 1981. "Wider, Stronger and Different Nets." *Journal of Research in Crime and Delinquency* 18:165-96.

Covey, Herbert and Scott Menard. 1984. "Community Corrections Diversions in Colorado." *Journal of Criminal Justice* 12:1-10.

Ezell, Mark. 1989. "Juvenile Arbitration: Net-Widening and Other Unintended Consequences." *Journal of Research in Crime and Delinquency* 26:358-77.

Flowers, G. T., T. S. Carr, and R. B. Ruback. 1991. *Special Alternative Incarceration Evaluation*. Atlanta: Georgia Department of Corrections. Unpublished manuscript.

Greenfeld, Larry A. 1992. *Prisons and Prisoners in the United States*. Washington, DC: U.S. Department of Justice, Bureau of Justice Statistics, NCJ-137002.

Hylton, J. H. 1980. *Community Corrections and Social Control: A Canadian Perspective*. Regina, Canada: University of Regina.

Jones, Peter. 1990. "Community Corrections in Kansas: Extending Community-Based Corrections or Widening the Net?" *Journal of Research in Crime and Delinquency* 27:79-101.

MacKenzie, Doris L. 1990. "Boot Camp Prisons: Components, Evaluations, and Empirical Issues." *Federal Probation* 54:44-52.

MacKenzie, Doris L. and Dale Parent. 1991. "Shock Incarceration and Prison Crowding in Louisiana." *Journal of Criminal Justice* 19:225-37.

MacKenzie, Doris L., James W. Shaw, and Voncile B. Gowdy. 1993. *An Evaluation of Shock Incarceration in Louisiana*. Washington, DC: U.S. Department of Justice, National Institute of Justice.

MacKenzie, Doris L. and Claire Souryal. 1991. "Boot Camp Survey: Rehabilitation, Recidivism Reduction Out Rank As Main Goals." *Corrections Today*, October, pp. 90-96.

———. 1993, September. *Multi-Site Study of Shock Incarceration: Process Evaluation*. Unpublished report to the National Institute of Justice.

Mainprize, Stephen. 1992. "Electronic Monitoring in Corrections: Assessing Cost Effectiveness and the Potential for Widening the Net of Social Control." *Canadian Journal of Criminology*, April, pp. 161-80.

Morris, Norval and Michael Tonry. 1990. *Between Prison and Probation: Intermediate Punishments in a Rational Sentencing System*. New York: Oxford University Press.

New York State Department of Correctional Services and New York State Division of Parole. 1990. *The Second Annual Report to the Legislature: Shock Incarceration in New York State*. Unpublished report by the Division of Program Planning, Research and Evaluation and the Office of Policy Analysis and Information.

———. 1991. *The Third Annual Report to the Legislature: Shock Incarceration in New York State*. Unpublished report by the Division of Program Planning, Research and Evaluation and the Office of Policy Analysis and Information.

———. 1993. *The Fifth Annual Report to the Legislature: Shock Incarceration in New York State*. Unpublished report by the Division of Program Planning, Research and Evaluation and the Office of Policy Analysis and Information.

Palumbo, D., M. Clifford, and Zoann Snyder-Joy. 1992. "From Net Widening to Intermediate Sanctions: The Transformation of Alternatives to Incarceration From Benevolence to Malevolence." Pp. 229-44 in *Smart Sentencing: The Emergence of Intermediate Sanctions*, edited by J. Byrne, A. Lurigio, and J. Petersilia. Newbury Park, CA: Sage.

Souryal, C. and Doris MacKenzie. 1993. "Shock Incarceration and Recidivism: An Examination of Boot Camp Programs in Four States." In *Intermediate Sanctions: Sentencing in the 90s*, edited by J. O. Smykla and W. L. Selke. Cincinnati, OH: Anderson.

Yokoyama, Minoru. 1986. "The Juvenile Justice System in Japan." In *Youth Crime, Social Control and Prevention*, edited by M. Brusten, J. Graham, N. Herringer, and P. Malinowski. Federal Republic of Germany: Centaurus-Verlags-Gesellschaft Pfeffenweiler.

———. 1989. "Net-Widening of the Juvenile Justice System in Japan." *Criminal Justice Review* 14:43-53

CJPR, VOL. 6, NO. 1/92, pp. 1-16

Adapting Conservative Correctional Policies To The Economic Realities Of The 1990s*

Alida V. Merlo
Westfield State College
Peter J. Benekos
Mercyhurst College

Abstract

This article reviews the impact that the punitive, "get tough" policies of the 1980s have had on corrections. With record breaking increases in prison populations, legislators and policy makers have had to confront the realities of fiscal constraints while responding to the conservative agenda on crime. The consequence has been to develop and expand alternatives to incarceration which can be both tough on criminals but cheaper than traditional prison punishment. However, intermediate punishments such as intensive probation, electronic monitoring, and shock incarceration may be widening the correctional net. In reviewing these developments, the authors examine ideologies and consequences, and observe that economic considerations will influence corrections policies in the 1990s.

Introduction

The United States has surpassed all other countries in the world in the number and rate of people incarcerated. According to the Sentencing Project, there are currently 1.1 million offenders in American prisons; and the incarceration rate is 455 per 100,000 (Butterfield, 1992:A16). Unfortunately, there appears to be no end to this trend. It is estimated that the prison population will increase by 30 percent by 1995. The doubling of the number of inmates between 1980 and 1990 has posed significant problems for the federal government and the fifty states (Butterfield, 1992:A16).

This paper examines the conservative policies underlying the record-breaking increases, the resulting dilemma of skyrocketing prison construction costs, and the search for effective alternatives.Ironically, the alternatives to incar-

* An earlier version of this paper was presented at the Annual Meeting of the Academy of Criminal Justice Sciences in 1992 in Pittsburgh, Pennsylvania.

ceration to which conservatives have been forced to turn bear a strong resemblance to liberal community correctional policies of the 1960s and early 1970s. This merger of conservative and liberal policies is not, however, because of some shared ideological belief. Rather, it is a function of simple economics—Americans cannot afford to continue incarcerating a million people a year.

Ideologies And Policies Of The 1980s

The current conservative agenda on crime can be reviewed in the context of the assumptions of correctional ideologies and the objectives of sentencing practices.

Liberal-rehabilitative ideology

Since the mid-twentieth century, a liberal perspective which emphasized reform and rehabilitation guided correctional policy. Shover and Einstadter explain that efforts to treat and improve offenders were influenced by the assumptions of the "medical model" (1988:24). In this model, crime was viewed as symptomatic of underlying deficiencies which could be diagnosed and corrected with appropriate treatments. The model emphasized the social factors of criminal behavior and relied on therapeutic intervention to rehabilitate the offender (Shover and Einstadter, 1988:25).

The medical model reflected a liberal-optimistic view of human nature and how to confront the problem of crime. For corrections, this required a focus on the individual and on the efforts to change behavior. Since it was "impossible to specify in advance just how much time" was necessary for this treatment to be successful, the concomitant of the medical model was indeterminate sentencing (Shover and Einstadter, 1988:25).

In their study of sentencing reform, Goodstein and Hepburn characterize the indeterminate sentence as the policy which prevailed in the 1900s based on the ideological assumption that individualized treatment of offenders would prevent future involvement in criminal activities (1985:12). The model emphasized an individualized sentencing structure that required judicial discretion to determine the needs and circumstances of the criminal. The model required that judges provide broad parameters, i.e., indeterminacy, in which correctional specialists and parole board authorities could evaluate treatment progress and determine the appropriate time for release.

This sentencing model is consistent with the liberal perspective on crime policy. It focuses on the rehabilitative goal of corrections and requires discretion for judicial sentencing, correctional treatment, and parole release. By the 1970s, however, critics were questioning the assumptions and the outcomes of the rehabilitative model and were reassessing the goals of sentencing (Fogel 1975; von Hirsch 1976). Several authors (von Hirsch, 1976; Cullen and Gilbert, 1982; Travis, 1982; Hepburn and Goodstein, 1986) have reviewed this period of sentencing history and have observed that disillusionment and dissatisfaction with rehabilitation provided an opportunity for conservative assumptions to be revived.

Conservative-punitive ideology

Conservatives viewed rehabilitation as the "coddling of criminals" that conveyed a concern and sympathy for offenders which should be more appropriately directed toward the victims of crime (Shover and Einstadter, 1988:30). Conservatives believed that crime was the result of inadequate control rather than illness. Additional assumptions were that criminal behavior was due to free will, individual choice, and hedonic calculation. Therefore, in order to deter criminals from their evil ways, the conservative perspective emphasized the necessity of structured consequences, i.e., punishment.

This conservative deterrence model included elements of retribution, incapacitation, and punishment. With an ideological shift from rehabilitation to deterrence, sentencing policy also shifted from discretion to determinacy and the search for "just deserts." In the effort to get tough, determinate sentencing policy was advocated by supporters who argued that certainty, swiftness, and severity of punishment would serve to deter criminals and reduce crime. Determinate sentencing would require judges to impose sanctions which were commensurate with the crime committed, not with the character of the criminal who committed them. This would reduce judicial and parole board discretion and, therefore, the disparity in sentences and punishments. For different reasons, the issue of "disparity" was a concern to both liberals and conservatives, and provided a common basis for seeking sentencing reform (Travis, 1982).

The shift from indeterminate to determinate sentencing practices and from rehabilitation to deterrence models signaled the emergence of new assumptions and objectives in crime control. Crime was not committed by offenders who were sick, but by criminals who made free-will decisions to commit crime. With this "paradigm" shift in the late 1970s and early 1980s, efforts to identify and develop treatment programs were replaced with initiatives to determine the "just" sentences to fit the crimes and to reduce disparity by removing judicial discretion with legislative schedules (Travis, 1982). The result was the development of mandatory sentences, sentencing commissions, and the creation of sentencing guidelines (Blumstein, Cohen, Martin, and Tonry, 1983; Champion, 1989; Lawrence, 1991; Tonry, 1991).

Sentencing reform

In the social and political context of this conservative approach to crime control, two important developments occurred in the 1980s: (1) get-tough sentencing reforms were implemented and (2) incarceration rates and prison populations increased.

As noted above, the shift from indeterminate to determinate sentencing not only signaled different assumptions but it was also indicative of new sentencing objectives. Sentencing "reforms" were initiated to establish (1) specific terms of incarceration, (2) equity in the sentencing process, and (3) reduction in judicial and administrative discretion (Pennsylvania Department of Corrections, 1991:2). The new principle was "just deserts" and the salient concerns were "honesty," "uniformity," and "proportionality" in sentencing (Katzenelson and McDanal, 1991:1).

In addition to the development of sentencing guidelines in the Federal Court System (Katzenelson and McDanal, 1991), several state legislatures introduced proposals to implement a standardization of punishment and to respond to the public's concern about crime (Aniskiewicz, 1991; Benekos, 1991; Lawrence, 1991). This concern was transformed into, and sustained, a get-tough momentum which also helped to politicize legislative sentencing.

The "lessons of Willie Horton" (The Sentencing Project, 1989) and the 1988 presidential election are recent reminders of how politics can distort policymaking. Throughout the 1980s, the "war" on drugs, the urban gang problem, and the fear of crime and violence were used to justify more severe criminal sanctions. Politicians capitalized on emotional issues and pursued short-term political gains (Aniskiewicz, 1991:8).

Since the 1970s, most states have revised their sentencing codes and several have adopted determinate sentencing. As part of these reforms, penalties were increased and mandatory sentences were legislated (Shover and Einstadter, 1988:51). The punishment frenzy of the 1970s and 1980s reflected conservative ideology and the emphasis on incarceration as the preferred get-tough punishment. As a result, prisons became synonymous with punishment and at the same time prison populations began to increase. While it is "difficult to determine to what extent" the sentencing reform movement contributed to this rise in prison populations (Shover and Einstadter, 1988:52), there is no question that the rate of incarceration and the number of prisoners confined in the United States have increased (Butterfield, 1992). In this context, prison crowding has become an administrative and legislative challenge for the 1990s.

State Of Corrections

Implications of conservative correctional policies

Even though more and more offenders are being sentenced to prison, there has not been any significant decrease in violent crime. According to the *Uniform Crime Reports*, the incidence of murder, rape, robbery and aggravated assault increased in 1990 over the previous year (Federal Bureau of Investigation, 1991). Official crime data from 1980 and 1986 further illustrate the difference noted between 1989 and 1990. The number of index crimes known to the police in 1990 was 8 percent higher than in 1980 and 10 percent higher than in 1986 (Federal Bureau of Investigation, 1991:50). These data exacerbate the public's fear of criminal victimization and the frustration with the status quo. Nationally, it is estimated that one adult in forty-three is under the control (in some form) of correctional authorities (Jankowski, 1991:1).

Not surprisingly, most states cannot keep up with the demand for more prison space. This fact has resulted in overcrowded institutions, inmate lawsuits, court ordered limits on institutional populations and court appointed masters. Camp and Camp report that on January 1, 1991, the average federal and state prison system had 25 percent fewer beds than the total number of inmates under its jurisdiction (1991:36). They report that fifteen states had court appointed monitors or overseers (1991:6), and fourteen states had emergency release procedures (most of them statutory) to deal with overcrowding (Camp and Camp, 1991:20). During 1990, 24,878 inmate lawsuits were filed in thirty-seven states, and 95 class action suits were filed in twenty-nine states (Camp and Camp, 1991:6).

Often, the public is unaware of these facts and the efforts to reduce prison populations with "back door" policies. For example, Austin reported that as Florida's prison population increased in 1990, credit for good-time was also increased to the level that prisoners served about one-third of their prison terms (1991:6). In response to prison crowding in Illinois, the legislature doubled the amount of good time which could be awarded with the result that sentences could be reduced by one-half (*Criminal Justice Newsletter*, 1991b:5). And in Texas, the "average prison inmate...serves less than 20 percent of his sentence" (*Criminal Justice Newsletter*, 1991a:6).

Prison overcrowding also impacts local corrections. As prisons attempt to deal with court-ordered limits on population, they funnel more and more inmates into the jails. In 1990, there were 403,019 adult offenders in jail (Jankowski, 1991:5).

The concomitant fiscal and regulatory stress associated with jail overcrowding has resulted in some dramatic reactions. For example, a sheriff in Arkansas transported fifty inmates from his jail to a diagnostic unit in the state prison system. In order to preclude the state prison officials from refusing to accept these felony transfers, he ordered his deputies to chain the thirteen women and thirty-seven men to trees in front of the unit. At that time, approximately 400 felons were being held in county jails in Arkansas awaiting prison beds (Vanagunas and England, 1988:196). Although the sheriff's actions were atypical, they illustrate how prison overcrowding overwhelms local officials and their institutions.

Economic realities and the consequences

The consequences of the over-utilization of incarceration sanctions are significant. Mauer contends that it costs $20.3 billion a year for the 1.1 million offenders currently in prison (Butterfield, 1992:A16). Although the costs of construction vary from state to state, some states reported that it cost $110,000 per bed for construction in 1987 (Castle, 1991:1). In 1990 alone, thirty eight states and the federal system reported construction costs in excess of $3.2 billion for 87,664 beds (Camp and Camp, 1991:44).

These figures do not reflect the construction costs for additional facilities and the economic constraints they represent for the public. Camp and Camp report that 812,649 new prison beds are anticipated based upon current and planned construction in the United States (1991:41). For example, Texas voters recently approved a $1.1 billion bond that will enhance the state's prison system over the next four years by adding 25,000 beds (American Correctional Association, 1992:3). Californians spend more than $1 million every day to pay the interest on the money that they borrow to build new prisons (Bennett, 1991:92).

As prison construction costs continue to soar, state and federal budgets continue to shrink. Funding required for prison construction projects simultaneously reduces the appropriations for other projects like education, highways, and waste disposal. Although Americans may fear crime and want to send a strong message to criminals, they are not necessarily prepared to continue to allocate a disproportionate share of their state's limited resources to construct and maintain these institutions (Merlo and Benekos, 1992).

Politics and policy

In spite of prison crowding, the conservative get-tough rhetoric and legislative "reforms" continue unabated. For example, the omnibus crime package before the Second Session of the 102nd Congress would have imposed the federal death penalty to about fifty additional crimes (*Congressional Quarterly*, 1992:273). One amendment to the Senate version of this bill (S 1241) would have imposed a ten-year mandatory federal prison sentence for using a firearm in a drug-trafficking crime and a twenty-year sentence if the firearm were discharged (Isikoff, 1991:32).

Representative Newt Gingrich (R) promised that his goal in the 102nd Session of Congress was to build more prisons. He contends that America should . . .

> build enough prisons so that there are enough beds that every violent offender in America is locked up and they will serve real time and they will serve their full sentences and they do not get out on good behavior. (Clymer, 1992:14)

Since polls continue to reveal that the public is concerned about crime and favors the death penalty, politicians will maintain conservative perspectives and talk tough about sentencing (Clymer, 1991). There are three reasons why this politicizing is disconcerting.

The first is that "if promised anonymity, conservatives readily concede there is more symbol than substance in their crime bill" (Clymer, 1991: E5). Get tough legislation is cheap; implementation in not. If these symbolic gestures had no consequence, then legislative policy predicated on the conservative assumptions would not seriously impact on the criminal justice system.

The second concern arises, however, because this politicalization of crime does have a negative impact on the system. Senator Alfonse M. D'Amato (R) of New York sponsored the amendment which would impose mandatory federal sentences on firearm violations. When asked about the impact of this amendment on federal courts, Senator D'Amato expressed disregard for the consequences and said he "could care a hoot" about the burden this legislation would create for the courts (not to mention the prison system) (Isikoff, 1991:32). In short, elected leaders are eager to introduce strategies that sound tough without concern for the feasibility of their implementation.

Third, if the public were adequately apprised of the costs, there is some evidence that it would likely opt for the less costly and less restrictive alternatives (Castle, 1991:2). Research conducted in California suggests that although the public prefers incarceration as the primary method to deal with offenders, it considers the alternatives appropriate sanctions when made aware of their existence and their reduced cost (Bennett, 1991).

This review of ideology and policy in the 1980s can be summarized in three points. First, the conservative assumptions and crime control policies are prevalent in the legislatures and popular with the politicians. While some researchers have found that the public supports rehabilitative interventions (e.g., Cullen, Skovron, Scott, and Burton, 1990), policymakers seem reluctant to embrace the issue.

Second, prison crowding not only distorts and compromises retributive sentencing objectives, it also is expensive public policy which is contributing to state budget problems while not necessarily providing better public safety to citizens. In other words, "the problem of overcrowded prisons (has) assumed priority over the objectives of determinacy" (Hepburn and Goodstein, 1986:360) and has become a public policy issue of its own.

Finally, in order to reconcile the above concerns (i.e., getting tough and dealing with rising costs of imprisonment), initiatives in policies and programs need to offer politicians "a possible way to be tough on crime (and criminals) and at the same time possibly reduce, or at least not exacerbate, prison crowding" (MacKenzie and Parent, 1991:236). The costs of incarceration and the number of offenders returning to prison suggest that the public would be receptive to alternative approaches and intermediate sanctions like private prisons, intensive probation, electronic monitoring and shock incarceration. To that end, legislators and policy makers are exploring these alternatives in the hope that they appeal to conservative voters and ideologies but cost less than existing correctional policies.

Alternatives And Intermediate Punishments

Privatization of prisons and jails

One way that some government agencies have coped both with the public's demand that more offenders be incarcerated and with dwindling budgets is to involve the private sector. Although federal, state and local governments have contracted with private providers for services for adult and juvenile offenders for a long time, total reliance on the private sector to own, manage and administer correctional facilities is a departure from that stance. In 1989, there were approximately two dozen adult confinement institutions operated by about twelve companies (Logan, 1990).

Private prisons are frequently advocated as an alternative to the traditional government owned and operated facilities because of their anticipated lower construction and administrative costs. However, very little research has actually been conducted on large privately administered prisons to prove that the costs are lower and that private vendors are more effective. Most of the research has examined smaller private facilities in locations where large, state administered maximum security prisons continue to incarcerate more troublesome offenders. In fact, no state has transferred the custody, care and control of its entire correctional population to the private sector. Even if such a transfer did occur, there is no reason to believe that the private sector could maintain the current increase in prison populations and save the state substantial amounts of money.

In addition to the fact that these facilities may end up costing as much as or more than the government's, there are some important ethical issues associated with the transfer of the state's authority to detain and punish offenders to a private corporation (Bowditch and Everett, 1987; Merlo, 1992). DiIulio (1988,1990) contends that if there is no moral difference between private corporations' and the state's incarcerating inmates, then there should be no reason to exclude the utilization of private police and private judges. Is the state prepared to have all of its justice components under private control? At a minimum, these cost and ethical concerns suggest that the government ought to exercise caution before embarking on a privatization strategy to address overcrowding and the expensive construction costs of building more prisons.

Intensive probation and electronic monitoring

As the number of offenders in prison has increased, so too has the number of probationers. In 1990, there were 2,670,274 adult offenders on probation (Jankowski, 1991:1). This means that probation caseloads have increased making "it difficult to provide adequate supervision for many of these offenders who are, in effect, then left unsecured in the communities they victimized" (Stewart, cited in Erwin and Bennett, 1987:1).

The alternative to sending these offenders to prison is to "improve" community supervision. The response has included intensive probation supervision programs and the increasing use of electronic technology (and house arrest) to provide more "control" over offenders (Ford and Schmidt, 1985; Erwin and Bennett, 1987; Morris and Tonry, 1990).

The goals of these intermediate sanctions are to provide some relief to prison crowding and, in comparison to "regular" probation, to increase the level of punishment for offenders (Erwin and Bennett, 1987). Harland and Rosen conclude that due to the increased level of supervision which these "new" programs permit, they emphasize incapacitation and specific deterrence (1987).

In assessing the merits and technological aspects of these alternatives (e.g., see Ford and Schmidt, 1985; Morris and Tonry, 1990), it is evident that community supervision has been transformed from a reintegrative to a retributive focus (Benekos, 1990). Studt characterizes this as a shift from service to surveillance (1972).

This get-tough approach with community corrections is a response to prison crowding and an attempt to offer a panacea which is tough on criminals but cheap on taxpayers. The intermediate punishments are promoted as cost-effective, tough sanctions which can help alleviate prison crowding. They are consistent with the conservative influence on the development of alternatives to incarceration. The get-tough model requires deterrence, incapacitation, and punishment, and intensive probation and electronic monitoring fit these objectives.

However, there are problems with these alternatives. Researchers and program evaluators have questioned some of the assumptions and consequences of these intermediate sanctions and alternatives (Byrne, Lurigio, and Baird, 1989; Petersilia and Turner, 1990; von Hirsch, 1990). Reliance on these programs also raises the issues of widening the net, expanding social control, and unrealistic expectations (Morris and Tonry, 1990). Offenders who previously might have been placed on probation or dismissed may now find themselves subjected to electronic surveillance and stricter supervision. The use of sophisticated technological devices does not necessarily preclude criminal activity and the failure rate may be as high or higher than that of traditional community-based alternatives.

Another development in community corrections is the imposition of "supervision fees" which are viewed as both an additional dimension of punishment and as a way "to help defray the continuing costs of corrections" (Leban, 1991:5). For example, Pennsylvania recently enacted legislation which requires a twenty-five dollar per month supervision fee for any offender who is under state or county probation, parole or accelerated rehabilitative disposition. Probationers in some states not only pay a monthly supervision fee but they also pay for the presentence investigations (Langston, 1988:92). "In part, the fees are designed to make up for reductions in state funds to pay salaries of county probation and parole officers" (Leban, 1991:5).

Although states can generate revenue through these procedures, there is concern that these fees "will turn probation and parole officers into bill collectors, with little time to exercise their parole or probation supervision functions" (Leban, 1991:5). With this theme of fiscal constraints in mind, the "alternatives" momentum has also had an impact on prison programs in the form of "shock incarceration."

Shock incarceration

If the traditional attitude toward incarceration has been that longer sentences equal more punishment, then the popularity of shock incarceration relies on the view that shorter sentences which provide for tougher conditions of incarceration can be equally punitive. In reaction to prison crowding and the need for more bed space, shock incarceration programs have been adopted as "an alternative to longer prison terms" (MacKenzie and Parent, 1991:225).

In return for these relatively shorter sentences—three to six months of incarceration—shock inmates are exposed to military training and drill, physical exercise, various treatment programs, and hard work. Intensive post-release supervision (or "after shock") is also a feature of the programs (Parent, 1989). Programs are highly structured and demanding in comparison to traditional imprisonment. As a result, not all inmates are eligible or selected for boot camp incarceration nor do all inmates successfully complete shock programs (Parent, 1989; MacKenzie and Parent, 1991).

Since the early 1980s when shock incarceration programs began to appear, the number has grown to the extent that several states have at least one program or are planning to implement a boot camp prison (MacKenzie and Parent, 1991). As noted above, the popularity of the boot camp concept primarily reflects the economics of corrections. However, in order to justify the shorter sentences in the conservative, get-tough political climate, the programs must emphasize the punitive as well as the cost-effective nature of shock incarceration (O'Daniel and Wells, 1991:1).

The importance of this punitive theme was also observed by MacKenzie and Parent in their evaluation of the Louisiana Shock Incarceration Program (1991). In considering the value of "intensive treatment" and "drill, hard labor, physical training and strict discipline," they acknowledged the political as opposed to the programmatic reality of boot camp incarceration (1991:236):

> If the program were changed to focus on therapy without the boot-camp atmosphere, perhaps the most important change would be the attitudes of the public and policymakers. It appears that policymakers are willing to trade longer prison terms for offenders for a program such as this if the program incorporates hard labor and strict discipline....A second reason policymakers appear willing to allow the shorter term in boot camp instead of a longer term in prison is because of the punishment aspects of the boot camp.

These intermediate and alternative punishments - private prisons, intensive probation, electronic monitoring, and shock incarceration - are some of the initiatives to deal with prison crowding and the increasing expense of incarcerative policies while upholding conservative objectives. Their acceptance to policymakers and the public depends on their compatibility with conservative ideology regarding crime and criminals. In other words, these sanctions must be tough on criminals but at the same time, safe to the community and less expensive than incarceration (Corrigan, cited in Gordon, 1990:100).

While these and other intermediate punishment programs (IPP) continue to receive popular support, Morris and Tonry are less optimistic that they can achieve their objectives (1990). In their critique of the "alternatives" movement, they maintain that the programs give "false promise of reducing the present overcrowding in American prisons and jails" (1990:4). Not only are they concerned about a widening of the net (as are others, e.g., Austin and Krisberg, 1982; MacKenzie and Parent, 1990), but they also perceive the potential for "jurisprudential and political problems" (1990:7). For example, they raise questions regarding enforcement, fair and equitable application to avoid bias, and control of judicial (and administrative) discretion to minimize "disparity and injustice" (7).

If conservatives were simply interested in the cheapest alternatives, they would probably resort to the halfway houses, work release and probation programs of the early 1970s. However, cost is not the only issue. The liberal ideology that accompanied these programs is not acceptable in today's political climate. Therefore, the search for alternative punishment-oriented programs which are also less costly than incarceration has become the rule. Alternative and intermediate sanctions may deal with only a small percentage of offenders, but the fact that they sound tough and cost less enhances their stature and increases the likelihood of their utilization and acceptance. These observations suggest that quick-fix, politically expedient responses to prison crowding may provoke another generation of policy issues and politicalization of crime and corrections.

Conclusion

If trends continue, the record breaking number of offenders in prison and jail, and on probation and parole, will increase all through the 1990s. Such a course implies a departure from the less stigmatizing sanctions of the 1970s, a greater exploitation of public frustration with crime, a greater willingness to punish offenders, and intolerance for even relatively minor crimes. The lack of empirical evidence to support a continuation of these policies does not appear to be an impediment.

Throughout this paper, the authors have argued that during the last twelve years, crime and what to do about it have become more politicized. As a result, conservative assumptions have prevailed and policies have reflected a sterner, tougher America. Second, the incarceration policies of the 1980s increased the rate of imprisonment and the population of offenders confined in jails and prisons. Prisons have failed to deter crime, however, and the recidivism rate among offenders is high. The high costs of this conservative public policy have prompted initiatives to develop alternatives which can alleviate prison crowding, be cost-effective, and still be tough on criminals. The intermediate punishment programs which have been developed rely to a large extent on community corrections to provide surveillance, control, and deterrence. The philosophy of get- tough has been filtered through the economic realities of fiscal limitations and community punishment has replaced community corrections.

These seemingly liberal-sounding alternatives are less costly, but there is no evidence that their usage will actually reduce the number of people incarcerated. They are currently being utilized in conjunction with incarceration and not as a substitute for it. Intermediate sanctions may result in greater increases in the number of people under correctional control, fewer constitutional procedural protections for offenders, and more unbridled discretion for criminal justice professionals.

Bibliography

American Correctional Association
1992 Texas governor, voters approve $1.1 billion prison construction. On The Line, January 15:1-6.

Aniskiewicz, R.
1991 The politics of prison reform in Indiana. Paper presented at the annual meeting of the American Society of Criminology, San Francisco.

Austin, J.
1991 The consequences of escalating the use of imprisonment. Corrections Compendium. (September).

Austin, J. and B. Krisberg
1982 The unmet promise of alternatives to incarceration. Crime And Delinquency. 28:374-409.

Benekos, P.
1991 Public policy and correctional reform: Politics of overcrowding. Paper presented at the annual meeting of the American Society of Criminology, San Francisco.

1990 Beyond reintegration: Community corrections in a retributive era. Federal Probation. (March):52-56.

Bennett, L. A.
1991 The public wants accountability. Corrections Today, 53(July):92-95.

Blumstein, A., J. Cohen, S. Martin, and M. Tonry, eds.
1983 Research On Sentencing: The Search For Reform, Volumes I and II. Washington: National Academy Press.

Bowditch, C. and R. S. Everett
1987 Private prisons: Problems within the solution. Justice Quarterly, 4 (September):441-453.

Butterfield, F.
1992 U.S. expands its lead in the rate of imprisonment. The New York Times (11 February):A16.

Byrne, J., A. Lurigio, and C. Baird
1989 The effectiveness of the new intensive supervision programs. Research In Corrections, 2(2):1-48.

Camp, G. M. and C. G. Camp
1991 The Corrections Yearbook - Adult Corrections. South Salem, NY: Criminal Justice Institute.

Castle, M. A.
1991 Alternative sentencing: Selling it to the public. In U.S. Department of Justice, National Institute Of Justice Research In Action: 1-5.

Champion, D., ed.
1989 The U.S. Sentencing Guidelines: Implications For Criminal Justice. New York: Praeger.

Clymer, A.
1992 A G.O.P. leader aims at 'welfare state' values. The New York Times (5 January):14.

1991 Politicans take up the domestic issues: Polls suggest why. The New York Times (15 September).

Congressional Quarterly
1992 Status of major legislation. 50(5): 273.

Criminal Justice Newsletter
1991a Texas parole board under fire: Prison crowding raises pressure. (1 May) 22:9.

Criminal Justice Newsletter
1991b Illinois 'good time' law eased prison crowding, study finds. (3 June) 22:11.

Cullen, F. and K. Gilbert
1982 Reaffirming Rehabilitation. Cincinnati: Anderson Publishing.

Cullen, F., S. E. Skovron, J. Scott, and V. Burton
1990 Public support for correctional treatment: The tenacity of rehabilitative ideology. Criminal Justice And Behavior, 17(1): 6-18.

DiIulio, J. J.
1990 The duty to govern: A critical perspective on the private management of prisons and jails. In D. C. McDonald, ed. Private Prisons And Public Interest. New Brunswick: Rutgers University Press: 155-178.

1988 What's Wrong With Private Prisons. The Public Interest, 92 (Summer): 66-84.

Erwin, B. and L. Bennett
1987 New Dimensions In Probation: Georgia's Experience With Intensive Probation Supervision (IPS). Washington: U.S. Department of Justice. National Institute of Justice. (January).

Federal Bureau of Investigation
1991 Uniform Crime Reports for the United States 1990. Washington, D.C.: U.S. Government Printing Office.

Fogel, D.
1975 We Are The Living Proof...The Justice Model For Corrections. Cincinnati: Anderson Publishing.

Ford, D. and A. Schmidt
1985 Electronically Monitored Home Confinement. Washington: U.S. Department of Justice. National Institute of Justice. (November).

Goodstein, L. and J. Hepburn
1985 Determinate Sentencing And Imprisonment: A Failure Of Reform. Cincinnati: Anderson Publishing.

Gordon, D.
1990 The Justice Juggernaut: Fighting Street Crime, Controlling Citizens. New Brunswick, NJ: Rutgers University Press.

Harland A. and C. Rosen
1987 Sentencing theory and intensive supervision probation. Federal Probation, 51 (4):33-42.

Hepburn, J. and L. Goodstein
1986 Organizational imperatives and sentencing reform implementation: The impact of prison practices and priorities on the attainment of the objectives of determinate sentencing. Crime And Delinquency, 32 (3):339-365.

Isikoff, M.
1991 The senate's crime bill with hidden costs. The Washington Post National Weekly Edition. (July 29-August 4): 32-33.

Jankowski, L.
1991 Probation And Parole 1990. Washington: U.S. Department of Justice. Bureau of Justice Statistics. (November).

Katzenelson, S. and C. McDanal
1991 Sentencing guidelines and judicial discretion in the federal court system. Paper presented at the annual meeting of the American Society of Criminology, San Francisco.

Langston, D. C.
1988 Probation and parole: No more free rides. Corrections Today, 50(August):90-93.

Lawrence, R.
1991 The impact of sentencing guidelines on corrections. Paper presented at the annual meeting of the Academy of Criminal Justice Sciences, Nashville.

Leban, J.
1991 Prison society supports a stay in implementing supervision fees for parolees and probationers. Corrections Forum, (December):5.

Logan, C. H.
1990 Private Prisons: Cons And Pros. New York: Oxford University Press.

MacKenzie, D. and D. Parent
1991 Shock incarceration and prison crowding in Louisiana. Journal Of Criminal Justice, 19(3):225-237.

McCarthy, B.
1987 Intermediate Punishments: Intensive Supervision, Home Confinement, And Electronic Surveillance. Monsey, NY: Criminal Justice Press.

Merlo, A. V.
1992 Ethical issues and the private sector. In P. J. Benekos and A. V. Merlo, eds. Corrections: Dilemmas And Directions. Cincinnati: Anderson Publishing Company: 23-36.

Merlo, A. V. and P. J. Benekos
1992 The politics of corrections. In P. J. Benekos and A. V. Merlo, eds. Corrections: Dilemmas And Directions. Cincinnati: Anderson Publishing Company: ix-xvii.

Morris, N. and M. Tonry
1990 Between Prison And Probation: Intermediate Punishments In A Rational Sentencing System. New York: Oxford University Press.

O'Daniel, L. and B. Wells
1991 Boot camp: A viable alternative to prison for the male Hispanic offender. Paper presented at the annual meeting of the Academy of Criminal Justice Sciences, Nashville.

Parent, D.
1989 Shock Incarceration: An Overview Of Existing Programs. Washington: U.S. Department of Justice. National Institute of Justice. (June).

Pennsylvania Department of Corrections
1991 Sentencing Reform Proposal. Camp Hill, PA.

Petersilia, J. and S. Turner
1990 Intensive Supervision For High-Risk Probationers: Findings From Three California Experiments. Santa Monica, CA: Rand.

The Sentencing Project
1989 The Lessons Of Willie Horton: Thinking About Crime And Punishment For The 1990s. Washington.

Shover, N. and W. Einstadter
1988 Analyzing American Corrections. Belmont, CA: Wadsworth Publishing.

Studt, E.
1972 Surveillance And Service In Parole. Washington: U.S. Department of Justice.

Tonry, M.
1990 Stated and latent functions of ISP. Crime And Delinquency, 36:174-191.

Travis, L., III
1982 The politics of sentencing reform. In M. Forst, ed. Sentencing Reform: Experiments In Reducing Disparity. Newbury Park, CA: Sage.

Vanagunas, S. and D. England
1988 The domino effect - state and federal crowding puts local jails on the receiving end. Corrections Today, 50 (August):196-199.

von Hirsch, A.
1990 The ethics of community-based sanctions. Crime And Delinquency, 36:162-173.

1976 Doing Justice: The Choice Of Punishments. New York: Hill and Wang.

A Comparison of Programming for Women and Men in U.S. Prisons in the 1980s

Merry Morash
Robin N. Haarr
Lila Rucker

This article examines programming for women in U.S. prisons in the 1980s, a decade marked by an increased number of incarcerated women and by court pressure to correct biases in programming. Data from a census of facilities and a sample of inmates reveal that regardless of gender, the prison experience does little to overcome marginalization from the workforce and leaves many who have a history of drug abuse, or who are parents, untouched by relevant programming. Moreover, gender stereotypes shape the nature of the work and vocational training, and women disproportionately receive psychotropic drugs for mental health treatment.

Rapid growth in the number of incarcerated women, recognition of their unique needs, and long-standing awareness of gender differences in prison programming have resulted in considerable concern about gender equality in U.S. prisons. Historically, correctional systems have provided fewer and less varied programs for women than for men (Shover 1991), and the current inadequacy of programs for incarcerated women has been noted in several works (Bershad 1985; CONtact 1981; Pollock-Byrne 1990; Ryan 1984; Weisheit and Mahan 1988). One facet of this inadequacy is that women's access to programs in correctional settings is less than that of men. Also, programming can be qualitatively different, shaped by stereotypical

---

MERRY MORASH: Professor and Director, School of Criminal Justice, Michigan State University. **ROBIN N. HAARR:** Doctoral candidate, School of Criminal Justice, Michigan State University. **LILA RUCKER:** Assistant Professor, Department of Criminal Justice, University of South Dakota.

The data used in this article were made available by the Inter-university Consortium for Political and Social Research. The data for the Census of State Adult Correctional Facilities, 1984 and the Survey of Inmates, 1986 were collected by the U.S. Department of Commerce, Bureau of the Census, under the direction of the Bureau of Justice Statistics. Neither the collector of the original data nor the consortium bear any responsibility for the analyses or interpretations presented here.

CRIME & DELINQUENCY, Vol. 40 No. 2, April 1994 197-221

notions about the nature, lives, and needs of women. A third dimension of inadequate programming is the failure to address the unique needs of women.

In past research, stereotypical programming was found in the area of work and vocational training. Studies have shown a tendency to restrict women's training opportunities to "female" occupations (e.g., cosmetology, sewing, food preparation) and to disproportionately involve women in "women's work" in the prison itself, although in recent years this tendency is reportedly decreasing (for a review, see Weisheit 1985). The emphasis on women's work is rooted in the early women's reformatories, which "were designed to rehabilitate by inculcating domesticity. In the early programs, inmates were mainly trained to sew, cook, and wait on tables. After parole, they were sent to positions as domestic servants where they could be supervised by . . . middle-class women" (Rafter 1993, pp. 8-9). Whatever the merits of these programs in the past, currently these experiences and training in these types of work traditionally done by women lead to those very occupations that pay poorly, have few if any medical or other benefits, and are subject to layoffs. After release from prison, such jobs offer minimal opportunity for self-support.

There has been much documentation of women inmates' unique needs. Between 1980 and 1990, the number of women arrested for drug crimes tripled, and this increase was much greater than for men (Bureau of Justice Statistics 1991). Consistent with this trend, one third of incarcerated women report being under the influence of a drug at the time of the offense, over half used drugs daily during the month before arrest, and nearly one fourth reported daily use of an addictive drug in that month. The increased number of incarcerated women reporting drug involvement may have been the result, in part, of greater severity in sentencing, rather than reflecting an actual shift in the number of women using drugs (e.g., see Rhode Island Justice Alliance 1990; LeClair 1990; Huling 1991; Daly 1987). Regardless of the reason for the shift, a growing proportion of women in prison need drug treatment, and this proportion is more than for men.

In addition to drug use, the Bureau of Justice Statistics (1991) has reported several other indicators of the special needs of incarcerated women:

- A high proportion of them (41%) report prior sexual or physical abuse.
- Two thirds of women in prison had children under 18 years old, and four out of five women had children living with them before incarceration.
- Less than one half of the women had been working during the month before arrest, and this rate is substantially lower than the three quarters figure for men.

Results from a recent American Correctional Association (1993) survey of imprisoned women reinforce the conclusion that many women in prison have emotional and drug-related problems, with high proportions having a history of suicide attempts, very serious drug problems, sexual and physical abuse, and of being a juvenile runaway (also see Gilfus 1988). Information on imprisoned women's backgrounds suggests that equitable treatment is not simply equivalent treatment, rather programming is needed to address the special difficulties of women (Rafter 1993, p. 7).

One explanation of inadequate correctional programming for women is that their small proportion in the total prison population has limited the resources available to them. Despite the rapid increase in the number of incarcerated women, they still represent under 6% of all inmates. The result is fewer facilities, and thus less variety in the programs offered, and also less pressure to meet unique needs of women. Their relatively small numbers can render women marginal in the eyes of correctional policymakers and also create an economy of scale problem for women's institutions; that is, it costs more per person to deliver programming to a small group of women than to a large group of men (Rafter 1990). Additionally, because there are fewer facilities for women, it is common for all security levels in women's institutions to be mixed together (Crawford 1988). Without a range of security classifications, it may be difficult to operate programs requiring less restrictive environments.

One particular area in which women's programming has been found to be inadequate is access to legal resources; for example, to assist in parental rights cases or the appeals process. Incarcerated offenders are legally entitled to access to law materials and lawyers necessary for protection of their rights. There have been class action suits claiming less adequate legal assistance in women's than men's prisons (Leonard 1982, p. 48) and, perhaps as a result of this inadequacy, women have been less likely than men to take their complaints about prison conditions to the courts (Alpert 1982).

The problems of stereotypical programming, programming that ignores women's special needs, and low levels of some types of programming, have all been manifested in the areas of medical and mental health treatment (including alcohol and drug treatment). Some researchers have offered evidence that women's correctional institutions are less likely than men's to have full-time medical staff or hospital facilities (Bershad 1985, p. 421). The lack of medical care is particularly problematic because women have a higher incidence of "asthma, drug abuse problems, seizure disorders, hypertension, diabetes, hepatitis, heart disorders, gastrointestinal problems, and genitourinary disorders than men" and many also have gynecological problems (Bershad 1985, p. 421; also see Yang 1990). Some of the difficulties that have been found involve limited access to prescribed medicines, delays in seeing a medical specialist, and lack of supervision for sick inmates.

Questions about the adequacy of mental health care for women center on both availability and appropriateness of the care received. In some contemporary prison settings, compared to men, women in prison have been more likely to receive mental health placement and related services (Steadman, Holohean, and Dvoskin 1991). This may be due, in part, to a historical tendency for woman's criminality to be attributed to mental illness and abnormality (Zedner 1991; Edwards 1986). The higher level of mental health services is also probably related to their greater need, which might be expected, given the high proportion of incarcerated women with a history of victimization (Brett 1993; Baskin, Sommers, Tessler, and Steadman 1989; Yang 1990, p. 1022). Additionally, gender stereotypes have an influence, as demonstrated by research showing that mental health diagnoses and services are more often used in response to violent or aggressive behavior on the part of women than equivalent behavior of men (Baskin et al. 1989).

Concerned with the appropriateness of mental health services, some writers have criticized the use of drugs as part of women's mental health treatment, claiming that they are used to control women rather than to alleviate symptoms of illness (Feinman 1986). Partially contradicting this view, a study of New York inmates showed that gender was not significantly related to drug therapy if the symptomatology of mental illness was moderate to high (Sommers and Baskin 1991). However, consistent with the criticism, when there were minimal symptoms of mental illness, women were more likely than men to be treated with drugs.

Other criticisms center on the failure to adapt substance abuse programs to women's special difficulties, which include low self-esteem, depression, loss of children, lack of family support, and involvement in destructive relationships with men (Passages Program n.d.).

LACK OF PARITY FOR INCARCERATED WOMEN

In response to contemporary gaps and inequities in programming for women, there have been several legal challenges centered on the equal protection clause of the 14th Amendment to the U.S. Constitution, "[n]o State shall . . . deny to any person within its jurisdiction the equal protection of the laws" (§ 2). As a result, several state correctional agencies have been under court supervision because of violation of the constitutional law (Bershad 1985; Leonard 1982; Van Ochten 1993). Legal challenges have concentrated on basic education, vocational training and work, medical care (including mental health and drug treatment), and access to legal assistance.

Advocates for women's rights continue to contend that despite court rulings, few programs have successfully departed from tradition to effectively address the needs of women in prison (Dobash, Dobash, and Gutteridge 1986). The unprecedented growth in the number of imprisoned women during the 1980s has brought increased attention to this problem.

The purpose of this article is to draw on indicators of prison programming derived from national data collection efforts to compare the programming in men's and women's prisons in the mid-1980s, a period which saw a rapid increase in numbers of incarcerated women and increased criticisms of programming for women. This comparison can reveal persisting inequities and allow us to determine whether they are related to security level and size of the facility—two factors that have been identified as contributing to inadequate programming. The analysis also can provide baseline data for future comparisons with the same indicators in the 1990s, when the effects of even more growth in inmate populations may be coupled with the constraints imposed by an economic recession and accompanying reductions in correctional services, under conditions of continuing court challenge. Finally, the research can shed some light on both the utility and the limitations of national data sets in providing indicators of the adequacy of programming for women.

METHODOLOGY

Data for the mid-1980s were collected as part of *The Survey of Inmates in State and Federal Prisons* (referred to below as the Survey) and the *Census of State Adult Correctional Facilities* (referred to below as the Census). Both the Survey and the Census provide the only national data of this type, and thus can be used to derive important social indicators of the level and type of programming. The Census is a mailed instrument filled out by correctional administrators. The Survey is a face-to-face interview conducted in prisons by U.S. Census Bureau employees. Both the Survey and the Census are repeated at 5- or 6-year intervals, and the Census includes all prisons, whereas the Survey uses a representative sample of prisoners, including an oversampling of female inmates that is designed to produce adequate numbers for analysis. The Survey and Census data correct the inadequacies of dated information or information on a very small number of facilities and programs that plagued much prior research on women in prison (for a summary, see Weisheit and Mahan 1988).

For the 1986 Survey, the population was all adult inmates who were housed in state-government operated correctional facilities. Data are available on 14,592 inmates, but because women were oversampled, this group includes 3,091 women. The data include information on program participation, as well as demographic characteristics, inmate background, drug use, and facility characteristics.

For the 1984 Census of State Adult Correctional Facilities, data were collected on all state-operated correctional facilities that were housing inmates on June 30, 1984. Coeducational institutions were omitted from the present data analysis. Data are available on programs, inmate activities, and institutional characteristics, such as size and custody levels.

Because of large populations, high incarceration rates, and a relatively large number of facilities for women, some states, such as California, New York, and Texas, are better represented by both data sets than are small states or states with limited use of incarceration. Thus, although the data do tell us about the typical situation of women imprisoned in the United States, they do not necessarily reflect accurately on each state's prisons. The results help us understand the situation of many women in prison and alert us to the need to look for specific problems and inequities at the state level or within particular institutions within a state.

The Survey relies on self-reports by inmates, supplemented with official record information for a limited number of variables and the Census relies on official reports supplied by prison administrators. To provide a check on the validity of information, the results of the Survey and the Census were compared whenever possible.

In addition to statistical techniques appropriate for comparing women and men and for comparing the facilities dedicated to each group, for the Survey data, multivariate analysis was used to control for offender background characteristics that might explain gender differences in programming. Facility size and security level were also considered in the analyses to determine the degree to which they explain gender differences. The multivariate analysis additionally allowed for comparison of the magnitude of the influence of gender on programming relative to the influence of other variables.

Dummy variable coding was used for several variables. For region, the omitted comparison category was West, and variables were created for Northeast, Midwest, and South. For the dummy variable coding of facility security level, the omitted value was "other," and variables were created for maximum, medium, and minimum security levels. The omitted value for race was other, and variables were created for White, Black, Asian or Pacific Islander, and Native American.[1]

There are missing data for some variables, and thus the totals do not sum to the full sample size for either the Survey or the Census. The degree of missing data is not extremely high, and the exact number of responses considered in each analysis are reported along with the findings.

FINDINGS

Size of Facility and Security Level

The expectation that women would be concentrated in medium and minimum security facilities that are relatively small compared to those for men was confirmed by the 1986 Survey data. Most women (55.5%) were in facilities housing 150 to 499 inmates, and just 15.4% were in the largest facilities, housing 1,000 or more persons. In contrast, 44.3% of the men surveyed were in facilities housing 1,000 or more inmates (Table 1). Men also tended to be concentrated in maximum security facilities and women in medium security facilities (Table 2).

Educational Programs

A slightly greater proportion of women compared to men had taken part in an academic educational program since admission. For women, the proportion was 48.6, and for men it was 45.0 (1,412 of 2,907 women vs. 4,841 of 10,757 men; $\chi^2 = 11.7$, $df = 1$, $p \leq .01$).

A logistic regression analysis indicated that, with other variables controlled, the probability of participation was increased slightly for women, by 20% after controls were introduced for racial and ethnic differences, prior work and educational experience, region of the country, and size and security level of the facility (Table 3). As might be expected, participation was somewhat (10%) more likely for persons with less prior education and no job just before incarceration. Hispanics also participated at a 20% higher rate than non-Hispanics, perhaps reflecting language-related programming. The chances of an inmate being in an academic program were 30% greater if that inmate lived in the Northeastern part of the United States, and 20% less if the inmate lived in the South. Those in large institutions were more likely to have participated; and those in the maximum security facilities had a 40% higher participation rate.

The Census provides information on participation in specific types of academic programs. Parallel to findings from the Survey, the Census shows that a higher proportion of women than men were involved in adult basic education programs (for 62 women's institutions, $\overline{X} = 10\%$, $SD = .16$; for 723

TABLE 1: Size of Institution by Inmate Gender, Survey

	Facility Size					
	Less Than 500		*500 to 999*		*More Than 999*	
Inmate Sex	%	n	%	n	%	n
Women	55.5	1,716	29.1	900	15.4	477
Men	31.4	3,582	24.2	2,764	44.3	5,054

$\chi^2 = 940.7$, $df = 2$, $p \leq .01$; 156 missing cases.

TABLE 2: Security Level of Facility by Inmate Gender, Survey

	Security Level							
	Maximum		*Medium*		*Minimum*		*Other*	
Inmate Sex	%	n	%	n	%	n	%	n
Women	19.2	563	57.8	1,694	19.6	576	3.4	99
Men	35.8	4,014	41.6	4,659	12.4	1,392	10.2	1,144

$\chi^2 = 544.6$, $df = 3$, $p \leq .01$; 508 missing cases.

men's institutions, $\overline{X} = 7\%$, $SD = .10$, $n = 723$; $F = 5.7$, $df = 1{,}783$, $p \leq .05$).[2] Women's and men's institutions did not differ significantly in the mean proportions of inmates in secondary education programs (for 59 women's institutions, $\overline{X} = .08$, $SD = .09$; for 704 men's institutions, $\overline{X} = .07$, $SD = .10$; $F = .56$, $df = 1{,}761$). They also did not significantly differ in the proportions in special education programs (for 68 women's institutions, $\overline{X} = .01$, $SD = .04$; for 749 men's institutions, $\overline{X} = .01$, $SD = .04$; $F = .01$, $df = 1{,}815$). However, there was a tendency for a greater proportion of inmates in women's than men's institutions to be in college courses (in women's institutions, $\overline{X} = .05$, $SD = .08$; for men's institutions, $\overline{X} = .03$, $SD = .07$; $F = 2.9$, $df = 1{,}830$, $p = .09$).

Work and Vocational Training

Regardless of the facility's level of security, women more often have work assignments than do men, and the nature of work reflects common gender stereotypes. The percentage of women with work assignments was 75.4 (2,192) whereas for men the percentage was 65.1 (7,010) ($\chi^2 = 110.4$; $df = 1$, $p \leq .05$). Women are disproportionately involved in cleaning (janitorial work)

TABLE 3: Logistic Regression Results for Prediction of Participation in Academic Programs, Survey

Predictors	B	SE	*Wald*	*Significance*	*Odds Ratio*[a]
Demographic					
Gender	.21	.05	19.1	.00	1.2
Race					
White	–.06	.09	.5	.47	.9
Black	–.02	.09	.1	.82	1.0
Asian, Pacific Islander	.27	.16	2.8	.10	1.3
Native American	–.17	.13	1.7	.19	.8
Hispanic	.19	.06	9.5	.00	1.2
Age	–.05	.00	387.0	.00	.9
Income	–.00	.00	10.4	.00	1.0
Years in prison	–.00	.00	10.4	.00	1.0
Last grade	–.05	.01	48.9	.00	.9
Unemployed	.07	.04	4.3	.04	1.1
Institution					
Region					
Northeast	.26	.04	47.6	.00	1.3
Midwest	.14	.04	15.0	.00	1.1
South	–.12	.03	18.0	.00	.8
Size	–.16	.02	118.7	.00	.8
Security					
Maximum	.30	.04	70.1	.00	1.4
Medium	.09	.03	8.8	.00	1.1
Minimum	.01	.05	.1	.82	1.0

NOTE: $\chi^2 = 1{,}252.4$, $df = 18$, $p \leq .01$; 1,525 missing cases.
a. Approximation of how much more likely the outcome is for people with the characteristic.

and kitchen work (Table 4). Men are overrepresented in farm and forestry, maintenance, and repair work.

The Census data confirm the gender difference in work assignments (Table 5). The comparison of women's and men's facilities on employment in prison industries showed that just 1% of men were employed in prison industries, whereas women did not do these kinds of work at all in most institutions. Similarly, an average of 5% of men were employed in highway maintenance, but this was a type of work in which women did not participate. Alternatively, a higher proportion of women were employed in textile-related work. Twice as many men as women were employed in physical plant and repair work.

Not only are the types of institutional work different for women and men, but men are more often paid than are women. The Survey data show that the

TABLE 4: Inmate Work Assignments by Sex, Survey

	Sex			
	Women		Men	
Type Work	%	n	%	n
Cleaning	21.3	459	16.9	1,169
Road and grounds maintenance	6.3	135	7.2	500
Food preparation/kitchen	22.5	485	18.8	1,300
Laundry	4.2	90	4.4	304
Medical services	1.6	35	1.2	83
Farm and forestry	.6	14	5.7	393
Goods production	9.6	206	6.4	443
Services (e.g., library)	14.9	320	11.5	797
Maintenance, repair	3.7	79	10.9	757
Other	15.4	331	16.9	1,169

$\chi^2 = 259.6$, $df = 9$, $p \leq .05$.

TABLE 5: Percentage of Inmates Employed in Various Types of Work for Women's and Men's Institutions, Census

	Women's Facilities			*Men's Facilities*			
	Average Proportion	SD	n	*Average Proportion*	SD	n	F
Work release	.04	.09	47	.03	.08	616	.8
Prison industry							
Furniture, make/repair	.00	.01	73	.01	.03	767	2.2
Shop	.00	.00	73	.01	.02	767	4.8**
Textiles	.04	.07	73	.01	.03	767	56.8*
Highway maintenance	.00	.01	73	.05	.14	767	7.9*
Forest/natural resources/ conservation	.02	.09	73	.03	.14	767	1.1
Clerical/hospital/crew	.02	.08	73	.02	.10	767	.0
Other[a]	.01	.04	73	.01	.06	767	.1
Prison maintenance							
Food service	.10	.09	73	.09	.07	767	1.2
Physical plant/repair	.02	.06	73	.04	.08	767	6.3*
Laundry	.02	.02	73	.02	.04	767	.2
Grounds/garden	.04	.07	73	.04	.07	767	.0
Construction	.04	.07	73	.04	.07	767	.8
Maintenance crews	.03	.07	73	.07	.03	767	.1
Clerical	.01	.04	73	.00	.02	767	2.9

a. Data processing, warehouse industry, sewing, machine repair.
*$p \leq .01$; **$p \leq .05$.

percentage of working women who received pay was 63.3 (1,383 of 2,186), in contrast to the 71.7% of the working men who were paid (4,957 of 6,970) ($\chi^2 = 47.8$, $df = 1$, $p \leq .05$).

Women and men did not report significantly different levels of participation in vocational programs during their incarceration (20.6% or 600 of 2,908 women reported receiving vocational education vs. 19.9% or 2,140 of 10,761 men; $\chi^2 = .8$, $df = 1$, $p \leq .05$); and the logistic regression confirmed no significant effect of gender (Table 6). Instead, the influencing variable was placement in a maximum or medium custody facility. In comparison with inmates in minimum security facilities, those in the maximum or medium security settings had a 20% greater likelihood of having received vocational programming. Living in the northeastern part of the United States also increased the odds by 20%. The Census provides evidence of differential involvement in various types of vocational training (Table 7). A higher proportion of men were in auto repair or in construction and building trade vocational programs, whereas women were disproportionately involved in office training.

Medical and Mental Health

A slightly greater percentage of women than men reported receiving medical services in prison (42.4% or 1,311 of 3,090 women vs. 40.2% or 4,619 of 11,501 men; $df = 1$, $\chi^2 = 5.2$, $p = .02$). The logistic regression showed that this gender difference was explained by control variables (Table 8), particularly women's more frequently reported need for medical care. Not unexpectedly, this need for care was the primary determinant of receiving medical care. There were lesser effects of other variables, with Native Americans 40% less likely than other prisoners to receive medical attention. Those in larger facilities were more likely to receive care. Inmates in the Northeast region were 30% more likely, and those in the South 20% less likely to report having received medical care.

The Census includes several questions about medical care facilities. All of the reporting women's facilities (47) had a contract with a licensed hospital, but 8.9% of the men's facilities did not ($\chi^2 = 4.5$, $df = 1$, $p = .03$). Women's institutions were less likely to share medical facilities with another institution (38.3% of the 47 women's facilities and 57.5% of the 605 men's shared facilities; $\chi^2 = 6.5$, $df = 1$, $p = .01$). Women's facilities were more likely to have a medical examining room on site (95.7% of the 47 women's facilities and 84.9% of the 608 men's; $\chi^2 = 4.2$, $df = 1$, $p = .04$). Similarly, more of the women's (74.5% of 47) than the men's facilities (58.2% of 607) had a dental

TABLE 6: Logistic Regression Results for Prediction of Participation in Vocational Programs, Survey

Predictors	B	SE	*Wald*	*Significance*	*Odds Ratio*[a]
Demographic					
Gender	.04	.06	.5	.00	1.0
Race					
White	.01	.11	.0	.95	1.0
Black	.04	.12	.1	.73	1.0
Asian, Pacific Islander	–.01	.20	.0	.96	1.0
Native American	.35	.16	4.9	.03	1.4
Hispanic	–.15	.07	3.8	.05	.9
Age	–.02	.00	45.8	.00	.9
Income	–.00	.00	9.5	.00	1.0
Years in prison	.10	.01	181.5	.00	1.1
Last grade	.01	.00	11.2	.00	1.0
Unemployed	.05	.04	1.1	.28	1.0
Institution					
Region					
Northeast	.19	.04	18.7	.00	1.2
Midwest	–.10	.04	5.8	.02	.9
South	–.11	.04	9.9	.00	.9
Size	–.08	.02	18.8	.00	.9
Security					
Maximum	.19	.04	18.3	.00	1.2
Medium	.17	.04	18.3	.00	1.2
Minimum	.08	.06	2.2	.14	1.1

NOTE: χ^2 = 1,329.7, df = 18, $p \leq .01$; 1,530 missing cases.
a. Approximation of how much more likely the outcome is for people with the characteristic.

office or laboratory ($\chi^2 = 4.8$, $df = 1$, $p = .03$). There were no statistically significant differences between women's and men's correctional facilities in the proportions with an in-house medical facility (for women's facilities, 12.8% of 47 facilities and for men's, 18.8% of 605 facilities; $df = 1$, $\chi^2 = 1.7$), with an infirmary with an overnight bed (for women's facilities, 55.3% of 47, for men's facilities, 45.8% of 607; $\chi^2 = 1.5$, $df = 1$), and with an infirmary with no overnight bed (for women's facilities, 17.4% of 46, for men's 21.1% of 589; $\chi^2 = .3$, $df = 1$).

Consistent with the general trend in the United States, more women than men were given psychotropic drugs during imprisonment (15.8% or 485 of the women vs. 8.9% or 1,026 of the men; $\chi^2 = 123.4$, $df = 1$, $p \leq .001$). There

TABLE 7: Percentage of Inmates Involved in Various Types of Vocational Training in Women's and Men's Institutions, Census[a]

	Women's Facilities			*Men's Facilities*			
Type of Training	*Average Proportion*	SD	n	*Average Proportion*	SD	n	F
Auto repair	.00	.01	73	.01	.03	767	5.3*
Sheet metal shop	.00	.00	73	.01	.03	767	2.7
Construction	.00	.01	73	.01	.04	767	7.2[a]
Office	.02	.05	73	.00	.01	767	97.5[a]
Other[b]	.04	.07	73	.03	.08	767	.8

a. For both women's and men's facilities, the average proportion of inmates participating in vocational training in some areas was less than 1%, and these areas are omitted from the analysis. They include drafting, data processing, and appliance repair.
b. Other vocational training includes heating, air conditioning and refrigeration, bartender, horticulture, commercial art, culinary, janitorial, cabinet making, watch repair, shoe repair, meat cutting, sewing, woodworking, and other areas.
$^{*}p \leq .01$.

TABLE 8: Logistic Regression Results for Prediction of Receipt of Medical Care, Survey

Predictors	B	SE	*Wald*	*Significance*	*Odds Ratio*[a]
Demographic					
Gender	.07	.07	.8	.36	.9
Race					
White	.04	.17	.1	.80	1.0
Black	–.18	.17	1.1	.29	.8
Asian, Pacific Islander	–.14	.26	.3	.58	.9
Native American	–.56	.22	6.6	.01	.6
Hispanic	–.03	.10	.1	.75	1.0
Age	–.02	.00	40.1	.00	.9
Income	–.00	.00	1.0	.31	1.0
Years in prison	.06	.01	34.3	.00	1.1
Institution					
Region					
Northeast	.26	.04	47.6	.00	1.3
Midwest	.14	.04	15.0	.00	1.1
South	–.12	.03	18.0	.00	.8
Size	–.16	.02	118.7	.00	.8
Security					
Maximum	.30	.04	70.1	.00	1.4
Medium	.09	.03	8.8	.00	1.1
Minimum	.01	.05	.1	.82	1.0

NOTE: $\chi^2 = 1{,}252.4$, $df = 18$, $p \leq .01$; 1,525 missing cases.
a. Approximation of how much more likely the outcome is for people with the characteristic.

is further evidence from the Census data of the higher proportion of women in institutions who were using psychotropic drugs at any given time, with the average proportion for women's facilities at .07 (*SD* = .09, number of institutions = 71), in comparison to the lower mean of .03 for the men's institutions (*SD* = .03, number of institutions = 736) ($F = 15.6$, $df = 1{,}806$, $p \leq .01$).

A number of factors other than gender might account for more frequent receipt of psychotropic drugs by women, and several of these alternative explanatory variables could be examined with the Survey data: need for care indicated by the offer to have a mental health professional see the woman at admission, prior mental hospital stay, and prior use of psychotropic drugs. Also, institutional characteristics or offender demographics might explain gender differences.

The logistic regression analysis showed that, even after taking these alternative explanatory variables into account, women were almost twice as likely than men to receive psychotropic drug treatment in prison (Table 9). As might be expected, the odds of receiving psychotropic medicine are increased most strongly (by a factor of nearly 8) by treatment with drugs before admission, and prior mental hospitalization increased the odds by just over 3.5. Being offered the opportunity to see a mental health professional at the time of admission, which can be viewed as an indication of need, doubled the odds of receiving psychotropic drugs. There also was a 30%, statistically significant, positive increase in odds related to being non-Hispanic.

Parallel to findings about gender and the use of psychotropic drugs, women were more likely than men to be offered an opportunity to see a mental health professional. The proportion of women offered this opportunity was 31.9 (911 of 2,855), in comparison to 26.5 of men (2,798 of 10,544) ($\chi^2 = 33.4$, $df = 1$, $p \leq .01$). The Census confirms that a greater proportion of women than men received psychological counseling, although there was no significant difference in the proportion receiving job or adjustment counseling (Table 10).

The logistic regression analysis showed that after controlling for other predictors, women were 60% more likely than men to be offered an opportunity to see a mental health professional (Table 11). Prior use of psychotropic drugs had a greater influence than gender, doubling the chances; prior hospitalization increased the chances by 70%, and being Asian, by 60%. In maximum security prisons, the odds were 20% greater of having been offered the chance to see a mental health professional, and in minimum security prisons they were 20% less.

Approximately the same proportion of women and men reported receiving drug treatment in prison (13.9% of 3,093 responding women, and 14.7% of

TABLE 9: **Logistic Regression Results for Prediction of Receipt of Psychotropic Drugs in Prison, Survey**

Predictors	B	SE	*Wald*	*Significance*	*Odds Ratio*[a]
Demographic					
Gender	.70	.08	82.3	.00	2.0
Race					
White	–.09	.13	.5	.47	.9
Black	–.32	.14	5.7	.02	.7
Asian, Pacific Islander	.03	.26	.0	.89	1.0
Native American	–.07	.21	.1	.72	.9
Hispanic	–.33	.11	9.0	.00	.7
Income	.00	.00	12.1	.00	1.0
Years in prison	.09	.01	97.3	.00	1.1
Hospital preadmission	1.27	.07	330.4	.00	3.5
Drugs preadmission	2.06	.08	593.6	.00	7.9
Offer mental health profession	.69	.06	112.7	.00	2.0
Institution					
Region					
Northeast	.06	.07	1.0	.33	1.1
Midwest	.05	.06	.7	.39	1.1
South	–.13	.05	6.5	.01	.9
Size	–.01	.03	.2	.66	1.0
Security					
Maximum	.13	.06	5.5	.02	1.1
Medium	–.11	.05	4.6	.03	.9
Minimum	–.17	.08	4.6	.03	.8

NOTE: $\chi^2 = 1{,}732.6$, $df = 18$, $p \leq .01$; 1,889 cases missing.
a. Approximation of how much more likely the outcome is for people with the characteristic.

TABLE 10: **Participation in Counseling at Women's and Men's Facilities, Census**

	Women's Facilities			*Men's Facilities*			
Type of Counseling	*Average Proportion*	SD	n	*Average Proportion*	SD	n	F
Psychological	.22	.24	55	.15	.21	663	6.1*
Employment	.07	.15	59	.04	.16	678	1.9
Adjustment	.13	.21	59	.09	.21	690	2.2

*$p \leq .05$.

TABLE 11: Logistic Regression Results for Prediction of Offer to See Mental Health Professional, Survey

Predictors	B	SE	*Wald*	*Significance*	*Odds Ratio*[a]
Demographic					
Gender	.15	.05	8.2	.00	1.6
Race					
White	.06	.10	.3	.59	1.1
Black	–.06	.10	.4	.54	.9
Asian, Pacific Islander	.49	.17	7.8	.01	1.6
Native American	–.05	.15	.1	.72	.9
Hispanic	–.09	.07	1.8	.18	.9
Income	–.00	.00	7.3	.01	.9
Years in prison	–.04	.01	27.6	.00	.9
Hospital preadmission	.51	.06	84.3	.00	1.7
Drugs preadmission	.68	.08	80.8	.00	2.0
Institution					
Region					
Northeast	.07	.04	2.9	.09	1.1
Midwest	.02	.04	.3	.59	1.0
South	.04	.03	2.0	.16	1.0
Size	–.01	.03	.2	.66	1.0
Security					
Maximum	.14	.04	13.9	.00	1.2
Medium	.01	.03	.1	.79	1.0
Minimum	–.25	.05	25.4	.00	.8

NOTE: $\chi^2 = 366.4$, $df = 17$, $p \leq .01$; 1,884 missing cases.
a. Approximation of how much more likely the outcome is for people with the characteristic.

11,556 responding men, $\chi^2 = 1.2$, $df = 1$, $p \geq .05$). The logistic regression showed that after control variables were introduced, women had a slightly reduced chance (15% less) of receiving drug treatment in prison (Table 12). Self-reports of drug dependency and cocaine use prior to incarceration were stronger predictors. There also were regional effects, with inmates in the Midwest least likely to receive drug treatment. Inmates in maximum security facilities were more likely to receive treatment, although inmates in large prisons had slightly less chance of receiving drug treatment.

Access to Legal Expertise and Materials

More women than men (40.6% or 1,169 of 2,879 women vs. 38.8% or 4,247 of 10,697 men) had contact with an attorney after incarceration ($df = 1$,

TABLE 12: Logistic Regression Results for Prediction Drug Treatment in Prison, Survey

Predictors	B	SE	*Wald*	*Significance*	*Odds Ratio*[a]
Drug history					
Ever dependent	.91	.07	191.0	.00	2.5
Ever used heroin	.00	.08	.0	.98	1.0
Heroin months before incarceration	.05	.09	.3	.58	1.0
Ever used methadone	–.09	.09	.8	.37	.9
Methadone months before incarceration	.07	.19	.2	.70	1.1
Ever used cocaine	.75	.07	117.8	.00	2.1
Cocaine months before incarceration	.12	.07	3.2	.07	1.1
Demographic					
Gender	–.29	.07	18.5	.00	.7
Race					
White	–.36	.18	4.2	.04	.7
Black	–.40	.18	4.9	.03	.7
Asian, Pacific Islander	–.08	.26	.1	.74	.9
Native American	.22	.22	1.0	.33	1.2
Hispanic	–.09	.09	1.2	.28	.9
Income	–.00	.00	1.9	.17	1.0
Years in prison	.04	.01	19.8	.00	1.0
Institution					
Region					
Northeast	.15	.05	7.9	.01	1.2
Midwest	–.06	.05	1.2	.28	.9
South	.17	.04	16.4	.00	1.2
Size	–.09	.02	18.6	.00	.9
Security					
Maximum	–.17	.05	10.5	.00	.8
Medium	.16	.04	13.5	.00	1.2
Minimum	.23	.06	13.9	.00	1.3

NOTE: $\chi^2 = 965.2$, $df = 23$, $p \leq .01$, 1,832 missing cases.
a. Approximation of how much more likely the outcome is for people with the characteristic.

$\chi^2 = 3.2$, $p = .07$). This difference was not statistically significant. After controls were introduced in the logistic regression, women were a bit (25%) more likely to have attorney contact, and this difference was statistically significant (Table 13). Most of the control variables only modestly influenced the odds of seeing an attorney.

TABLE 13: Logistic Regression Results for Prediction of Attorney Contact, Survey

Predictors	B	SE	*Wald*	*Significance*	*Odds Ratio*[a]
Demographic					
Gender	.22	.05	22.4	.00	1.3
Race					
White	–.16	.13	1.6	.21	.8
Black	–.13	.13	1.0	.32	.9
Asian, Pacific Islander	–.13	.20	.4	.50	.9
Native American	–.10	.17	.4	.53	.9
Hispanic	–.34	.06	32.1	.00	.7
Income	–.00	.00	7.2	.01	1.0
Years in prison	.10	.01	222.6	.00	1.1
Institution					
Region					
Northeast	.31	.03	67.7	.00	1.4
Midwest	.16	.04	19.7	.00	1.2
South	–.25	.03	76.4	.00	.8
Size	–.02	.01	3.4	.06	1.0
Security					
Maximum	.24	.04	44.8	.00	1.3
Medium	.09	.03	8.4	.00	1.1
Minimum	–.20	.05	19.1	.00	.8

NOTE: $\chi^2 = 572.6$, $df = 16$, $p \leq .01$; 599 missing cases.
a. Approximation of how much more likely the outcome is for people with the characteristic.

Since admission, fewer women than men had used law books or other legal materials provided by the prison (33.4% or 960 of 2,879 women vs. 41.7% or 4,461 of 10,705 men) ($df = 1$, $\chi^2 = 65.3$, $p \leq .01$). When control variables were introduced in the regression analysis, women still had somewhat lower odds of using legal materials (Table 14). Native American and White offenders also had lower levels of use. In the Northeast, more offenders used materials, and in the South fewer. There was greater use in maximum security prisons and slightly increased use in the larger prisons and for those who had been incarcerated for a long period.

Parent-Child Relations

The Survey did not include data on participation in parenting programs, but it is clear from the Census that counseling regarding parenting was almost

TABLE 14: **Logistic Regression Results for Prediction of Use of Legal Materials, Survey (N = 12,994)**

Predictors	B	SE	*Wald*	*Significance*	*Odds Ratio*[a]
Demographic					
Gender	–.15	.05	10.1	.00	.9
Race					
White	–.32	.14	5.6	.02	.7
Black	.01	.14	.0	.95	1.0
Asian, Pacific Islander	–.25	.20	1.6	.21	.8
Native American	–.45	.18	6.4	.01	.6
Hispanic	–.31	.06	24.7	.00	.7
Income	–.00	.00	6.7	.01	1.0
Years in prison	.09	.01	188.4	.00	1.1
Institution					
Region					
Northeast	.39	.04	107.5	.00	1.5
Midwest	.04	.04	1.5	.22	1.0
South	–.27	.03	89.1	.00	.8
Size	.06	.01	17.7	.00	1.1
Security					
Maximum	.24	.04	44.6	.00	1.3
Medium	.00	.03	.0	.99	1.0
Minimum	–.06	.05	1.5	.22	.9

NOTE: $\chi^2 = 738.1$, $df = 16$, $p \leq .01$; 601 missing cases.
a. Approximation of how much more likely the outcome is for people with the characteristic.

exclusively used in women's facilities. The average proportion of men participating was less than 1% ($SD = .01$, $n = 759$), but for women the average proportion participating was 4% ($SD = .09$, $n = 68$) ($F = 178.5$, $p \leq .01$). Given the very high proportion of women with children, and of those planning to assume responsibility for their children on release, there would appear to be much more need than availability of parenting programs for women. There appears to be even less adequate programming for men.

IMPLICATIONS AND CONCLUSION

National data sets are relevant to the development of criminal justice policy, for they overcome the persistent problem of identifying national conditions and trends for a system that is fragmented and diverse. Social indicators of the characteristics of women in prison as well as comparisons of these indicators for women and men have been the focus of several government publications (e.g., Bureau of Justice Statistics 1991), and the data sets are particularly detailed in their inclusion of information on the offenders' employment, education, drug, and criminal histories. It also is important to have data from which to derive indicators of programming in correctional facilities, both to assess program adequacy and to identify gender and other biases. Program data make it possible to draw connections between indicators of need (for example, prior responsibility for children) with both program availability and involvement (for example, parenting programs).

Although the Census and the Survey include questions that provide some valuable insights into correctional programming, there are some limitations in these data. The specific difficulties that women experience with medical programming (delay, lack of high-risk pregnancy care, availability of hospital facilities, care for HIV positive inmates, etc.) are important enough to warrant specific questions, and reports of pregnancy and HIV positive status would shed light on program needs. In the mental health and substance abuse treatment areas, questions about the availability of certain types of programming (programs addressing self-esteem, prior victimization, etc.) would be needed to generate useful indicators of the success in adapting general program models to women's special needs. Other information on parenting that would be helpful would be the types of programming available, including visitation and access to assistance with parental rights. For women, involvement in vocational choice advising may be as important as the availability of particular types of work experience and training, because inmates are influenced by stereotypes about appropriate occupations. For all areas of programming, information on intensity of involvement (length of time and hours per week) would reflect on the program's potential to effect change.

Of course, there are resource limitations, both in terms of funding and time, that constrain additions to any survey instrument. Yet, in light of the importance of fully documenting women offenders' needs and programming to address these needs, an expanded set of questions would be useful for at least a subsample of women and men. Social indicator information can play a major role in stimulating social change, for it highlights problem areas and helps to create the conditions needed for change.

Turning now to the basic findings of our research, even allowing for underreporting of program participation by both inmates and administrators, a striking result of the analysis is the very low level of participation by both incarcerated men and women in work, vocational training, mental health programs (including substance abuse treatment), and parent counseling programs. Prior to incarceration, many offenders were marginally involved in the workforce and had a history of mental health problems or substance abuse. A very high proportion of women in prison are parents with responsibility for their children up to the point of incarceration, and many men in prison are fathers. A growing proportion of women in particular, but also of men, have a history of drug abuse. Regardless of gender, for most offenders, incarceration in the 1980s was a continuation or an exacerbation of marginalization from meaningful work or related vocational training, and there was no substantial counterbalance brought by programming related to such key areas as substance abuse or parenting.

Although the core of the prison experience is similar for women and men, it is also shaped by gender relations. The organization of gender includes the differences in power, activities, and experiences that happen because of one's sex. The common themes of women immersed in women's work—cleaning, cooking, working as secretaries or with textiles, or in the home raising children—are mirrored in the prison. In men's institutions, the emphasis is on different types of work and training, and there is little emphasis on parenting.

Gender arrangements in the larger society have implications for the programming available both to women and to men. Imprisoned fathers, as much as imprisoned mothers, would seem to need parenting-related programming to manage relationships with children during incarceration and to prepare for release by improving parenting skills. Through work assignments and the allocation of resources to particular programs, women are more often called on to do women's work, both within the institution of the prison and in preparation for family responsibilities during and after incarceration. Although there are some alternative programs affecting some women in prison (Weisheit 1985), the summary information provided by the Survey and the Census shows that on the whole, prisons in the 1980s continue to reinforce a traditional organization of gender.

That women receive more programming related to children is not in itself negative, for they usually had custody of the children before incarceration. However, the very minimal programming for fathers and their children supports current arrangements; it does not challenge men to take more responsibility for children, nor does it prepare them to do so.

Another outcome is the reinforcement—through the typical prison work or vocational training experience—of women's employment in areas that are not financially rewarded. Because such small percentages of inmates are in any sort of work or training, percentage differences reflect tendencies rather than dramatically different experiences for women and men. However, even among inmates who are not themselves involved in sex-stereotyped work or training, the patterns within the institution are apparent. The message conveyed by the type of work available in the 1980s and the symbolism of more women than men working for no pay, is not subtle.

The data do not reveal why a higher proportion of women than men participate in educational programming, but this finding again reflects some societywide patterns. Women in the United States often work in jobs for which they have more than the required education because they are denied access to jobs open to men with equivalent levels of education. In the same vein, it is well-known that when educational levels are constant, men earn more than women. In and outside of prison, women are not less educated than men, but they fare more poorly in employment.

Like the experiences of work and training, the disproportionate use of psychotropic drugs for women mirrors and reinforces gender-related differences in the U.S. context. There has been no empirical demonstration that more imprisoned women than men have the kinds of mental illnesses that respond to psychotropic drug treatment. Why, then, are drugs more often used for women?

Findings of Baskin et al. (1989) raise the possibility that drugs are more often used in prison to control aggressive women than men. Perhaps aggressive women are more subject to medical control than similar men because they are viewed as particularly abnormal or dangerous, as more completely deviating from appropriate behavior. This would be one way that gender organization might influence mental health treatment.

Gender organization also could result in a failure to develop mental health programming that deals with the problems of women offenders, which are rooted in their status as women. Little is known from empirical research about the extent to which the documented high levels of child sexual abuse, adult battering, and exploitation by men who manage the drug and sex trades contribute to mental illness among women inmates. Research has failed to ask key questions about the connection between girls' and women's victimization and negative psychological outcomes (for exceptions, see Chesney-Lind 1989). The frequent use of psychotropic drugs should be examined in relation to the etiology of incarcerated women's mental health problems, with attention to the appropriateness of drug therapy for women whose difficulties result from victimization.

In addition to the direct influences of gender on the prison experience, there are differences in women's experiences because of the type of facility in which they are concentrated. The smaller, lower security facilities where women tend to be housed are characterized by lower proportions of inmates receiving educational programming, vocational programming, medical care, and an offer to see a mental health professional. Also, in smaller, less secure facilities, a lower proportion of inmates use legal materials. Then, too, there is less likelihood of drug treatment or of attorney contact in minimum security facilities. These findings suggest an economy of scale problem in programming for women. However, because women are typically incarcerated for less violent offenses than men, it certainly does not make sense to house them in more secure, large facilities (Immarigeon and Chesney-Lind 1992). Rather, the findings raise the question of whether alternatives could be used for a greater number of women, making various resources in the community accessible to them.

The logistic regression analyses showed differences in programming related not only to gender, but also to region and ethnic or racial group. Using the Western region for comparison, offenders in the South received less programming and those in the Northeast had more, which suggests the need for federal policies that provide incentives and resources for improvements in the program-poor states.

Differences related to race and ethnicity could not be fully explored with the available data, but the indicators suggested some important disparities that should be further examined. For instance, we need to know more about the negative association of Native American status with medical care. Also, is the more frequent offer to Asians of the opportunity to see a mental health professional a result of their greater need, or of stereotypes of Asians or other groups? Similarly, are Hispanics less likely than other offenders to receive psychotropic drugs for mental health treatment because of their mental health needs or because of stereotypes about them or other groups?

Along with regional residence, race, and ethnicity, gender is a system of division and stratification that shapes the experience of incarceration. Given the history of corrections in the United States, it is not surprising that the amount and emphasis of programming in prisons, as revealed by the indicators derived from the Survey and the Census, essentially reproduce the gender arrangements in the larger society. There are, of course, alternative programs and practices that challenge current arrangements, but the full picture suggests that these were not the norm in the mid-1980s, a point of rapid expansion in the prison population, especially for women, and of increased legal challenge regarding the equity in programming for women.

NOTES

1. The standard procedure for working with dummy variables is to create one less variable than the number of values for the measure being converted to a dummy variable. For race, variables were created for four racial groups (White, Black, Asian or Pacific Islander, Native

American) and for each variable, all respondents were coded as 1 or as 0, indicating membership in that group or nonmembership in that group, respectively. No variable was created for people in other racial groups. This omitted group is considered in interpreting the regression results. For example, a significant positive beta value for White indicates that in comparison to the other category of racial groups, individuals who are White are more likely to be in the numerically coded, higher category of the dependent variable.

2. The symbol $\overline{X}$ signifies mean.

REFERENCES

Alpert, Geoffrey P. 1982. "Women Prisoners and the Law: Which Way Will the Pendulum Swing?" *Journal of Criminal Justice* 10:37-44.

American Correctional Association. 1993. "Legal Issues and the Female Offender." *Female Offenders: Meeting Needs of a Neglected Population*, edited by American Correctional Association. Laurel, MD: Author.

Baskin, Deborah R., Ira Sommers, Richard Tessler, and Henry J. Steadman. 1989. "Role Incongruence and Gender Variation in Prison Mental Health Services." *Journal of Health and Social Behavior* 1989:305-14.

Bershad, Lawrence 1985. "Discriminatory Treatment of the Female Offender in the Criminal Justice System." *Boston College Law Review* 26:389-438.

Brett, Crista. 1993. "From Victim to Victimizer." Pp. 26-30 in *Female Offenders: Needs of a Neglected Population*, edited by the American Correctional Association. College Park, MD: American Correctional Association.

Bureau of Justice Statistics. 1991. *Women in Prison*. Washington, DC: U.S. Government Printing Office.

Chesney-Lind, Meda. 1989. "Girls' Crime and Woman's Place: Toward a Feminist Model of Female Delinquency." *Crime & Delinquency* 35:5-29.

CONtact, Inc. 1981. *Women Offenders*. Lincoln, NE: Corrections Compendium.

Crawford, Jane. 1988. *Tabulation of a Nationwide Survey of State Correctional Facilities for Adult and Juvenile Female Offenders*. Laurel, MD: American Correctional Association.

Daly, Kathleen. 1987, January. "Survey Results of the Niantic Interviews December 1983 and May 1986." mimeo.

Dobash, Russell P., R. Emerson Dobash, and Sue Gutteridge. 1986. *The Imprisonment of Women*. Oxford, UK: Blackwell.

Edwards, Susan S. 1986. "Neither Bad Nor Mad: The Female Violent Offender Reassessed." *Women's Studies International Forum* 9:79-88.

Feinman, Clarice. 1986. *Women in the Criminal Justice System*. New York: Praeger.

Gilfus, Mary E. 1988. "Seasoned by Violence/Tempered by Law: Qualitative Study of Women and Crime." Ph.D. dissertation, Brandeis University, Waltham, Massachusetts.

Huling, Tracy. 1991. "Breaking the Silence." Correctional Association of New York, March 4. mimeo.

Immarigeon, Russ and Meda Chesney-Lind. 1992. *Women's Prisons: Overcrowded and Overused*. San Francisco, CA: National Council on Crime and Delinquency.

LeClair, Daniel. 1990, October. *The Incarcerated Female Offender: Victim or Villain?* Research Division, Massachusetts Division of Correction. mimeo.

Leonard, E. 1982. *Women in Crime and Society*. New York: Longman.

Passages Program. n.d. "You Never Know What Is Really Going on With You Until Somebody is Willing to be Your Mirror." Madison, WI: Wisconsin Division of Corrections.

Pollock-Byrne, Joycelyn M. 1990. *Women, Prison and Crime*. Pacific Grove, CA: Brooks/Cole.

Rafter, Nicole Hahn. 1990. *Partial Justice: Women, Prisons and Social Control*. New Brunswick, NJ: Transaction Books.

———. 1993. "Equity or Difference?" Pp. 7-11 in *Female Offenders: Meeting Needs of a Neglected Population*. College Park, MD: American Correctional Association.

Rhode Island Justice Alliance. 1990. "Female Offender Survey, Rhode Island Adult Correctional Institutions, Women's Division." mimeo.

Ryan, T. E. 1984. *Adult Female Offenders and the Institutional Programs: A State of the Art Analysis*. Washington, DC: National Institute of Corrections.

Shover, Neal 1991. "Institutional Corrections: Jails and Prisons." Pp. 379-98 in *Criminology: A Contemporary Handbook*, edited by J. F. Sheley. Belmont, CA: Wadsworth.

Sommers, Ira and Deborah R. Baskin. 1991. "Assessing the Appropriateness of the Prescription of Psychiatric Medications in Prison." *Journal of Nervous and Mental Disease* 179:267-73.

Steadman, Henry J., Edward J. Holohean, and Joel Dvoskin. 1991. "Estimating Mental Health Needs and Service Utilization Among Prison Inmates." *Bulletin of the American Academy of Psychiatry and the Law* 19:297-307.

Van Ochten, Marjorie. 1993. "Legal Issues and the Female Offender." Pp. 31-36 in *Female Offenders: Meeting Needs of a Neglected Population*. Laurel, MD: American Correctional Association.

Weisheit, Ralph. 1985. "Trends in Programs for Female Offenders: The Use of Private Agencies as Service Providers." *International Journal of Offender Therapy and Comparative Criminology* 29:35-42.

Weisheit, Ralph and Susan Mahan. 1988. *Women, Crime and Criminal Justice*. Cincinnati, OH: Anderson.

Yang, S. Steven. 1990. "The Unique Treatment Needs of Female Substance Abusers in Correctional Institutions: The Obligation of the Criminal Justice System to Provide Parity Services." *Medicine and Law* 9:1018-27.

Zedner, Lucia. 1991. "Women, Crime, and Penal Responses: A Historical Account." Pp. 307-62 in *Crime and Justice: A Review of Research*, edited by M. Tonry. Chicago: University of Chicago Press.

Growth-Centered Intervention: An Overview of Changes in Recent Decades

BY TED PALMER, PH.D.
*Senior Researcher, California Youth Authority**

THROUGHOUT THE 1980's, American corrections struggled with issues of institutional crowding, rising costs, and controlling offenders' behavior. These were its central themes or strongest currents. To many practitioners and policy makers they resembled a troubled sea.

Simultaneously, other currents were stirring, ones that were calmer, submerged at first, and considerably stronger before 1980. These involved rehabilitation or habilitation, which may be called growth-centered intervention. By the mid-'80's these currents became somewhat stronger, and, as it were, they returned to view. Toward the end of the decade much of their strength was back.

This article briefly reviews these issues and currents. It focuses on the reemergence of intervention in particular—its growth-centered version especially—and it discusses its prospects in the 1990's and beyond. It tries to provide perspective, interpretation, and possible direction mainly to practitioners, policy makers, researchers, and students.

The Era of Incapacitation

The 1980's was mainly an era of incapacitation and short-term behavior-control. This was corrections' chief response to the public's concern with safety *now*. It was a response which reflected a hope and belief that emerged in the mid-to-late 1970's, namely, that swift and certain punishment, by itself, could provide enough deterrence to produce high levels of immediate protection, and perhaps long-term safety as well. Further, this response reflected a correctional philosophy called the justice model. This model, which began to dominate corrections by the mid-1970's, emphasized punishment and downplayed rehabilitation as well as alternatives to incarceration (Fogel, 1975; von Hirsch, 1976).

As the 1990's approached and the volume of crime remained high, it became clear that the above hope and model had not produced the desired level of protection, whether short-term or long. Nor had crowding and costs declined. Despite this, the justice model will probably remain dominant during the 1990's; and incapacitation, plus intensive supervision combined with fines, restitution, etc., will likely remain corrections' main strategy.

This situation reflects the importance of incapacitation's and intensive supervision's contribution. For instance, though these approaches do not provide the *desired* level of short- and certainly long-term protection, they do provide *considerable* short-term safety. In this regard they reduce criminal and delinquent behavior or at least dampen their spread, and in so doing they partly address the public's main concern. Moreover, incapacitation and intensive supervision perform this function at a monetary price that may remain barely manageable in most jurisdictions for at least several years.

"Hidden" Costs

Yet, heavy or exclusive reliance on such a strategy can also have hidden (or not so hidden) costs, ones which are substantial and might include the following: continued or increased institutional crowding, with its many attendant problems; absence or paucity of serious programming within and outside lockup; little focus on long-term change in offenders even when some programming exists; and diversion of resources from broad activities such as delinquency prevention. These "costs" mainly but not entirely apply to incapacitation. Some can involve high recidivism rates and a resulting "revolving door" relationship between lockup and the streets. Several states and systems, e.g., California and its department of adult corrections, clearly exemplify this relationship (Blue Ribbon Commission, 1990).

Still, corrections' present strategy does help, and problems such as the above should not be entirely attributed to it. Nevertheless, this strategy leaves much to be desired; as a result, it should at least be complemented by other strategies or approaches and to some extent replaced by them. One such strategy involves *intervention*, particularly that form which does not center on punishment and incapacitation itself. Historically, this strategy is broader than, but sometimes identified with, rehabilitation.

The Reemergence of Intervention

As suggested, in the 1980's a then-secondary approach existed, one with strong roots in the 1960's and earlier. This approach is generally called rehabilita-

***Opinions expressed in this article are those of the author and do not necessarily reflect the California Youth Authority's official position.**

tion or, less often, habilitation. It is a major form of intervention, one which not only emphasizes the goal of internal change and growth but which recognizes the role of external controls and is sometimes called treatment. Rehabilitation tries to build—and build on—an individual's skills and interests rather than rely on punishment, fear, public humiliation, physical pain/discomfort, or incapacitation itself. At least, it tries to minimize the latter factors.

Developments in Recent Decades

From the 1960's to early-1970's there was a broad surge of confidence regarding rehabilitation's ability to change and control offenders on a short- as well as long-term basis. This high optimism was quickly followed by widespread pessimism during 1975-81, a period which was triggered by Martinson's mid-1970's critique of rehabilitation's presumed effectiveness. By 1983-84 evidence for his "relatively-little-works" view *and* for an alternative, "several-things-sometimes-work" view had been marshalled and became increasingly known. As a result, a mixed and unsettled atmosphere emerged regarding effectiveness. More precisely, some confusion and considerable uncertainty existed (Greenberg, 1977; Martinson, 1974; Palmer, 1974, 1978; President's Commission, 1967; Warren, 1971).

Yet, one thing became clear: Neither the deep pessimism of 1975-81 nor the global optimism of the 1960's seemed justified. Instead, more moderate positions had taken shape and soon began to prevail, especially among researchers and academicians (Empey, 1978; Gendreau & Ross, 1979; Glaser, 1975; Martin et al., 1981; Palmer, 1978, 1983; Romig, 1978; Sechrest et al., 1979). This included a relatively open-minded skepticism, on the one hand, and a more cautious optimism, on the other. Meanwhile, most practitioners believed programming was helpful but many had doubts about the extent of that help. Other individuals were neutral but not uninvolved.

During the rest of the '80's intervention gained strength in terms of *focus, direction, and legitimacy*. Its new or increased focus mainly resulted from its relevance and responsiveness to a growing interest by both the public and policy makers in addressing serious or multiple offenders. This interest reflected not only America's growing volume of crime, but widely accepted studies which showed that relatively few offenders accounted for half of all recorded crimes, many of which were violent (Hamparian et al., 1978; Strasberg, 1978; West & Farrington, 1977; Wolfgang et al., 1972).

Common Ground

Intervention's new direction or emphasis resulted from the fact that many individuals, some "skeptics" included, largely agreed on the following three principles for working with serious or multiple offenders, among others: (a) *multiple modality programs were needed*; (b) *increased intensity of contact was important*; (c) *greater attention had to be paid to offenders' needs and characteristics*, e.g., to matching those factors with particular program elements (Palmer, 1983, 1984). These principles gave new direction and impetus to program development in several states, beginning around 1985. Included was intensive probation programming for juvenile recidivists and various intensive parole programs for serious adult offenders. These programs, of course, were also in response to institutional crowding, rising costs, and the desire for increased protection from non-incarcerated offenders (Armstrong, 1988a, 1988b; Barton & Butts, 1990; Byrne et al., 1989; Fagan & Hartstone, 1986; Greenwood & Zimring, 1985; Gruenewald et al., 1985; Krisberg et al., 1989; U.S. Department of Justice, 1988; Van Voorhis, 1987).

The Re-legitimization of Intervention

Throughout 1975-81, several justice model proponents and followers of Martinson's early views virtually declared intervention "illegitimate," i.e., inappropriate or, at best, seldom needed (Greenberg, 1977; van den Haag, 1975; Wilson, 1975). Nevertheless, supported by its above-mentioned *relevance*, intervention regained considerable "legitimacy" in the 1980's. First, it regained pragmatic legitimacy. This occurred when it became clear that intervention often did provide practical assistance—simply put, concrete help—whether educational, vocational, psychological, or in interceding with others. Punishment and incapacitation were not, by themselves, designed for that. Secondly, intervention slowly regained moral legitimacy. This occurred when it became increasingly obvious that various stereotypes, such as the 1970's *Clockwork Orange* characterization of treatment as dehumanizing and inhumane, were intrinsic to neither intervention in general nor rehabilitation in particular—that, in fact, they seldom pertained beyond the early-to-mid 1970's. This applied to Mitford's (1971, 1973) widely known descriptions as well. If anything, instances of dehumanized "treatment" frequently emerged in the 1980's in connection with punishment and crowded institutions, rarely in relation to treatment as described above.

Further, intervention regained substantial scientific legitimacy. This occurred as several meta-analyses and literature reviews of experimental programs found converging evidence that most such efforts reduced recidivism when compared to their control programs; and for all programs combined the average reduction was moderate, i.e., 10-12 percent[1]. These reductions, and others which were considerably larger, e.g., 25 percent or more, made those programs directly relevant to public protection, especially when large numbers of offenders and therefore many potential offenses were involved (Andrews et al., 1990; Davidson et al., 1984; Garrett, 1985; Geismar & Wood, 1985; Gendreau & Ross, 1987; Gottschalk et al., 1987; Lipsey, 1989, 1991; Mayer et al., 1986; Palmer, 1975, 1984; Panizzon et al., 1991).

Finally, intervention regained—actually, retained—its philosophical legitimacy. This occurred toward the end of the decade as the following became clear: Neither justice model proponents nor others had provided convincing arguments that rehabilitation (a) should be considered intrinsically inappropriate as a major correctional goal, (b) was in fact unimportant or perhaps even harmful, and (c) should be secondary to punishment in any event, whether for short- or long-term goals.

On such grounds, intervention, particularly rehabilitation, had "fought its way back" from the artificially created, near-"illegitimacy" of previous years, and from its very real, partial banishment as well. This re-legitimization is a major development in American corrections, one whose implications are substantial.

The Tacit Consensus

Even by the mid-1980's, one product of intervention's early gains in terms of focus, direction, and legitimacy was the following tacit consensus among many practitioners and researchers (soon afterwards, this consensus also included various policy makers): (a) In contrast to the clearly pessimistic outlook and the actively rejecting attitude of 1975-81, some forms of intervention *could* probably reduce the recidivism of key offenders. In this regard, and because it often produced educational, vocational, and other gains, (b) rehabilitation/habilitation might be possible and useful after all.[2]

Though essentially self-evident by 1990, and seemingly simple and basic in any event, this consensus, in the mid-1980's, represented a major shift in tone and attitude from the preceding decade.

Supported by this developing consensus, and given direction by the agreed-upon principles (multiple modality programming, increased intensity of contact, and greater attention to offender needs/characteristics), program-development efforts began moving toward the same level that existed during 1965-75. By the late 1980's many practitioners and researchers were seriously focusing on the task of discovering and rediscovering practical methods and strategies, and of developing/evaluating possibly improved approaches. In this regard, many individuals, former skeptics included, were moving in similar directions and supporting similar goals.

Into the '90's

As the 1990's begin, intervention has a recognized and generally accepted role with serious and multiple offenders, sometimes including "special populations" such as sex offenders and substance abusers. Through the 1990's and beyond, this role can be performed via several approaches, including skill-development methods, control/surveillance techniques, psychologically oriented programs, and combinations of all three. In this respect intervention can draw on approaches that have existed in one form or another for over 30 years; yet it can utilize new approaches as well. Its role can be played with high- and middle-risk youths and adults and it can doubtlessly extend beyond serious, multiple offenders. In this regard, intervention's relevance or responsibility can be broad.

Current Limitations

Given its heavy responsibility—present and future—intervention's current limitations should be well understood; so should its present inability to guarantee certain levels of success. For instance, as of 1990 no *categories* ("types") of programs exist that usually—e.g., in at least two of every three such programs (*individual* programs)—produce *large* recidivism-reductions with typical, heterogeneous client-samples. Moreover, such reductions do not even occur one-third of the time, and this applies whether or not those samples mostly contain serious, multiple offenders. Here, "large reductions" means 25 percent or more, and "type" refers to a program's principal or most conspicuous component, e.g., vocational training or group counseling. As indicated, however, moderate reductions are common.

This absence of even a few generally reliable and, simultaneously, rather powerful and widely applicable *categories* of programs has major implications. For instance, it makes it impossible to presently recommend any categories as such to policy makers, i.e., recommend them on an across-the-board basis. More specifically, one cannot claim that any randomly selected individual program which falls within a given category, e.g., within the set of programs labeled "vocational training," will quite likely produce large recidivism-reductions compared to standard programs. One reason for this limitation is as follows: Individual programs often differ from each other on various dimensions, even though they may share a label such as "vocational training" or "individual counseling." As a result, many may also differ from others in their relevance to particular offender-groups that are found within the overall client samples, e.g., to younger vs.

older offenders, or to fearful vs. assertive. Those programs may therefore vary in their ability to reduce illegal behavior, and some—depending, e.g., on the dominant client-sample and the particular *mix* of clients—may not reduce it at all.

Moving Forward via Knowledge-Building

Though categories of programs cannot be recommended carte blanche, the individual programs that comprise them need not all be discarded and the categories themselves thereby eliminated. For instance, the above-mentioned meta-analyses showed that in each of several program categories, e.g., educational training or cognitive-behavioral, many individual programs that comprised those respective categories did reduce recidivism, though many others did not. Even if, say, only two out of every five of a given category's individual programs (not, e.g., the desired 67 percent or more) reduced recidivism to a statistically reliable degree, *those* two could still play important roles. Moreover, they could do so even if their reductions were moderate instead of large, e.g., 10-12 percent rather than 25 percent or more. A 10 percent reduction would mean, e.g., that 900 offenses rather than 1,000 could be expected; in addition, many of the 100 that could be avoided would probably be violent.

To make solid progress, corrections should of course reproduce programs, e.g., the "two out of five," that have shown success; moreover, it should discard or substantially modify the rest. This would increase the percentage of successful programs within each given category and could eventually make the category itself more useful to decision makers. Through research and other means, corrections should also adapt its existing programs to new settings and conditions.

To help achieve these goals, researchers and practitioners need detailed information not only about the defining features of promising programs but about factors that probably make them relevant to various kinds of offenders. Such information could provide a sound basis for program-building. It could, e.g., lead to better matching of new programs with given individuals and settings, and it could thereby increase the degree to which those programs reduce illegal behavior.

Despite these important possibilities the following should be kept in mind. Though correctional intervention gained considerable strength in the 1980's, similar progress or at least a comparable rate will not necessarily occur in the '90's. However, brisk progress can indeed occur if a number of the following objectives are achieved in connection with experimental studies:

(a) A higher percentage than in 1960-90 should be well-designed, and many fewer should be of questionable quality.

(b) To test reliability, a higher percentage should be replications or partial replications of programs that showed substantial success.

(c) To test and increase generalizability, a higher percentage should be systematic variations of programs that have already shown success under one or two sets of conditions.

(d) Wherever possible, studies should describe the main offender subgroups that comprise the overall sample, and separate outcome-analyses should be conducted for each such group.

(e) Intervention processes, e.g., techniques and strategies, should be examined closely and described more often and fully than before.

Beyond Tokenism

Knowledge gained from such studies can help intervention avoid being left to function in a very limited capacity or as mere window dressing and a token of humanitarian concern. All in all, intervention's potential within American corrections extends beyond that of providing, at most, modest assistance to many offenders and perhaps somewhat more to those actively seeking it or in obvious need. As a result, rehabilitation or habilitation, e.g., can and should be developed as more than essentially an appendage to either a management-and-control centered strategy or a punishment-oriented strategy. In the 1980's, intervention's relevance and potential were again partly recognized. In the 1990's, its gains as well as potential should be actively supported by practitioners, policy makers, and others. They should not be left to fade because of other valid priorities.

Nevertheless, even if considerable knowledge is gained and carefully planned programs become increasingly valued options, the public's overriding desire for short-term protection will probably remain the largest single influence on corrections in the 1990's. For this reason, and because they address that desire very directly and visibly, the control-centered approaches and relatively short-term goals that dominated corrections in the 1980's will likely remain in the forefront and will probably absorb most resources. Though this may occur at the expense of continued, serious overcrowding, it should not and probably will not occur at the price of ignoring intervention. Given substantial progress, and as growth-centered intervention and longer-term goals plus community-programming are increasingly used, the mix of available options will broaden and corrections *as a whole* will have more relevance and strength. This, however, should not in turn detract from crime-and-delinquency prevention efforts and from the fact that broad social changes are needed as well.

Finally, with regard to theory, a recently described "habilitation/developmental" (H/D) framework could add a critical dimension or emphasis to today's main perspective and tomorrow's program development (Palmer, 1991). Current perspectives mainly emphasize sociological factors and downplay the psychological or personal/developmental, factors of importance with many offenders (Elliott et al., 1979; Hawkins & Weis, 1985). In addressing various gaps and in providing direction for both expanded and more focused correctional efforts, an H/D framework would implement the three earlier-mentioned principles in an individualized way and could apply to more than serious, multiple offenders. It could also refocus knowledge-building and the interpretation of findings.

Closing Thoughts

In reflecting on the past three decades one quickly realizes that correctional intervention has already accomplished much and has a good deal to build on. Nevertheless, many approaches and combinations are still untried, and considerable growth can occur in the next few decades. More specifically, although many individual programs can already help many offenders, corrections as a whole has a long way to go before it can offer practitioners and policy makers a large number of highly reliable, cost-effective, yet also powerful approaches. Nevertheless, though American corrections often struggles to simply survive the day, the development of such approaches—while it may take considerable time—remains an exciting challenge to persons with confidence in the power of knowledge-building and well-documented practical experience. By the year 2000, intervention, through hard and carefully planned work, could be well along the way.

Toward this end, however, it should be firmly kept in mind that rehabilitation and habilitation, in particular, *are* part of corrections, not illegitimate or alien forces. Together with other contributions, theirs can help this field overcome or reduce its difficulties, much as they jointly help individuals address their own, and thereby progress.

NOTES

[1]The 10-12 percent average reduction resulted from combining all programs that yielded a positive outcome (meaning, *any* reduction in recidivism) with all programs that yielded a negative outcome, as well as those in which no differences were found between the experimental and control programs. When only those programs which yielded a positive outcome were examined, the average recidivism-reduction wes approximately 20 percent.

[2]Other aspects of the consensus were: (c) Most standard forms and typical variants of intervention, e.g., variants of individual or group counseling, were no longer considered intrinsically demeaning or necessarily onerous to offenders. (d) When viewed as a package that included definite external controls and "accountability," e.g., unpleasant consequences for infractions and illegal behavior, some forms of intervention, e.g., the community-based, were now considered less risky to the public than before, for selected offenders.

REFERENCES

Andrews, D. et al. (1990). Does correctional treatment work? A clinically relevant and psychologically informed meta-analysis. *Criminology, 28*(3), 369-404.

Armstrong, T. (1988a). National survey of juvenile intensive probation supervision. (Part I). *Criminal Justice Abstracts, 20*(1), 342-348.

Armstrong, T. (1988b). National survey of juvenile intensive probation supervision. (Part II). *Criminal Justice Abstracts,* 20(2), 497-523.

Barton, W., & Butts, J. (1990). Viable options: Intensive supervision programs for juvenile delinquents. *Crime and Delinquency, 36*(2), 238-256.

Blue Ribbon Commission on Inmate Population Management: Final Report. (1990). Sacramento: California State Legislature.

Byrne, J., Lurigio, A., & Baird, C. (1989). The effectiveness of the new intensive supervision programs. *Research in Corrections,* 2(2), 1-75.

Davidson, W. et al. (1984). Interventions with juvenile delinquents: A meta-analysis of treatment efficacy. Washington, DC: National Institute of Juvenile Justice and Delinquency Prevention.

Elliott, D., Ageton, S., & Canter, R. (1979). An integrated theoretical perspective on delinquent behavior. *Journal of Research in Crime and Delinquency, 16*(1), 3-27.

Empey, L. (1978). *American delinquency: Its meaning and construction.* Homewood, Il: Dorsey.

Fagan, J., & Hartstone, E. (1986). Innovation and experimentation in juvenile corrections: Implementing a community reintegration model for violent juvenile offenders. San Francisco: The URSA Institute.

Fogel, D. (1975). *We are the living proof. The justice model for corrections.* Cincinnati, OH: The W.H. Anderson Company.

Garrett, C. (1985). Effects of residential treatment on adjudicated delinquents: A meta-analysis. *Journal of Research in Crime and Delinquency, 22,* 287-308.

Geismar, L., & Wood, K. (1985). *Family and delinquency: Resocializing the young offender.* New York: Human Sciences Press.

Gendreau, P., & Ross, R. (1979). Effective correctional treatment: Bibliotherapy for cynics. *Crime and Delinquency, 25,* 463-489.

Gendreau, P., & Ross, R. (1987). Revivification of rehabilitation: Evidence from the 1980s. *Justice Quarterly, 4*(3), 349-407.

Glaser, D. (1975). Achieving better questions: A half century s progress in correctional research. *Federal Probation, 39,* 3-9.

Gottschalk, R., Davidson, W., Gensheimer, L., & Mayer, J. (1987). Community-based interventions. In H. Quay (Ed.), *Handbook of Juvenile Delinquency.* New York: Wiley & Sons.

Greenberg, D. (1977). The correctional effects of corrections: A survey of evaluations. In D. Greenberg (Ed.), *Corrections and punishment.* Beverly Hills, CA: Sage Publications.

Greenwood, P., & Zimring, F. (1985). *One more chance: The pursuit of promising intervention strategies for chronic juvenile offenders.* Santa Monica, CA: The Rand Corporation.

Gruenewald, P., Laurence, S., & West, B. (1985). National evaluation of the New Pride replication program. Executive summary. Walnut Creek, CA: Pacific Institute for Research and Evaluation.

Hamparian, D., Schuster, R., Dinitz, S., & Conrad, J. (1978). *The violent few.* Lexington, MA: Lexington Books.

Hawkins, J., & Weis, J. (1985). The prevention of delinquency through social development. *Journal of Primary Prevention, 6,* 73-97.

Krisberg, B. et al. (1989). Demonstration of post-adjudication non-residential intensive supervision programs: Assessment report. San Francisco: National Council on Crime and Delinquency.

Lipsey, M. (1989, November). The efficacy of intervention for juvenile delinquency. Paper presented at American Society of Criminology Annual Meeting. Reno.

Lipsey, M. (1991). Juvenile delinquency treatment: A meta-analytic inquiry into the validity of effects. Russell Sage Foundation.

Martin, S., Sechrest, L., & Redner, R. (1981). New directions in the rehabilitation of criminal offenders. Washington, DC: The National Academy Press.

Martinson, R. (1974). What works?—Questions and answers about prison reform. *The Public Interest, 35*, 22-54.

Mayer, J. et al. (1986). Social learning treatment within juvenile justice: A meta-analysis of impact in the natural environment. In S. Apter & A. Goldstein (Eds.), *Youth violence: Progress and prospects*. New York: Pergamon.

Mitford, J. (1971, March). Kind and usual punishment in California. *The Atlantic Monthly, 227*, 45-52.

Mitford, J. (1973, August). The torture cure. *Harpers, 247*, 16-30.

Palmer, T. (1978). *Correctional intervention and research: Current issues and future prospects*. Lexington, MA: Lexington Books.

Palmer, T. (1975). Martinson revisited. *Journal of Research in Crime and Delinquency, 12*, 133-152.

Palmer, T. (1983). The "effectiveness" issue today: An overview. *Federal Probation, 47*(2), 3-10.

Palmer, T. (1991). The habilitation/developmental perspective: A missing link in corrections. *Federal Probation, 55*(1).

Palmer, T. (1974). The Youth Authority's Community Treatment Project. *Federal Probation, 38*(1), 3-14.

Palmer, T. (1984). Treatment and the role of classification: A review of basics. *Crime and Delinquency, 30*(2), 245-267.

Panizzon, A., Olson-Raymer, G., & Guerra, N. (1991). Delinquency prevention: What works/what doesn't. Sacramento: Office of Criminal Justice Planning.

President's Commission on Law Enforcement and Administration of Justice. (1967). *The challenge of crime in a free society*. Washington, DC: U.S. Government Printing Office.

Romig, D. (1978). *Justice for our children*. Lexington, MA: Lexington Books.

Sechrest, L., White, S., & Brown, E. (1979). *The rehabilitation of criminal offenders: Problems and prospects*. Washington, DC: The National Academy of Sciences.

Strasberg, P. (1978). *Violent delinquents: A report to the Ford Foundation from the Vera Institute of Justice*. New York: Monarch Press.

U.S. Department of Justice. (1988). A private-sector corrections program for juveniles: Paint Creek Youth Center. Washington, DC: Office of Juvenile Justice and Delinquency Prevention.

van den Haag, E. (1975). *Punishing criminals*. New York: Basic Books.

Van Voorhis, P. (1987). Correctional effectiveness: The high cost of ignoring success. *Federal Probation, 51*(1), 56-62.

von Hirsch, A. (1976). *Doing justice: The choice of punishments*. New York: Hill and Wang.

Warren, M. (1971). Classification of offenders as an aid to efficient management and effective treatment. *Journal of Crime, Law, Criminology, and Police Science, 62*, 239-258.

West, D., & Farrington, D. (1977). *The delinquent way of life*. London: Hienemann.

Wilson, J. (1975). *Thinking about crime*. New York: Basic Books.

Wolfgang, M., Figlio, R., & Sellin, T. (1972). *Delinquency in a birth cohort*. Chicago: University of Chicago Press.

Journal of Offender Rehabilitation, Vol. 17 (1/2), 1991. Pp. 119-132.

☐ MEASUREMENT AND APPRAISAL

Using Situational Factors to Predict Types of Prison Violence

Pamela Steinke
University of California, Davis

ABSTRACT This study tested situational factors as predictors of types of individual aggressive incidents in a male prison population. The majority of past research on predicting individual incidents of prison violence has seriously downplayed situational factors. The situational variables used covered three general questions: Where? When? and Who Else?. Incidents of violence were categorized by whether the occurrence of an infraction involved aggressive behavior directed at staff, another inmate, self, or property. This study found that situational variables did serve as predictors of these categories of violence. These results support the position that background or personality factors, when used without situational factors, may not provide a complete understanding of prison violence.

Past research predicting disruptive or violent behavior in prison has largely conceived of these behaviors as indicative of the coping level of the inmate. The focus is necessarily on the inmate and the question centers around which types of inmates engage in these behaviors. The underlying or explicit presumption is that if an inmate does engage in these behaviors that inmate is "maladjusted" and if an inmate does not engage in these behaviors that inmate is "well adjusted." This line of thinking is infused with a bias in favor of the individual at the expense of the situation within which the incident occurred, suggesting that there may be a correspondent inference bias (Jones & Davis, 1965) in prison researchers. Prison researchers assume that there must be some dispositional characteristic of the individual that accounts for this behavior and so research continues in this direction while situational factors are ignored.

RELATED STUDIES

The current prison research environment presents a classic case of the fundamental attribution error (Ross, 1977), the tendency to attribute the cause of a behavior to an individual's character or personality even in the face of very strong situational determinants.

The specific variables used in predicting prison adjustment [Note 1] or incidents of violence have been heavily weighed in the direction of background variables such as race, age, and commitment offense (Brown & Spavecek, 1971; Coe, 1961; Flanagan, 1980; Flanagan, 1983) or personality factors such as MMPI scores (Jones, Beidleman, & Fowler, 1981; Panton, 1979). The usefulness of this type of prediction study has been questioned on a number of grounds (Henderson, 1986; Megargee & Carbonell, 1985; Shawver, Clanon, Kurdys & Friedman, 1985). The personality inventories that are most often used, contain little situational or contextual information (Furnham & Henderson, 1982) which hampers their ability to aid in predicting violence that necessarily includes not only a person but also a situation.

This bias may have arisen because of the necessity of classification of inmates. Classification of inmates for housing and program purposes has, for good reason, focused on use of variables centered in the individual. Classification for purposes of programing and prison management, while it includes the goal of violence reduction, is not, however, equivalent to violence prediction for purposes of violence prevention. Because classification serves to fit a group of individuals with a housing area, it necessarily includes the use of situational factors in carrying out its objective. Classification uses information about the person and the situations available in the given prison in making a determination. While it is often assumed that these two functions (classification and adjustment prediction) will involve the same variables (e.g., Louscher, Hosford & Moss, 1983; Wright, 1988) this assumption may not be founded.

Situational Studies

Studies on situational factors contributing to incidents of violence in maximum security psychiatric or forensic settings have found differences in physically aggressive behavior depending on location, housing unit, and time of day of assaults (Dietz & Rada, 1983; Harris & Varney, 1986). Harris and Varney found that much of the variability in assaultive behavior was due to environmental factors even when patients were initially noted to be characteristically violent. They concluded that assaultiveness was "due to the interaction of environmental and internal factors" (p. 188).

There have been a few studies conducted on the relationship between situational factors and individual incidents of violence in prison populations. Henderson (1986) researched incidents both within and outside of prison, as described by the perpetrator, and found eight different clusters, in part based on situational factors, which roughly corresponded to eight different types of violence as previously described in other research. Kratcoski (1988) examined situational factors of inmate violence toward guards and found that location of assault, time of day of assault, and work experience of the correctional officer assaulted, all varied systematically as a function of the assaultive behavior. Other situational studies have focused on issues of crowding or density (e.g. Cox, Paulus & McCain, 1988; Megargee, 1976). High levels of density have been shown to be related to disruptive behavior in several different types of prisons (Cox, Paulus & McCain; Jan, 1980).

The current project examined disciplinary infractions through the use of the situational information provided by the institution rather than individual characteristics of inmates. The perspective taken here emphasizes the fact that the incidents arise out of the combination of features both as part of the inmate and as part of the situation. As Flanagan (1983) notes, "the processes that lead to charging an inmate with a disciplinary infraction are situational in nature-involving a complex interplay between inmate, officer, and the setting in which the interaction occurs" (p. 37). In addition, given that some infraction occurs, it is not necessarily the case that an act of violence will be included as part of that infraction. It was predicted that the likelihood that the infraction involved violence would be, in part, determined by the situation.

The purpose of the present study was to test the prediction that, given the occurrence of an infraction, situational variables could be identified as predictors of whether this infraction included an individual act of violence. If so, specific situational variables should be identifiable for each of the different types of individual violence that occurred in the given prison population. The types of individual violence found on the unit under investigation were distinguished by the target of the violent behavior. This study examined violence toward staff, another inmate, self, and property. Individual violence is usually defined as acts of violence against others, but, as Toch (1976) points out, violence may also include acts of self-inflicted violence. No study to date has looked at each of these types of violence separately given a set of situational predictors.

The situational variables used in this study have been implicated by previous research and, for the most part, are noted on infraction reports. The predictor variables used were location of incident, housing wing of inmate, temperature, shift, job assignment of reporting officer, and the involvement of other inmates. The only variable not taken from infraction reports was ambient temperature. Due to an absence of air conditioning on inmate housing units, hot temperatures could be related to aggressive incidents. Studies done outside the prison environment have indicated a possible linear relationship between heat and assaultive behavior (Cotton, 1986; Harries & Stadler, 1983, 1988) though some evidence suggests that if there is a relationship, it may be curvilinear (Bell & Fusco, 1989).

In a study done in a Federal prison, Megargee (1976) found no relationship between heat and assaultive behavior. Location of incident, time of day of incident, and housing unit of inmate have been indicated as possible predictors of assaultive behavior in psychiatric hospitals (Harris & Varney, 1986; Dietz & Rada, 1983); location, time of day, and characteristics of the reporting officer have been found to be related to staff assaults in prison (Kratcoski, 1988); and location, time of day, and the presence of others have been found to be helpful in distinguishing types of violence occurring in and outside of prison (Henderson, 1986).

METHOD

The prison in which the present investigation was conducted is a medium security, state prison in California and the unit studied housed 500 men who were identified as having some psychiatric or behavior problems while incarcerated. All data were obtained from infraction reports (CDC-115s) for a one year period (June 87 to May 88). Cases were identified by reports rather than by inmates or subjects. Of the total 911 infraction reports identified 809 had some penalty assessed so were retained for the current study. All variables were dummy coded for nominal scale. Because of the categorical nature of the dependent variables, logistic regression was used (Aldrich & Nelson, 1984). Logistic regression or logit analysis works on a non-linear probability model in the case of dichotomous dependent variables. As in linear regression, logit coefficients are interpretable as the independent contribution of each regressor in predicting the outcome. Logistic regression or logit analysis was chosen over discriminant analysis as a means of analyzing the data because of its fewer limitations and better suitability to this type of predictive analysis (Darlington, 1990).

All predictor variables except temperature were taken from the incident report. Maximum daily ambient temperatures were obtained from the National Weather Service and the highest maximum temperatures were coded. "Hot" was defined as 85 degrees or more. The situational variables used covered three general questions: *Where? When?* and *Who Else?*.

"Where?" represented both the site in the prison at which the incident occurred and the type of residence [wing] in which the inmate was housed. Locations coded were job, school, or appointment site; dorm; corridor or hall (including grill gates and sally ports); shower, dining, or recreation area; and cell. The "cell" category was used as the base category in dummy coding because of its lack of public situational features. Type of housing wings coded were observation, disciplinary or restricted movement, chronic or outpatient psychiatric. The psychiatric wings were used as the base category because of the unique environmental features of the inpatient wing (i.e. mental health staff, air conditioning).

"When?" represented both whether the incident occurred in days with extreme heat as defined above and the shift on which the incident occurred. The base category for temperature was all days which had a maximum temperature that was less than 85 degrees. Shift categories were day shift (7:00-14:59), afternoon shift (15:00 to 22:59), night shift (23:00-06:59). Night shift was used as the base category in dummy coding.

"Who else?" represented both who wrote up the report and whether any other inmates were actively involved in the incident. Categories for who wrote up the report were correctional officer assigned to the wing on which the inmate was housed, correctional officer assigned other than where the inmate was housed, medical technical assistant or other staff. The last category was used as a base category. The active involvement of other inmates was coded using the "no other inmates" category as the base category. The variable representing other inmates was not used in the models for violence toward another inmate or self because the active involvement of other inmates is part of the definition of the first and the involvement of other inmates is incompatible with the second.

The four types of violence representing the criterion variables were coded from the description of the offense. The operational definition of violence here was one used by Wilds (1973) as "hostility translated into physical action that has intent to cause harm to people or destruction to property" (p. 429). Using this definition the terms "violence" or "aggression" can be used interchangeably. Categories of aggression used as criterion variables were violence toward (1) staff; (2) another inmate; (3) self; and (4) property. Each category was predicted from the population of all infractions occurring within the one year period for the unit studied. A separate logit analysis was done for each type of violence.

RESULTS & DISCUSSION

Violent incidents comprised just over 50% of all infractions. Of the total 809 infractions, 82 involved aggressive behavior toward staff, 128 involved aggressive behavior toward another inmate, 53 involved aggressive behavior toward self, and 153 involved aggressive behavior toward property. Overall goodness of fit of the model was calculated for each equation. The measure used was one suggested by Aldrich and Nelson (1984) where pseudo R-squared = c/(N + c), with c being the chi-square statistic for overall fit and N being the total sample size. This measure ranges from 0 to 1. Using this measure the overall goodness of fit for violence toward staff was .08, toward another inmate was .21, toward self was .06, and toward property was .23.

Logit analyses also revealed that there were significant predictors for each type of aggression. The results of the analyses are given in Table 1 by the coefficient estimates of each situational variable with corresponding t values. Significance levels are given for those variables that, relative to the base category, correspond with a significant increase or decrease in the likelihood of each type of aggression occurring. The Job/School/Apartment category was taken out of the equations for self and property; the Shower/Dining/Recreation area category was taken out of the equation for self because these were zero-entry categories, retention of which would create problems in the statistical analyses. This reduced the N for these two equations as is noted in Table 1.

Violence toward staff was more likely to occur in areas where inmates were active but not in a highly structured manner (i.e. corridors and dining, recreation, and shower areas) rather than in

Table 1: Coefficient Estimates of Each Situational Variable for Likelihood of Each Type of Violence

Factor	Staff N = 809	Inmate N = 809	Self N = 623	Property N = 749
Site				
Job/School/Appointment site	-.10	2.43*		
Dorm	.23	4.54**	-.58	-.33
Corridor/Hall	1.73**	4.17**	-2.20**	-4.03**
Shower/Dining/Recreational area	1.56**	5.20**		-2.93**
Residence				
Observation	.94**	-.32	.27	.89**
Disciplinary	1.23**	-.70*	.90*	.79*
Temperature = Hot	.25	.59*	-.22	.15
Shift				
Day	.16	.50	-.90*	-.08
Afternoon	.32	.45	-.31	-.73*
Reporter				
Officer/same unit	-.19	.58	-.34	1.36**
Officer/another unit	-.80	-.33	-.08	1.18**
Other inmates involved	-2.62**			-2.76**

*p = .05 **p = .01

cells, dorms or highly structured activities such as jobs or school. Inmates living on non-psychiatric housing floors (i.e. disciplinary, restricted movement or observation floors) were more likely to act violently toward staff. Inmates were more likely to be alone rather than with other inmates when acting aggressively toward staff. Contrary to findings in both a state and a federal prison (Kratcoski, 1988), staff assaults were not found to occur significantly more during the day or to be related to characteristics of the reporting staff.

Violence toward another inmate was more likely to occur anywhere inmates were allowed to congregate. This concurs with findings from a maximum security psychiatric unit where few assaults occurred in patient rooms (Harris & Varney 1986). Outside the cell, however, inmate aggression was less likely to occur in the structured activities of the job and school. There was a small but significant trend for inmate aggression to occur more when the temperatures were hot which supports findings of a positive linear relationship between heat and aggression (Cotton, 1986; Harries & Stadler, 1983, 1988) but goes against Megargee's (1976) finding that there was no relationship between heat and aggression in a Federal prison population. Inmate aggression was less likely to occur when inmates were housed on disciplinary floors.

Violence toward self was less likely to occur anywhere outside of the inmate's cell or dorm area. It was significantly less likely to occur in the corridor or hall areas and, as noted above, never occurred at a job, school or appointment site or in the dining, shower or recreation area. This is probably related to the private nature of this type of violence. Aggression toward self occurred more in the cells of inmates housed on floors with restricted movement and was less likely to occur during the day.

Violence toward property occurred less when an inmate was outside the cell or dorm areas and, as previously noted, never occurred while an inmate was at school, a job, or an appointment. Aggression toward property was more likely to occur on non-psychiatric units and less likely to occur in the afternoon. In contrast to all other types of violence, aggression toward property was significantly more likely to be reported by a correctional officer than by other staff.

GENERAL DISCUSSION

The use of information on situational factors need not lead to the claim that purely situational factors could ever completely explain violent behavior. As Bandura (1981) states, a search for purely situational causal determinants of behavior is "an unproductive pursuit of the psychological Grail" (p. 30). Rather, the point of the present study is to underscore the fact that there are non-random patterns to the type of behaviors people exhibit in varying situations. As the results here indicate, violent behavior in a male prison population is no exception. There is a need, therefore, to increase our understanding of the situational factors that will help us to predict the likelihood of violent behaviors occurring in prison, in effort to prevent their occurrence.

While personality and background variables should not be ignored, they should be supplemented. Exclusive use of background variables produces what some psychologists have termed "destiny studies" (Shawver, et al., 1985) because they "tell us how things are likely to turn out but they do not give us a clue as to what we can do to influence things to turn out better" (p. 2). One cannot hope to change an inmate's age, sex or prior convictions during incarceration. The exclusive use of MMPI scales presents similar problems. Because of their tendency to categorize people based on criteria that is difficult to alter, they too act as destiny variables. Changing a person's MMPI score is neither a very realistic goal nor a necessarily helpful goal.

Prediction based solely on personality or background factors also has had its share of empirical problems. These factors when used alone have yielded a high number of false positives (Megargee & Carbonell, 1985) and have accounted for less than 30% of the variance in prison adjustment studies (Carbonell, Megargee & Moorhead, 1985). In a review of the literature on the previous use of eight MMPI scales in predicting adjustment to prison by use of criteria indicating the occurrence of disruptive behavior (e.g., segregation, disciplinary infractions), Megargee and Carbonell reported that many of the studies gave contradictory results or found no relationship.

The use of classification variables for violence or adjustment prediction is inherently problematic because only one aspect of the incident is being measured. In a study of the usefulness of different classification systems in predicting adjustment to prison, Wright (1988) found that whether the system focused on psychological (Megargee's MMPI Typology), situational (Toch's Prison Preference Inventory) or background (Risk Assessment) variables none were superior to the others. Each predicted some outcomes and not others and each explained no more that 20% of the variance. This suggests that there is a need to re-think how violence prediction is best done and what the variables for future study should be.

Ideally, what is needed is an ecological approach to understanding prison violence, one that focuses on the relationship between the person and the environment (Flynn, 1976). Only when researchers find ways to capture the necessarily interacting variables of the person and the situation can they begin to tell the whole story of prison violence (Jones, Beidleman & Fowler, 1981; Monahan, 1981). As Monahan states, "It can be argued that the inclusion of situational variables is the most pressing current need in the field of violence prediction" (p. 130). It is clear that the study presented here does not tell the whole story but only a small part of the story. Its importance lies in the fact that it tells the part that needs to be heard most at this time.

Research Note

1. The term "adjustment" will be used in describing other studies, but because the present investigation is a situational study, disruptive or violent behavior is herein conceptualized quite differently.

References

Aldrich, J.H. & Nelson, F.D. (1984). Linear probability, logit, and probit models. Sage university paper series on quantitative applications in the social sciences, 07-045. Beverly Hills: Sage Publications.

Bandura, A. (1981). In search of pure unidirectional determinants. Behavior Therapy, 12, 30-40.

Bell, P.A. & Fusco, M.E. (1989). Heat and violence in the Dallas field data: Linearity, curvilinearity, and heteroscedasticity. Journal of Applied Social Psychology, 19, 1479-1482.

Brown, B.S. & Spavecek, J.D. (1971). Disciplinary offenses and offenders at two differing correctional institutions. Corrective Psychiatry and Journal of Social Therapy, 17, 48-56.

Carbonell, J.L., Megargee, E.I., & Moorhead, K.M. (1984). Predicting prison adjustment with structured personality inventories. Journal of Consulting and Clinical Psychology, 52, 280-294.

Coe, R.M. (1961). Characteristics of well adjusted and poorly adjusted inmates. Journal of Criminal Law, Criminology, and Police Science, 52, 178-184.

Cotton, J.L. (1986). Ambient temperature and violent crime. Journal of Applied Social Psychology, 16, 786-801.

Cox, V.C., Paulus P.B. & McCain, G. (1984). Prison crowding research. American Psychologist, 39, 1148-1160.

Darlington, R.B. (1990). Regression and linear models. New York: McGraw Hill.

Dietz, P.E. & Rada, R.T. (1983). Interpersonal violence in forensic facilities. In J.R. Lion & W.H. Reid (Eds.), Assaults within psychiatric facilities, 47-59. New York: Grune & Stratton.

Flanagan, T.J. (1980). Time served and institutional misconduct: Patterns of involvement in disciplinary infractions among long-term and short-term inmates. Journal of Criminal Justice, 8, 357-367.

Flanagan, T.J. (1983). Correlates of institutional misconduct among state prisoners. Criminology, 21, 29-39.

Flynn, E.E. (1976). The ecology of prison violence. In A.K. Cohen, G.F. Cole, & R.G. Bailey (Eds.), Prison violence, 115-133. Lexington, MA: Lexington Books.

Furnham, A. & Henderson, M. (1982). A content analysis of four personality inventories. Journal of Clinical Psychology, 38, 818-825.

Harries, K.D. & Stadler, S.J. (1983). Determinism revisited: Assault and heat stress in Dallas, 1980. Environment and Behavior, 15, 235-256.

Harries, K.D. & Stadler, S.J. (1988). Heat and violence: New findings from Dallas Field Data, 1980-1981. Journal of Applied Social Psychology, 18, 129-138.

Harris, G.T. & Varney, G.W. (1986). A ten-year study of assaults and assaulters on a maximum security psychiatric unit. Journal of Interpersonal Violence, 1, 173-191.

Henderson, M. (1986). An empirical typology of violent incidents reported by prison inmates with convictions for violence. Aggressive Behavior, 12, 21-32.

Jan, L. (1980). Overcrowding and inmate behavior. Criminal Justice and Behavior, 7, 293-301.

Jones, E.E. & Davis, K.E. (1965). A theory of correspondent inferences: From acts to dispositions. In L. Berkowitz (Ed.), Advances in experimental social psychology, Vol. 2, 216-266. N.Y.: Academic Press.

Jones, T., Beidleman, W.B., & Fowler, R.D. (1981). Differentiating violent prison inmates by use of selected MMPI scales. Journal of Clinical Psychology, 37, 673-678.

Kratcoski, P.C. (1988). The implications of research explaining prison violence and disruption. Federal Probation, 52, 27- 32.

Louscher, P.K., Hosford, R.E., & Moss, C.S. (1983). Predicting dangerous behavior in a penitentiary using the Megargee typology. Criminal Justice and Behavior, 10, 269-284.

Megargee, E.I. (1976). Population density and disruption behavior in a prison setting. In A.K. Cohen, G.F. Cole, & R.G. Bailey (Eds.), Prison violence, 135-144. Lexington, MA: Lexington Books.

Megargee, E.I. & Carbonell, J.L. (1985). Predicting prison adjustment with MMPI correctional scales. Journal of Consulting and Clinical Psychology, 53, 874-883.

Monahan, J. (1981). Predicting violent behavior. Beverly Hills, CA: Sage Publications.

Panton, J.H. (1979). Escape (Ec) and prison adjustment (Ap) scales. Journal of Clinical Psychology, 35, 101-103.

Ross, L.D. (1977). The intuitive psychologist and his shortcomings: Distortions in the attribution process. In L. Berkowitz (Ed.), Advances in experimental social psychology, Vol. 10. New York: Academic Press.

Shawver, L., Clanon, T.L., Kurdys, D., & Friedman, H. (1985). Predicting and improving parole success with P.A.S. Federal Probation, 40, 34-37.

Toch, H. (1976). A psychological view of prison violence. In A.K. Cohen, G.F. Cole, & R.G. Bailey (Eds.), Prison violence, 43-51. Lexington, MA: Lexington Books.

Wilds, C.E. (1973). Evaluation of a method of predicting violence in offenders. Criminology, 11, 427-435.

Wright, K.N. (1988). The relationship of risk, needs, and personality classification systems and prison adjustment. Criminal Justice and Behavior, 15, 454-471.

Author's Note

Pamela Steinke is at the Department of Psychology at the University of California, Davis, CA 95616.

The author is indebted to the contributions of Lois Shawver, Doug Kurdys, and Freddie Gravely for their ideas during the preliminary phases of this project and for their help in identifying appropriate data sources.

Imprisonment in the American States*

William A. TAGGART, *New Mexico State University*

Russell G. WINN, *New Mexico State University*

This study examines eight rival hypotheses concerning determinants of state incarceration rates in 1984. Multiple measures of crime, economics, social characteristics, demographics, ideology and culture, sentencing and parole reforms, alternatives to corrections, and institutional conditions are evaluated in light of their ability to account for cross-sectional variation in incarceration practices. Initially the analysis reveals that all eight hypotheses are associated with imprisonment. However, in light of statistical controls, the explanatory power of most variables is greatly diminished or found to be indirect rather than direct. The two factors having the greatest direct impact on incarceration are crime and culture.

In recent years substantial attention has been devoted to better understanding the use of imprisonment in the United States. The impetus for this attention was the discovery of a "crisis in corrections" (Gottfredson and McConville, 1987) which followed a dramatic increase in prison population during the last two decades. Maguire and Flanagan (1991:604) reported that between 1975 and 1989 the number of inmates held in state and federal penal institutions almost tripled, achieving a record number surpassing 680,000. The burden of this growth has fallen on the American states; 90 percent of the individuals serving prison sentences in 1989 were incarcerated in state correctional facilities (Maguire and Flanagan, 1991:607). The policy and administrative consequences are numerous and far-reaching and, in the opinion of many, place state prisons on the verge of total institutional failure (Flanagan, 1975; Gottfredson and McConville, 1987).

Not surprisingly, states are the subject of much research on the use of imprisonment (e.g., Galster and Scaturo, 1985; Garofalo, 1980; Wirt, 1983).

* Direct all correspondence to William A. Taggart, Department of Government, Box 30001, Dept. 3BN, New Mexico State University, Las Cruces, NM 88003. Earlier versions of this paper were presented at the 1990 meeting of the Western Political Science Association and the 1991 meeting of the Western and Pacific Association of Criminal Justice Educators. Work on this project was made possible while the first author was Visiting Professor of Political Science, University of North Carolina at Chapel Hill. He would like to thank Richard Richardson and Gordon Whitaker for arranging this appointment.

SOCIAL SCIENCE QUARTERLY, Volume 74, Number 4, December 1993

What is noteworthy about this body of literature is its limited explanatory power concerning incarceration practices and its failure to evaluate competing hypotheses for any more than a few states (Zimring and Hawkins, 1991). As a result, scholars continue to call for systematic investigations explaining these significant interstate differences (e.g., Blumstein, 1987; Zimring and Hawkins, 1991).

The objective of this study is to improve our knowledge in this area by evaluating the explanatory power of eight propositions in accounting for cross-sectional variation in state incarceration rates. In the next section the eight hypotheses concerning imprisonment are briefly outlined, with an elaboration of the data and methods employed in the present analysis.

Prior Research and Methodology

What determines why states have different incarceration rates? There appears to be no shortage of theories, though some factors are mentioned more frequently than others to explain the level of punitiveness found across political units (Zimring and Hawkins, 1991). The explanatory power of eight reasonably distinct, though overlapping, influences on state incarceration rates are evaluated in our analysis: (1) crime, (2) economics, (3) social characteristics, (4) demographics, (5) ideology and culture, (6) sentencing and parole reforms, (7) alternatives to corrections, and (8) institutional conditions. Similar conceptualizations have appeared in the public policy literature as influential determinants of other policy outputs in the American states, providing additional justification for selection of hypotheses and variables (Dye, 1987). It is not expected that any one factor will completely explain state-level incarceration practices. Rather this effort seeks to describe the confluence of environmental and institutional forces which account for differences in imprisonment.

The dependent variable, a state's incarceration rate, is the (year-end) number of prisoners per 100,000 population (estimated) in 1984. Inmate figures are reported by the individual states and published by the U.S. Department of Justice (1987c). Lacking strong theoretical guidance, 1984 was selected to create a reasonable time lag between dependent and independent variables, since most of the latter are based on the 1980 U.S. Census. The independent variables are grouped into a series of hypotheses reflecting the eight influences mentioned above. Unless noted, data for the independent variables are derived from standard summary publications associated with the decennial census.

Hypothesis 1: Crime. As a source of influence on incarceration rates, crime would appear to be an obvious candidate. Corrections is a legitimized governmental response to this basic social problem. The nature of the relationship between crime and imprisonment is viewed in a direct, mechanistic fashion: as the crime rate increases, so does the level of incarceration (e.g., Carroll and Cornell, 1985; Garofalo, 1980; Skogan, 1990). Thus, it is postulated that states with higher crime rates will have higher incarceration rates. Two measures of crime in 1980 are considered, violent crimes per 100,000 population and property crimes per 100,000 (U.S. Department of Justice, 1983b).

Hypothesis 2: Economics. While invoking considerable controversy, there are at least two noncompeting perspectives concerning the influence of economics on punishment practices. One of these originates in the study of public policy and views economics as representing the relative wealth or resources available to support institutional corrections (e.g., Taggart, 1989; Wirt, 1983). Richer states are better able to finance prisons, and therefore can assume the burden of higher incarceration rates. The second view treats economics as a condition creating the need for imprisonment, placing an emphasis on the overall health and vitality of the economy. Hence, it is postulated states with harsher economic conditions will have higher incarceration rates. The percentage of individuals living below the poverty level in 1980 is used as an indicator of economic health, while median family income in 1980 is employed as a measure of wealth.

Hypothesis 3: Social Characteristics. Several commentators have noted a relationship between incarceration rates and basic social characteristics (e.g., Blumstein, 1982; Garofalo, 1980). Besides gender, three social features stand out in these works. The first is race and ethnicity where it is argued that imprisonment levels are higher in states with larger minority populations (e.g., Carroll and Cornell, 1985). Some interpret this as an indicator of institutionalized racism, while others reason it is a case of minority group members committing proportionately more crimes and going to prison at a greater rate (see Blumstein, 1982, 1988; Hindelang, 1978; Klein, Petersilia, and Turner, 1990). Ethnicity is measured as the percentage of the male population that was nonwhite in 1980.

A second social characteristic is age, where it has been noted that incarceration rates are higher in states with larger proportions of the population in the "peak imprisonment age" group (e.g., Blumstein, 1988; Carroll and Cornell, 1985; Flanagan, 1975). The peak age group is usually defined as falling somewhere between 18 and 30 years of age, with this group having the highest incarceration rate. This suggested a second 1980 measure: the percentage of the male population between 20 and 29 years of age.

A final twist is provided by Blumstein (1982), who reported that black males in their twenties have an incarceration rate 25 times higher than the general population. He concluded it is the nexus of age *and* race which is the single best predictor of imprisonment levels, as states with greater proportions of black males in the most at-risk age group have higher incarceration rates. Thus, a third measure, the percentage of the male population that was nonwhite and between the ages of 20 and 29 in 1980, is considered.

Hypothesis 4: Demographics. While related to Hypothesis 3, a broader view on the influence of social features concerns basic population characteristics (e.g., Carroll and Doubet, 1983). Researchers have contended that states experiencing greater population pressures suffer more social ills and that this leads to a greater reliance on imprisonment (Skogan, 1990). This view includes such considerations as population size, population density, population change, and increasing urbanization. Consequently, four variables are examined: population in 1980, population density in 1980, the absolute change in population density between 1970 and 1980, and the percent change in population for the same period.

Hypothesis 5: Ideology and Culture. Several investigators have suggested that state incarceration practices reflect differences in the ideological and cultural orientations of citizens (e.g., Harrigan, 1991; Skogan, 1990; Wirt, 1983). Ideology is postulated to manifest itself in many ways, but generally it is argued that liberalism is associated with lower levels of punitiveness in the states and conservatism with higher levels. Ideology is examined using two common measures. The first is the percentage vote for presidential candidate George McGovern in 1972, which has been found to be associated with a number of measures of state policy liberalism (e.g., Nice, 1983). A validated measure of conservatism has been provided by Wright, Erikson, and McIver (1985), a scale based on state-level public opinion data.

Similarly, Wirt (1983) drew on Elazar's (1972) work concerning political culture to understand imprisonment. Wirt reported that incarceration rates are higher in states with traditional cultures, where government's primary role is defined as promoting and maintaining social order. At the other extreme, he found that states with moralistic cultures have lower incarceration rates, in part because citizens are less likely to engage in unacceptable behaviors. Using Elazar's findings, Sharkansky (1969) provided a nine-point scale of political culture which arrayed states from moralistic (score of one) to traditionalistic (nine).

Hypothesis 6: Sentencing and Parole Reforms. In response to public concerns over mounting crime and a call for more punitive sanctions, numerous states have enacted laws designed to increase the certainty and severity of court-imposed sentences. These actions impact upon the "inflow" of individuals into the correctional system (Skogan, 1990). One such innovation has been the adoption of determinate sentencing, requiring specific sentences for particular crimes, thus reducing judicial discretion in sentencing. Some suggest this has had an adverse impact on prison populations through increased inflow (e.g., Blumstein, 1987; Nagin, 1979). Others counter that many states have made an effort to link inflow to capacity in order to better regulate prison populations, thereby holding incarceration rates down (e.g., Clarke, 1984). Thus, both a negative and positive relationship between determinate sentencing and incarceration rates is predicted. A dummy variable indicating the absence (0) or presence (1) of determinate sentencing as of 1983 is employed (U.S. Department of Justice, 1983a).

A second initiative associated with inflow is mandatory sentencing (Blumstein, 1988; Skogan, 1990). These laws stipulate a required sentence for certain felony convictions. States typically apply these sentences to more publicly visible crimes, such as using a handgun during the commission of a crime. A major criticism of mandatory sentencing has been its adverse impact on incarceration levels, in part because some individuals who might have otherwise avoided prison are now serving time. More importantly, mandatory sentencing laws dictate a fixed sentence which cannot be reduced through early release or parole. To examine the impact of such laws on incarceration rates, an additive index was constructed covering the four most common types of offenses subject to mandatory sentences: violent crime, habitual offender, use of firearm, and narcotic/drug crime (U.S. Department of Justice, 1983a). The more laws adopted by a state as of 1983, the higher its score, with values ranging between zero and four.

States also have modified the other end of the correctional system, the "outflow" side. Statutes have been promulgated to reduce the flow of inmates out of prisons, again in the name of greater punitiveness. The intent is to reduce the amount of discretion associated with the granting of early release or parole. States enacting these reforms have found inmate populations rising (e.g., Nagin, 1979; Skogan, 1990). Two outflow reforms are considered: the adoption of systemwide parole guidelines and the elimination of prison-granted credits toward early release (U.S. Department of Justice, 1983a). The former is a binary variable indicating the absence (0) or presence (1) of systemwide parole guidelines in 1983. State adoption represents a step taken to minimize leniency and uncertainty in the granting of parole. The second variable is a three-category measure concerning the elimination of early release credits as of 1983: states retaining early release credits for program participation *and* good behavior (0); states giving credit for *one* of the two (1); and, states not granting either type of credit (2).

Hypothesis 7: Alternatives to Corrections. A second major way states seek to control inflow is to provide alternatives to incarceration. The use of probation and community-based facilities are two common examples. Justifications for these alternative placements include reducing both the number of people incarcerated and the costs of corrections, suggesting states which make greater use of these alternatives would have lower incarceration rates (e.g., Scull, 1977). However, a number of writers have argued that this is not true (e.g., Walker, 1989). Instead of reducing incarceration, these alternatives merely extend the "net of social control," capturing offenders who might otherwise receive no punishment. To examine the impact of alternative programs on imprisonment, three 1984 measures are employed: the number of probationers per 100,000 population (U.S. Department of Justice, 1987a); the total designed or planned capacity of community-based facilities as reported by the states; and the ratio of community capacity to prison capacity (U.S. Department of Justice, 1987b).

Hypothesis 8: Institutional Conditions. Most agree that state correctional agencies or departments have an independent effect on incarceration practices. While this area of influence covers a host of structural and administrative factors, two dimensions of institutional conditions will be examined. The capacity of a state's prison system is mentioned with some frequency as a relevant variable (e.g., Blumstein, 1988), though disagreement exists over the postulated direction of the relationship. One view, according to Zimring and Hawkins (1991:76–77), is that "capacity drives population" and the other is that "capacity serves to limit" population. Thus, both a positive and negative association between capacity and incarceration is predicted. Prison capacity in 1984 is measured two ways: the total planned institutional capacity as reported by the states and the actual prison population as a percentage of planned population (U.S. Bureau of the Census, 1984).

A second institutional feature is the organizational ability of correctional agencies to serve a given level of imprisonment. Beyond physical space, prison administration requires a sufficient resource and personnel base to operate at even the most minimal level. Corrections must therefore compete for favorable levels of funding (Skogan, 1990; Zimring and Hawkins, 1991). State prisons enjoying relatively greater success can sustain a higher incarceration rate. Gray and Williams (1980) provided a measure of organizational strength, indicating the ability of corrections to acquire new resources compared to other criminal justice agencies. As coded, correctional agencies with higher rankings were comparatively more successful in obtaining funds in the late 1970s.

The analysis is based on correlational and multiple regression techniques for the 48 contiguous states. Zero-order correlation coefficients are examined initially, and then OLS regression is employed to assess the relative influence of variables for each hypothesis.[1] Based on these results, more complex models are estimated permitting the simultaneous evaluation of the hypotheses.

Analysis of State Incarceration Rates

In Table 1 Pearson's zero-order correlation coefficients for state incarceration rates and each of the independent variables are reported. There is at

[1] To keep the analysis simple, Pearson correlation coefficients are reported, regardless of measurement scale. For variables measured at the nominal and ordinal levels, more appropriate statistics did not suggest different conclusions. A copy of the full correlation matrix is available from the authors.

TABLE 1

Eight Hypotheses Concerning State Incarceration Rates in 1984: Pearson's Zero-Order Correlation Coefficients ($N = 48$)

Hypothesis/Variables	Correlation with Incarceration Rate
Hypothesis 1: Crime in 1980	
1. Violent crimes per 100,000 population	.69**
2. Property crimes per 100,000 population	.42**
Hypothesis 2: Economics in 1980	
1. Median family income	.05
2. Percentage of individuals below poverty level	.29*
Hypothesis 3: Social characteristics in 1980	
1. Percent of males between 20 and 29 years of age	.09
2. Percent nonwhite males	.58**
3. Percent nonwhite males between 20 and 29 years	.66**
Hypothesis 4: Demographics in 1980 and between 1970 and 1980	
1. Population	.19
2. Population density	−.07
3. Change in population density	.36*
4. Percent change in population	.31*
Hypothesis 5: Ideology and culture	
1. Percent vote for McGovern in 1972	−.41**
2. Conservatism in the early 1980s	.30*
3. Political culture circa 1970	.65**
Hypothesis 6: Sentencing and parole reforms as of 1983	
1. Adoption of determinate sentencing (0 = no; 1 = yes)	−.16
2. Mandatory sentencing index	.43**
3. Adoption of systemwide parole (0 = no; 1 = yes)	.18
4. Early release credit provision index	−.03
Hypothesis 7: Alternatives to corrections in 1984	
1. Probationers per 100,000 population	.38**
2. Designed capacity of community-based facilities	.41**
3. Ratio of community-based capacity to prison capacity	.02
Hypothesis 8: Institutional conditions	
1. Percent prison capacity in 1984	.08
2. Corrections organizational strength in 1977	.03
3. Designed capacity of prison facilities in 1984	.41**

*$p < .05$.
**$p < .01$.

least limited support for all of the hypotheses. The variables displaying the strongest relationships are associated with crime, social characteristics, ideology and culture, alternatives to corrections, and the two demographic measures addressing change. Almost all of these measures are significant at conventional levels (.05 or less). Violent crime is more strongly associated with incarceration than property crime, and generated the largest correlation found in the table. Likewise, change in population density produced a higher correlation than percent change in population. In terms of social characteristics, the variable measuring the interaction of age and race is strongly associated with incarceration as is percent nonwhite males. Lastly, two of the three indicators of alternatives to corrections (probation rate and capacity of community-based facilities) and ideology and culture (McGovern vote and political culture) are significantly related to imprisonment.

The results for the remaining three hypotheses are less clear. Institutional conditions, economics, and sentencing and parole reforms each produced one significant correlation. For instance, of the sentencing and parole reform variables only mandatory sentencing is significantly associated with incarceration. Similarly, percent prison capacity and corrections organizational strength are not significantly related to incarceration, but absolute prison capacity does appear to be relevant. In the latter case, the direction of the relationship is positive, supporting the "build and fill" hypothesis that capacity drives imprisonment. Lastly, in terms of the economic hypothesis, incarceration rates are more closely linked to poverty rather than wealth.

The next step in the analysis was to regress all the variables for each hypothesis on incarceration rates using both a forced and stepwise procedure. This was done for each hypothesis to determine the unique contribution of each variable while controlling for closely related variables. The results, not shown in tabular form, help clarify the initial findings. For the five hypotheses generating more than one significant variable in the bivariate analysis, the regression estimates indicated model redundancy with one exception. That is, when examined simultaneously, only one variable per hypothesis achieved significance: violent crime for the crime hypothesis; the percentage of nonwhite males between 20 and 29 years of age for the social characteristics hypothesis; change in population density for the demographic hypothesis; and political culture for the ideology and culture hypothesis. Only in the case of the alternatives to corrections hypothesis did more than one variable remain significant, with both the capacity of community-based facilities and the probation rate achieving significance. For the other three hypotheses, economics, sentencing and parole reforms, and institutional conditions, the variables identified previously were the only ones to stand out in this stage in the analysis: percentage of individuals below poverty level, mandatory sentencing, and absolute prison capacity.

Based on these results, a total of nine variables, one per hypothesis plus

TABLE 2

Multiple Regression Analysis of State Incarceration Rates

Variable	Slope (Standard Error)	Beta Weight
1. Violent crimes per 100,000	0.165 (0.050)**	.54
2. Percent individuals below poverty	−1.386 (2.892)	−.07
3. Percent young nonwhite males	1.587 (6.272)	.04
4. Change in population density	−0.897 (0.730)	−.14
5. Political culture	15.445 (4.010)**	.57
6. Mandatory sentencing index	−0.652 (7.087)	−.01
7. Capacity of community-based facilities	0.003 (0.019)	.01
8. Probationers per 100,000	0.040 (0.022)	.20
9. Capacity of correctional facilities	−0.001 (0.001)	−.13
Constant	10.364 (38.279)	
Adjusted R^2	.66	

$^{**}p \leq .01$.

two for the alternatives to corrections hypothesis, were retained for further analysis. The incarceration rate was regressed simultaneously on these nine variables in order to assess their relative influence on imprisonment.[2] The results summarized in Table 2 are mixed. Only two variables display a strong positive association with imprisonment: violent crime and political culture. The probation rate is also positively related to incarceration, though the association is not as strong ($p = .08$). None of the remaining variables contribute significantly to our understanding of incarceration when examined together. Prison capacity, mandatory sentencing, percent young nonwhite males, poverty, community corrections capacity, and change in density have little direct influence on incarceration rates based on both their standard errors and standardized coefficients. These findings are not altered when looking at reduced model specifications or when employing stepwise procedures.

[2]Numerous specifications were examined, including a model which incorporated all of the variables. The results of these analyses are not reported because they add little to the discussion.

These results are supportive of arguments that incarceration practices in the states reflect patterns of crime and culture. Sentencing and parole reforms, institutional conditions, social characteristics, economics, and demographic change seem to have little direct bearing on imprisonment. Many of the variables failing to demonstrate a significant relationship with incarceration did generate coefficients in the postulated direction and, in the bivariate analysis, assumed rather large values. In light of statistical control, these associations are found to be spurious and are the product of a third variable related to both incarceration and these independent variables.

Consistently throughout this analysis violent crime has stood out as one of the most important variables. This variable is also correlated with many of the other measures included in this study. Further, many of the hypotheses generated to explain levels of punishment acknowledge a relationship to crime and suggest that this linkage influences incarceration. Hence, the impact of some variables on incarceration may be indirect rather than direct.

To better understand these linkages, a simple path model was estimated using the nine independent variables identified previously. Figure 1 summarizes the results of this procedure, three features of which deserve comment.[3] First, in terms of direct effects on the incarceration rate, the results are consistent with those reported in Table 2: violent crime, culture and, less imporantly, probation are directly associated with incarceration. None of the remaining six variables have a direct impact on the incarceration rate. Second, the three remaining socioeconomic measures have an indirect effect on imprisonment through their significant impacts on rates of crime and, to a lesser extent, the use of probation. Indeed, when one looks at the total effect of each variable, poverty and percentage of young nonwhite males have similar influences, almost double the direct impact of probation or the indirect effect of change in density.[4] In terms of total impact, crime is the most important variable (.51), followed by culture (.45), young nonwhite males (.25), and poverty (.20). Use of probation (.12) and change in population density (.11) are least relevant. Finally, adoption of mandatory sentencing laws, absolute prison capacity, and community-based corrections are directly influenced

[3] Six regression equations were estimated. First, violent crime was regressed on the four variables linked to a state's socioeconomic environment on the assumption that crime stems from general social conditions. Four equations were then estimated using prison capacity, the probation rate, community-based capacity, and mandatory sentencing as dependent variables, with the four socioeconomic measures and crime serving as independent variables. Lastly, incarceration was regressed, as before, on all nine variables. To keep the model understandable, paths not shown in Figure 1 failed to generate an unstandardized coefficient significant at a rather liberal .10 level. Each equation was reestimated until the retained variables satisfied the .10 requirement.

[4] The total effect of a variable is equal to the sum of its direct path and, for each intervening variable, the product of its indirect path times the direct path. For example, the total effect of crime is .45 plus .48 times .12 or .51.

FIGURE 1

Path Model of State Incarceration Rates in 1984

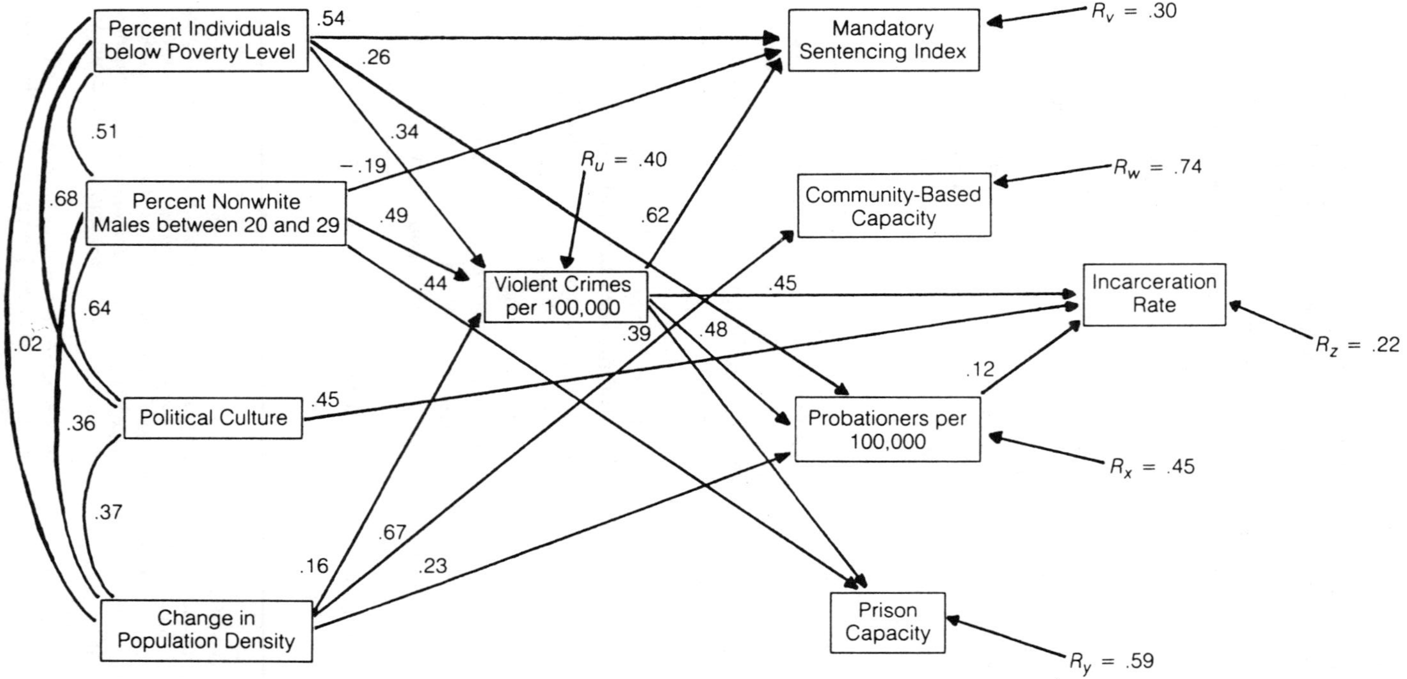

by crime and both directly and indirectly influenced by the environmental measures, but none affects incarceration. Their observed simple association with imprisonment is due to these multiple relationships.

Discussion

This paper has examined eight rival hypotheses concerning determinants of state incarceration rates. The findings suggest imprisonment is shaped primarily by the broader environment, which is beyond the immediate control of state policymakers. Moreover, those factors more readily controlled by policymakers, such as sentencing and parole reforms and institutional conditions, are themselves a product of these environmental characteristics and have limited impact on incarceration practices. The analysis indicates the causes of imprisonment are traceable directly or indirectly to societal conditions such as crime, culture, race, poverty, and increasing urbanization. Punishment reflects the social and cultural diversity of the states, not the efforts of policymakers to manipulate the criminal justice system.

Our modest effort to improve upon existing research in this area by evaluating several explanations of incarceration within a common framework suggests much remains to be done in future studies. While this analysis considered many common hypotheses, other possibilities certainly exist. For example, we have not explored the possible effects of court orders on incarceration practices. Similarly, the improvement of certain measures considered in this study, particularly those of a binary nature, may prove useful. It may be the case that it is not the adoption of mandatory sentencing laws which is relevant but rather the length of the mandated sentences. Further, the dynamic nature of many of these hypotheses cannot be captured adequately within a cross-sectional framework. Longitudinal investigations must be conducted before more definitive conclusions are possible. This analysis does suggest future researchers should be prepared to explore relatively complex models of incarceration. The crisis in corrections would suggest that time is of the essence. SSQ

REFERENCES

Blumstein, Alfred. 1982. "On the Racial Disproportionality of United States' Prison Populations." *Journal of Criminal Law and Criminology* 73:1259–81.

———. 1987. "Sentencing and the Prison Crowding Problem." Pp. 161–78 in Stephen D. Gottfredson and Sean McConville, eds., *America's Correctional Crisis: Prison Populations and Public Policy*. New York: Greenwood.

———. 1988. "Prison Populations: A System Out of Control." Pp. 231–66 in Michael Tonry and Norval Morris, eds., *Crime and Justice: A Review of Research*, vol. 10. Chicago: University of Chicago Press.

Carroll, Leo, and Claire P. Cornell. 1985. "Racial Composition, Sentencing Reforms, and Rates of Incarceration, 1970–1980." *Justice Quarterly* 2:473–90.

Carroll, Leo, and Mary Beth Doubet. 1983. "U.S. Social Structure and Imprisonment: A Comment." *Criminology* 21:449–56

Clarke, Steven H. 1984. "North Carolina's Determinate Sentencing Legislation." *Judicature* 68:140–52.

Dye, Thomas R. 1987. *Understanding Public Policy.* 6th ed. Englewoods Cliffs, N.J.: Prentice-Hall.

Elazar, Daniel J. 1972. *American Federalism: A View from the States.* 2d ed. New York: Harper & Row.

Flanagan, John. 1975. "Imminent Crisis in Prison Populations." *American Journal of Corrections* 37:20–36.

Galster, George C., and Laure A. Scaturo. 1985. "The U.S. Criminal Justice System: Unemployment and the Severity of Punishment." *Journal of Research in Crime and Delinquency* 22:163–89.

Garofalo, James. 1980. "Social Structure and Rates of Imprisonment: A Research Note." *Justice Systems Journal* 5:299–305.

Gottfredson, Stephen D., and Sean McConville. 1987. "Introduction." Pp. 3–11 in S. D. Gottfredson and S. McConville, eds., *America's Correctional Crisis: Prison Populations and Public Policy.* New York: Greenwood.

Gray, Virginia, and Bruce Williams. 1980. *The Organizational Politics of Criminal Justice.* Lexington, Mass.: Lexington Books.

Harrigan, John. 1991. *Politics and Policy in States and Communities.* 4th ed. New York: Harper Collins.

Hindelang, Michael J. 1978. "Race and Involvement in Common Law Personal Crimes." *American Sociological Review* 43:93–109.

Klein, Stephen, Joan Petersilia, and Susan Turner. 1990. "Race and Imprisonment Decisions in California." *Science* 247:812–16.

Maguire, Kathleen, and Timothy J. Flanagan. 1991. *Sourcebook of Criminal Justice Statistics 1990.* U.S. Department of Justice, Bureau of Justice Statistics. Washington, D.C.: U.S. Government Printing Office.

Nagin, Daniel. 1979. "The Impact of Determinate Sentencing Legislation on Prison Population and Sentence Length: A California Case Study." *Public Policy* 27:69–98.

Nice, David C. 1983. "Representation in the States: Policymaking and Ideology." *Social Science Quarterly* 64:404–11.

Scull, Andrew T. 1977. *Decarceration.* Englewoods Cliffs, N.J.: Prentice-Hall.

Sharkansky, Ira. 1969. "The Utility of Elazar's Political Culture: A Research Note." *Polity* 2:66–83.

Skogan, Wesley G. 1990. "Crime and Punishment." Pp. 378–410 in Virginia Gray, Herbert Jacob, and Robert B. Albritton, eds., *Politics in the American States: A Comparative Analysis.* 5th ed. Glenview, Ill.: Scott, Foresman.

Taggart, William A. 1989. "A Note on Testing Models of Spending in the American States: The Case of Public Expenditures for Corrections." *Western Political Quarterly* 42:679–90.

U.S. Bureau of the Census. 1984. *Statistical Abstract of the United States, 1984.* Washington, D.C.: USGPO.

U.S. Department of Justice, Bureau of Justice Statistics. 1983a. *Setting Prison Terms*. Washington, D.C.: U.S. Government Printing Office.

———. 1983b. *Sourcebook of Criminal Justice Statistics—1982*. Washington, D.C.: U.S. Government Printing Office.

———. 1987a. *BJS Bulletin—Probation and Parole in 1985*. Washington, D.C.: U.S. Government Printing Office.

———. 1987b. *1984 Census of State Adult Correctional Facilities*. Washington, D.C.: U.S. Government Printing Office.

———. 1987c. *Prisoners in State and Federal Institutions*. Washington, D.C.: U.S. Government Printing Office.

Walker, Samuel. 1989. *Sense and Nonsense about Crime: A Policy Guide*. 2d ed. Pacific Green, Calif.: Brooks/Cole.

Wirt, Frederick M. 1983. "Institutionalization: Prison and School Policies." Pp. 287–328 in Virginia Gray, Herbert Jacob, and Kenneth V. Vines, eds., *Politics in the American States: A Comparative Analysis*. 4th ed. Boston: Little, Brown.

Wright, Gerald C., Jr., Robert S. Erikson, and John P. McIver. 1985. "Measuring State Partisanship and Ideology with Survey Data." *Journal of Politics* 47:469–89.

Zimring, Franklin E., and Gordon Hawkins. 1991. *The Scale of Imprisonment*. Chicago: University of Chicago Press.

DEMOCRATIZING PRISONS

HANS TOCH
State University of New York at Albany

Experiments in prison reform have often included efforts to democratize prisons. Such experiments were especially popular during the progressive era. Today, democratization efforts are congruent with management literature that describes employee participation and total quality of management initiatives through which organizations try to improve the quality of their products and services. Prison democratization can combine opportunities for staff involvement with enhanced prisoner participation. Inmates can be afforded a greater role in classification and programming decisions, and in determining policies that affect the quality of prison life. Such participatory approaches help to normalize prison life and contribute to the resocialization of offenders.

In 1924, a town in West Virginia wanted to become the site of the first federal reformatory for women. To attract this prize the town donated 202 acres of prime pasture adjoining a river, a railroad, and a neighboring farm that became available at distress prices.

The Alderson Reformatory opened on February 22, 1928, and on that date its 200 inmates adopted a constitution setting up what they called "cooperative clubs" in each of the prison's 14 cottages. The constitution said that the inmates resolved "to improve the life of our cottages, thence [of] the whole institution, and finally [of] the families and communities to which we hope to return." The inmates also declared that they would show themselves "capable of taking responsibility" and earning "the trust reposed in us" (Harris, 1936, pp. 344-345).

The way the Alderson cooperative clubs worked is illustrated by the minutes of a typical session, which read (in part) as follows:

> Our meeting of the Co-operative Club was held Monday, October 19, 1931, with Lulu chairman and Carrie secretary, and was opened with the Sentence Prayer in concert. We took in six new members who were: Mary, Virginia, Charity, Georgia, Maude, and Willie.

This article is a revised version of an address given at the Scottish Prison Service College, Polmont, June 24, 1993.

THE PRISON JOURNAL, Vol. 73 No. 1, March 1994 62-72

Our Secretary, Carrie, read the pledge to them and each signed it, and it was witnessed by our Warder [correction officer]. The minutes of the last meeting were read, and stood approved.

The opening of business was to elect a new Committee girl. When the votes were counted, Annie had the most and was made our new Committee girl. She thanked the Club and said she would do her best in every way she could.

As several of the girls had gone home, new ones had to be put on the different assignments as follows:

1. Lights	Lulu and Blanche
2. Promptness	Carrie
3. Courtesy	Mabel
4. Cleanliness	Blanche
5. Librarian	Elizabeth
6. Entertainment	Annie

Also, the Fire Drill was reorganized. . . .

Reports were asked from the different Committee assignments; there were no complaints. . . .

We talked of the Hallowe'en party, and Annie was given the assignment for Entertainment.

No further business, the meeting was voted adjourned. (Harris, 1936, pp. 348-349)

The inmates at Alderson willingly undertook civic obligations, and they farmed out assignments to each other. They made decisions about the running of their cottage and expended effort to implement these decisions. They elected representatives to groups concerned with activities in the institution as a whole and staged events that made for highlights in the daily regime of the prison.

A second valued innovation that was taken seriously at the Alderson Reformatory was the Classification Committee, which met two mornings of each week. The concept of the Classification Committee had been imported from another institution, but Alderson's version was self-consciously democratic. In the words of the warden of the prison,

An important departure from the procedure followed [elsewhere] is the inclusion in our classification meetings of the warder of the cottage where the inmate under consideration is living. In our small units the head of the cottage comes to know her group intimately, and the fact that she is expected to make a verbal report on the personal peculiarities and difficulties of her charges at these formal meetings undoubtedly tends to sharpen her observation and quicken her interest. She cannot confine her attention to a few even if she would lean in that direction, for she has a pride in being able to answer the searching questions asked about the progress or retrogression of all her wards.

> Unquestionably these classification meetings are exceedingly educational for all who participate in them. Several warders attend each meeting and not only hear their own cases discussed, but learn how other warders are facing the common problems successfully. They become familiar with the significance of the physician's and the psychologist's reports and asks questions if matters are not clear. When a new medical term occurs, I ask the doctor to tell us what it means, and frequently she gives us a short account of the symptoms and remedies of the ailment mentioned. This clinic [case conference], for such it is, is far more educational for the staff than formal courses could ever be. When a new warder comes, one of the first things we have her do is to attend a classification meeting. All members of the staff, whether they deal directly with inmates or not, get a better understanding of what it is all about if they attend these meetings occasionally. (Harris, 1936, p. 329)

Alderson's classification process was not only a training process and an exercise in staff involvement but also a way to do participatory sentence planning for the prisoners, including an opportunity for the prisoners to express their desires, interests, and preferences, and to ventilate their grievances. The warden (Mary Harris) testified that

> the women are always asked at these meetings if they wish to continue with their work assignments; if not, why. When possible, adjustments and changes, if they seem reasonable, are made. When they cannot be made, an explanation is given of the situation. These fixed dates for reconsideration are almost without exception kept to the day, and everyone knows that she is going to be given a hearing at a definite time. If at that time she does not ask for a change, she gets no sympathy from her mates when she complains afterwards. They say: "You were up for classification. Why didn't you ask for a change?" It is the recognized clearing house for complaints and dissatisfactions. (Harris, 1936, p. 332)

To put this story in perspective, one must re-emphasize that the account refers to procedures that were followed between 1928 and 1935 and that the institution later became a more conventional prison (Giallombardo, 1966). One must also note that both staff and inmates were the objects or targets of innovations.[1]

Prisons in theory are susceptible to any trends and fashions in organizational reform that are prevalent in the private or public sector. In other words, when administrators outside prisons have found a better way of running things, their ideas and experiments can carry implications for the prison. The obverse also holds, of course: Alderson's cooperative clubs and classification committees, for example, could have been adopted by schools or hospitals.

It is not a priori obvious whether democratization or participatory trends in society are relevant to prisons, or whether prisons can afford to ignore them. Some otherwise progressive countries have chosen the second option. That course of action was adopted in Yugoslavia, for instance, when there was a Yugoslavia. There, industrial enterprises were in theory self-managed, with workers making production decisions and allocating budgets (Blumberg, 1973; Zwerdling, 1980). Apartment complexes were run by tenants. Health decisions were made in municipal conclaves of providers and consumers. But prisons were run with paramilitary staff hierarchies. There were inmate groups, but they were described as gripe sessions, which is a far cry from self-management.

Yugoslavia is an interesting example because it is a country where organizational democracy had been institutionalized in an effort to avoid substituting state autocracy for private managerial autocracy. In this connection, it is ironic that perestroika envisioned a similar trend in Russia, under the heading of privatization—workers acquiring shares of enterprises and electing managers to manage them.

Different societies have had different reasons for vertically rearranging organizations. In Scandinavia, for instance, it has been a matter of importing democracy from the streets into the workplace (Thosrud, 1984). Elsewhere, the goal has fit most neatly under a heading such as human resource management (Likert, 1967). The premise is that people work more effectively when they are involved in making decisions that govern their work, and that organizations are more effective when they deploy the intelligence, wisdom, and judgment of all of their members, particularly those on the front lines—those in the bowels of organization. A second premise is that involvement brings a sense of ownership and buys loyalty, dedication, and commitment.

Another way of stating the human resource argument is that the classic hierarchical, top-down management model may have outlived its day, even on the assembly lines where it was born (Morse & Reimer, 1956; Special Task Force, 1973). The most recent version of this argument sees organizational democracy as the only means to achieve quality of products or services (Lawler, Mohrman, & Ledford, 1992). When we now produce quality cars, we advertise in commercials that we have had assembly line workers involved in the quality control process, as they do in Japan (Ouchi, 1981).[2] And if one can make this claim for assembly lines, the question arises how one can pretend to do quality social work, or nursing, or teaching, or police work, with managers attempting to second-guess the decisions that professional or paraprofessional employees make or subjecting them to detailed prescriptions and instructions. A second question is how one can expect workers in the human services to carry out policies that offer implementation problems that supervisors who are not on the front lines might not anticipate.

Some human service managers can, of course, argue, "We manage workers who make fateful decisions, and we have to protect people from the damage these workers could do, and ourselves from the law suits that could eventuate from their mistakes." Teachers might not cover their lessons, nurses might poison patients, police might punish suspects, and correction officers might brutalize inmates. How can we prevent these sorts of contingencies other than through eternal vigilance, painstaking monitoring, and unsparing discipline?

Ironically, one of my own experiences with participatory involvement began against the backdrop of this concern in a police department that was having problems with uses of force by officers against civilians and was getting an exceedingly bad press. Some colleagues and I were invited in as researchers and confirmed that a minority of officers were repeatedly involved in violent encounters and saw themselves doing excellent police work in the process. I listened to the officers recounting incident after horrifying incident with evident pride while I shuddered at what they were describing to me (Toch, 1992).

The police department at issue was very tightly managed but could not fire the problems officers because it was hard to make airtight cases in individual incidents. The aggressive officers were also, as a group, productive officers and had many arrests to their credit. In one sense, they would never have been missed, but in another sense, the organization would have hated to lose them.

What we as consultants did in response to this situation was to set groups of violence-involved officers to work addressing the violence problem. We had seven of the officers seconded to us and had them study police-citizen violence. We also trained them as group leaders. We put them in charge of three other groups of violence-experienced officers to work on solutions to the problem. The groups advanced a number of useful ideas, but their most innovative and influential solution was a peer review panel run by experienced policemen for other officers who were recurrently involved in incidents. The panels in short order retrained scores of problem officers and gathered the statistics to prove it (Toch & Grant, 1991). There is no way of estimating how many police careers they saved and how many incidents they prevented in which citizens would have been hurt. What outcome statistics suggest is that the officers succeeded where management had failed and did so because they were close enough to the problem to understand its nuances and carried credibility with other officers. And I suspect that it also helped that the prescription they implemented was their prescription, not that of someone sitting behind a desk in an office.

Some of the same colleagues and I later worked with groups of correction officers in four large prisons. Each group originated proposals for prison reform—two designed for their own institution and two for the system at large. The ideas for these proposals evolved in the groups after systematic dissection of problems that the officers thought needed solution. The proposals were worked through by subgroups who reported to a larger group and then wrote up the proposals with some editing assistance from us. The officers in these subgroups were those who had shown intense interest in the problems and their solution and had a substantial investment in their product. They would have become dedicated implementers of the ideas they originated, in the event of their adoption. But although some of the ideas were adopted, in only two cases did officers get credit for contributions (Toch & Grant, 1982).

At this point, one must mention one other important strategy for change that is relevant to prison staff—and to guards in particular. The notion in question is that of job enrichment, which means roughly what the words job ENRICHment suggest. Again, the concern is with how we can motivate people at work, and the suspicion is that pay, fringe benefits, and other material commodities do not suffice as incentives (Herzberg, Mausner, & Snyderman, 1993).

The assumption is that it is work itself that can motivate, provided that it is interesting and that it offers variety, complexity, feedback, and a sense of completion when it is done—that a person can go home at the end of a long day and say, "I have accomplished something which has contributed modestly to human betterment. I get a sense of satisfaction from these accomplishments." The presumption in corrections is that the tasks of guarding, counting, and escorting people may not provide such satisfaction, and that one may have to supplement traditional custody tasks by introducing other tasks, such as assisting prisoners or helping to rehabilitate them (Toch, 1978).

Some prison systems have followed the enrichment route but not across the board: They have enriched some of their custody jobs, but not others; they consequently ended up with two kinds of officers, the old kind and the enriched variety. This arrangement can work, but it also can become somewhat problematic, and occasionally, seriously problematic.

A case in point is that of the Norfolk (Massachusetts) Prison Colony, founded by Howard Gill in 1931. According to an article in *Corrections Magazine*, Norfolk was "a very special institution—the best hope of a whole generation of prison reformers" (Serill, 1982, p. 25). The article pointed out that "the State Prison Colony at Norfolk was the crucible in which many treatment and other programs were tested—the casework approach, the inmate council, the simulation of 'normal' society behind prison walls. The documents associated with Norfolk . . . are full of observations that seem as applicable today as they did in 1931" (Serill, 1982, p. 32).

Unfortunately, one thing that these documents make clear is that Gill saw one set of officers as the core of his enterprise and another as ancillary, or as a necessary evil. His core staff were House Officers, who, according to Gill's manual, "live with the men throughout the twenty four hours of every day while they eat, sleep, work and play, [and] their influence upon the inmate is the most constant and influential factor in maintaining morale and in promoting constructive, wholesome attitudes and adjustments to the institution and to life in general" (Commons, 1940, p. 32).

Gill's other guards made up a Custodial Division, which (according to the same manual) "is operated under a semimilitary type of organization, with periodic drill and instruction periods, and its regulations provide for continuous observation and frequent periodic, systematic checking of all inmates and their activities throughout the entire 24-hour day" (Commons, 1940, p. 22). The custodial officers had no meaningful inmate contacts, and their views were disregarded or disrespected, even on matters of prisoner discipline. These officers came to resent what they saw as unbridled anarchy and delighted in feeding examples of licentiousness to legislators and newspaper reporters. Gill's second mistake was to import professional classification personnel, who sat in resplendent architectural isolation and second-guessed the opinions of the House Officers. This created another destructive rift in his staff.

As for prisoners, Norfolk did have an elected council and prisoner committees that dealt with every subject under the sun. Observers agree, however, that the Norfolk experiment was most exciting when the institution was small and intimate and staff and prisoner involvement in governance was direct and immediate.

In general, inmate representative governance has had a checkered and, to date, unpromising history. The standard complaint has been that the wrong inmates arrange to get themselves elected and that they advance selfish and parochial interests to the detriment of the common good (DiIulio, 1987). This charge is the same as in the outside world: When you rely on representative democracy, politicians take over the process and prostitute it.

In prisons, we must also worry about the impact on staff of what we do with inmates. It is axiomatic that prisoner participation in the absence of staff participation lowers morale. There is no complaint more plaintive than that of an officer who says "the Inmate Council regularly meets with the warden, but he does not listen to our views, and I cannot get to see him." Democracy in theory should not lend itself to zero sum games.

Several types of direct participation are possible in prisons. One is to involve inmates in the day-to-day running of small institutions and small subdivisions of large institutions. The second is involvement of prisoners in specialized groups that are concerned with some aspect of prison administration, including inmate-staff task forces that deal with problems of topical interest. The third approach is to have prisoners individually participate in their own management, sharing critical decisions along the way, and reviewing their progress at key junctures in their careers. Needless to say, these approaches are combinable, and a prison system can aspire to offer as many avenues of participation as possible.

One important conception that achieved popularity in the 1960s saw democracy as a vehicle of personal reform or of "social therapy" (Jones, 1968). One learns to be prosocial by working with others and to govern oneself through involvement in governance. As one learns, one assists others to learn and is assisted by others in doing so. Some even argued that inmate learning and staff development must go hand in hand in institutional settings. Such was the belief of the psychiatrist Maxwell Jones, who said in more mellow moments that he didn't know who needed therapy the most, his colleagues or his clients.

There are many examples of programs such as the Alderson classification teams in which staff acquire new responsibilities that permit them to provide new services that benefit inmates. Staff develop because they learn and exercise new skills. Prisoners acquire new roles, new ways of interacting with each other and with staff. Such social learning benefits are available even where they are not explicit, as in groups concerned with bread-and-butter issues or issues of governance or policy, in which prisoners and staff can interact around shared or intersecting concerns.

One can orchestrate groups to achieve desired intersections: A group that deals with issues of visitation, for example, could contain inmates and staff with very large families or those who have recently married. The presumption would be that custodial and inmate perspectives could be softened by shared concerns about the maintenance of family ties, which would be a common goal for the group. The problem-solving exercise would be meaningful and consequential, and it could even lead to further cooperation if inmates and staff were charged with coordinating modified visitation arrangements or were asked to monitor the impact of innovations in visitation.

Problems can be addressed proactively before they arise to culminate in disruptive crises. Institutional violence prevention, as example, can be a subject of concern to staff and inmates that benefits from conjoint deliberation. As in the police example, prisoners who in the past have been sources of problems can become members of violence prevention task forces, and their expertise can be valuable if invoked. Past incidents of violence can be reviewed for lessons they may convey about future incidents. Prisoners and officers can meet separately and report to each other or to plenary sessions. Groups from different institutions can interact and pool suggestions.

Special skills and interests can be exploited in selecting participants in governance bodies. An advisory group to the prison kitchen, for example, could contain persons who have worked in restaurants, grown vegetables, or become famous because of the amount of food they consume. Former accountants could be enlisted to review budget decisions. A budget may seem an unlikely subject for participation, but at least one prison warden in the United States routinely presents his budget to prisoners and asks them if they would prefer to repair broken windows or buy television sets, given budgetary constraints.

Service consumption can become a passive or an active enterprise, and the latter is preferable to the former. A passive consumer can be forced into a regressive, dependent stance, which some students have described as a "gimme" posture (Fogel, 1985). Such a person's role becomes that of a mendicant, who is given to whining and tends to grouse and complain. An active consumer exercises options among available alternatives or invents options, given existing resources.

Gradations of consumer activism (or active consumerism) can be envisaged in prisons. Inmates can be afforded choices of services or combinations of services. Such choices can involve mindfully trading off something one would like to attain something else one would like, given existing constraints: A program one might want, for example, can be available at a relatively distant location, or require that one arise at dawn, or that one live in substandard accommodations. Choices can also be subject to review: An inmate may agree to try a program for size, with the explicit provision that he or she can opt out of it after a reasonable time (Morris, 1974).

The most common form of active consumerism is a quid pro quo arrangement, in which the prisoner agrees to participate in a set of experiences that the staff feels he or she can use in exchange for actions the staff promises to take on his or her behalf, such as recommendations for early release.[3] Contracts can also provide for admission into a desired program after completion of a less desired one, or for conditional increments in quality of life. The common denominator of such arrangements is that the prisoner has mindful control over the sequence of events, in negotiation with staff members.

More active participation involves the creation of new options by consumers, as in consumer cooperatives. A staff role in such arrangement can be one of sponsorship or facilitation. Staff members might arrange adjoining housing, for example, to permit a group of inmates to engage in some constructive activity or to create a social milieu that affords a commodity (such as privacy) the inmates might want (Toch, 1992). Or the staff may provide modest funds or facilities so that prisoners can engage in self-educational pursuits not otherwise available in the prison.

Active consumerism involves adult-to-adult transactions between prisoners and staff. It requires prisoners to do something to get something. And it lets prisoners engage in assessment, deliberation, and planning in determining their future. This process gives prisoners an enhanced stake in the outcome and motivates them to validate the choices they have made. The prison remains physically confining but becomes psychologically liberating to a limited degree. The experience is also one that prepares prisoners for more responsible participation in the opportunity structures of society at large.

NOTES

1. Alderson was not the first effort at prison democracy but is unique in its concern about staff members in the design of the experiment. The best known early democratizing venture was that of Thomas Matt Osborne at Sing Sing prison, which was a radical experiment in inmate self-governance. Osborne's Mutual Welfare League was initiated at the Auburn Penitentiary in 1914 as the Good Conduct League. In Sing Sing, it survived Osborne's tenure, and was abolished—after a riot—in 1929 (Tannenbaum, 1933).

2. This claim can be substantiated because the most current approach to human resource management—which is called total quality management (TQM)—was introduced to Japan after World War II by W. E. Deming (1986), and universally adopted in Japan before being re-exported to the United States. TQM advocates rank-and-file involvement in policy decisions and input from consumers in the definition of qualitative production goals. The approach has been experimentally introduced in many goverment agencies (see, e.g., Keehley, 1992; National Governors' Association, 1992), including some correctional bureaucracies.

3. A recent development in corrections has been the revival of arrangements in which release decisions are affected by prisoner participation in educational, vocational, or rehabilitative programs. One way in which this can be done is through use of presumptive parole certificates, which increase the probability of parole.

REFERENCES

Blumberg, P. (1973). *Industrial democracy: The sociology of participation.* New York: Schocken.

Commons, W. H. (1940). Official manual of the state prison colony. In C. R. Doering (Ed.), *A report on the development of penological treatment at Norfolk Prison Colony in Massachusetts.* New York: Bureau of Social Hygiene.

Deming, W. E. (1986). *Out of crisis*. Cambridge: Massachusetts Institute of Technology, Center for Advanced Engineering Study.

DiIulio, J. J., Jr. (1987). *Governing prisons: A comparative study of correctional management*. New York: Free Press.

Fogel, D. (1985). *"We are the living proof . . . ": The justice model for corrections*. Cincinnati, OH: Anderson.

Giallombardo, R. (1966). *Society of women: A study of women's prisons*. New York: Wiley.

Harris, M. (1936). *I knew them in prison*. New York: Viking.

Herzberg, F., Mausner, B., & Snyderman, B. B. (1993). *The motivation to work*. New Brunswick, NJ: Transaction Books.

Jones, M. (1968). *Beyond the therapeutic community*. New Haven, CT: Yale University Press.

Keehley, P. (1992, August). TQM for local governments: The principles and prospects. *Public Management*, pp. 10-18.

Lawler, E. E., Mohrman, S. E., & Ledford, G. E. (1992). *Employee involvement and total quality management*. San Francisco: Jossey-Bass.

Likert, R. (1967). *The human organization: Its management and value*. New York: McGraw-Hill.

Morris, N. (1974). *The future of imprisonment*. Chicago: University of Chicago Press.

Morse, N., & Reimer, E. (1956). The experimental change of a major organizational variable. *Journal of Abnormal and Social Psychology, 52*, 120-129.

National Governors' Association, Office of State Services. (1992). Total quality management initiatives in state government. *Management briefs* (Attachment). Washington, DC: Author.

Ouchi, W. (1981). *Theory Z: How American business can meet the Japanese challenge*. Reading, MA: Addison-Wesley.

Serill, M. S. (1982, August). New debate over a famous prison experiment. *Corrections Magazine*, pp. 25-32.

Special Task Force to the Secretary of Health, Education and Welfare. (1973). *Work in America*. Cambridge: MIT Press.

Tannenbaum, F. (1933). *Osborne of Sing Sing*. Chapel Hill: University of North Carolina Press.

Thosrud, E. (1984). The Scandinavian model: Strategies of organizational democratization in Norway. In B. Wilpert & A. Sorge (Eds.), *International perspectives on organizational democracy*. New York: Wiley.

Toch, H. (1978). Is a "correction officer", by any other name, a "screw"? *Criminal Justice Review, 3*, 19-36.

Toch, H. (1992). *Violent men: An inquiry into the psychology of violence*. Washington, DC: American Psychological Association.

Toch, H., & Grant, J. D. (1982). *Reforming human services*. Beverly Hills, CA: Sage.

Toch, H., & Grant, J. D. (1991). *Police as problem solvers*. New York: Plenum.

Zwerdling, D. (1980). *Workplace democracy: A guide to workplace ownership, participation and self-management experiments in the United States and Europe*. New York: Harper & Row.

MEASURING PRISON DISCIPLINARY PROBLEMS: A MULTIPLE INDICATORS APPROACH TO UNDERSTANDING PRISON ADJUSTMENT*

PATRICIA VAN VOORHIS
University of Cincinnati

This article examines the validity of alternative indicators of prison adjustment. The analysis compares four types of adjustment measures (e.g., official disciplinary citations, staff assessments, inmate survey measures, and inmate interview measures), which provide multiple measures of 1) aggressive behaviors, 2) insubordination, 3) drug and alcohol use, and 4) victimizations. Data were collected in a low-maximum security federal penitentiary for males. The multiple indicators analysis revealed agreement among measures of insubordination. For other measures, staff data tended to agree with official data, and self-report survey measures tended to agree with the interview measures. Bivariate and multivariate analysis showed that the effects of psychological, demographic, and criminal record variables on prison adjustment varied substantially across criterion measures.

Optimal adjustment of prison inmates is of paramount concern to those charged with maintaining safe and humane prisons. In response, scholars have generated a wealth of research identifying factors associated with poor adjustment.[1] These studies address the early prisonization research (e.g., Clemmer 1940; Irwin and Cressey 1962; Sykes 1958; Thomas 1970; Wellford 1967), the correlates of prison maladaptation (e.g., Flanagan 1980, 1983), the needs of prison inmates (e.g., Toch 1977), coping and stress patterns (e.g., Hokanson et al. 1976; Megargee and Bohn 1979; Toch 1975, 1977;

---

* Data for this project were obtained through a grant awarded to the University of Cincinnati by the National Institute of Justice (85-IJ-CX-0063). The content of this article is attributable to the author and does not reflect the official position or policies of the U.S. Department of Justice.

1 In most of the prison research, the term *prison adjustment* is used in a generic sense and later is defined further according to a specific form of maladjustment, such as stress, aggression, rule infractions, sick calls, or victimizations. In this article, maladjustment is confined to aggression, insubordination, drug/alcohol use, and victimizations. Although there is no single, agreed-upon conceptualization of adjustment, almost all prison studies include an official measure of citations for rule infractions.

JUSTICE QUARTERLY, Vol. 11 No. 4, December 1994

Toch and Adams 1989; Van Voorhis 1994; Zamble and Porporino 1988), environmental interactions (Toch 1977; Wright 1991) and classification (Megargee and Bohn 1979; NIC 1982; Quay 1983, 1984; Van Voorhis 1994; Wright 1986, 1988). Understandably, the predictors or independent variables are the central focus of most studies. These have varied considerably across studies; criterion measures of poor adjustment have not. Most often, adjustment is operationalized as rule-breaking behavior and is indicated as official citations for disciplinary infractions. Alternatively, a growing number of studies employ self-report or staff evaluation measures.

Regardless of the choice of criterion measures, certain criminologists' admonitions are clear: we are devoting insufficient attention to the quality of measurement and data (e.g., Gottfredson and Gottfredson 1980; Hindelang, Hirschi and Weis 1981; Sampson 1989), particularly with respect to criterion variables (e.g., Farrington and Tarling 1985; D. Gottfredson 1987; Gottfredson and Gottfredson 1980). Concern about the adequacy of criterion measures has extended more recently to prison research (e.g., Hewitt, Poole, and Regoli 1984; Light 1990; Poole and Regoli 1980; Schafer 1984; Van Voorhis 1994; Wooldredge 1991). These researchers pose questions that are vital to our understanding of prison problems: 1) Are prison criterion measures valid, or are they limited in other important ways? 2) If they are limited, might these limitations affect our understanding of prison adjustment?

In addressing these issues, this article explores the quality of selected prison adjustment criterion measures. Following the two questions posed above, we first employ Campbell and Fiske's (1959) Multitrait-Multimethod Matrix to compare the validity of official, self-report, and staff evaluation measures of aggression, insubordination, drug use, and victimizations. Although we cannot examine all facets of prison adjustment, it is possible to address the second question by illustrating how results for identical predictive models change across different measures of the same adjustment problem. Specifically, these illustrations examine personality and demographic predictors of aggression, insubordination, drug use, and victimizations.

The primary intent of this study is to achieve a fuller understanding of the three types of criterion variables and to offer a clearer impression of the strengths, weaknesses, and optimal uses of alternative measures. The study employs data collected from a recent study of psychological prison classification systems (Van Voorhis 1994) which was funded by the National Institute of Justice.

MEASUREMENT OF PRISON ADJUSTMENT

Table 1 presents an overview of criterion measures used in studies cited frequently within the past 20 years. One can see that most of the studies employ official disciplinary citations as a criterion variable. The more recent studies, however, show increased use of self-report and (more importantly) mixed criterion measures. Staff evaluation measures are used less frequently. The limited array of literature examining the adequacy of these measurement options is reviewed below.

Table 1. Summary of Criterion Variables Used in Recent Prison Studies

Citation	Sample Size	Research Issue	Criterion Variable
Adams 1993	3,426	Prison and postprison adjustment of former mental health patients	Official: disciplinary citations, disciplinary punishments, aggression, postprison failures
Carbonnell, Megargee, and Moorhead 1984	1,313	MMPI and CPI scale correlates of prison adjustment	Official: disciplinary and sick call reports, days in segregation; staff evaluations of work and prison adjustment (mixed)
Edinger 1979	2,063 1,455	Classification efficacy of Megargee MMPI system	Official: disciplinary citations
Edinger, Reuterfors, and Logue 1982	369	Classification efficacy of Megargee MMPI system	Psychological inventories and diagnoses
Ekland-Olson, Barrich, and Cohen 1983	—	Effects of overcrowding on disciplinary reports	Official: disciplinary reports
Flanagan 1980	701 765	Correlates of prison dispositions	Official: disciplinary infractions and dispositions
Flanagan 1983	758	Demographic correlates of infractions	Official: annual disciplinary infraction rate
Gaes and McGuire 1985	627	Effects of crowding and other variables on prison violence	Official: assault incidents
Goetting and Howsen 1986	5,586	Correlates of rule-breaking behaviors	Self-report: officially reported rulebreaking
Hanson, Moss, Hosford, and Johnson 1983	337	Comparative efficacy of four classification systems	Official: disciplinary reports, days in administrative segregation, days of good time forfeited; staff: work performance measures (mixed)
Hewitt, Poole, and Regoli 1984	391 inmates 44 guards	Comparison of self-report and official measures of rule breaking	Official: disciplinary reports; self-report: rule breaking; staff: estimates of rule breaking (mixed)
Holland and Holt 1980	293	Adequacy of staff predictions of disciplinary problems	Official: disciplinary citations, transfers, escapes

Table 1 (continued)

Citation	Sample Size	Research Issue	Criterion Variable
Jones, Beidleman, and Fowler 1981	141	MMPI and demographic correlates of adjustment	Violent behaviors
Light 1991	694	Understanding assaultive events	Official: citations for assault
Louscher, Hosford, and Moss 1983	520	Classification efficacy of Megargee MMPI system	Official: disciplinary data, use of administrative detention and protective custody
MacKenzie 1987	755	Interaction of age, attitudes, and anxiety on prison adjustment	Official: disciplinary citations; self-report: aggression, psychological inventories (mixed)
Megargee and Bohn 1979	1,164	Validation of the Megargee MMPI system	Official: disciplinary and sick call reports, days in segregation; Staff evaluations of work and prison adjustment, educational evaluations (mixed)
Megargee and Carbonell 1985	1,214	MMPI scale correlates of prison adjustment	Official: disciplinary and sick call reports, days in segregations; staff evaluations of work and prison adjustment (mixed)
Myers and Levy 1978	100	Factors associated with the intractable inmate	Staff identification of intractable inmates
Nacci, Teitelbaum, and Prather 1977	37 (institutions)	Effects of population density on serious rule infractions	Official: serious rule infractions
Poole and Regoli 1980	182	Effects of race on institutional rule breaking	Official: disciplinary reports; self-report: number of rule violations during month before survey (mixed)
Scott, Mount, and Duffy 1977	168	MMPI correlates of adjustment	Official: prison escapes
Silverman and Vega 1990	783	Demographic and personality correlates of stress	Psychological inventories
Tischler and Marquart, 1989	17,305	Gender effects on disciplinary infraction rates	Official: disciplinary reports
Toch 1977	408	Environmental needs of prison inmates	Self-report: interview, Prison Preference Inventory
Toch and Adams 1987	9,103	Coping and maladaptation of prison inmates	Official: disciplinary reports, transfers; staff: mental health data (mixed)
Van Voorhis 1988	52	Comparative efficacy of 5 classification systems	Official: disciplinary citations, protective custody

Table 1 (continued)

Citation	Sample Size	Research Issue	Criterion Variable
Van Voorhis 1993	179 190	Psychological determinants of prison adjustment	Official: disciplinary citations; self-report: indexes of rule-breaking behavior and stress; staff: Megargee Prison Adjustment and Work Performance measures (mixed)
Van Voorhis 1994	179 190	Comparative efficacy of 5 classification systems	Official: disciplinary citations; self-report: indexes of rule-breaking behavior and stress; staff: Megargee Prison Adjustment and Work Performance measures (mixed)
Walters 1991	80	Classification efficacy of Lifestyle Criminality Screening Form	Official: transfers; staff: ratings of disciplinary problems (mixed)
Walters, Scrapansky, and Marrlow 1986	86	Characteristics of emotionally disturbed military offenders	Official: disciplinary citations, days in psychiatric hospital; staff: social and vocational adjustment, psychological assessments (mixed)
Wright 1986	942	Development of transactional classification methods	Official: citations for aggressive behavior, sick calls; self-report: Prison Adjustment Questionaire (mixed)
Wright 1988	942	Comparative efficacy of 4 classification systems	Official: citations for aggressive behavior, insubordination, sick calls; self-report: Prison Adjustment Questionaire (mixed)
Wright 1991	339	Environmental needs of prison inmates	Official: citations for aggressive behavior, sick calls; self-report: Prison Adjustment Questionaire (mixed)
Zamble 1992	25	Long-term prison adaptation	Official: penalties, medical problems; self-report: psychological inventories (mixed)
Zamble and Porporino 1988	98	Coping and adaptation to stress	Official: penalties, medical problems; self-report: psychological inventories (mixed)

Official / Citation Measures of Disciplinary Behaviors

Most of the criticism of prison adjustment measures is directed toward official citation measures. Like official crime data, measures formed from prison records of disciplinary citations may "tell us as much about reactions of guards as they do about the activity of inmates" (Poole and Regoli 1980:945). Measures can be marred by officers' selective perceptions of groups of inmates (Boyd 1976; Carroll 1974; Hawkins and Tiedeman 1975; Poole and Regoli 1980) or by their anticipation of difficulties during periods of crisis or overcrowding (Schafer 1984). Some types of citations, such as insubordination, may be used unjustly (Flanagan 1980; Schafer 1984) or may be "fitted" to offensive behavior, as when an officer first decides to discipline an inmate and then finds the rule that best fits the situation (Light 1990; Lombardo 1980).

Organizational factors also may affect the accuracy of citation data (Light 1990). In some organizations, for example, a citation may be viewed as indicating an officer's inability to control the inmate rather than the inmate's inability to adhere to prison rules (Lombardo 1980). Such institutions would look with disfavor on the issuance of citations (Hewitt et al. 1984). Changes in policies and procedures or historical events also can affect changes in citation patterns (Light 1990; Schafer 1984).

The potential for not detecting clandestine incidents is high with official data. Sexual offenses in particular are believed to be underreported (Bowker 1980; Lockwood 1980). In addition to inaccuracy, one must consider the unwieldiness of official data. Typically such data are highly skewed (Megargee and Carbonnel 1985; Wooldredge 1991) and can evidence very low base rates. This is especially true for aggression and victimization measures and creates a number of difficulties, including 1) unstable correlates (S. Gottfredson 1987), 2) a dearth of significant findings based on official data, which then may be found using another data source (e.g., Megargee and Bohn 1979; Megargee and Carbonnel 1985; Van Voorhis 1994), 3) in the case of prediction studies, the problem of overprediction or too many false positives (Clear 1988; S. Gottfredson 1987), and 4) the practice of combining too many criterion measures (each with different reliability and validity) into one composite indicator. Poor base rates also generate design decisions that accommodate the base rate/variability problem but mar the research in other ways, such as 1) creating samples so large (in the thousands) that even the weakest of correlations produces significance, and 2) representing several types of institutions in a single sample, when institutions differ so greatly that the models should be disaggregated.

Self-Report Measures of Disciplinary Behaviors

Self report data, one alternative to the citation data, also warrant caution. As with self-report crime data (Hindelang et al. 1981), the most obvious concern is the inmates' honesty and the resulting accuracy of the data (Wooldredge 1991). In addition, inmates may be unwilling to participate, thereby affecting the representativeness of the data (Wooldredge 1991). Perhaps more subtle than the question of honesty is whether self-report data can be affected by inmates' perceptions, just as official data may be affected by staff members' perceptions. In earlier analyses of these data, for example, we assumed that the self-report data may have shown differential perceptions of attribution. Thus in some instances, some individuals may report more infractions than others because they are quicker to define their behavior as stepping over the line (Van Voorhis 1994).

Despite these difficulties, self-report measures of prison adjustment offer numerous advantages. The most obvious is the opportunity to identify a greater proportion of the prison offenses while at the same time improving the variability of the data over that obtained with official citation data. The measurement error inherent in the citation data translates typically into an underestimation of prison infractions. Evidence of this was found in the research conducted by Hewitt et al. (1984) in which officers saw more than 200 instances of inmate fighting which were not reported, and by Poole and Regoli (1980), in which a comparison of official with self-report data showed a 75 percent discrepancy between the official data (17%) and the self-report data (95%) on rule infractions.

Staff Measures of Disciplinary Behaviors

A third type of criterion measure employs staff evaluations. The most common, the Megargee Prison Adjustment Rating Form and the Megargee Work Performance Rating Form, are routine instruments of case management in most federal prisons. These were developed to provide a more workable alternative to official measures of prison adjustment (e.g., see Fowler and Megargee 1976; Megargee 1972). Most of the measures are five point scales.

Although the staff measures have not received much critical examination, one could speculate that the staff data might suffer from some of the same biases that plague official citation data because both measures reflect staff members' perceptions of inmates. Indeed, the research conducted by Hewett et al. (1984) and by Poole and Regoli (1980) suggests that this is the case.

An unrelated problem is the difficulty of obtaining staff members' evaluations: one must ask busy employees to complete additional paperwork (see Van Voorhis 1994). Overcrowded prison conditions aggravate this situation, because even when the easiest, most efficient observation forms are used, staff members have few opportunities to observe inmates on dimensions identified by the instruments (Van Voorhis 1994). They also may underrate behaviors, such as anxiety, which inmates make less visible in an effort to appear less vulnerable (Bowker 1980).

A final difficulty (one which we encountered in the classification study) concerns staff members' tendency to rate inmates at the scale midpoint (or average). This problem indicated a reluctance to issue negative evaluations unless they were extremely negative. Concern emanated (as some employees told us) from heightened fear of inmates' litigation against staff members (Van Voorhis 1994).

The staff data, however, have distinct advantages. Most notably, researchers benefit by the ability to construct scales that help smooth the distribution and prevent the skewness of data that is such a bane to the researcher using official measures. This advantage in itself may produce more workable tests in which researchers obtain more significant and more theoretically relevant findings with the staff criterion measures than with the official measures (Megargee and Bohn 1979; Megargee and Carbonnel 1985; Van Voorhis 1994). The trade-off, however, is the loss of the opportunity to tap discrete events. In the present study, for example, staff members were asked to rate tendencies such as "how aggressive is this inmate?" on a five-point scale, which may or may not reflect actual aggressive incidents.

In considering the three types of measures, each data source appears to have its advantages as well as its unique source of measurement error. It is not clear, for example, that official prison data is inherently flawed and therefore should be replaced by other outcome measures. In fact, the ideal, according to Farrington and Tarling (1985), is to use multiple measures of outcome. This could facilitate construction of a composite measure, but often the differences between the data sources are so profound that it is better to use each measure separately. For our purposes, the availability of alternative indicators provides a valuable opportunity to explore these issues in greater detail.

MEASUREMENT THEORY: THE IMPORTANCE OF MULTIPLE MEASURES

Our problem is one of measuring the abstract concept of prison adjustment, which is common to many theories and investigations in corrections. Even when we subdivide that concept into component problems such as aggression, drug and alcohol use, insubordination, and victimizations, the path from the abstract concepts to empirical indicators of the same is a crucial task of social science, which is achieved with varying degrees of success and ease. Theoretically an epistemic correlation, one between the indicator and the theoretical concept, would tell us how well we had measured the abstract concept (see Sullivan and Feldman 1979). The epistemic correlation would be the true indicator of the measure's validity, but we cannot correlate an indicator with an abstract concept. It is possible, however, to test the relationship between an indicator of a concept and an alternative indicator of the same concept. Even more useful would be a systematic comparison of correlations among both similar *and* dissimilar measures.

One such approach, the Multitrait-Multimethod Matrix, was proposed by Campbell and Fiske (1959) in the late 1950s as a vehicle for facilitating the measurement of validity. This process focuses on a comparison of two notions, convergent validity and discriminant validity. Simply put, indicators of identical concepts should converge, or show high correlations; indicators of different concepts should not. On the Campbell and Fiske scheme, the extent to which we see convergence across similar constructs and divergence across dissimilar ones is the extent to which we can place confidence in the validity of any single indicator.

The matrix is shown in Table 2. Required for its use are at least two different traits measured in at least two different ways. The matrix displays four different types of correlations. The first type (R), shown in the major diagonals, consists of reliability coefficients (e.g., interrater, split-half, internal consistency).

The second type of correlation (V) shows the measure of association between different measures of similar traits. These are of crucial importance because they represent the construct validity of the trait under consideration. The criteria set forth by Campbell and Fiske (1959) assert that these correlations should be significant and at least of moderate strength. They are located in the internal diagonals between the triangles.[2]

[2] The staff measures do not form a diagonal line, because there were fewer staff criterion measures than official and self-report measures.

Table 2. Multitrait-Multimethod Matrix

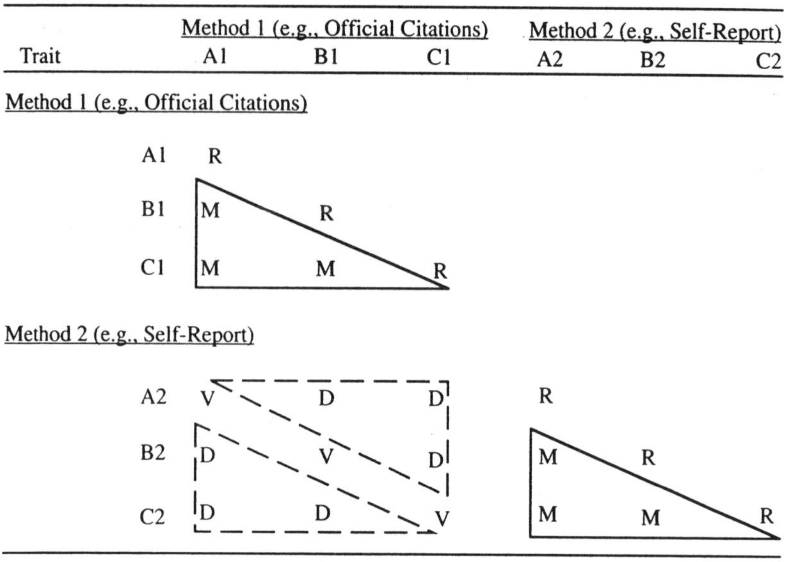

		Method 1 (e.g., Official Citations)			Method 2 (e.g., Self-Report)		
Trait		A1	B1	C1	A2	B2	C2
Method 1 (e.g., Official Citations)							
	A1	R					
	B1	M	R				
	C1	M	M	R			
Method 2 (e.g., Self-Report)							
	A2	V	D	D	R		
	B2	D	V	D	M	R	
	C2	D	D	V	M	M	R

Source: Campbell and Fiske (1959)

A third type of correlation (M) exists between different traits measured by the same method, such as between a self-report measure of aggressive behaviors and a self-report measure of victimization experiences. These are enclosed in the solid triangles. Although a valid relationship between these different traits will produce a correlation, *strong* correlations are considered to be artifacts of the identical measurement strategies. Validity coefficients (V) are expected to surpass M coefficients.

The remaining correlation (D) occurs between different traits measured in different ways (different-trait, different-methods correlations) and appears within the dashed lines. These should conform to a similar pattern in each triangle. If, for example, a self-report measure of victimizations correlates with an official measure of aggression, similar relationships should be noted in other triangles.

Finally, each validity correlation is expected to be stronger than all different-trait, different-method coefficients located in the same row or column as the validity coefficient but within the dashed triangles adjacent to the validity coefficient.

Researchers do not agree on how closely the data must conform to the Campbell and Fiske criteria to be considered valid (Sullivan and Feldman 1979). In fact, some of the criteria are quite difficult;

presumably, factors other than validity (or reliability) could affect the magnitude of the correlations between measures.[3] Moreover, measures of similar constructs may operationalize the construct in slightly different ways that accommodate the measurement medium. Self-report measures of aggression, for example, are noted to tap less serious forms of aggression, just as self-report crime measures tap less serious crimes than official measures. Thus, although the multitrait, multimethod matrix is a valuable means of assessing validity, it also can be used to acquire a clearer understanding of the strengths and weaknesses of different data sources. We employ it for these two purposes in this study. In doing so, we can ultimately examine how our understanding of empirical measures also might qualify knowledge.

METHODOLOGY

Data for this study were obtained at the federal penitentiary in Terre Haute, Indiana from September 1986 to July 1988. The penitentiary is rated Level 4/5, a low-maximum security facility on the Federal Bureau of Prisons (FBOP) security continuum.

Sample Selection

A total of 179 penitentiary inmates participated in the larger study. Participants were selected randomly from a pool of potential subjects who met the following criteria: 1) newly admitted and identified for participation within one month of prison intake, 2) not anticipating an early release or transfer, and 3) able to read, write, and speak English. Participation was voluntary; the response rate was 76 percent.[4]

The present study uses a subsample of the larger sample, the 111 inmates (62%) for whom a complete set of follow-up data was available. This decision was made in order to keep the various tests as comparable as possible and to avoid tests that could differ by as much as 68 subjects, depending on the follow-up variable. Most of the data attrition occurred on an inmate survey rather than on the citation measures or staff rating forms. It is important to note that data attrition on the survey was not necessarily due to an inmate's refusal to complete a self-report account of his behavior while in prison. The survey was not a part of the original study design; in fact, it was implemented eight months later than the ideal follow-up point (see Van Voorhis 1994 for additional details). At that

[3] Some examples would be 1) the level of measurement (e.g., interval versus dichotomous), 2) the distribution of cases on each indicator, and 3) the dispersion or range of values on each indicator.

[4] See Van Voorhis (1994) for further details concerning sample selection.

point, paid work assignments and transfers contributed to the data attrition problem. Nevertheless, the subsample of surveyed inmates does not differ significantly from the entire sample on background factors such as age, race, education, employment status, prior record, and WAIS-R (Shipley) scores.

Sample Characteristics

Members of this subsample ranged in age from 19 to 63 (mean=33, median=31). Fifty-one percent of the participants were white; African Americans, American Indians, Hispanics, and Asians comprised the other 49 percent. Forty-four inmates (40%) were married. At the time of their arrest, 69 (66%) of the subjects were unemployed, 46 (42%) had not finished high school, and an additional 23 (21%) had acquired a GED.

Prior adult and/or juvenile records characterized 96 percent of the sample; 67 percent had served one or more prior prison terms. Many of the same subjects showed poor adjustment to prior sanctions, including prior prison escapes (17, 20%), probation revocations (28, 41%), and parole revocations (26, 46%).

The subjects were convicted of a broad array of federal offenses, including 1) drug-related offenses (26%), 2) violent offenses (16%), 3) fraud (5%), 4) theft (1%), 5) illegal operations (5%), 6) bank crimes (27%), 7) postal crimes (2%), 8) firearms and weapons charges (18%). Fifty-two percent (56) of the participants used weapons while committing the offense that led to their conviction.

Data Collection

At admission to prison, project staff members administered psychological classification instruments to inmates and obtained social, demographic, and criminal record data. They tracked participants for six months in order to obtain follow-up data consisting of official reports of disciplinary infractions, staff assessments of prison adjustment and work performance, and self-report surveys. In addition, an intake interview obtained inmates' perceptions of how they would cope with prison difficulties.

Measurement of Personality Variables

Four personality variables are introduced as independent variables for a portion of the subsequent analyses. We do not put these forward in order to study personality, but rather to illustrate how that study is affected by one's choice of a criterion variable. The four types considered (aggressive, dependent, neurotic, and situational) were obtained from the Jesness Inventory Classification

System (Jesness and Wedge 1983). These descriptions of personality types are somewhat self-explanatory except for the situational type, which is described in several correctional classification systems (e.g., Jesness and Wedge 1983; Quay 1983, 1984; Warren et al. 1966) as an inmate who became involved in criminal behavior as a response to a recent crisis or emotional change. Such inmates typically do not have extensive prior records or prison experience.

Measurement of Criterion Variables

Table 3 shows the distributions of inmates across the criterion variables that form the focus of this study. We employed four very different measurement strategies; these are described in greater detail below. Measures of all four traits (aggression, victimizations, insubordination, drug and alcohol use) were obtained from the prison records, the interview, and the survey. Staff evaluation forms provided data only on aggression and insubordination.

Table 3. Frequency and Percentage Distribution of Disciplinary, Interview, Survey, and Staff Variables

Variable	N	Percentage[a]	Reliability
Official Disciplinary Citations			
Aggression[b]			NC
No citations	106	96	
1 or 2	4	4	
	110	100	
Insubordination[b]			
No citations	93	84	NC
1 or 2	17	17	
	110	100	
Official Protection from Victimization[c]			
No instances	106	95	NC
Protection	5	5	
	111	100	
Drug and/or Alcohol Citations[b]			NC
None	102	93	
1 or 2	8	7	
	110	100	
Self-Report Intake Interview Rating Items[d]			
Will Fight If Necessary (Aggression)			
No	32	32	
Yes	69	68	87%
	101	100	
Believes in Doing His Own Time (Insubordination)			
Yes	76	74	
No	27	26	61%
	103	100	
Concern with Personal Safety While Incarcerated (Victimization)			
No	92	89	
Yes	11	11	88%
	103	100	

Table 3 (continued)

Variable	N	Percentage[a]	Reliability
Will Use Drugs or Alcohol to Deal with Prison Difficulties			
No	98	95	
Yes	5	5	79%
	103	100	
Self-Report Follow-Up Survey Items[e]			
Aggressive Behaviors			
None	76	69	
1	26	24	.71
2 or more	8	08	
	110	101	
Will Tell Staff When I Don't Think They Are Doing Their Job (Insubordination)			
No	86	77	
Yes (not helpful)	15	14	na
Yes (helpful)	6	6	
Yes (very helpful)	3	3	
	111	100	
Victimizing Experiences			
None	57	51	
1	47	42	
2 or more	7	6	.75
	111	100	
Drug or Alcohol Use			
None	80	73	
1	22	20	
2 or more	8	7	.55
	110	100	
Staff Evaluations (Megargee Prison Adjustment Measures)[f]			
Verbal and Physical Aggressiveness			
Very passive	4	4	
Not aggressive unless provoked	52	47	
Not aggressive	43	39	.63
Hostile	10	9	
Extremely hostile	2	2	
	111	100	
Response to Supervision			
Excellent	5	4	
Good	47	42	
Fair	44	40	.75
Resists/ignores suggestions	13	12	
Very poor	2	2	
	111	100	
Fails to Obey Rules			
No	99	89	
Yes	12	11	.51
	111	100	

[a] Percentages may not sum to 100 because of rounding.
[b] Rate of incidents (number of incidents/N months follow-up)×100.
[c] Dichotomous item indicating whether or not the inmate received official means of protection during the monitoring period.
[d] Reliability figures represent percentage of interrater reliability.
[e] Cumulative indexes; reliability represented by Cronbach's alpha.
[f] Average of three evaluations taken at the fourth, fifth, and sixth month of the monitoring period. Reliability represented by Cronbach's alpha.

Definitions of each measure are shown in the appendix. As can be seen, definitions are not identical across similar measures. For example, the offense of insubordination in this setting referred to violations of staff orders or prison policies. It was easier to locate a staff evaluation measure that fit the official disciplinary definition than to fit interview or survey measures to that designation. Nevertheless, the interview measure "doing one's own time" appeared to be a reasonable measure of insubordination because the inmates who were *not* doing their own time were likely to bring unnecessary difficulties upon themselves. The survey item, which referred to the inmate's report that he would tell staff members when they weren't doing their job, fits some notions of insubordination in its indication that staff members would be confronted.

The items also differ in whether they tap actual events or tendencies. Indeed, two of the measures, the interview items and the staff evaluations, have no reference to events. Interview items tap the inmate's preferred methods of coping with prison difficulties; staff ratings reflect the staff's perceptions of an inmate's tendency to behave in a certain way.

Officially recorded disciplinary infractions and victimizations. These data were obtained by examining each inmate's central file six months after admission. The research staff recorded disciplinary reports and records of protective custody. For three of the measures (aggression, insubordination, and drug/alcohol citation), an incident was coded as an official citation after a disciplinary hearing had confirmed the citation. To correct for the different follow-up periods that had occurred for 4 percent of the subjects, we divided the total number of disciplinary citations by the number of follow-up months available and multiplied the result by 100. The remaining item, denoting prison victimizations, is dichotomous and indicates whether or not the inmate received official forms of protection.

Interview rating items. Within one month of admission, inmates participated in a long interview in which they were asked to discuss whether they expected difficulties while in prison and, if so, how they planned to cope with them. In more direct questions, they were asked whether they would fight if necessary or seek help from prison officials. Interrater reliability ranges from a low of 61 percent (belief in doing one's own time) to a high of 88 percent (expresses a need for personal safety).

Unlike the other follow-up measures, these items are proscriptive and were not designed to represent actual behaviors. We sought to determine what the inmate considered doing (or needing) rather than whether he had engaged in these behaviors.

Self-report (survey) items. Follow-up surveys were administered to inmates at least four months after prison admission. With the exception of one item (will tell staff when they are not doing their job), the measures shown in Table 3 are cumulative indexes that combine two or more items under the broader behaviors of aggression, victimization, or drugs and alcohol. Each item within the respective indexes asked the inmate to indicate the number of times he had experienced a given event or engaged in a particular behavior. The options were 1) "never," 2) "once," 3) "a few times (2-8 times)," and 4) "many times (more than 8 times)." The index scores represent an average of all the items contained in the index.

Because the survey was not implemented until nine months after the beginning of the project, and because we needed to obtain data on as many cases as possible, the follow-up time period was often longer than four months. In this sample, for example, follow-up time frames ranged from three to 36 months (mean=7.2 months, median=6 months). Correlations, however, between a variable denoting the number of months intervening between prison admission and the completion of the follow-up survey and each of the survey variables, were not significant. As a result, no corrections were made to the measures.

Reliability measures (Cronbach's alpha) range from .55 (drugs/alcohol) to .75 (victimizations). Even though the variability on scales such as these is decidedly superior to the disciplinary data discussed above, the scales are, nevertheless, somewhat skewed.

Staff evaluation measures (Megargee Prison Adjustment Form). The Megargee Prison Adjustment Form (Megargee 1972) was administered during the fourth, fifth, and sixth month following prison admission. The score for each variable represents an average of the three evaluations. Measures of aggression (mean=3.3) and response to supervision (mean=3.3) consist of five-point scales; the obedience measure is dichotomous. Measures of internal consistency range from a low of .51 for obedience to a high of .75 for response to supervision.

To facilitate the task of interpreting the research findings, we coded all items so that high scores reflect the dysfunctional behavior. This may be misleading for two measures which are not unidimensional, the interview and the staff aggression measures. Low scores on these measures are also somewhat problematic because they represent a degree of passivity, which is not considered to be adaptive in this type of prison environment (Bowker 1980).

Summary comparison of follow-up measures. It is obvious that if we had limited our analysis to the official measures, we would have achieved a misleading picture of prison adjustment. A cursory overview of Table 3 shows that the official disciplinary data underestimate the extent of prison difficulties. Although we are not confident in estimating the exact size of the discrepancy,[5] we can agree with Poole and Regoli (1980) that self-report data identify more incidents than do the official data. It is also apparent that the distributions for official disciplinary infractions and victimizations are quite limited.

RESULTS

The analysis begins with a multitrait-multimethod matrix for the prison adjustment measures shown in Table 4. Discussion of these findings follows the four criteria set forward above.

Criterion 1: The validity coefficients should be significant and sufficiently large.

An overview of Table 4 shows that significant findings occur in many, but certainly not all, cases,. The most obvious pattern to these validity tests is the correspondence between the two self-report measures (interview and survey) and (to a lesser extent) between the official citation data and the staff evaluations. Three of the four survey measures were validated by an interview measure of the same behaviors, and vice versa. Two of the three staff measures proved to be related significantly to official citations. With only one exception (citations for insubordination), none of the official disciplinary measures were validated by the self-report measures (interview or survey).

In contrast to this pattern is the relatively strong correspondence among most measures of insubordination. Here staff and official assessments often agreed with self-report measures. In fact, the strongest validity correlations involved the staff and survey data: correlations between the two insubordination measures—response to supervision and obeys orders—and the survey measure of insubordination were .21 and .29 respectively. This finding is somewhat surprising in view of the less-than-ideal correspondence among the definitions of each insubordination variable. It may be attributable to the fact that insubordinate inmates are more visible than others; by definition, insubordination cannot be hidden from one's superiors or fellow inmates.

---

5 It is possible that the self-report measures are tapping less serious incidents, but all items on the self-report index theoretically could have resulted in an official citation. The data, however, do not show us why some incidents did not result in a citation (e.g., unobserved, not viewed as serious).

Table 4. Multitrait-Multimethod Matrix for Aggression, Insubordination, Use of Drugs and Alcohol, and Victimizations by Official Prison Data, Interview Data, Self Report Data, and Staff Ratings

	Official Disciplinary Reports				Interview				Self-Report (Inmate) Data				Staff Ratings		
	Aggress.	Insub.	Victim.	Drugs	Aggress.	Insub.	Victim	Drugs	Aggress.	Insub.	Victim	Drugs	Aggress.	Respsup	Obeys
Official Disciplinary Reports															
Aggression	1.00														
Insubordination	.00	1.00													
Victimizations	-.04	.01	1.00												
Alcohol/Drugs	-.05	-.04	-.06	1.00											
Self Report Interview Rating Items															
Aggression	-.06	.05	-.14*	.19**	1.00										
Insubordination (Does his own time)	.01	.15*	.07	-.09	-.21**	1.00									
Victimization	.27***	-.07	.07	.00	.10	-.13*	1.00								
Alcohol/Drugs	-.04	.01	-.05	.08	.16*	-.13*	.07	1.00							
Self Report Survey Measures															
Aggression	.05	.16**	-.12*	-.04	.16**	.08	.03	.05	1.00						
Insubordination (Tells staff when they're not doing their job)	.04	.09	-.10	.06	.17**	-.04	-.01	.11	.15*	1.00					
Victimization	.08	-.03	.05	-.08	-.21**	.08	.20**	-.02	.24***	.08	1.00				
Alcohol/Drugs	-.10	.14*	-.07	.12	.10	-.08	-.10	.23**	.37***	.04	.14*	1.00			
Staff Ratings															
Aggression	.25***	.10	-.16*	.04	.03	.11	.03	.08	.04	.06	-.02	.06	1.00		
Response/Superv.	.23***	.17**	-.06	.16**	.04	.15*	.01	.13*	.09	.21**	.07	.24***	.54***	1.00	
Obeys Rules	.10	.10	.02	.05	-.03	.12	-.05	.11	.19**	.29***	.22***	-.03	.16*	.26***	1.00

*p ≤ .10; **p ≤ .05; ***p≤ .01

On other measures, such as aggression, victimizations, and drug and alcohol use, correspondence depended more strongly on the measure. Taken as a whole, only nine of 21 validity tests produced significant results, and one could argue that these were not strong correlations. On a more optimistic note, 13 of the 15 criterion measures were validated by at least one other measure of the same construct.

Criterion 2: Each validity coefficient should be larger than all different-trait, different-method coefficients located in the same row or column as the validity coefficient but within the dashed triangles adjacent to the validity coefficient.

Of the nine significant validity correlations noted above, six are larger than their respective different-trait, different-methods correlations, or of a similar magnitude. One of the smaller validity correlations involves a correlation between a survey measure of victimization and the interview measure of aggression, which is higher than the correlation between the interview measure and the survey measure of aggression. As will be explained shortly, however, valid relationships appear to exist between aggression and victimizations.

Criterion 3: Each validity coefficient should be larger than coefficients involving different traits but similar measurement strategies.

Differences in the other direction are assumed, on this scheme, to be attributable to measurement effects. Several of the validity coefficients noted above do not meet this criterion. Findings for the staff rating forms in particular suggest that the data are affected by a response set on the part of the staff members; in view of staff members' tendency to rate most inmates at the mean (see Table 3), this finding is not surprising.[6] To a lesser extent, the survey data also showed intercorrelations. Subsequent analyses of these data, however, did not present the types of problems (e.g., duplicative results) that one might expect to find with severe cases of response sets.

---

6 Perhaps this situation is aggravated by the fact that the staff evaluation forms were established tools of case management. They became a part of the inmates' record and affected decisions made on his behalf. Thus it is entirely possible that if these evaluations were used solely for research and not at all for the prison records, researchers might find less conservative responses.

Criterion 4: Each triangle (both the solid and the slashed) should produce the same pattern of correlations.

Although the patterns within each triangle are not identical, we found important patterns in several of the triangles. In several instances, for example, aggression measures correlated with victimization measures. The study yielded a total of 12 such tests; six produced significant, sometimes relatively strong relationships. The observation that some of these correlations are positive and some are negative is more explainable than it would appear to be. Most of the negative relationships involve an aggression variable that taps passivity as well as aggressiveness (e.g., the interview variable and the staff variable). In contrast, the positive correlations are actual victimizations and actual aggressive behavior, as shown by the survey items ($r=.24$, $p \leq .01$). Taken together, these findings suggest that passivity and fear of victimization contribute to an inmate's being victimized. Once actual behaviors are considered, however, the line between the victimizers and the victimized becomes thin. Positive correlations here mean that inmates both act aggressively and experienced their aggression reciprocated from their fellow inmates.

Table 4 also reveals a pattern of relationships between insubordination variables and aggression variables, both within the solid triangles (e.g., staff measures, survey measures, and interview measures) and within the dashed triangles (e.g., interview and survey, survey and disciplinary, disciplinary and staff, and survey and staff evaluations). The negative relationship between the interview measure of insubordination and the interview measure of aggression, in contrast to the other positive relationships, may be attributable to the manner in which the constructs are operationalized. The ideas of staying out of trouble and of fighting, but only if necessary, *are* compatible in prison cultures.

Another pattern is evident in the drug measures: these are observed to be related to insubordination in five instances and to aggression in three, thus suggesting that drug/alcohol use relates to a variety of additional difficulties.

The failure to obtain greater correspondence between staff data and inmate data suggests that researchers risk portraying different impressions of prison adjustment, depending on their choice of criterion measures.

Prison Adjustment across Different Criterion Measures

Because different data sets portray prison adjustment differently, it makes sense to suggest that these differences in portrayals then might affect the covariates of prison adjustment in important ways. Accordingly, we examined the role of personality and demographic factors on prison disciplinary behaviors. These variables were selected to illuminate measurement issues, not the matter of personality and prison adjustment. More in-depth discussions of personality and prison adjustment are available elsewhere (Van Voorhis 1993, 1994).

The first analysis, appearing in Table 5, shows the bivariate measures of the relationship between four personality traits and measures of aggression and victimizations. The findings with respect to aggression suggest that our understanding of aggressive behavior is best offered by the self-report and the staff data. The official data suffer from low base rates and extremely skewed distributions. Both the staff and the self-report data, however, show that aggressive personality types evidence aggressive behaviors. Both measures reveal something that the citation data do not show: the neurotic inmates also evidence aggressive tendencies. This finding is quite consistent with descriptions of the neurotic personality. Dependent and situational inmates appear to be more aggressive on self-report data than on staff and official data, but their relative position as the least aggressive inmates is similar to that shown on the staff data. Only the findings for the tests of the staff data are significant.

Table 5. Effects of Personality Variables on Official, Self-Report, and Staff Measures of Aggression and on Official and Self-Report Measures of Victimizations

	Aggression									Victimizations					
	Official Aggression[a]			Self-Report Index[b]			Staff Rating			Official Victimization			Self-Report Index[c]		
Measure	%[d]	$\bar{X}$	N	%[e]	$\bar{X}$	N	%[f]	$\bar{X}$	N	%	$\bar{X}$	N	%[g]	$\bar{X}$	N
Aggressive	5	1.34	57	32	1.27	56	17	2.85	57	4	1.04	57	49	1.31	57
Neurotic	0	0.00	18	50	1.37	18	11	2.80	18	0	1.00	18	44	1.41	18
Dependent	7	0.98	15	27	1.12	15	0	2.57	17	7	1.06	15	53	1.32	15
Situational	0	0.00	18	16	1.11	19	0	2.62	19	11	1.10	19	47	1.34	19
							chi-square=6.7* Tau$_c$=-.16**								

[a] Rate per month × 100.
[b] Scale includes use of verbal threats, insults and attacks on others. Alpha=.71. Higher values denote aggression.
[c] Scale includes threats and insults from other inmates, attacks and pressures for sex. Alpha=.75. Higher values denote victimizations.
[d] Percentage with at least one disciplinary report.
[e] Percentage scoring 2.0 and above on this scale, indicating aggressive infractions.
[f] Percentage rated higher than 3, indicating unsatisfactory performance.
[g] Percentage scoring 2.0 and above, indicating victimizations.
*p≤.10; **p≤.05; ***p≤.01

Official criterion measures of victimizations are also marred by low base rates and by the fact that this sample is not large enough to compensate for those rates. Neither test was significant.

Personality effects on insubordination and on drug and alcohol measures are shown in Table 6. Results across insubordination measures show a relatively high rate of official citations for the situational inmates. On self-report measures, however, these inmates indicate that they are not over assertive with superiors, and staff members rate them as responding well to authority. Both the survey and the staff evaluation tests produced significant results. This strange reversal of findings for the situational inmates (high citations for less serious infractions and good performance in self-report and staff data) was found frequently in the larger study, even with different diagnoses of situational types (Van Voorhis 1994).

Table 6. Effects of Personality Variables on Official, Self-Report, and Staff Measures of Insubordination and on Official and Self-Report Measures of Drug and Alcohol Use

	Insubordination									Drug and Alcohol Use					
	Official Citations[a]			Self-Report Index			Staff Rating			Official Citations[a]			Self-Report Index		
Personality Type	%[b]	$\bar{X}$	N	%[c]	$\bar{X}$	N	%[d]	$\bar{X}$	N	%[b]	$\bar{X}$	N	%[e]	$\bar{X}$	N
Aggressive	14	2.68	57	32	1.56	57	18	2.79	57	12	2.08	57	25	1.24	57
Neurotic	6	1.85	18	11	1.11	18	17	2.88	18	6	1.00	18	67	1.83	18
Dependent	13	1.96	15	27	1.48	15	13	2.73	15	0	0.00	15	7	1.06	15
Situational	33	5.55	18	0	1.00	19	0	2.52	19	0	0.00	18	11	1.14	19
					mr=.28**									mr=.43***	
				chi-square=9.8***									chi-square=20.3***		
					Tau_c=-.22**			Tau_c=-.11*			Tau_c=-.11*				

[a] Rate per month × 100.
[b] Percentage with at least one disciplinary report.
[c] Percentage scoring 2.0 and above on this scale, indicating insubordination.
[d] Percentage rated higher than 3, indicating unsatisfactory performance.
[e] Percentage scoring 2.0 and above on this scale, indicating drug or alcohol use.
*p≤.10; **p≤.05; ***p≤.01

Neurotic inmates report far more incidents of drug use than do inmates classified into the other personality groups. On official citation measures, however, aggressive inmates are slightly more likely than neurotics and others to be cited for drug and alcohol violations.

Multivariate analyses. We expanded this exploration to a multivariate test of the role of personality in comparison with more traditional predictors of adjustment. This step is useful primarily in examining the comparative effects of demographic and personality factors. At this point, given the constraints of a limited sample size, we present these findings as tentative and as warranting further research. The findings nevertheless offer important suggestions.

Table 7 shows a pattern suggesting that demographic factors emerge primarily on the models which employ official measures of disciplinary problems, but not on the self-report measures or the staff measures (with the exception of a correlation between age and staff ratings of insubordination). Race, which correlates moderately high with official citation data, is not found to be a significant predictor of self-report insubordination; this finding is analogous those for the crime data.

Table 7. Effects of Personality Variables and Background Variables on Official, Self-Report, and Staff Measures of Aggression and Insubordination and on Official and Self-Report Measures of Drug and Alcohol Use (Beta)

	Aggression			Insubordination			Drug and Alcohol Use	
	Official	Self-Report	Staff	Official	Self-Report	Staff	Official	Self-Report
Aggressive	.02	.16	.27*	.17	.02	.03	.22	.11
Neurotic	-.09	.17	.17	.13	-.18	.11	.11	.47***
Dependent	ref	ref	ref	ref	ref	ref	ref	ref
Situational	-.07	-.01	.07	.26**	-.21*	-.09	.02	-.02
Revoke/Escape	-.14	-.01	-.04	.00	-.03	-.08	-.01	-.02
Prior Time	.07	-.02	-.01	.09	-.02	—	.21**	.04
Age	-.10	-.07	-.06	.17*	-.07	-.18*	-.06	-.12
Race	.06	-.03	.09	.26***	.01	.13	.05	-.05
R^2	.05	.05	.06	.12	.08	.10	.08	.20
F	.75	.78	.99	2.04**	1.33	1.58*	1.31	3.63***

*p≤.10; **p≤.05; ***p≤.01

As in the bivariate findings reported in Tables 5 and 6, the effect of personality changes in important ways across data sources.[7] With few exceptions, findings are similar to those noted in Tables 5 and 6. The one exception occurs on the staff insubordination model, where the effect of the situational factor is now insignificant; perhaps it is attenuated by controlling for age and race.

DISCUSSION

Although these findings compellingly illustrate the importance of criterion measurements to our understanding of prison adjustment, they warrant three cautions. First, a larger sample will be

[7] The victimization models also are not compared because the official victimization variable was dichotomous and therefore did not meet the assumptions of OLS. Regression of the predictor variables on the self-report measure of victimization, however, reveals a frequently observed racial correlate whereby whites are more likely than others to be victimized (see Bowker 1980).

needed if we are to explore this question further. Although the sample was large enough for the bivariate analysis comprising most of this paper, the multivariate analysis (Table 7) was conducted on a sample size of only 111 inmates. As a result, relatively high betas did not achieve significance because of limited degrees of freedom. In addition, a larger sample would have afforded an opportunity to cross-validate findings to check the possibility that some of the findings might have been attributable to chance, particularly in view of the large number of tests we performed.

Second, having initiated a much different study than what we present here, we did not collect the data needed to explore these results further. Thus it is not possible to determine whether differences across criterion measures are due to officers' use of discretion, to their difficulties in detecting certain behaviors, or to differences in perceptions held by inmates and by staff.

Third, the task of comparing these measures was somewhat challenging. Measures were not identical across similar behaviors, and a strict application of the Campbell and Fiske design might have required greater similarity. These data, for example, do not equate severity of offenses. Nevertheless, the analysis selected measures typically available to prison researchers, ones which historically have been crucial to our knowledge of prison adjustment.

In the larger study of crime causation, crime measurement has received ongoing scrutiny; corrections scholars have devoted less attention to a similar inquiry. Yet, in examining the prison criteria, we observe some of the same issues as plague the crime data: 1) official data underestimate the actual magnitude of problem behaviors in prison; 2) extralegal correlates are found with official data (and, to a lesser extent, with the staff data) that are not found with self-report data; 3) we may debate the same issue of observers' bias versus respondents' honesty; and 4) low base rates plague official measures.

Despite these precautions, the preceding analyses produced some favorable results: 1) 13 of the 15 criterion measures were validated by at least one measure of the same behavioral problem, and 2) results of bivariate and multivariate analyses of these data produced valuable findings and patterns that lend themselves to reasonable interpretations. Yet it is obvious that these findings depended largely on the type of criterion measure used; this is an important area for discussion at this point.

Our understanding of the impact of psychological classification types would have been marred seriously by limiting our criterion measures to official citation data. One gains, for example, an entirely different understanding of neurotic inmates when we compare the official understanding of their behavior with their own. Also, situational inmates create an impression with the staff which seems to fit their own perceptions of their intentions. The results of the citation data analysis, however, suggest that things break down during their early days in the institution, at least in regard to less serious forms of behavior. A more comprehensive account of the relationship between personality and prison adjustment is available elsewhere (Van Voorhis 1993, 1994). Relevant to this inquiry, however, is the fact that personality effects will be detected on some types of measures and not on others. This is understandable because in all likelihood, personality is related not only to the behaviors in question, but also to whether one will 1) be caught committing a prison infraction, 2) define one's own behavior in a negative light, 3) express fear of victimizations, and 4) present a favorable impression to the staff.

Findings for demographic factors also appear to depend on our choice of criterion variables. In earlier analyses, age, race, and prior prison escapes or probation/parole revocations were related to official data (and in one case to a staff measure), but not to self-report or to most of the staff measures. Similar findings have been noted for comparisons of official with self-report crime measures (Farrington 1985). Despite their consistency, findings such as these have disturbing implications for the use of prison risk assessment classification systems because typically they are constructed through the use of citation data and because they identify demographic, social, and prior record measures as predictors.

Unfortunately, it is more difficult to propose solutions than to identify strengths and weaknesses of the various indicators of correctional behavior. Traditional applications of multiple indicators are not likely to help this situation. Results such as these, for example, argue against the development of composite indexes of adjustment. The differences in patterns of agreement among similar measures do not appear to support the combination of these measures. Even on the criterion measures of insubordination, which showed the greatest overall agreement whether furnished by staff or by inmates, effects differed across different measures of insubordination.

Alternatively, we could select the most adequate measures from among all that were tested. For example, if staff and self-report measures of aggression are validated by at least one other measure of aggression, why not use them rather than the official data, which pose base rate problems? Perhaps we would prefer the self-report indicators of substance abuse to official data, especially because self-reported drug abuse does not present the problem of tapping a less serious form of behavior. With proper precautions, such observations might suggest greater use of staff data *and* self-report data, at least for research purposes. Such use, would increase the opportunity to study problems such as aggression, which traditionally have been difficult to examine because of low base rates (e.g., see Monahan 1981; Steadman and Cocozza 1974; Monahan and Steadman, 1994).

This approach would appear to be advisable, but how might we respond to the policy maker who argues that official data represent objective, observable, and verifiable actual events? Such data would withstand legal challenges far better than a staff member's assessment of a tendency. Official data also direct us toward clear criteria for decision making because the correlates of predictive models are demographic and record factors. If we then incorporate these factors into risk assessment measures, we have constructed an instrument that will not require staff members to make subjective assessments.

This research, however, has bolstered our confidence in official data in only limited ways. We can be somewhat optimistic about the observation that official citations for aggression correlated with staff assessments of aggressive behavior. We also might be tempted to observe that the official insubordination measure *was* validated by correlations with several alternative measures. Yet this observation might prove less optimistic once we observed that most of these were correlations with recalcitrant attitudes of inmates who failed to "do their own time" or who were critical of staff members' performance. Such findings prompt us to ask, with other scholars, "Which comes first—the rule violation or the irritating behavior?" (Flanagan 1980; Light 1990; Lombardo 1980; Schafer 1984). This consideration is underscored by the fact that *most* disciplinary infractions *are* for insubordination. Thus studies that combine all disciplinary infractions into a single indicator may be studying mostly insubordinate behaviors.

Moreover, this and other studies make it apparent that the theoretically relevant findings emerge more frequently from staff and self-report measures than from citation data (Megargee and Bohn 1979; Megargee and Carbonnel 1985; Van Voorhis 1993). In part this may be due to limited base rates and uneven distributions of the citation data, but one cannot ignore the effects of omitting unobserved behaviors (Monahan and Steadman, 1994).

The conclusions at this point would appear to favor multiple indicators of adjustment, used with precautions pertinent to the measurement. Most commonly, the result would be a comparison of similar models across separate analyses for each criterion. As with those analyses of the crime data which wisely employ multiple criterion measures, the results represent a balanced comparison of findings for similar models across different measures of the same problem behavior, tempered by knowledge of the limitations and benefits of each data source. Such a process seems far superior to overreliance on official citation data. It is definitely preferable to the design decisions that sometimes are required if one is to use official data.

The results of this study suggest that most criterion measures of prison adjustment are reasonably valid, but that different types of measures pose different sources of potential bias and measurement error. Most important, as with the crime data, we have a reasonably clear understanding of *how* these data perform and where the biases are; our research should strive to reflect that understanding.

REFERENCES

Adams, K. (1983) "Former Mental Patients in a Prison and Parole System: A Study of Socially Disruptive Behavior." *Criminal Justice and Behavior* 10:358-84.

Bowker, L. (1980) *Prison Victimization.* New York: Elsevier.

Boyd, J. (1976) "Race of Inmate, Race of Officer, and Disciplinary Proceedings at a Federal Correctional Institution." *FCI Research Reports* 8:1-31.

Campbell, D. and D. Fiske (1959) "Convergent and Discriminant Validation by the Multitrait-Multimethod Matrix." *Psychological Bulletin* 56:81-105.

Carbonnel, J., E. Megargee, and K. Moorhead (1984). "Predicting Prison Adjustment with Structured Personality Inventories." *Journal of Consulting and Clinical Psychology.* 52:280-94.

Carroll, L. (1974) *Hacks, Blacks, and Cons: Race Relations in a Maximum Security Prison.* Lexington, MA: Lexington Books.

Clear, T. (1988) "Statistical Prediction in Corrections." *Research in Corrections* 1:1-39.

Clemmer, D. (1940) *The Prison Community.* New York: Rinehart.

Edinger, J. (1979) "Cross Validation of the Megargee MMPI Typology for Prisoners." *Journal of Consulting and Clinical Psychology* 47:234-42.

Edinger, J., D. Reuterfors, and P. Logue (1982) "Cross-Validation of the Megargee MMPI Typology: A Study of Specialized Inmate Populations." *Criminal Justice and Behavior* 9:184-203.

Ekland-Olson, S., D. Barrick, and L. Cohen (1983) "Prison Overcrowding and Disciplinary Problems: An Analysis of the Texas Prison System." *Journal of Applied Behavioral Science* 19:163-76.

Farrington, D. (1985) "Predicting Self-Reported and Official Delinquency." In D. Farrington and R. Tarling (eds.), *Prediction in Criminology*, pp. 150-73. Albany: SUNY Press.

Farrington, D. and R. Tarling (1985) "Criminological Prediction: An Introduction." In D. Farrington and R. Tarling (eds.), *Prediction in Criminology*, pp. 2-33. Albany: SUNY Press.

Flanagan, T. (1980) "Time Served and Institutional Misconduct: Patterns of Involvement in Disciplinary Infractions among Long-Term and Short-Term Inmates." *Journal of Criminal Justice* 8:357-67.

——— (1983) "Correlates of Institutional Misconduct Among State Prisoners." *Criminology* 21:29-39.

Fowler, M. and E. Megargee (1976) "Psychometric Characteristics of Megargee's Work Performance and Interpersonal Adjustment Rating Schedules." *Criminal Justice and Behavior* 3:361-70.

Gaes, G. and W. McGuire (1985) "Prison Violence: The Contribution of Crowding versus Other Determinants of Prison Assault Rates." *Journal of Research in Crime and Delinquency* 22:41-65.

Goetting, A. and R. Howsen (1986) "Correlates of Prisoner Misconduct." *Journal of Quantitative Criminology* 2:49-67.

Gottfredson, D. (1987) "Prediction and Classification in Criminal Justice Decision Making." In D. Gottfredson and M. Tonry (eds.), *Prediction and Classification: Criminal Justice Decision Making*, pp. 1-20. Chicago: University of Chicago Press.

Gottfredson, D. and M. Gottfredson (1980) "Data for Criminal Justice Evaluation: Some Resources and Pitfalls." In M. Klein and K. Teilmann (eds.), *Handbook of Criminal Justice Evaluation*, pp. 97-118. Beverly Hills: Sage.

Gottfredson, S. (1987) "Prediction: An Overview of Selected Methodological Issues." In D. Gottfredson and M. Tonry (eds.), *Prediction and Classification: Criminal Justice Decision Making*, pp. 21-51. Chicago: University of Chicago Press.

Hanson, R., C. Moss, R. Hosford, and M. Johnson, M. (1983) "Predicting Inmate Penitentiary Adjustment: An Assessment of Four Classificatory Methods." *Criminal Justice and Behavior* 10:293-309.

Hawkins, R. and G. Tiedeman (1975) *The Creation of Deviance: Interpersonal and Organizational Determinants*. Columbus, OH: Merrill.

Hewitt, J., E. Poole, and R. Regoli (1984) "Self-Reported and Observed Rule Breaking in Prison: A Look at Disciplinary Response." *Justice Quarterly* 1:437-47.

Hindelang, M., T. Hirschi, and J. Weis (1981) *Measuring Delinquency*. Beverly Hills: Sage.

Hokanson, J., E. Megargee, S. O'Hagan, and A. Perry (1976) "Behavioral, Emotional, and Autonomic Reactions to Stress among Incarcerated Youthful Offenders." *Criminal Justice and Behavior* 3:203-34.

Holland, T. and N. Holt (1980) "Correctional Classification and the Prediction of Institutional Adjustment." *Criminal Justice and Behavior* 7:51-60.

Irwin, J. and D. Cressey (1962) "Thieves, Convicts, and the Inmate Culture." *Social Problems* 10:142-55.

Jesness, C. and R. Wedge (1983) *Classifying Offenders: The Jesness Inventory Classification System*. Sacramento, CA: California Youth Authority.

Jones, T., W. Beidleman, and R. Fowler (1981) "Differentiating Violent and Nonviolent Prison Inmates by Use of Selected MMPI Scales." *Journal of Clinical Psychology* 37:673-78.

Light, S. (1990) "Measurement Error in Official Statistics: Prison Rule Infraction Data." *Federal Probation* 54:63-68.

——— (1991) "Assault on Prison Officers: Interactional Themes." *Justice Quarterly* 8:243-61.

Lockwood, D. (1980) *Prison Sexual Violence*. New York: Elsevier.

Lombardo, L. (1980) *Guards Imprisoned: Correctional Officers at Work*. New York: Elsevier.

Louscher, P., R. Hosford, and C. Moss (1983) "Predicting Dangerous Behavior in a Penitentiary Using the Megargee Typology." *Criminal Justice and Behavior* 10:263-68.

MacKenzie, D. (1987) "Age and Adjustment to Prison: Interactions with Attitudes and Anxiety." *Criminal Justice and Behavior* 14:427-47.

Megargee, E. (1972) "Standardized Reports of Work Performance and Inmate Adjustment for Use in Correctional Settings." *Correctional Psychologist* 5:48-54.

Megargee, E. and M. Bohn (1979) *Classifying Criminal Offenders: A New System Based on the MMPI*. Beverly Hills: Sage.

Megargee, E. and J. Carbonell (1985) "Predicting Prison Adjustment with MMPI Correctional Scales." *Journal of Consulting and Clinical Psychology* 53:874-83.

Monahan, J. (1981) *Predicting Violent Behavior: An Assessment of Clinical Techniques*. Beverly Hills: Sage.

Monahan, J. and H. Steadman (1994) "Toward a Rejuvenation of Risk Assessment Research." In J. Monahan and H. Steadman (eds.), *Violence and Mental Disorder: Developments in Risk Assessment*, pp. 1-17. Chicago: University of Chicago Press.

Myers, L. and G. Levy (1978) "Description and Prediction of the Intractable Inmate." *Journal of Research in Crime and Delinquency* 15:214-28.

Nacci, P., H. Teitelbaum, and J. Prather (1977) "Population Density and Inmate Misconduct Rates in the Federal Prison System." *Federal Probation* 41:26-31.

National Institute of Corrections (NIC) (1982). *Classification: Principles, Models, and Guidelines*. Washington, DC: U.S. Department of Justice.

Poole, E. and R. Regoli (1980) "Race, Institutional Rule Breaking, and Disciplinary Response: A Study of Discretionary Decision Making in Prison." *Law and Society Review* 14:931-46.

Quay, H. (1983) *Technical Manual for the Behavioral Classification System for Adult Offenders*. Washington, DC: U.S. Department of Justice.

——— (1984) *Managing Adult Inmates: Classification for Housing and Program Assignments*. College Park, MD: American Correctional Association.

Sampson, R. (1989) "The Promises and Pitfalls of Macro-Level Research." *The Criminologist* 14:1-11.

Schafer, N. (1984) "Prisoner Behavior, Staff Response: Using Prison Discipline Records." Paper presented at annual meetings of the Academy of Criminal Justice Sciences, Chicago.

Scott, N., M. Mount, and P. Duffy (1977) ""MMPI and Demographic Correlates and Predictions of Female Prison Escape." *Criminal Justice and Behavior* 4:285-300.

Silverman, M. and M. Vega (1990) "Reactions of Prisoners to Stress as a Function of Personality and Demographic Variables." *International Journal of Offender Therapy and Comparative Criminology* 34:187-96.

Steadman, H. and J. Cocozza (1974) *Careers of the Criminally Insane*. Lexington, MA: Lexington Books.

Sullivan, J. and S. Feldman (1979) *Multiple Indicators: An Introduction*. Beverly Hills: Sage.

Sykes, G. (1958) *Society of Captives*. Princeton: Princeton University Press.

Thomas, C. (1970) "Toward a More Inclusive Model of the Inmate Contraculture." *Criminology* 8:251-62.

Tischler, C. and J. Marquart (1989) "Analysis of Disciplinary Infraction Rates among Female and Male Inmates." *Journal of Criminal Justice* 17:507-13.

Toch, H. (1975) *Men in Crisis: Human Breakdowns in Prison*. Chicago: Aldine.

——— (1977) *Living in Prison*. New York: Free Press.

Toch, H. and K. Adams (1989) *Coping: Maladaptation in Prisons*. New Brunswick, NJ: Transaction.

Van Voorhis, P. (1988) "A Cross Classification of Five Offender Typologies: Issues of Construct and Predictive Validity." *Criminal Justice and Behavior* 15:24-38.

——— (1993) "Psychological Determinants of the Prison Experience." *The Prison Journal* 73:72-102.

——— (1994) *Psychological Classification of the Adult Male Prison Inmate*. Albany: SUNY Press.

Walters, G. (1991) "Predicting the Disciplinary Adjustment of Maximum and Minimum Security Prison Inmates Using the Lifestyle Criminality Screening Form." *International Journal of Offender Therapy and Comparative Criminology* 35:63-71.

Walters, G., T. Scrapansky, and G. Marrlow (1986) "The Emotionally Disturbed Military Criminal Offender: Identification, Background, and Institutional Adjustment." *Criminal Justice and Behavior* 13:261-85.

Warren, M.Q. and the Staff of the Community Treatment Project (1966) *Interpersonal Maturity Level Classification: Diagnosis and Treatment of Low, Middle, and High Maturity Delinquents*. Sacramento: California Youth Authority.

Wellford, C. (1967) "Factors Associated with the Adoption of the Inmate Code." *Journal of Criminal Law, Criminology, and Police Science* 58:197-203.

Wooldredge, J. (1991) "Correlates of Deviant Behavior among Inmates of U.S. Correctional Facilities." *Journal of Crime and Justice* 14(1):1-25.

Wright, K. (1986) "An Exploratory Study of Transactional Classification." *Journal of Research in Crime and Delinquency* 23:326-48.

——— (1988) "The Relationship of Risk, Needs, and Personality Classification Systems and Prison Adjustment." *Criminal Justice and Behavior* 15:454-71.

——— (1991) "A Study of Individual, Environmental, and Interactive Effects in Explaining Adjustment to Prison." *Justice Quarterly* 8:217-42.

Zamble, E. (1992) "Behavior and Adaptation in Long-Term Prison Inmates: Descriptive Longitudinal Results." *Criminal Justice and Behavior* 19:409-25.

Zamble, E. and F. Porporino (1988) *Coping, Behavior, and Adaptation in Prison Inmates*. New York: Springer-Verlag.

Appendix. Descriptions of Criterion Variables

Official Citation Data	
Aggression	Number of citations for violent behaviors (e.g., threats, fights, attacks) per month multiplied by 100
Insubordination	Number of citation for insubordination per month multiplied by 100
Victimizations	Whether or not the inmate received protective custody or attention from the psychology department in response to his request for protection
Drug and alcohol use	Number of citations for drug and alcohol per month multiplied by 100
Staff Evaluation Data	
Aggression	(1) Very passive and meek (2) Not aggressive unless provoked (3) Generally doesn't carry a chip on his shoulder (4) Hostile to others (5) Extremely hostile and aggressive
Response to supervision	(1) Excellent (2) Good (3) Fair (4) Resists/ignores suggestions (5) Very poor
Fails to obey rules	(1) No (2) Yes
Self-Report Interview Data	
Aggression	Will fight if necessary (no/yes).
Insubordination	Believes in doing his own time (yes/no).
Victimizations	Concern for personal safety while incarcerated
Drug and alcohol use	Will use drugs/alcohol as a means of dealing with prison difficulties (offered spontaneously) (no/yes).
Self-Report Survey Data	
Aggression	Cumulative index: About how many times have you: verbally threatened other inmates, physically attacked other inmates, verbally insulted other inmates?
Insubordination	Single item relative to coping styles: Will tell staff when I don't think they are doing their job: no, yes (not helpful), yes (helpful), yes (very helpful).
Victimizations	Cumulative index: About how many times have you been: threatened by other inmates, physically attacked by other inmates, insulted by other inmates, pressured for sex by other inmates?
Drug and alcohol use	Cumulative index: About how many times have you: used illegal drugs in here, drunk alcoholic beverages in here?

Acknowledgments

Morgan, Kathryn D. "Factors Influencing Probation Outcome: A Review of the Literature." *Federal Probation* 57 (1993): 23–29. Reprinted with the permission of the Administrative Office of the U.S. Courts.

Andrews, D.A., Ivan Zinger, Robert D. Hoge, James Bonta, Paul Gendreau, and Frances T. Cullen. "Does Correctional Treatment Work? A Clinically Relevant and Psychologically Informed Meta-Analysis." *Criminology* 28 (1990): 369–404. Reprinted with the permission of the American Society of Criminology.

Antonowicz, Daniel H. and Robert R. Ross. "Essential Components of Successful Rehabilitation Programs for Offenders." *International Journal of Offender Therapy and Comparative Criminology* 38 (1994): 97–104. Reprinted with the permission of Sage Publications, Inc.

Chayet, Ellen F. "Correctional 'Good Time' as a Means of Early Release." *Criminal Justice Abstracts* 26 (1994): 521–38. Reprinted with the permission of Willow Tree Press, Inc.

Chesney-Lind, Meda. "Patriarchy, Prisons, and Jails: A Critical Look at Trends in Women's Incarceration." *Prison Journal* 71 (1991): 51–67. Reprinted with the permission of Sage Publications Inc.

Corbett, Ronald and Gary T. Marx. "No Soul in the New Machine: Technofallacies in the Electronic Monitoring Movement." *Journal of Offender Monitoring* 7 (1994): 1–9. Reprinted with the permission of the Academy of Criminal Justice Sciences.

Crouch, Ben M. "Is Incarceration Really Worse? Analysis of Offenders' Preferences for Prison Over Probation?" *Justice Quarterly* 10 (1993): 67–88. Reprinted with the permission of the Academy of Criminal Justice Sciences.

Dickinson, George E. and Thomas W. Seaman. "Communication Policy Changes from 1971 to 1991 in State Correctional Facilities for Adult Males in the United States." *Prison Journal* 74 (1994): 371–82. Reprinted with the permission of Sage Publications Inc.

Feeley, Malcolm M. "The Privatization of Prisons in Historical Perspective." *Criminal Justice Research Bulletin* 6 (1991): 1–10. Reprinted with the permission of the Criminal Justice Center.

Macallair, Dan. "Reaffirming Rehabilitation in Juvenile Justice." *Youth and Society* 25 (1993): 104–25. Reprinted with the permission of Sage Publications, Inc.

Geerken, Michael R. and Hennessey D. Hayes. "Probation and Parole: Public Risk and the Future of Incarceration Alternatives." *Criminology* 31 (1993): 549–64. Reprinted with the permission of the American Society of Criminology.

Kelly, William R. and Sheldon Ekland-Olson. "The Response of the Criminal Justice System to Prison Overcrowding: Recidivism Patterns Among Four Successive Parolee Cohorts." *Law and Society Review* 25 (1991): 601–20. Reprinted with the permission of the Law and Society Association.

Klofas, John M., Stan Stojkovic, and David A. Kalinich. "The Meaning of Correctional Crowding: Steps Toward an Index of Severity." *Crime and Delinquency* 38 (1992): 171–88. Reprinted with the permission of Sage Publications, Inc.

MacKenzie, Doris Layton and Alex Piquero. "The Impact of Shock Incarceration Programs on Prison Crowding." *Crime and Delinquency* 40 (1994): 222–49. Reprinted with the permission of Sage Publications, Inc.

Merlo, Alida V. and Peter J. Benekos. "Adapting Conservative Correctional Policies to the Economic Realities of the 1990s." *Criminal Justice Policy Review* 6 (1992): 1–16. Reprinted with the permission of the Indiana University of Pennsylvania.

Morash, Merry, Robin N. Haarr, and Lila Rucker. "A Comparison of Programming for Women and Men in U.S. Prisons in the 1980s." *Crime and Delinquency* 40 (1994): 197–221. Reprinted with the permission of Sage Publications, Inc.

Palmer, Ted. "Growth-Centered Intervention: An Overview of Changes in Recent Decades." *Federal Probation* 56 (1992): 62–67. Reprinted with the permission of the Administrative Office of the U.S. Courts.

Steinke, Pamela. "Using Situational Factors to Predict Types of Prison Violence." *Journal of Offender Rehabilitation* 17 (1991): 119–32. Reprinted with the permission of Haworth Press, Inc.

Taggart, William A. and Russell G. Winn. "Imprisonment in the American States." *Social Science Quarterly* 74 (1993): 736–49. Reprinted from Southwestern Social Science Quarterly, by permission of the authors and the University of Texas Press.

Toch, Hans. "Democratizing Prisons." *Prison Journal* 74 (1994): 62–72. Reprinted with the permission of Sage Publications Inc.

Van Voorhis, Patricia. "Measuring Prison Disciplinary Problems: A Multiple Indicators Approach to Understanding the Prison Adjustment." *Justice Quarterly* 11 (1994): 679–709. Reprinted with the permission of the Academy of Criminal Justice Sciences.